Liberation Theologies, Postmodernity, and the Americas

Liberation Theologies, Postmodernity, and the Americas

David Batstone

Eduardo Mendieta

Lois Ann Lorentzen

Dwight N. Hopkins

Routledge
London   New York

Published in 1997 by
Routledge
29 West 35th Street
New York, NY 10001

Published in Great Britain by
Routledge
11 New Fetter Lane
London EC4P 4EE

Copyright © 1997 by Routledge

Printed in the United States of America on acid-free paper.

Cover art: "Last Supper of Chicano Heroes"
Mural artist: José Antonio Burciaga
"The idea [for this mural] arose from [another] I was designing on the mythology and history of maiz, corn. I had intended to depict the Last Supper; Christ and his 12 apostles were to be portrayed dining on tortillas, tamales and tequila instead of bread and wine. I dropped that idea when some students expressed dismay at my mixing humor with religion. That's when I decided to replace the religious figures with 13 Chicano heroes. The mural is now in the dining hall of Casa Zapata, the Chicano-theme student residence at Stanford [University]."

—extracted from the *Los Angeles Times*, May 3, 1988

Library of Congress Cataloging-in-Publication Data

Liberation theologies, postmodernity, and the Americas / edited by
    David Batstone . . . [et al.].
        p.   cm.
    Includes bibliographical references and index.
    ISBN 0-415-91658-5 (alk. paper. — ISBN 0-415-91659-0 (pbk. :
alk. paper)
        1. Liberation theology.   2. Postmodernism—Religious aspects—
Christianity.   3. Sociology, Christian—America.   I. Batstone,
David B., 1958– .
    BT83. 57.L483   1997
    230'.0464—dc21
                                                              96-54817
                                                              CIP

Dedicated to all bordercrossers

Contents

Acknowledgments

D avid, Eduardo, and Lois thank the Faculty Development Fund
of the University of San Francisco, which made much of
this research possible, and the generous support of Dean Stanley
Nel and former Associate Dean Gerardo Marin. We also thank our
incredible assistants Michelle Myers, José Espinosa, and Adam
Renner. Our stimulating colleagues at USF are too numerous to
mention although we single out Daniel Kendall, S.J., chair of the
Theology and Religious Studies Department, for special recognition.

Dwight thanks Clark Gilpin (dean), the faculty, and students at
the Divinity School of the University of Chicago, for their intellectual support, and Linda E. Thomas for her several readings of his
chapter in progress. David is grateful for the thoughtful suggestions
of Jonathan Gill toward revising his chapter. We acknowledge Jim
Morgan and Marna Anderson, who alerted us to Gustavo Gutiérrez's lecture in San Salvador, which we subsequently turned into a
chapter with Gutiérrez's assistance.

We thank the *Journal of Hispanic/Latino Theology* and its editor,
Orlando Espín, for publishing early versions of two of the essays
and for dedicating an entire issue to the question.

We were fortunate to have gifted translators in Pedro Lange-
Churión, Amós Nascimento, and Elizabeth Wing. And of course we
are thrilled by our contributors and are grateful for their hard work
and their creativity, which made this volume possible.

Finally, we wish to thank our families and loved ones: Wendy,
Jade, Zachary, Jesse, Bill, Gerardo, Eva, Jenny, Emily, and Turtle.

Introduction

David Batstone
Eduardo Mendieta
Lois Lorentzen
Dwight N. Hopkins

L ed by voices who raise up their spiritual, economic, cultural, and political experiences at the margins of social power in the postmodern exigencies of the Americas, liberation theology demystifies the pretensions of the Eurocentric subject. At its roots, liberation theology attempts to rebuild theology in view of the history of massive suffering produced by empire and to affirm marginalized faith communities in their creation of a new humanity. The existence of millions of people who are not recognized as human beings by the prevailing social systems call into question those systems and the religious structures that validate them.

Its many-sided grounding and method of de-centering one dominating voice put liberation theology in natural dialogue with postmodern analyses. Postmodern thinking also concerns itself with the limitations and underside of rationality and of subjectivity. It is a "decanonization" of conventional authorities, since it assumes that no thinking is free from time, place, or interest. Much like postmodernity, liberation theology situates itself as a way and language of the "outposts," a delegitimizing of the center of knowledge and of power.

In the process of our collaborative work on this text, we agreed on the above conceptual and practical convergences. As the conversation deepened and progressed, however, we found ourselves

1

uncovering a constellation of continuing contradictions and persis-
tent problems. For instance, could some forms of postmodern
thought be "new forms of cultural imperialism," as some Latin
American critics claimed? Do liberation theologies naively supplant
one metanarrative with a new metanarrative of the oppressed? Are
the contradictions irreconcilable? What does this debate mean for
social strategies that resist domination? And why have both postmodern analyses and liberation theologies thrived on American
soil? Why have they emerged almost simultaneously? What are the
relationships between political economy in the Americas and these
modes of discourse?

Modern thinkers, and to a large extent their postmodern children,
often treat religion as a regressive system for interpreting material
reality. But liberation theology, while suspicious of all existing ideologies and institutions that are in a relationship to systems of dominant power, turns to religious narratives and to spiritual forces as
resources for understanding material realities. These tensions forge
a subtext for the current debates ranging over cultural identity and
self-image in North and South Americas, and reflect global realign-
ments that transgress regions, religions, and linguistic differences.
Such problematical discourses and pressing concerns are not reserved merely for philosophers and theologians.

The Americas

The Americas in the title of this anthology is an essential point of
reference for this book; through it we situate ourselves in geo-political space while foregrounding the role that America plays within
the cartography of the social imaginary of Western culture. To situate oneself, to place oneself, to name oneself within and through a
site in geo-political space means to acknowledge one's locatedness
and thus one's particular and circumscribed perspective. This is not
relativism, nor does it have to turn into some sort of enlightened
liberal ethnocentrism (à la Rorty). Acknowledgment of one's locatedness is recognition that purported universality is always bought
at the expense of other people's history, land, resources, uniqueness,
and hope; it is even bought at the expense of our own internal heterogeneity. We are situating ourselves and acknowledging the privileges entailed by our global site. Perhaps our vantage point allows
us a broader horizon of survey, but it also presupposes that there

are perspectives that we are either ignoring or occluding. Acknowledging our place in geo-political dimensions is not a means for disavowing responsibility, shrugging off our privileges, but rather a way of saying that our knowledge is particular, compromised by our site of enunciation, the place from which we survey, oversee, and name social reality. We call this acknowledgment of how our knowing and understanding are a privilege and how they affect others the imperative of hermeneutical humility. This locating ourselves is a way of laying the ground work for substantive dialogue, but also and perhaps most importantly, it is a way in which we make ourselves accountable.

Indeed, universality is a way of concealing one's responsibilities, one's accountability, one's interests. Universality is a way of saying one is everywhere and nowhere—universality is a way of saying one sees *sub specie aeternitatis*, that is, as if from God's perspective. How, then we must ask, could the Other incriminate me, call me to responsibility, ask of me to give an account of my judgments, pronouncements, perspectives, when I, the One, the universal subject, the "unencumbered self," is not in social space? Universality produces an anamorphosis of the social imaginary—it distorts the representations it produces of others and of ourselves. Placing ourselves is a way of acknowledging how the mirror in which the social imaginary sees itself is warped by sheer materiality and sociality. For us, America is the site of our privilege, the loci of our own sociality and materiality, with its sexism, racism, classism, ecological pillage, and economic rapacity, but also with its idealism, democratic temper, protest tradition, many languages, and diverse ethnic-racial groupings.

Moreover, Americas in the title of this anthology foregrounds the rich and complex role that America has played in the hermeneutical horizon of Western culture. No event has altered more radically the horizon of expectations of Western society than the "discovery" of the New World. Western culture is as much a detritus of Christianity as it is the result of its "invention," "discovery," "colonization," and "evangelization" of America. Conversely, America is as much a detritus of Christianity as it is the extension and transformation of Europe and its culture. The "discovery/invention" of America altered the surface of Western culture's map in many ways: politically, economically, socially, and religiously.

Politically, without America we would not have the revolutionary spirit of mass democracy that has become our nation's most prized ideal. To this day, the democracy of the United States of America remains the oldest in the world as it continues to inspire and to fire the imaginations of cultures and movements in the process of political independence. Without the riches extracted from the New World, Europe would not have emerged from the economic stagnation in which it wallowed for close to a millennium. America was the cornucopia of material resources that allowed Europe to obtain a differential advantage over other world empires of the fifteenth century. Up through the sixteenth century, Europe remained a peripheral outpost of the Eurasian continent, of which Europe is a mere peninsula. Socially, America became the land of the poor, the underclass, the dregs, the heretics and heathen of Europe. America was the land where the European went to regenerate and to mutate into a new being—Whitman's democratic creature, Emerson's imperial self, and Vasconcelos' "cosmic race."

Most importantly, and this is what we want to underscore with our reference to it in our title, America transformed Christianity as much as it transformed Europe. America became "God's new Israel," the new Jerusalem, the new Eden, the wilderness into which humanity went to reform and to purify itself. America was a religious imperative, the sedimentation of a Christian ideal, a result of the catalyzing of messianic and millenerian imperatives and their social stratification and regimentation. America, in John Winthrop's famous phrase, was to become the "city upon the hill," where Israel's God was to walk in its midst. America was to be the new Jerusalem. As such, however, America became the place where Christianity rediscovered its intrinsic humanism in the figure of Bartolomé de las Casas, the defender of the "indians." America became the land for Christianity's melting pot of syncretism, heterogeneity, and heterodoxy. African Americans, Amerindians, Europeans, Latin Americans, Asian Americans, Pacific Islanders, (Protestants, Catholics, Moslems, and Jews) came together to give birth to denominations, churches, religions, sects, and the "civil religion" of a society that replaced constitution for creed without disavowing or eschewing religious fervor and discipline. Black, womanist, feminist, American Indian, gay, and Latin American liberation theologies made America the land of the second reformation. The self-images of America, whether as the utopian site of Western culture, the latest outpost, the farthest frontier, the decadent epitome, or the recaptured innocence, are deeply implicated in the future of Christianity.

Postmodernity interrogates the complicity of both Western ideals and Christianity's idolatry in the form of its monotheism in the great catastrophes of the twentieth century, as well as the ecocide, genocide, and slavery of the last centuries of Europeanization of the world. But, postmodernity is America: it is Disneyland, Jazz, Ellison, Marquez, Borges, Chinese New Year, Los Angeles, New York, Buenos Aires, Medellín, Che and the Zapatistas, Wounded Knee, Arrested Development, Sitting Bull, and Carlos Vivez. Postmodernity is Western Christian humanism's rediscovery of historicity and particularity, challenging its fetishization of universality. *Cur Deus Homo*: and God became human in the form of the courageous amerindian whom de las Casa defended, or the black slaves whose acts of resistance were forms of religion.

This is what our title suggests: postmodernity, the Americas, and Christianity in the form of critical liberation theologies form part of a constellation of forces and coordinates. The meaning and fate of one is implicated and incriminated by the others. Each one is a coordinate in the cognitive mapping of contemporary society. As we enter the twenty-first century, the substance, content, and meaning of Americas, postmodernity, and Christianity will undergo profound transformation partly determined by the shifting ground of each element in this triad.

Postmodernism

We need to ask whether or not the term postmodern is at all useful. Is it better than post-industrial, post-fordist, post-capitalist, or post-colonial? Does the term throw light on a set of societal processes that is not illuminated by other categories? Does the term postmodern occlude certain social realities by the fact that it hijacks our attention by zooming in on the "post" of the "modern"? Indeed to the extent to which the postmodern still depends on the modern, despite its shift due to a preposition, we can say that the postmodern is more of the modern under the guise of its exhaustion. The postmodern, already in its name, indicates how much it is determined by the coordinates and cardinal points of the modern. If this is the case, we need to ask how is it that the postmodern is still the modern, modernity under a different facade? Indeed, postmodernity as the highest stage of modernity must be the continuation of the colonial, destructive, cannibalizing, and rapacious practices of the modern, but now let loose. But, this quick moralistic dismissal of postmodernity fails to come to terms with the fact that the post-modern also presents itself as a critique of the modern, of Modernity. The postmodern, it can be argued, is the recapturing of the moral, ethical, historical dimensions that had been suspended by the homogenizing tendencies of Modernity.

Furthermore, postmodernity as an epochal condition points to the transformation that Western societies have undergone. Modes of production, social relations, and the ideologies that both occluded and critically examined these and their interactions have changed. "All that was solid has melted into thin air," noted Marx. First world, industrialized nations have become obsolete for globalized finance capital. Economies are de-industrialized, while workers become mere providers of ethereal services. With the de-industrialization of economies and the globalization of capital, the nation state has become less important. The welfare state is under attack. The conditions that gave birth to it no longer apply. Workers are not clients of a state that mediates between capitalist and labor movements. Workers are no longer entitled because there is nothing to which they can make a claim. The economy, which was subject to national imperatives (the New Deal and National Socialism were cases of this interaction), has become autonomous. It owes no allegiance to nation, to community, or to laws. Although some of us in the First World live in increasingly de-industrialized nations, we can talk about hyper-capitalism, or the complete rule of automatized and self-determining capital (no longer owned by the bourgeoisie, but by corporate conglomerates). While economies have become de-industrialized, the market has expanded. The primary mode of integration into society is not through entry into the production process, but through entering the circle of consumption, of market frenzy. Whereas for industrial capitalism being a producer was of primary importance, under globalized capital, being a consumer is the determining factor. The difference is no longer between workers and bourgeoisie, but between consumers and the destitute—those who not only have nothing to sell in the labor market, but most importantly, those who cannot afford to buy anything.

The transformation of the economy has entailed a whole new set of contradictions and social relations. The increasing marginalization and obsolescence of the nation state has meant that its mediating role has decreased, which means that the gains that workers made are coming under attack (for example, the welfare state, education, social security, etc.). Similarly, the privatization of social services has meant the dismantling of a state supported infra-structure (such as roads, public transportation, schools, and universities). Public phones no longer work because now people have cellular phones in their coat pockets. Public schools are falling apart in the inner city, while in the suburbs they are standardized with the latest technology due to the direct financing of rich communities. Health care, instead of becoming the universal right of every citizen, has become the luxury of those who can afford such a service. Bluntly and tersely, the postmodern as an epochal condition underscores in its celebration of camp, kitsch, and retro the other side of a social reality in which we wallow in private affluence while squatting in public squalor.

As de-industrialization takes its toll on infra- and super-structure, the work day dwindles, not so that we can be farmers in the morning, fisherfolk in the afternoon, and poets in the evening, but so that companies do not have to pay for workers' benefits. The right to work has become the prerogative to hire on a per hour basis without incurring the down-sides of a salaried worker with rights and benefits. This is not a workers' economy; it is a consumers' economy. How you make your living in order to consume does not matter. What matters is that you consume and participate in the bacchanalia and frenzy of boundless and useless consumption.

If we are to understand more precisely what postmodernity means, however, we need to have a general sense of what Modernity is and was about; for Modernity co-exists with postmodernity just as the non-contemporaneous synchronicities of the "medieval" and "pre-modern" co-exist within Modernity (see Habermas's essay). Every epoch paints its past according to its image of itself. The image we are proposing here is to a large extent determined by the referentiality of Modernity vis-à-vis postmodernity.

Modernity was based on the following set of fundamental assumptions. These assumptions served as the archimedean points that helped Modernity propel itself into a false universality, a universality that in turn entailed the colonization, slavery, and "Europeanization" of the world. These assumptions were also the pillars that supported the immense edifice of Modernity: an edifice that was at once train station, auction block, panopticon, gas chamber, laboratory, office building, factory, and educational/correctional/legislative institution. Modernity was the court house of world judgment—*Weltgeschichte ist ein Weltgericht*. The assumptions that determined the coordinates of the episteme of Modernity were:

1. *Unity of self, society, reason, history*: Modernity was based partly on the notion of the stability, univocity, and homogeneity of all of these social constructs. It prescribed the unity of self, as autonomy, the unity of society, as homogeneity, the unity of reason, as the synthesis of the different faculties under one coordinating reason (*Vernunft*), and the unity of history in terms of its teleology (history, perceived as the seamless progression of industrial development, growth of freedom, growth of consciousness, growth of civility, etc.).

2. *The mimesis of representation and perception*: Modernity's affirmation, of course, of the unity and stability of selves, societies, and history was based on the assumption that its knowledge claims were accurate and truthful. This in turn was based on the notion that there was an uncontaminated isomorphism between mind and world, and that representation mimetically reproduces perception. Evidently, this mimesis also presupposed the idea that the mind was a faultless, non-convex mirror that reflected faithfully and accurately nature.

3. *Evaluative and normative teleologies*: Modernity was and is an evaluation of history in terms of normative teleologies. Modernity took over from Western Christendom the belief in a *Heilsgeschichte*, a divine plan of history that guarantees the better, purer outcome of the slaughter bench of history. Indeed, teleology became a means for reconciling a modern world to its own theodicy, which explains why Christian theodicy became a demonology in Marx's hand. Be that as it may, Modernity is above all based on the conflation of historicity and history, a surreptitious conflation of European ontogenesis with world phylogenesis—a substitution of world historical development for the western experience of that development.

It is almost impossible to say which item has had supremacy over another. They are inextricably entwined in an embrace that makes it difficult to determine at which point the drive to colonize and to manage the world—to use an expression of Dussel—was justified and legitimated (a) by an appeal to the inevitability of history, as in manifest destiny, the white man's burden, the logic of capitalist development that necessitated that it give birth to its grave diggers, the inevitability of the revolution; (b) by the legislative notion that selves had to be unified for them to be held accountable and be imputed moral autonomy, or that, as in the case with women and blacks, they could not be full citizens because they were inferior, children, *unmündig,* immature and unworthy according to the language of the European Enlightenment; or (c) by the idea that our culture understood best what was happening in the world because of its purer, truer, epistemic means.

All these presuppositions and prejudices collaborated with one or the other to make Modernity a world pursuit, one in which subordination and control reached its most extreme levels and broadest reach.

Postmodernity, as that which purportedly comes after Modernity, where the "post" is not necessarily temporal but epistemological, is thus said to be the crises and critique of some of those projects, goals, presuppositions, and ideals. Insofar as postmodernity criticizes them, whether through parody, parataxis, metonym, hyper-reflexivity, intertextuality, historization, or detotalization, postmodernity pries open Modernity so as to liberate some of its own best normative contents. At a more conceptual level, the following are some of the ways in which postmodernity confronts Modernity and thus defines itself.

1. *The self-affirmation and naming of the Other:* they will represent themselves, rather than let themselves be represented. The postmodern as the age of difference and the Other.

2. *Historicization of history:* the rediscovery of the difference between history and historicity.

3. *Significance of language:* The contamination by language of the entire ideology of structure and mimesis, of representation and perception. There is nothing outside the text, and everything, even the self-reflexivity of language, is refracted and distorted by the materiality and contingency of language.

4. *Emphasis on technology:* The collapse of metanarratives because of the success of science, on the one hand, but also because of the re-historization of history. Science was pursued in the name of progress, but progress is canceled and vitiated by the perpetual innovation of science/technology (as in the films *Blade Runner, Brazil,* and *Twelve Monkeys*).

5. *Fragmentation of the subject:* Heterogeneity of selves, history, reason, due partly to the success of the market economy but also to the disintegration of univocal, stable, homogeneous narratives. The Enlightenment's "unencumbered self" (Kant) is replaced by multiple situated and heterogeneously constituted selves. Postmodernity

is not the death of the subject, but rather the re-politicization of agency. Agency is the site of convergence of the power vectors of history, rationality/irrationality, and social geography.

6. *Question of perception:* The de-naturalization of "reality" and "perception" with its accompanying call for a critique of the political economy of representation. Whereas high Modernity presupposed the givenness of both an ontologically stable object and an epistemologically unified subject who represented to itself that object in the camera obscura of its "mind," the postmodern professes the constructedness of both "object" and "subject." These, instead, are seen as positionalities, localities made possible or disabled by a cartography of power and legitimate sites of enunciation. The question becomes who is authorized to name what as a legitimate object of inquiry. The postmodern, therefore, raises the issue of the political economy of the discursive regime of truth production.

7. *The death of the "intellectual":* The intellectual was one of the most dear products created by the epistemic legitimacy granting machines of Modernity. With the dismantling of both "object" and "subject," the privileged site that the intellectual occupies is also called into question. To a great extent, as Zygmut Bauman notes, postmodernity is about the crisis of the intellectual as the "legislator" of Modernity.

8. *The suspicion of any "revolutionary" project:* Foucault asked the question, "Is revolution still desirable?" Under Modernity the political was determined by its extreme, revolution. This is clear in Schmitt and in Parsons, who go back to Hobbes, Locke, and Rousseau. In modernity, revolutions become rituals of regeneration through expiatory violence. But as long as revolutions are epitomes of the "state of emergency," the possibility for justice is suspended. Postmodernity abandoned the politics of revolution, through a revolution of politics, in which the political became the condition of possibility of ethics, agency, and critical representation. Who is accountable to whom, who can know what, and how can something be made into an object of investigation are eminent political questions. These questions pertain to the fundamental issues of the production, distribution, and allocation of representational power, the power to name oneself, and to name others.

9. *Demystifying of fetishisms:* A simultaneously complicit and critical demystification of all fetishisms: be they of reason, or sci-

ence, social organization, genius, art, literature, progress, autonomy, universality, history, or innocence. Postmodernity's motto: *Any religion is already bad religion*.

10. *The death of history:* The end of history as understood by the European imperial project announces the death of its utopian dream, which for others was a nightmare. Postmodernity, thus, as the pronouncement of the death of history, the collapse of all metanarratives, turns into the following challenge: how to think utopia and/or emancipation without a teleology; or, how to think liberation without either a metaphysical (god, nature, reason) or historical (progress, *Heilsgeschichte*, technology, etc.) alibi.

Liberation Theologies

The coronation of Christianity as the state religion in the fourth century under Emperor Constantine transformed theology into the queen of the sciences, making philosophy a mere ancillary. To theology was granted the cognitive privilege of weaving and presiding over a symbolic universe that gave meaning and legitimacy to the social order. By its sacramental powers human nomos was transubstantiated into divine cosmos, and cultural products canonized into supra-mundane facticities. In only a few centuries, the church had achieved what its Savior had but taught his disciples to pray, "on earth as it is in heaven." The emperor's church was God. This was the hubris of a church that had forgotten its humble origins.

It would be, however, inaccurate to suggest that as Christianity became the theology of the Roman empire, neither empire nor church were transformed radically. Between the fourth century and our time, there have been as many, if not more, Christianities as there have been descendants of the Roman empire. If there have been Asian, North African, Middle-Eastern, and Western European Christianities, there have also been several Romes: Rome, Athens, Constantinople, and Berlin. Nevertheless, what was originally a small sect in one of the colonial outposts of the Roman empire, expanded, grew, and adapted into an imperial ideology that ruled almost unchallenged for over a millennium. With this in mind, perhaps it would be more appropriate to talk of many Christianities than one christendom, where the latter refers to the entire ideological edifice that legitimated both external and internal colonization. It is in christendom that we have the antecedents of what we now critically call modernity. For much like Plato's cave, christendom saw and read the entire world as a projection of a divine semiology where everything was a cipher of a divine message. This is an eminently qualitative and teleological world view: qualitative because everything is seen as being a repository of divine will and self-disclosure; teleological because everything then becomes proleptic of a final revelation, the arrival of the *Parousia*, or the final judgment.

Since modernity's birth, or many births (e.g., 1492, the Renaissance, the Reformation, the French and American revolutions, and Capitalism), theology has reacted to the claims and challenges presented to it by modernity, even as modernity itself arose out of the Christian worldview. Here it must be noted that the term "modern" enters our vocabulary in the fifth century during the transition from the Roman world to the Christian world. Modernity as the age of the absoluteness of Reason, translated theology into absolute doubt and apologetic accommodation (although to a certain extent all theology is but this, *apologetic modus vivendi*). Modern theology, since its so-called father, F. Schleiermacher, has tried to accommodate to the locale assigned to it by the discursive boundaries that Modernity dictated. Modern theology—mostly Protestant, for Roman Catholic theology only started engaging the world in the twentieth century—has negotiated, since Descartes gave primacy to the "cogito," around the borders established by Modernity's gerrymandering of social-cognitive space. It is this mapping of social space and cultural semiology (perhaps a redundancy) that is contested as much by liberation theologies as by postmodernity.

In so far as modern theology, however, accepted and complicitiously legitimated the discursive boundaries and categories dictated by Modernity, it was its twin and assistant. This is where liberation theology steps in. Liberation theology is a demystifying critique of theologies of modernity and of their complicity with Modernity—the modernity of colonialism, and neocolonialism, of the genocide of the Amerindian, Africans, and Jews, of the subordination of women and of the so-called heathen-pagan.

With the advent of modernity, nevertheless, the cultural influence of theology waned dramatically. The epistemological turn toward autonomous reason presented a direct challenge to theology's trinitarian grounding in revelation, tradition, and authority. Modernity sought to free the subject from the hierarchical ordering of knowledge and to contest every non-empirical regulation of social relations. Theology has lived ever since in a state of perpetual crisis. This hermeneutical contestation signifies in consciousness what was occurring in the political economy of a European empire in transition. An emerging mercantile class was demanding broader participation in the production and distribution of resources and goods. It was in their material interest to regulate social relations on the basis of a principle of exchange, yet codified in the legal structures of a modern nation-state. All other non-market valuations were consigned to the private realm of individual conscience and reason. This gerrymandering of social-cognitive space into public/private boundaries was replicated in modernity with other perceptual dyads: secular/religious, history/myth, rational/emotive, subject/object, freedom/authority, and civilized/primitive.

In the North Atlantic countries, Christian theology generally accommodated itself to these discursive boundaries. Protestantism carried out much of this reconstructive work until the twentieth century when Roman Catholicism began its own process of reconciling itself to the modern world. Stripped of its moorings in the public domain, religious consciousness laid claim to the interior dimensions of the self, alternatively defining its primary locus as feeling, spirit, moral piety, or irrational belief. The church, once the warden of the social order, was now its chaplain. Despite these changing historical roles, the Christian church and its theology consistently buttressed the expansion of empire. The majority of the church, regardless of where it stood in its conflict with modernity, blessed colonialism, neo-colonialism, extreme stratification of wealth, centuries of genocide of Amerindians, blacks, and Jews, the subordination of women, the persecution of the sexual other, and the social exclusion of the pagan. During the last five centuries theology has glorified all of these historical projects as divine constructions of reality. The conquest and colonization of the Americas that began in 1492 is but one piece of historical evidence.

Liberation theology arises in response to this corporal violation of human dignity, both as negative critique and emancipatory inspiration. Simultaneously arising out of the black church in the United States, feminist networks in North Atlantic countries, and grassroots religious communities in Latin America, liberation theology demystifies the production of theology in culture. Because it gives interpretive priority to sites of pain, social marginality, and freedom praxis, liberation hermeneutics expose the material alliances of every other theological and ethical system. While modernity aimed to release the subject from historical contingency, liberation theology aims to bring the subject to historical accountability. Truth-claims in liberation theology therefore do not belong to a universe complete in itself. Nor are they pre-existent to and independent of the historical events in which women and men act as agents. Its truth-claims emerge when theory meets practice. Theologies of praxis boldly cross modernity's discursive borders, making the private public and the public private.

In practice liberation theology uses a variety of socio-analytic mediations to analyze the causes of suffering and the incentives for emancipation and their reproduction in a political economy. The influence of Marx cannot be either underestimated or overgeneralized. For Latin American liberation theologians living under conditions of economic deprivation, marxian categories of class stratification and relations of production are extremely useful for explicating social reality. Black and feminist liberation theologies, although not ignoring Marx, have found more fruitful dialogue with social theories that uncover the social overlappings of race, gender, and class construction. The fact that liberation theology's reflection is therefore parasitic and subservient to material culture is not contradictory to its method. Liberation theology presumes that every cultural theory, be it theological or otherwise, works out of an ideological framework. Its rejection of modern theology is not based on modern theology's inability to transcend culture, but its denial of its own material location and interest.

Liberation theology's response to Modernity parallels and perhaps even anticipates the critiques of postmodernism. Both movements operate self-consciously within the limits of rationality and subjectivity, while decanonizing universal truth-claims with an appeal to the contingencies of time and place. Both liberation theology and postmodernity also celebrate fragments of local knowledge that cannot be synthesized or unified to consume the worlds of others; in principle, difference is neither a cause for exclusion nor contradiction. Hence liberation theology and postmodernism both relativize the absolute claims of dominant ideologies from the margins of social existence. Despite these similarities, their points of divergence are far from trivial. Postmodernism for the most part views religion as a regressive (read: superstitious, primitive, atavistic) fetish that masks material reality. Liberation theology, of course, is a reflection on praxis informed by religious faith.

Not only does liberation theology rely on religious narratives and spiritual experience as guides for interpreting material reality, it has faith in transcendent values that give structure and meaning to human existence. While these values remain constant, the means of actualizing them are in need of constant revolution and reconstruction. So faith is the pedagogical process of humanity learning to be human. Liberation theology accepts that Feuerbach and Marx were not entirely off-base when they surmised that the countenance of the God that we picture is the projection of what we have not yet become. But what Marx took as a negation of faith, liberation theology contends with Feuerbach, provides an avenue for its affirmation. Religious dogma is merely sedimented pedagogy, while its epistemic nucleus is the principle of liberation.

Moreover, this *principium liberationis* turns on a principle of hope and a principle of remembrance. In order for there to be sustained resistance to the violation of life by current systems of power, a people must be informed by narratives that manifest alternative ways of being. Hearing the dangerous hopes and liberating memories of the poor and powerless who were once liberated by their faith evokes the inspiration to write emancipatory narratives in the present. In lieu of being passive victims of oppression, the socially marginal can become agents of their own freedom. There is no hope without liberation, but no liberation if the future is empty of remembrance. Hope without anamnesis is empty, anamnesis without hope is blind, both without liberation are powerless.

Postmodernism is ill at ease with narratives of emancipation since it deems it ludicrous to point toward a meta-discourse that might legitimate action, values, or meaning. In a world of rapidly changing configurations or knowledge, where lies the foundation for a privileged description of reality, both its problems and its resolutions? Postmodernism considers engagement in utopian discourse as a potentially dangerous form of deception of oneself and others. It further rejects the notion of an enemy who is to be overcome, a clearly delineated demarcation along ideological lines, or a binary division such as economic class that might guide a political struggle. Not that postmodernism would suggest that struggles against domination and exploitation have ceased, but it perceives the complex and circular relations that exist between the mechanisms of domination and exploitation as resistant to revolutionary transformation. Individuals and communities are both effects of power and elements of its articulation. Instead of concentrating

attention on the motivation or interests of groups, classes, or individuals, critical analysis should concern itself with the mechanisms
of power.

Liberation theologians claim that to miss the face of the poor is
to miss the whole point of theologies of liberation. Our primary
concern in this volume is not to resolve the intriguing intellectual
challenges posed by the meeting between theologies of liberation
and postmodernism, but rather to call into question prevailing
social systems that refuse to recognize millions of the world's people as human beings. By calling into question those systems and the
religious, intellectual, and ideological structures that validate them,
we move closer to changing them. We wonder, as do some postmodern thinkers, if meta-narratives are obsolete, and if marginal
ideologies still mirror centers of domination. Yet, we also wonder
with some liberation theologians, if postmodernism is "toothless in
the face of oppression." Our concern is what this debate means for
social strategies that resist domination and advance the full humanity of the powerless.

Thus our concern is whether postmodernity and theologies of liberation situate themselves as ways and languages of the margins,
delegitimizers of the centers of knowledge and of power. We must
raise a note of caution here. How does one talk about the marginalized without reducing the victim, or producing a reification of the
victim, which is as condescending as is any fixed concept? We must
take care to attend to the multiple and fluid forms that victimization takes rather than reducing the victim to a new Other, and thus
finding ourselves again representing others rather than attending to
how they are self-represented. By what means can the victim speak
in the swirl of capital, words, and information that is our late twentieth century reality?

What we seek, in part, from our exploration of the meeting of theologies of liberation and postmodernity is guidance for political
action. Ideally our practice is that of political art, as Yúdice puts it,
which realizes that seeking articulations among the marginalized
and oppressed is as critical to the survival of the non-poor as well
as it is to the world's victims. A global configuration shaped by
flows of capital to the non-poor of deindustrialization, of a blurring
of "third" and "first" world as Detroit and Bombay move closer to
each other, of massive environmental deterioration that increasingly affects the poor, of rapacious consumption by some few yield-

ing increased hunger of too many others, of high levels of regional wars and conflicts, of large geographical pockets of human rights violations (e.g., Guatemala, East Timor, Philadelphia, Pennsylvania), or of rampant economic, physical, sexual, and psychological abuse of far too many of the world's women, of a homogenization of culture as indigenous peoples disappear while McDonalds appear everywhere, pose interconnected problems. These interconnected problems demonstrate that hegemony has far from ended, in spite of postmodernism thought's pointing to decentering and fragmentation. As noted earlier, postmodernity often seems to be the highest stage of modernity, continuing destructive, consumptive, and cannabilistic practices, which are currently often glorified or even made chic and trendy through media representations.

We return to the victims of the world. Will this debate help make their lives better? What social movements, practices, and strategies are required "by any means necessary" for large-scale transformation? What tools (intellectual, practical, social) are at our disposal to meet the Goliath of the new world order? The primary concern of the editors and contributors of this volume is to develop new paradigms for understanding the distribution of power and knowledge in the Americas and to engage in the praxis of liberation theology for acknowledgment of the complete humanity of the poor, not only in the Americas, but, indeed in the entire postmodern world.

The essays in *Liberation Theologies, Postmodernity, and the Americas* open up new horizons and prisms as they participate in the dissolution of the discursive boundaries that have gerrymandered theology apart from the other social sciences, thus naming its sometimes not-so-silent complicity. These essays exemplify the kinds of challenges that liberation theologies must meet while also illustrating the ways in which other fields of human activity and self-understanding have been transformed by liberation theologies. With this in mind, we have organized the contributions to this volume in the following three sections:

Part One: Dangerous Hope and Liberating Memory: In a time in which the wells of utopian energies seem exhausted and collective memory turns into xenophobic and expurgatory violence, the imperative to dream otherwise and to recollect responsibly have all become the more pressing. Liberation theologies emerged as responses to this imperative, as the following essays illustrate.

Franz Hinkelammert's contribution establishes the concreteness of liberation theology with its necessary emphasis on orthopraxis— the appropriate practice with and on behalf of the poor. The option for the poor is both God's and humanity's choice for the liberation of the poor. It is in the poor that we find mutual recognition between human beings, hence the presence of God. Hinkelammert, in addition, offers an insightful historical recreation of the cause, sense, and purpose of Latin American liberation theology, starting with the late 1960s and ending with the present. Today's task for liberation theology is a critique of neoliberal political economy and a pursuance of a Christian tradition critical of the law.

Elsa Tamez explores the utopian thought of a liberation praxis as expressed in Qohélet or Ecclesiastes. In a twist on postmodernist thought's rejection of the alleged utopianism of liberation theology, Tamez demonstrates that for Qohélet, a harsh realism leads to a rejection of the present while calling us to live in "utopian" fashions within the rejected present. The affirmation of material life, bread, wine, and the beloved, occurs within a thorough analysis of material groundedness and political economy.

The essay by Gustavo Gutiérrez, the Peruvian priest who shook up the religious world in the late 1960s with his call for the Christian church to make a "preferential option for the poor," develops a theology. He revisits the hermeneutical precedence of "the poor" in liberation theology and links their destiny to the ultimate negotiation of life and death. Gutiérrez does not try to justify "preference" for the poor on the basis of social theory, but locates it in religious faith. He concludes by explicating the spiritual practices that facilitate one's capacity to materialize this option in history.

A surprising response to the alterity, vulnerabilities, and religious pluralism of postmodern life occurs in the contribution by Maria Clara Bingemer. Bingemer clearly analyzes the context of contemporary Christianity within an increasingly secularized world, inter-religious dialogue, political transformation, and the concrete realities of Brazil. Yet she emerges from this context and analysis claiming that the challenge to Christianity in a world of religious pluralism is to maintain a high Christology, the scandal of faith in Jesus Christ.

Josué A. Sathler and Amós Nascimento examine liberation theology, postmodernity, and the Americas through an analysis of the ideology of syncretism in Brazil. They critically interpret postmodernity in liberation theology, the history of conservative attitudes toward miscegenation and syncretism, an anthropological and sociological approach to religious syncretism, the theological debate around syncretism (here critiquing liberation theology for a racist posture), and finally call for a consideration of African cultures and religions as constitutive parts of the Americas, and not as elements needing syncreticization and christianization.

Part Two: Crossing Borders: Remapping the Sacred/Secular: Modernity was and still is the most exacting regimentation of social space and cognitive mappings. The valencies of heathen, irrational, primitive, religious, and pre-modern paradoxically have come to assume greater social weight even as they stand under critique. The following essays deliberately situate themselves at the borders of those categories calling for a type of cognitive *mestizaje*. Sharon Welch opens up with a challenge to reconstitute the vocabulary of political struggle. Welch believes liberation theology could benefit from the critiques of poststructuralist theory, particularly its appreciation for the fallibility of human relations and the unexpected results of political action. While a vocabulary of moral absolutes may motivate immediate political energy, Welch doubts their efficacy for sustained political struggle.

Lois Ann Lorentzen analyzes women's writing from El Salvador's "secret" wartime prisons in order to test the cogency of Lyotard's skepticism toward emancipatory narratives in liberation thought. Lorentzen provides a close reading of *Nunca Estuve Sola* [I was never Alone] by Nidia Díaz and *Las carceles clandestinas de El Salvador* [El Salvador's Clandestine Prisons] by Ana Guadalupe Martinez, to show the role of *testimonio* in political resistance and liberation discourse. Lorentzen agrees with Lyotard that emancipatory narratives risk replicating dominant discourse and power structures. Yet, she concludes that a hermeneutic of suspicion applied to emancipatory narratives that are viewed as *transitional*, can yield powerful narratives that are both postmodern and liberation texts.

David Batstone charts the borders of a "postmodern hermeneutic of liberation" that is conscious of the paradoxes and limitations of their interplay. Batstone believes that representations of material culture move across multiple domains of knowledge. He therefore uses testimony, aesthetics, and critical rationality to depict the flow of emancipation in history, linking each portrait in order to illustrate the role of imagination in the production of knowledge.

Mark McClain Taylor argues that a postmodernism that is not

infused with an hermeneutics of liberation will likely obscure the social and economic oppression of the global economy. Taylor presents a case of how certain forms of postmodernism legitimate neoliberalist economic policies and silence the strategies that historically have served to resist the kind of domination neoliberalism produces. He then points towards a direction for proponents of postmodern discourse to re-position themselves in an ethos of political struggle.

Robert Warrior takes up some of the paradoxical dimensions of Modernity in the U.S.A. through the rescue of William Apess, a Pequot and Methodist critic of Puritanism and betrayed Modernity. Warrior's redemption of Apess, as part of the establishment of a Native American intellectual tradition and critique of American obliviousness to its colonial and imperial past (and present), delineates simultaneously a fascinating hermeneutical device: a critique of the rhetoric of ancientness and novelty. It is this rhetoric that allows modernity to exile Native Americans from history to some mythological past, as well as allowing postmodernity to utilize Native Americans to exemplify a novelty that similarly eviscerates their history.

Part Three: Postmodern Praxes and Liberation Theories: The hybridization of social life and the contingency of all conceptual tools have rendered all praxis postmodern, or, problematic. It is not surprising that for many, postmodernity stands for the collapse of Western culture. Without universal principles, it is claimed, ethics and moral theory become obsolete. Postmodernity, thus, has become a shibboleth for moral relativism and the paralysis of ethical censure and moral accountability. Equally facile, however, would be a retreat to unquestioned religion and religiosity out of the need to provide a moral compass for a polycentric world. The essays in the last section gravitate around this challenge.

Dwight N. Hopkins provides a critical interrogation of postmodernity and black theology of liberation vis-à-vis an encounter between James H. Cone and Michel Foucault. Citing the postmodern experience of African Americans long before cultural intellectuals coined the word (postmodern), Hopkins offers a constructive resolution of the encounter by localizing four areas of difference and commonality between Cone and Foucault—power, race and culture, methodology, and telos.

A prolific German theologian, Edmund Arens's work emerges from the mediation between Habermas's and Apel's post-linguistic grounding of the social sciences and philosophy, on the one hand, and political and liberation theologies, on the other hand. At stake in the debate between political theology and Habermas' reformulation of critical theory is precisely the role theology plays vis-à-vis the demands and still outstanding promises of Modernity that the postmodern critique has made the more relevant and obvious. Moreover, Arens challenges Habermas's engagement with Metz in the following essay. For Arens, there is no liberation without communication, but also no communication without liberation.

Jürgen Habermas, in a significant exchange with Johannes Baptist Metz, articulates important challenges that Christianity faces at the turn of the twenty-first century. Insofar as Metz engages Habermas and vice versa, we take this to be a confrontation and dialogue by proxy with liberation theologies. Metz claims that anamnestic reason is that faculty that allows reason to criticize itself in terms of remembrance. Remembrance thus becomes normative and imperative, if reason is to be liberating. A forgetful reason that approaches freedom as an utopia empty of mournful remembrance is oblivious to suffering, tragedy, remorse, and gratitude. The unconditionality implicit in this reappropriation of theodicy, Habermas suggests, is sublimated and refunctioned with a theory of communicative action and a discourse ethics. For philosophy not only can appropriate the semantic contents of Christianity, it can also come to its help and self-clarification.

Eduardo Mendieta's essay shows the complicity between a certain reading of Christianity and the project of Modernity, which is also read as an eminently European project. Mendieta, however, suggests that although there are resemblances between postmodernity and liberation theologies, due to historical, methodological, and political reasons, they nevertheless remain very different projects. What is at issue in liberation theology is the question of the other in a very specific historical, economic, political, social, erotic, pedagogical situation. Moreover, Mendieta suggests, for liberation theologies the axes of praxis and understanding are both spatial and temporal. In this situated praxis and reflection are profiled a planetary and polycentric approach that not only anticipates the postmodern, but already inaugurates its superseding, the transmodern, and postcolonial.

Enrique Dussel points out that it is not just postmodernity's exaltation of otherness that threatens the possibility of ethics, so does modernity's idolatry of universality, unity and oneness, in the form of formalism. Taking as a point of departure liberation theology's insight that the telos of liberation is pointed to by the epiphany of God's otherness in the suffering face of the poor, Dussel reformulates many of the insights of discourse ethics in order to articulate an ethics of liberation that supersedes the dichotomy between the formal and material, universality and particularity, sameness and difference. In the age of glib globalization and fatal exclusion, the poor, the victims, those for whom liberation theology and philosophy, as well as the critical theory of the Frankfurt school, make a preferential option, demand praxes beyond the modernity/postmodernity divide and critical reflection that prefigures a still possible liberation.

Part I

Dangerous Hope & Liberating Memory

1

Liberation Theology in the Economic and Social Context of Latin America

Economy and Theology, or the Irrationality of the Rationalized

Franz J. Hinkelammert

Liberation theology is concrete theology, historical theology. For this reason it is appropriate to question the historical context of this theology. Its development can be observed in the agitated history of Latin America of the last three decades. Consequently, we are going to encounter a liberation theology that reflects on, is reflected by, and re-elaborates the very history of which it consciously forms a part.

As concrete theology, liberation theology inserts itself into Latin American society. Base communities, popular movements, and even political parties are key places from which this theology unfolds. Not only does liberation theology speak out of these concrete places but it reflects their historical situation in its own development. Therefore its analyses are tightly linked with theories of social science. Its concrete analyses cannot be deduced from its theological positions, but at the same time its theological positions cannot be independent from the results of its concrete analysis.

However, liberation theology is not a social science; rather it is theology. In relation to its concrete analysis of historical situations, this theology is developed as a theological dimension of actual historical situations. As such, it is exposed to the risk of being mistaken. It does not have absolute truths specified in an a priori manner. In terms used often by liberation theologians, the question is not orthodoxy, but *orthopraxis*. The problem of liberation theology is to find the appropriate praxis for a given situation. Therefore it is in a continual state of gradual development, in which the problems change and new knowledge must be acquired for confronting them. It is living theology.

Yet, a theology can be pronounced as such even before entering in the concrete analysis and the corresponding *orthopraxis*. As theology it precedes *praxis*. Preceding praxis is a collection of empty beliefs. The existence of God, its trinitarian character, redemption, etc., upon being professed as acts of faith, independent from their historical and concrete insertion, become nothing more than empty abstractions that compose a dogmatic whole without content. Liberation theology's problem is not to deny these beliefs, but to question their significance. Therefore, its question is not "Does God exist?" but "Where is God present?" and "How does God act?". The point of departure for liberation theology is, then, the question of the concrete and historical place in which God reveals (it)self.

Liberation theology is born from the answer it gives to these questions. The answer of liberation theology is given through what these theologians call "the option for the poor." This option for the poor is God's option, but equally is the option of human beings, inasmuch as they want freedom. Freedom is liberation of the poor. It is not an act made by others who have the obligation to liberate the poor, and see them as objects. Without mutual acknowledgment between subjects, in which poverty becomes the negation of the acknowledgment, there is no option for the poor. Human subjects cannot recognize each other without recognizing themselves as corporeal, natural, and needed beings. Poverty is a living negation of this acknowledgement. From liberation theologians' point of view, human beings cannot liberate themselves without a mutual acknowledgment between subjects. Therefore, the poor person as subject, who is within a relationship of recognition, is the place in which it is decided whether this recognition is effective or not. As a result, the other side of mutual acknowledgement between human subjects as natural needy beings is the option for the poor.[1]

The absence of this mutual recognition between human beings is present in the poor then. According to liberation theology, God is present wherever this acknowledgment occurs. The fact that this has not happened demonstrates a human relationship bereft of God. The existence of the poor attests to the existence of a Godless society, whether one explicitly believes in God or not. This absence of God is present wherever someone is crying out. The absence of God is present in the poor person. The poor are the presence of the absent God.

Out of this reflection, liberation theology is born as concrete theology, although theologians may express this differently. In this way liberation theology can interpret historical reality. God's absence is a place that can be pointed to. One can protest God's abandonment and God's absence, one can reclaim the assumption of responsibility for this absence, and one can call for the acknowledgement of God, which can also mean a call for this absence to be transformed into presence. The presence of God is no longer an internal emotion, but rather is transformed into praxis (orthopraxis). Its criteria lie in actual reality. God is present if there is no poverty. God's presence is a doing, a praxis.

In this sense, liberation theology is orthopraxis. God does not dictate what needs to be done. God's will is to liberate the poor, but the path of freedom has to be searched out. That which ends up being God's will depends on an analysis of reality. Therefore one cannot know God's will without an analysis of reality that never ignores social sciences. And the results of social sciences fall directly upon what, for liberation theology's orthopraxis, is God's will.

Orthodox theology is different. It stands by its dogmatic affirmations without positioning them within an historical context. Because of this it is easy for orthodoxy to place itself next to domination. Domination is always abstract; it reclaims validity independent of concrete and historical situations. However, it calls attention to the fact that, in the dispute between liberation and orthodox theology there are hardly ever discussions about dogmatic groupings. Orthodoxy affirms it, as does liberation theology. There is no religious conflict in this sense. This situation is completely different from the conflicts of Europe's Middle Ages. Currently, the conflicts revolve around the contents of the dogmatic whole. The schism between the occidental and oriental churches comes undone with the trinitarian formula, that is to say, the presence and origins of the Holy Spirit. The conflict of the Middle Ages had to do with the question of the resurrection of the body. During the Reformation the conflict was predominantly of this type also, i.e., over the interpretation of the Eucharist and the meaning of the saints' heaven.

Economy and Theology at the Beginnings of Liberation Theology

The conflict over liberation theology, then, has had little to do with discrepancies relating to the dogmatic whole. The corresponding discussion, therefore, is not about theological content in the formal sense, but rather about the concrete meaning of these contents. But given that orthodox theology is exclusively dogmatic, this discussion confronts the orthodox position, which reduces the theological content to the pronouncement of empty eternal truths, with the position of liberation theologians, which defends the historical concretization of this same faith. Thus, the use of the social sciences in liberation theology plays a key role within this conflict.

This conflict emerged in the public for the first time during the Popular Unity Party's government in Chile from 1970–1973. Liberation theology had already risen in the previous years, especially during the late sixties. It did not rise primarily in the academic environment but through pastoral activity in the churches, for at that time mainly priests and pastors worked with the poor of Latin American countries. Their first publications appeared as mimeographed manuscripts and were distributed at meetings or by mail. At the end of the sixties the first books appeared (Assmann, Gutiérrez, Miguez Bonino, Juan Luis Segundo). This way of thinking rapidly influenced seminaries and theology departments and created a current of opinion in Latin America, was expressed most intensely in Chile after the electoral victory of the Popular Unity Party in 1970.

Since its inception liberation theology has been closely linked to the popular movements of the sixties. In Chile these movements searched for public expression just as much in the Popular Unity Party as in the Democratic-Christian party. These movements looked for the economic and social integration of popular groups. This problem became more pronounced during the sixties, manifesting itself in the marginality of the poor, felt mostly in the shantytowns of the urban centers, but also in the countryside with the farmers who lacked land and with the small land holder, and in a standstill in employment. Although industrial production continued to expand, this mostly created increases in work productivity, not increases in employment. These factors characterized marginality as structural exclusion and not as a phenomenon of simple transition.

This situation explains the fact that popular movements pushed for changes within social and economic structures. During the sixties many popular movements still hoped for a possible solution from reformist capitalism, sponsored by the Chilean Christian Democracy. However, especially after 1968, popular movements oriented themselves toward the Popular Unity Party. At this time the division in the Democratic-Christian Party occurred in Chile, after which part of this party went on to support the Popular Unity Party.

A profound experience corresponded with the changes in political orientation of these popular movements. It became evident that indeed there was no possibility of economic and social integration within the structural logic of capitalism. This orientation was at first expressed in terms of the need for non-capitalistic development, but later was articulated in terms of a socialist development.

The majority of liberation theologians shared this experience of the incapacity of the logic of capitalist structures to create a society capable of solving the economic and social problems of popular groups. They also shared the interpretation that integral development could not be effective without profound change in the actual capitalist structures. Therefore, they formed a Latin American organization that represented many liberation theologians under the name "Christians for Socialism." They had their first important meeting in Santiago de Chile in March of 1972. It possessed an ecumenical character and it was there that many liberation theologians, Catholic as well as Protestant, met and organized themselves.

The critique of capitalism and the search for an alternative for the transformation of capitalist structures, brought about a conflict with not only orthodox theology but also with the Catholic Church. This church had been a tight ally of the Christian Democracy Party during the sixties. Upon the latter's turning toward anti-socialist and anti-communist positions, the Catholic Church took the same route. Nevertheless, it was very difficult to rebut the experience of liberation theologians and the theory of dependence, which undergirded it. Besides, today, after thirty years of capitalism in Latin America, we can see that the liberation theologians' interpretation of it—and of the theory of dependence—has been completely confirmed, although it has become more difficult to understand the

alternatives than it was thirty years ago. Indeed, taken Latin American's capitalism to the extreme, the marginalization of the population has become more acute and has transformed itself into
exclusion without destination.

Because of this, orthodox theology and the Catholic Church of
Chile might have argued with liberation theology, but without justification. Furthermore, there were no major discrepancies at the
level of the dogmatic whole of their faith, and the critique of capitalism by liberation theologians, at least in its strongest version,
was irrefutable. Therefore, they did not enter into any discussion
with the debate, rather they simply dedicated themselves to denunciation.

The Denunciation of Liberation Theology

An orthodox theology that acts in the name of a dogmatic whole
with the pretense of eternal truth cannot make itself concrete historically. Therefore, in order to confront liberation theology, one
cannot dismantle it without denouncing, however irrelevantly and
even perversely, the manner by which this theology concretizes
itself. Orthodox critics cannot enter into the discussion of concretization, because in this case one would have to accept that theology is and has to be concrete and historical theology.

Denunciation remains as a way out for orthodoxy. And since liberation theologians return many times to Marxist theory to think out
their lived experiences, the orthodox denounces liberation theology
for being Marxist. In a modern bourgeois society, nevertheless, Marx
is—in an Orwellian sense—the non-person that all the world must
attack in order to demonstrate its fidelity to the values of the self-
proclaimed "Free World." Marx is for the free world what Trotsky is
for the Soviet world: the non-person in which evil is supposedly
incarnated. Therefore the denunciation of the Marxist social analysis of liberation theology implies an irrational and ideological condemnation of this theology, without any need to answer to its
concrete challenges. The concrete disappears. There is no need to
discuss or argue. The other always already reveals itself as enemy.

In order that the denunciation serve this goal, Marxist thought is
transformed into a great magic, from which there is no escape.
Whoever comes close gets lost. It is a great turbulence, not theory,
but rather the temptation of evil. Cardinal Ratzinger sums up well
the vision of this Lucifer:

Marxist thought constitutes a totalizing conception of the world in which numerous facts of observation and descriptive analysis are integrated in a philosophical and ideological structure which imposes the meaning and relative importance that they recognize. . . .The separation of heterogeneous elements that compose this hybrid epistemological amalgamation come to be impossible, in such a way that believing to accept only that which is presented as analysis ends with the obligation of accepting the ideology at the same time.[2]

In fact, liberation theologians had only said that the option for the poor is in conflict with the logic of the capitalist structure. Therefore, taken seriously and realistically, this option must overcome this logic. According to critics, this overcoming is called socialism. A real exchange would have to address the question of whether or not this is what liberation theologians maintain. Yet there is not one word about this.

The reason for this rejection is not because that liberation theologians have used Marxist theory. The condemnation was the same even when the theologians had not referred to Marx. But, according to critics the result, that the option for the poor is in conflict with the logic of capitalist structure, proves its marxism. Ideological condemnation prohibits the question, and once the question is prohibited, there is no need to address an answer.

Along with the magical denunciation of marxism, appears the anti-utopic condemnation. The anti-utopic denunciation is nothing but the other face of this magical anti-marxism. Once again a denunciation is substituted for the discussion of concrete and historical situations. Nor does a discussion of the utopic or an analysis of the problematic appear. Liberation theologians asked for structural changes so that society could confront the solution of the problem of poverty. They were not asking for the realization of utopias. They had a realistic objective, although the realism of this goal surpassed the possibilities of their current living situation, that of capitalistic society.

Liberation theologians recognized the utopic dimensions of their political goals and coupled them with a critique of the utopic contents in relation to the realistic structural changes. The anti-utopic denunciation of pro-capitalist forces, however, did nothing more than demonize them, avoiding the dialogue.[3] This led to a situation in which the Chilean Catholic Church made the strongest condemnation of the "Christians for Socialism" group after the military coup, when the group was already being persecuted by the terrorism of the State of National Security.

The formal condemnation of the group "Christians for Socialism" has its own history. The condemnation was decided in secret, without being published, at the Chilean Episcopal Conference in April of 1973. Two days after the military coup d'etat of September 11, 1973, an additional document was passed by the same Episcopal Conference. Their condemnations were put in circulation October 26, 1973, and definitively published in April 1974. During this period more than sixty priests were exiled from Chile and some were tortured. Many lay members of "Christians for Socialism" were either killed, tortured, or detained. State terrorism effectively repressed the "Christians for Socialism."[4]

Liberation Theology and the Dictatorship(s) of National Security

The Chilean Military coup of September 11, 1973 signified a caesura for the Christians for Socialism, and for liberation theologians in general. It was not a traditional military coup in which a military group assumes power over the government while assuring the continuity of the preexisting bourgeois society. The Chilean Military coup was a coup of National Security. The military government took over the task of reconstructing the Chilean bourgeois society from its roots and following a preconceived ideological scheme. A society established itself, which according to abstract principles was one without any relation to Chilean history. For the first time in present history a clearly neoliberal regime appeared in Chile. Through state terrorism, an abstract model of government, deduced from the principles of totalized capitalist market, was imposed. Hence the jacobin character of this coup d'état.[5]

The politics of the military junta prompted a change in the entire society. It was not simply a question of eliminating any trace left by the Popular Unity Party's politics, but of actually transforming the capitalism that had previously existed. This capitalism had been one of reforms, of an interventionist character, which had given way to the existence of an expansive civil society in which popular organizations had held a legitimate and important place. The ideologists of the military junta saw in the capitalist reformation the foundation of the Popular Unity Party's rise. In fact, the Popular

Unity Party had only further carried out the same reformism of the actual capitalist structure but to such a degree that it had put the very capitalist structure in check. Therefore, the military junta took two main lines of action. On the one hand, they directed themselves against all popular organizations in order to destroy them completely, especially the syndicates, the local organizations, and the cooperatives. As these organizations had strong social and political roots, this objective implied the destruction of all popular parties. The terrorism of the State played its principle role here. The politics of terror lasted more than a decade and succeeded in eliminating whatever popular power had previously existed. On the other hand, the politics of the junta also directed itself towards the change of the State. The reformist and interventionist, market-based State was the other face of the popular movements' strength. It was transformed into an anti-reform and anti-intervention State serving a totalized market. The privatization of State functions in the economic, social, and public enterprise arenas shaped for Latin America the first case of a systematic application of abstract outlines brought in by the leaders of this process from the Chicago School of Economics. This concerns precisely the politics that soon after was assumed everywhere by the IMF under the name of structural adjustment.[6]

In this new environment the reflections of Latin American liberation theologians became inscribed. Although a rupture was not produced in this theology, important matrixes were changed. Whereas in the period preceding the Chilean coup a liberationist focus had prevailed, there now prevailed a focus on resistance. There had always been an intense effort on transformation in the ecclesial base communities. But this work had been strongly interwoven with the work of popular organizations. Now, popular organizations were persecuted and had lost much of their force; therefore base communities played a much greater role. In many parts of the country these communities transformed themselves into the only places of popular activity, maintaining the churches as protected spaces from repression. (In place of the popular organizations, many human rights defense groups appeared. Only in Central America was the situation different, especially in Nicaragua and El Salvador. But this tendency began to reverse during the eighties.)

At the center of liberation theology now appeared the themes of idolatry and of the God of life confronting the gods of death. The theme of idolatry had a long tradition extending back to Jewish roots. According to this tradition the idol is a god whose existence and veneration leads to death. Whether the idols exist or not is not as important as the fact that the idol exists, but rather the idol is seen as a force toward death, which is venerated as a god. The idol is a god of death, which therefore confronts the God of life. Consequently, the God of life is seen as a god whose existence and veneration produce life and not death. Since liberation theology holds that corporal life is the final resort of pure, whole life. Although the body does not live except as a body with a soul, neither does the soul live except with the body (*Gratia suponit naturam*).

Thus, for liberation theologians the problem is not one of theism and atheism, but one of idolatry and the God of life. The position contrary to belief is not unbelief. Faith in God can be idolatry or not, just as atheism can be. An atheism whose experience leads to death is idolatry; one whose experience leads to life is not. Life and death are the criteria, not abstract metaphysics. There are also atheists in the family of God. Nevertheless the affirmation of life continues to be seen as starting from the mutual recognition between subjects who perceive themselves as natural and needed human beings. Hence, life and death again confront the option for the poor. Nevertheless the poor now have a new dimension. They are not only poor, but also victims, as they are persecuted by the apparatus of state repression.

Starting from this examination of idolatry and its victim, liberation theology analyzes further the processes of victimization. Orthodox theology is now confronted as a theology of "sacrificiality," or of a God who desires sacrifices. Liberation theology develops a strong criticism of this theological sacrificiality based on an analysis of the sacrificiality of the economic and social systems of Latin America. An entire history of sacrificiality is discovered in the very conquest of America and of the early reactions in support of the indigenous. Liberation theologian Gustavo Gutiérrez returns to the discussion of the theology of the conquest and reclaims the figure of las Casas as a key ancestor of liberation theology.[7]

Yet some theologians go deeper into the subject of the problematic in the relation between economy and theology, especially at DEI (*Ecumenical Department of Investigation*) in Costa Rica (Assman/ Hinkelammert 1989). The theme of sacrificiality is also focused on in terms of the economic and social systems (Hinkelammert 1991).

The sacrificiality of Western culture itself is discovered and the non-sacrificial judeo-christian tradition is reclaimed.

The Conflict Around Liberation Theology

There has always been a latent conflict between liberation theology on the one side and orthodox theology and the churches that support it on the other. We have already seen how this conflict broke out towards the end of the Popular Unity Party's government and during the first year of the Chilean military junta. But with the Rockefeller report of the late sixties another conflict opened up: the conflict between political power and the empire.

Liberation theology ends up being a danger to empire for various reasons. One important reason is ideological, playing an important part during the cold war. This Manichean confrontation needed clear trenches. The empire interpreted itself as the christian (western) world, a reign of god facing a reign of atheist evil. Although the foundation of bourgeois society's legitimacy is not Christian but rather rests on secular myths, the religious dimension is also essential in anchoring itself in transcendence. To believe in God and to fight on capitalism's side against enemies seemed to be the same. This identification is even stronger in the U.S. than in Europe, although it also exists there. This leads to what in the U.S. is called civil religion, which is the underlying religiosity of the actual way of life in the U.S. It is the religiosity that includes all of the specific religions. Therefore, the religious tolerance facing diverse faiths has as its condition the respect accorded these in the framework of the civil religion. Religion is considered a private affair insomuch as it inscribes itself in the civil religion as in public religiosity.

Liberation theology threatened this religious homogeneity—even christianity—of the empire. This was much more sensible, so much more that liberation theology had a positive reception in various churches in the U.S. and Europe, including in the general public. Consequently, the Manichean condemnation of popular movements, their protests, and the demand for structural changes were not carried out easily since important currents of these movements expressed themselves in their religious faith (that is, in their theology). At the same time, certain sectors of the U.S. and European general publics began to doubt the simplicity of cold war ideology.

A similar shift happened among Latin America's popular movements, but from the opposite perspective (e.g., reacting to the orthodox "left"). Liberation theology was one of the currents of thought which allowed a way out of the narrowness of Marxist orthodoxy, especially as it was promoted by the Marxist literature edited by the Moscow Academy of Sciences. This orthodoxy very soon ran its course because it did not succeed in relating to the reality in which the members of these popular movements lived. It was as abstract in its lack of connection to this reality as were market-based ideologies.

Thus an important contribution for these popular movements was the rise of a theology that thought of the world from a similar point of view as these movements and that allowed faith to exist as a participant in the struggles of these movements. Although the majority of theologians were not antimarxist, and actually found inspiration in Marxist thought for the analyses of their reality, they maintained a critical position, one that effectively reinforced these popular movements.

All of this was sufficient reasoning for the empire to react. The Rockefeller Report of the late sixties gave the signal. The very same empire now began to develop its theology, which at first promoted the negation of and later the recuperation of liberation theology.

In the sixties theological centers of a completely new character appeared. The first was the department of theology of the American Enterprise Institute directed by Michael Novak. Its reason for existence was to protest against liberation theology in Latin America and in the U.S. It was followed soon after by the Institute of Religion and Democracy, directed by Peter Berger, an entity that had the same purpose but acted more at a state level of political organizations and churches in the U.S. Michael Novak's books, which appeared in Spanish, were distributed by the impresarial organizations in Latin America and by the U.S. embassies on the continent. Michael Novak made trips for conferences and round tables in Latin America that were organized by embassies or impresarial organizations. The European impresarial organizations followed the American Enterprise Institute and organized their respective theological centers. Even the Pentagon formed a group of specialists in this field to take part in the Pan-American military organizations. Similarly in the late eighties the International Monetary Fund (IMF), headed by secretary Michel Camdessus,

developed its own theological reflection. The principle daily papers
became voices of the new theology of empire. The Santa Fé document of 1980, which formulated the electoral platform for Reagan's
presidency, detected the front between the popular church and liberation theology in Latin America as one of the principle preoccu-
pations of U.S. National Security.

Through the mid-eighties the arguments used against liberation
theology by the proponents of empire were similar to those used by
orthodox theology. Principally, they attacked the Marxist analyses
that appeared as the theoretical element of the concretization of liberation theology and its utopic formulations for a liberated future.
But there is at least one noticeable difference: anti-utopianism of
this imperial theology is much more extreme than the anti-utopianism of orthodox theology and anti-liberationist churches.

Certainly, theological orthodoxy reproached liberation theologians as having a false utopia. But they did not reproach the utopia
itself. As christian orthodoxy, it maintained its own vision of the
coming kingdom of God, and of the heavens. Critics could not
reproach liberation theology for its hope in a kingdom of God.
Therefore, this theological orthodoxy reproached it for interpreting
this reign in material, bodily, and earthly terms—a false concept of
the kingdom. The orthodox kingdom of God understands itself as a
kingdom of pure souls, for whom corporeality is something ethereal, even ephemeral. The kingdom of God imagined on the part of
liberation theologians is a New Earth, it is "this earth without
death," it is a kingdom in which corporeal needs are satisfied.
Orthodoxy sees this as "materialistic," that is to say, as a false hope,
to which it counterpoises its vision of "true" hope. But it does not
deny the vision of the coming kingdom of God.[8]

The imperial theology of the seventies and of the first half of the
eighties is different. It is clearly anti-utopic setting a world without
hope against the utopic vision of a world with hope. Although it
continues to utopianize the market, understanding the market as a
place of "providence" tending towards equilibrium, it does not
establish relations between market-based utopia and the kingdom
of God. Therefore, solidarity appears as human perversion and
atavism.[9]

It has to do with a theology that corresponds to the manicheanism of the Cold War. The authority sees itself in a struggle between
God and the devil, and sees utopia as that which is incarnated in

the kingdom wrongly presented by the devil, and sees itself as a reign of realism, one which does not need utopias. The confrontation of god-devil corresponds, therefore, to the confrontation of realism-utopia. This extreme manicheanism was interpreted by Popper as They who desire heaven, produce hell (Popper 1971).

But this vision of utopia causes problems within the conservative coalition which in the eighties. We have already seen that in its clarity it is not acceptable for actual orthodox theology. But neither did it serve the political coalition of christian fundamentalism in the U.S., one of the pillars of Reagan's government. This fundamentalism is highly utopic and messianic with a wholly apocalyptic vision of history.[10] Thus its own existence daily contradicted the cold war ideology on which its imperial theology is based. The Christian orthodox utopia contradicted the imperial theology's initial anti-utopia.

At the same time as the visible disintegration of the socialist countries took place, a growing utopianism of the actual empire was also produced. The politics of structural readjustment with their disastrous effects on third world countries needed promises of a better future in order to legitimize themselves. The infernos produced on earth demanded the promise of coming heavens. With its conversions and gospel of the market, neoliberalism transformed itself into a religion.

Imperial Theology's Attempt to Co-opt Liberation Theology

After all of this, a transformation in the imperial theology was produced. This theology passed from the negation of liberation theology to its co-option. In the mid-eighties this co-option was in full effect, although it had been notable in Latin America ever since the Chilean military coup d'etat.[11]

In 1985 David Stockman, who came from a fundamentalist background, resigned from his position as chief of budget for Reagan's government and he published a book entitled *The Triumph of Politics*. He reproached Reagan for having been a traitor to the clean model of neoliberalism and for having favored populism. Stockman's book develops a neoliberally positioned, academic theology, that does not denounce utopias, but presents neoliberalism as the only efficient and realistic means to realize them. It attacks the socialist "utopias" in order to reclaim them in favor of the attempted neoliberal realism. According to Stockman, it is not the utopia that threatens, but the false utopia against which he contrasts his "realist" utopia of neoliberalism.[12]

Michel Camdessus, Secretary General of the IMF, echoes the transformed theology of empire grounding it in certain key theses of liberation theology. In a conference on March 27, 1992 he directed the National Congress of French Christian Impresarios in Lille.[13] Mid-discussion he summarizes his central theological theses:

> Surely the Kingdom is a place: these new Heavens and this new earth of which we are called to enter one day, a sublime promise; but the Kingdom is in some way geographical, the Reign is History, a history in which we are the actors, one which is in process and that is close to us since Jesus came into human history. The Reign is what happens when God is King and we recognize Him as such, and we make possible the extension, spreading of this reign, like a spot of oil, impregnating, renewing and unifying human realities. "Let Thy Kingdom come. . . ."

He immediately counterpoises the power of this world and the Kingdom of God:

> One grounds itself on power, the other on service, one, supported by force, orients itself toward possession and monopoly, the other, toward sharing; one exalts the prince and his barons, the other exalts the excluded and weak; one draws up borders, the other links; one supports itself with the spectacular and immediate, the other prefers the discrete germination of the mustard seed. They are complete opposites! and at the heart of these differences is that which condenses them: the King identifies himself with the POOR. . . . In this Kingdom, who judges, who is King? In the gospel the answer is given to us in a formidable, solemn manner with the announcement and perspective of the Final Judgement: today- my judge and my king, is my Brother who is hungry and thirsty, who is a stranger, who is naked, sick or imprisoned. . . .

Camdessus contrasts power, possession and monopoly, the prince and his barons, borders, the spectacular and immediate to service, sharing, the excluded and weak, bonds, and the germination of a mustard seed. He contrasts pride and humility. Nevertheless, he claims that the IMF, structural adjustment, and the entire neoliberal concept of the society incarnate precisely the humility and pride of those exercising resistance, arriving at the following conclusion:

> Our mandate? It resounded in the synagogue at Nazareth, and from the Spirit we are given the receiving of that which the apostles of Jesus denied to accept: precisely the realization of the promise made in Isaiah (61, 1–3) beginning with our present history! It is a text of Isaiah which Jesus explained; it says (Luke 4, 16–23): "The spirit of the Lord is upon me. He has anointed me in order to announce the good news to the Poor, to proclaim liberation to captives and the return of sight to the blind, to free the oppressed and proclaim the year of grace granted by the Lord." And Jesus only had one short response: "Today this message is fulfilled for you that you should listen." This today is our today and we are part of this grace of God, we who are in charge of the economy (the administrators of a part of it in any case): the alleviation of suffering for our brothers and the procurers of the expansion of their liberty. It is we who have received the Word. This Word can change everything. We know that God is with us in the work of spreading brotherhood.

A liberation theologian could have written the text of the secretary general of the IMF. Camdessus formulated the center of liberation theologians' evangelical interpretation, especially the promise of God's kingdom and the option for the poor.

Nevertheless the cited text is only one part of the conference. The anterior and posterior parts contradict key tenets of liberation theology, disparaging "populisms." In the language of the Fondo "populisms" summarizes all possible attitudes and politics that do not assume the strict positions of the IMF's structural adjustment. The speech, therefore, is virulently directed against:

> All of these forms of populist demagoguery which are current and we know where they will lead: to hyperinflation and through it— because the market had not heard the promises- to the economic debacle, of the increase in misery and the return of "forceful" regimes, that is to say, of the end of freedom.

In this way the conference was transformed from an option for the poor to an option for the IMF. Those who wanted anything different from what the IMF's structural adjustment politics conceded, produced "the economic debacle, the increase in misery and the return of the 'forceful' regimes, that is to say, of the end of liberties". This would damage the poor. Therefore, those who are on the side of the poor, by force have to stay with the Fondo. There are no alternatives.

As Camdessus was speaking to a mostly Catholic audience, he also addressed traditionally social Catholic doctrine:

> Of course, the marketplace is the most effective mode of economic organization for increasing individual and collective richness; we should not have an attitude of embarrassment that some generations of our social catholic brothers felt with respect to the market: this "yes, but . . .". The matter is resolved and the Holy Pope left the point very clear in the *Centesimus annus*. For the effectiveness that it assures, the market can permit greater solidarity. From this point of view, the marketplace and solidarity do not oppose each other but rather can be reunited. Besides, the impresarial economy, as you well know, is an economy of responsibility wherein human beings can develop to their fullest dimensions.

Outside of the market no possible activity remains, even solidarity is in practice as a result of the marketplace. Therefore, Camdessus presented the IMF as the great world organism whose responsibility is the exercise of solidarity. Furthermore, according to Camdessus, there is a definitive kingdom beyond history that does not meddle in the matters of the marketplace. He concludes:

> The citizen of the Kingdom—we will refer to him in this way—is in the vanguard of courage so that all forms of fear, mistrust, egoisms, "this idolatry" as Saint Paul calls it (Ephesians 5, 5) recede, and so that finally the field of sharing expands, where the Kingdom already impregnates human reality, and in which human beings find a little more space, freedom and happiness. This, knowing full well that "there will always be poor among us." Which means to say, among other things—and it is indebted to Jesus' saying it—that the Kingdom will not be realized on this earth, not at least until the day on which "He will make all things new." We cannot realize this work

of impregnating human realities without our hearts and our intelligences expanding and being renewed, "full of Grace from on High." For those who exercise our type of work, in this urgency of service to humanity, there is no other solution—I am sure and at the same time far from knowing—than saintliness, or if you wish, of "refashioning" the New Man: that one formed from the earth but that—I return to Saint Paul—"Since Christ came from Heaven, as he belongs to Heaven." Formed from the earth but pertaining to the heavens: the key is there and in Prayer in order to receive this gift.

It is the total declaration of the empire without any escape, neither on earth nor in the heavens. The IMF politics have been transformed into God's will on this earth. Not a will expressed by any Sinai, but by reality itself. Reality is such that, when human actions attempt structural adjustments, the results necessarily will be worse than the situation that is trying to be changed. There is no alternative because the search for one inevitably leads to the worsening of the situation. For this reason, to opt for the poor is to opt for realism. Capitalism has transformed itself into "total capitalism," as Friedman calls it (Sorman 1994). Preferential opting for the poor and preferential opting for the IMF are identified with each other.[15]

Of course, for churches, a great temptation appears. In the vision opened up by Camdessus, one can opt for the poor without entering into any conflict with the powers that be. Great harmony seems to have been achieved. And liberation theology is now part of the orthodoxy itself. The New Man has returned as an official of the IMF.[16]

The empire now appears as absolute and closed. Nothing remains outside of it. It is better not to look for alternatives. When the punishment is greater than what can be achieved in the search for an alternative, it is preferable not to search. In such a situation, power dictates what reality will be like. In between power and reality a circuit is established in which reality tautologically confirms the theses of those in power.[17]

Liberation theologians perceive this condition of an absolute and closed empire as an apocalyptic situation in the judeo-christian tradition. In such a situation there are no visible ways out and there can be no concrete projects for change. According to tradition, the apocalypse is revelation. The apocalypse reveals that, faced with an absolute and closed empire, an unknown alternative exists. Total power of the empire reveals its weakness, but its fall is not seen as a product of an intentional political action. The name of this empire is Babylonia.

This reading of the apocalypse entails analyses of the known apocalyptic texts, as well as the analyses of their economic, social, and political contexts. One rediscovers the fact that these apocalyptic texts have appeared in historical situations similar to ours. The believers found themselves face-to-face with an impregnable empire from which there must have been an, albeit unknown, escape.

Apocalypse does not signify catastrophe. As revelation, the apocalypse reveals that the monster is a giant with clay feet whose fall will leave open the future for realizing alternatives.[18] This reading of the apocalypse, as it now appears in liberation theology, is not directly comparable with the reading of the apocalypse made by Christian Fundamentalists in the U.S. For the latter, the apocalypse is again only a catastrophe that comes by God's will, in the form of inexorable historical law. The world is condemned to perish and its salvation is achieved by a god-judge upon the consummation of history itself. History's own law is human catastrophe. But, the recuperation of liberation theology that Camdessus tried to achieve is perfectly compatible with such a world vision.

Certain liberation theologians' current reading of the apocalypse does not coincide with any of these meanings. The absolute and closed empire of today, as were the Roman, Hellenic, and Babylonian empires, is a Babylonia. As such, it is a giant with feet of clay. It falls, but the reason for its fall cannot be a voluntary human act. It falls due to unintentional effects resulting from its own omnipotence. There is no metaphysical law of history that makes it fall. It falls because "suddenly a stone is detached, without intervention of any human hand and, comes to hit the statue on its iron and clay feet and it pulverizes them."[19]

The apocalyptic situation also inspired wisdom literature. One of the greatest testimonies of this literature, that today has been reclaimed by liberation theology, is the book "Ecclesiastes" of the Bible, which was written in the third century B.C. Faced with an unshakable and disastrous empire, Ecclesiastes has a more or less tragic sense of life. The lament over the loss of a sense of life prevails Ecclesiastes has much in common with certain currents of contemporary postmodernism. Upon the return by some theologians to the reading of the apocalypse, this problematic also appears today in liberation theology.[20]

The Challenge of Liberation Theology:
The Irrationality of the Rationalized

As we saw precisely with the IMF, the negation of liberation theology was the construction of an anti-liberation theology. This anti-theology is an inversion of liberation theology.

Again the fact that these two contrary theologies cannot be distinguished on the level of a clearly theological discussion stands out. At this level liberation theology does not visibly distinguish itself from the anti-theology presented by the IMF. The conflict seems to be over the application of a theology shared by both sides. The theology of the empire—the theology of the IMF *is* the theology of the empire—assumed the key elements of liberation theology: the preferential option for the poor and the hope for the kingdom of God, incarnated in the *orthopraxis*. At least this is all of its obvious appearance.

On a different level, another problem returns which we have seen at the beginning of this article. There we analyzed the fact that liberation theology arose in such a way that the conflict with orthodoxy did not appear as a religious conflict because no religious dogma was questioned. The conflict appeared as a conflict over the concretization of a common faith. The preferential option for the poor and the incarnation of the kingdom of God in the economic and political world were the instruments of this actualization. As a concretized theology, liberation theology was seen as one of conflict.

These days, imperial theology assumes these positions. Imperial theology is in agreement with the preferential option for the poor and with the economic and social incarnation of God's kingdom. It presents itself as the only realist path for fulfilling these demands.

Surely the theology of the empire distorts liberation theology's option for the poor. From liberation theology's point of view, this option is the consequence of a mutual acknowledgement between human subjects. The poor are a sign of the loss of the acknowledgment which verifies that all human social relations are distorted. Imperial theology can only focus on the poor as an object of the others who are not poor.

Under the claims of imperial theology, the option for the poor can no longer identify any specification and natural affinity for liberation theology. Now, the question is over the realism of the con-cretization. No preconceived faith can give the answer. One cannot decide the truth of one of the positions without returning to empir-ical sciences, especially economic sciences. It is they who decide. As a result, they transform themselves into carriers of the criteria of truth about the theologies. Indeed, with neoliberal economic poli-tics in their hand, the option for the poor is transformed into an option for the IMF. From the point of view of a political and critical economy, the option for the poor is transformed into the demand for an alternative society, in which everyone has a place. Theology as theology cannot decide. Scientific results recognize the concrete content of theology.

For this reason, the recuperative intentions of liberation theology force the development of new problematics. In order to continue supporting the option for the poor in terms that respect the poor as a subject—something specific to liberation theology—this option has to be linked in a specific way with the mutual acknowledgment between embodied and needed subjects.

This leads to the need for the development of liberation theology along two lines. The first refers to the critique of the neoliberal political economy and its respective utopianization of market law. The second refers to the Christian tradition of a theology critical of the law. Both constitute space for a discussion that today is often summed up as "economy and theology." This confirms the rele-vance of economic analysis for the discernment of faith content.

The first line of the critique of a neoliberal political economy could be summed up as follows: the rationalization by competitive-ness and efficiency (profitability) reveals the profound irrationality of the rationalized. Efficiency is not efficient. Upon reducing ratio-nality to rentability the present economic system transforms itself into irrationality. It unties destructive processes that cannot be con-trolled from the parameters of rationality that it has chosen. The exclusion of a growing number of persons from the economic sys-tem, the destruction of the natural bases of life, the distortion of all social relationships and consequently, of actual mercantile relations are the nonintentional results of this reduction of rationality to rentability. The market laws of total capitalism destroy society and its natural environment. By making absolute these laws by way of the myth of the automatism of the market, these destructive ten-dencies become uncontrollable and convert themselves into a threat for human survival itself.

This critique leads to an analysis of rationality that includes the irrationality of the rationalized. It deals with the development of a concept of a natural and social circuit of human life that has to globalize and to condition the halfway-ended rationality that underlies the calculation of rentability. This excludes the neoliberal totalization of market law for integrating mercantile relations into social life. The neoliberal politic, however, treats the market as the constituent element of all social relations, in this way leading to its politics of total capitalism.[21]

With analyses of this type, liberation theology is faced once again with the need to confront Marxist thought.[22] Marxist thought is the existing theoretical body that precisely critiques the irrationality of the rationalized. Upon confronting this problem today, any conceptualization will develop thoughts close to those developed first by Marx. The Marxist critique still presents problems for liberation theology. It has to do with Marxist hope in being able to solve the problems of absolute capitalism by completely overcoming capitalism itself. With the neoliberal totalization of capitalism, marxism led to a totalization analogous to that in which we live. Liberation theology has to overcome the totalizations, if it indeed wants to contribute to the building of a new faith. Yet however criticized these totalizations, the conceptualizations of the critique of the irrationality of the rationalized are indispensable in order to constitute an adequate concept of the rationality of human behavior. The theory of rational behavior, as stated by Max Weber, does not go beyond the reductionism of rational behavior to its expressions in terms of a means-ends rationality, i.e., the measurable in terms of profitability and efficiency.

This brings us to the second line of liberation theology's necessary development in today's world. The critique of the irrationality of the rationalized must be expressed in theological terminology itself. This occurs today precisely because of the recuperation of a long theological tradition of the critique of the law, which begins in the gospels themselves and has its first theological elaboration with Saint Paul of Tarsus, especially in his letter to the Romans. In fact, it is the first production of the critique of the irrationality of the rationalized that exists.[23]

Liberation theologians emphasize the key elements of Pauline theology in their critique of law. On the one hand, Paul makes visible that the law, insomuch as it is a law of fulfillment, leads those who fulfill it or who are obliged to fulfill it to death. Even the law that serves life leads to death. Here, law is any law. Therefore, the privileged law State, which appeared as the Roman Empire for the first time in history, is not the maximum expression of humanity, but rather, is a threat. The law does not save by its being fulfilled. On the other hand, Paul considers sin not as an infraction of the law. Sin, in the way it is dealt with in Paul's vision, is committed in fulfilling the law. Infractions of the law are secondary. Therefore, sin is committed with the good conscience of fulfilling the law.[24] Traces of this thought were still maintained in the European Middle Ages: *Suma lex, maxima injustitia*. Or the more ironic opposite: *Fiat injustitia, pereat mundus* (that the law be fulfilled even if the world must perish).

In this sense, the critique of the law already develops the problem of the irrationality of the rationalized. For this reason, liberation theologians can reclaim this theology in relation to market law. On the one side, the law of the market leads to the death of humanity. On the other side, a sin is committed in fulfilling the law of market and it is committed with the good conscience of fulfilling the maximum law of humanity. Christian freedom returns therefore, in the sense pronounced by Paul, as a freedom that is sovereign before the law. The free subjects are free to the degree that they are able to make the law relative with respect to their own needs. Freedom is not in the law, but rather in the relationship subjects have *with* the law. Considering market-based law, freedom consists precisely in being able to subordinate and even to break the law, if the needs of the subjects demand it. The mutual acknowledgement between embodied and needy subjects implies unequivocally the acknowledgement of the relativization of any law as a function of this acknowledgment. Upon mutually acknowledging each other as subjects, they recognize themselves as sovereign before the law. Law is valuable only to the degree that it does not impede this mutual acknowledgment.

The option for the poor can now be taken back in a sense in which imperial theology will never accept it. The mutual acknowledgement between embodied and needed subjects implies the option for the poor, and because of this implies at the same time the sovereignty of the subject over the law. Without this sovereignty there can be neither mutual acknowledgement between subjects nor the option for the poor. This reconceptualization also demands a reconceptualization of the kingdom of God (Sung 1994).

Therefore, liberation theology denies not only the making absolute of market law in "total capitalism," but also of any metaphysical law of history. The making absolute of the law—that is to say, its transformation into metaphysical law of history—is totalization, which in the end leads to totalitarianism. Its motto is always that one of "the end of history," and the negation of all alternatives (Assman 1994).

With this result, liberation theology leads not only to a critique of capitalism, but also to one of modernity itself. It arrives at the confirmation of a crisis of Western society itself.

Nevertheless, it is not postmodern. Postmodernists take great care to analyze the law of the market law as a metaphysical law of history. They attack from all sides metaphysical laws of history. But, the law of the market as the only case today of the imposition of a metaphysical law of history, is not even mentioned. They conceal the metaphysical laws of history in force today in the name of the critique of so many laws of past history.

Translated by Elizabeth Wing

Notes

1. Emanuel Levinas's philosophy is one of the sources of this thinking. Refer to his *Totalidad y Infinito: Ensayo sobre la Externidad*. Ediciones Sigueme, Salamanca, 1977 and his *De otro modo de ser, o mas alla de la esencia*. Ediciones Sigueme, Salamanca, 1987. In a later work Levinas summarizes the position, when speaking of loving one's neighbor: "What does 'as yourself' mean? Buber and Rosenzweig here had their greatest problems with translation. They said: 'as yourself', does this not mean that one loves the self more? In place of the translation mentioned for you, they translated: 'love your neighbor, he is like you'. But if one already agrees to separate the last word of the hebrew line, 'kamokha', from the beginning of the verse, it can all be read in another way: 'Love your neighbor; this creation is like you, yourself'; 'love your neighbor, you are he'; 'this love for your neighbor is what you are'." Levinas, Emanuel: *De Dieu qui vient a l'idee*. J. Urin, Paris, 1986. p. 144.

2. Ratzinger, *Libertatis nuntius*, VII, 6. See also Hinkelammert, Franz: "Befreiung, soziale Sunde und subjektive Verantwortlichkeit" in Venetz, Hermann-Josef, and Vogrimler, Herbert, ed. *Das Lehramt der Kirche und der Schrei der Armen*. Edition Exodus y Liberacion, Freiburg/Munster, 1985. p. 60–76.

3. Comblin summarizes this critique of utopia by liberation theologians: "The future has been planned by God and stays always out of humanity's reach: it is the renewed man, the man of the new alliance. . . . The future is lived by living the present. One cannot sacrifice the present to the future, but the opposite rather, the future should be lived and realized in the present in

the form of image or likeness. Not to sacrifice the present man in the light of future brotherhood and peace, but to live this future peace in an imperfect present, but a valid and real image. On the other hand, the present has no meaning in the immediate satisfaction that it bestows, but in the image of the future which it allows to be realized." Comblin, *Mensaje*, July, 1974. p. 298. See also Hinkelammert, Franz: *Ideologias del Desarollo y Dialectica de la Historia*. Editorial Universidad Catolica de Chile. Paidos, Buenos Aires, 1970.

4. The same Cardinal of Santiago, Raul Silva Henriquez, declared in a trip to Italy, that the Christians for Socialism had taken a path which "as a matter of fact, made them renounce their Christianity. . . ." (Avvenire, according to *Mercurio*, 10–25–73).

5. The analysis Hegel makes of jacobism, clearly affirms the Chilean military coup d'état and its previous politics: ". . . when these abstract conclusions came into power, they afforded for the first time in human history the prodigious spectacle of the overthrow of the constitution of a great actual state and its complete reconstruction *ab initio* on the basis of pure thought alone, after the destruction of all existing and given material. The will of its re-founders was to give it what they alleged was a purely rational basis, but it was only abstractions that were being used; the Idea was lacking, and the experiment ended in the maximum of frightfulness and terror" (Hegel, *Philosophy of Right*, trans. by T. M. Knox, Oxford: The Clarendon Press, 1942), Paragraph 258, p. 157). This jacobism, with its disposition to state-sponsored terrorism is also notable in many later cases of the Chilean military coup, in which the schematics of the neoliberal ideology were imposed. One of the coup's mottos comes directly from Saint-Just: "No freedom for the enemies of freedom." On the French Revolution refer to: Gallardo, Helio: "La revolucion francesa y el pensamiento politico" in *Pasos*, (DEI. San José), 1989, Nr. 26 Nov/Dec.

6. Milton Friedman later called this move the politics of "total capitalism."

7. The theology of the victim also has roots in German theology of the Nazi era. See Gutiérrez, Gustavo: "Los limites de la teologia moderna: Un texto de Bonhoeffer" in Gutierrez, Gustavo: *La fuerza historica de los pobres: Seleccion de trabajos*. CEP. Lima, 1979; and Hinkelammert, Franz: "Bonhoeffer" in *Teologia alemana y teologia latinoamericana de la liberacion: Un esfuerzo de dialogo*. DEI. San José, Costa Rica. 1990.

8. "The Marxist doctrine of the final hour is a promise of intra-worldly salvation. Karl Marx secularized the fate of the Jewish people—slavery in Egypt and the exodus to the promised land—as the hope of the messianic salvation of the Old Testament in order to transpose them to our time, the period after Jesus Christ—a disturbing reduction and an imitation (Nachaffung: behave as a monkey) of the salvation which was given to all of humanity through Jesus Christ. Marxism is an anti-gospel." (Hoffner, Josef: *Christliche Gesellschafts-lehre*, Kevalear 1975. p.171–172.)

9. "The traditional and socialist societies offer a unitarian vision. They arouse in all activity a *symbolic solidarity*. The human heart is hungry for this bread. Atavistic memories besiege every free man. *The 'paramo' (high barren plain) which we find in the heart of democratic capitalism is like a field of war on which many individuals wander amidst cadavers*. But this desert, like the

dark night of the soul in the journey of mystics, fulfills an indispensable intention. . . . Of course the transcendental dominium is mediated by literature, religion, family and similar institutions; but in the last instance, it is centered around the interior silence of each person." Novak, Michael. *The Spirit of Democratic Capitalism*. An American Enterprise Institute/ Simon and Schuster Publication, N.Y. 1982.

"In conclusion: The 'children of light' are in many ways a greater danger for biblical faith than the 'children of darkness'." Novak, op.cit. p.71. Novak, Michael. *El Espiritu del Capitalismo Democratico*. Ediciones Tres Tiempos: Buenos Aires, 1983.

10. Refer to Pentecost, J. Dwight. *Eventos del Porvenir: Estudios de Escatologia Biblica*. Editorial Vida: Miami, 1984 or Lindsay, Hal. *La Agonia del Gran Planeta Tierra*. Editorial Vida: Miami, 1988. (*The Late Great Planet Earth*. Zondervan Publishing House: Grand Rapids, MI, 1970.) During the seventies more than 15 million copies of Lindsay's book were sold.

11. "The Declaration of the Principles" of the Chilean military government of 1974 makes this clear.

12. Stockman presents himself as a converted leftist, who at one time was partisan to a false utopia, but who has now discovered the true utopia: "In a deeper sense, however, the new doctrine [he even speaks of the "gospel of the offering"] of the offering was nothing but a re-working of my old social idealism in a new form and, as I thought, matured. The world could begin again from the start. The economic and social crises, that are getting bigger, could be overcome. The oldest evil inheritors of racism and pauperization could also be overcome with profound reforms which are born of political causes. But most of all, the doctrine of the offering offered an idealist alternative to the sense of a time of cynicism and pessimism."

13. The quotes that follow are translated from the published text: Camdessus, Michel: Marché-Royaume. La double Apparteanace. Documents EPISCOPAT. Bulletin de secrétariat de la conférence des éveques de France, Nr. 12. Juillet-Aut. 1992. Camdessus presented a similar conference before Christian businessmen in Mexico.

14. At a conference at the Semana Social de Francia/ Social Week of France in 1991, Camdessus also confronted the option for the poor with what he calls populism: "Let us be careful with our judgments so that we may never confuse the preferential option for the poor with populism" (p. 100). See Camdessus, Michel. Liberalisme et Solidarite a l'echelle mondiale. XXX, Concurrence et Solidarite. L'économie de marché presqu'ou? Actes de Seminaries sociales de France tenues a Paris in 1991, Paris, ESF editeur, 1992.

15. In this sense, Hugo Assmann cites Roberto Campos: "In rigor, nobody can directly opt for the poor. The option that they have to make is for the inversionist, they who create work for the poor." In Assmann, Hugo: *Economia y Religion*. DEI: San José, 1994. p.101. See also Moll, Peter G.: "Liberating Liberation Theology: Towards Independence from Dependency Theory." *Journal of Theology for Southern Africa*. March, 1992; Haigh, Roger S. J.: *An Alternative Vision: an Interpretation of Liberation Theology*. Paulist, N.Y.; Sherman, Amy L.: *Preferential Option: A Christian and Neoliberal Strategy for Latin America's Poor*. Grand Rapids, MI. 1992.

16. Refer to: Assmann, Hugo/Hinkelammert, Franz J.: *A Idolatria do Mercado: Ensaio sobre Economia e Teologia*. Vozes, Sao Paulo, 1989.

17. Hannah Arendt skillfully describes this network: "The affirmation that the Metro of Moscow is the only one in the world is only a lie while the Bolsheviks do not have the power to destroy all the rest. In other words, the method of infallible prediction, more than any other totalitarian, propagandistic method, denotes its final objective of world conquering, given that only in a world completely below its control can the totalitarian dominator possibly make reality all of their lies and accomplish the fulfilling of all of their prophecies." Arendt, Hannah. *The Origins of Totalitarianism*. Taurus, Madrid 1974, p. 435. She continues, "Then, all discussion around the accurate or erroneous of the prediction of a totalitarian dictator results as fantastic as discussing with a professional assassin about whether their future victim is alive or dead, given that killing the person in question the assassin can immediately apportion the test of veracity of their declaration" (435). In an interview Camdessus describes this mechanism as seen from the IMF, asking, "What would the social cost be of the measures to place public finances in order?" and answering, "The question is what would the cost be for the people of Costa Rica to not adjust their structures? The cost might be the interruption of internal financing, reduction of inversion/investment??, the paralyzing of an agreement for recognition of debt, and the interruption of importing. The cost might be a recession. . . . Our position is not exactly that of recommending nor imposing measures, our position is one of dialogue. . . . But, the fact that the goals have not been respected and that we may have suspended the expenditure, does not signify a punishment but a reality which the country faces by adapting their politics. Later, we will pay." Interview with Michel Camdessus, director-general of the IMF. (*La Nacion*, San José, 3–5–90.)

18. Perhaps the best description of the apocalyptic situation is the following from the prophet Daniel: "You, oh king, have seen this vision: a statue, an enormous statue of extraordinary brilliance, of terrifying aspect, arises before You. The head of this statue was of pure gold, its chest and arms of silver, its belly and loin of bronze, its legs of iron, and its feet part iron and part clay. You are looking, when *suddenly a stone is unfastened, without the help of any hand, comes and hits the statue's feet of iron and clay and pulverizes them.* Then everything was left pulverized at once: iron, clay, bronze, silver, and gold. . . . And the stone that had hit the statue converted into a great mountain that filled all the earth." (Dan. 2. 31–35).

19. Cf., Richard, Pablo, "El pueblo de Dios contra el imperio. Daniel 7 en su contexto literario e historico" in *Ribla*, Nr. 7. DEI, San José, 1990. Also, Richard, Pablo, *Apocalipsis: Reconstruccion de la esperanza*. DEI: San Jose, 1994; Mesters, Carlos, *Apocalipsis: La esperanza de un pueblo que lucha*. Rehue: Santiago de Chile, 1986; Foulkes, Ricardo, *El apocalipsis de San Juan: una lectura desde America Latina*, Buenos Aires, 1989; Rowland, Christopher: *Radical Christianity: A Reading of Recovery*, Orbis: New York, 1988.

20. Cf., Tamez, Elsa: "La razón utópica de Qohélet" in *Pasos*, Nr. 52. DEI: March/April 1994.

21. Gallardo, Helio: "Radicalidad de la teoriá y sujeto popular en América

Latina" in *Pasos*: Numero especial, 3/ 1992. DEI: San José, Costa Rica. And: Hinkelammert, Franz J.: "La lógica de la expulsión del mercado capitalista mundial y el proyecto de liberación" *Pasos*: Numero especial, 3/ 1992.

22. Cf., the respective works of Enrique Dussel, *La produccion teórica de Marx: un comentario a los "Grundrisse"*. Siglo XXI: Mexico, 1985; *Hacia un Marx desconocido: Un comentario de los Manuscritos del 61–63*. Siglo XXI: Mexico, 1988.

23. The book most emphasized in this sense is: Tamez, Elsa: *Contra toda condena: La justificacion por la fe desde los excluidos*. DEI: San José, 1991. Cf. also, Hinkelammert, Franz J.: *Las armas ideologicas de la muerte*. DEI: San José, 1981. Second Edition, revised and expanded with an introduction by Pablo Richard and Raul Valdes.

24. This leads to an analysis of sacrificiality as being a result of the law. The law, upon being treated as totalitarian, demands human sacrifices. This was clear in early Christianity. All of the Evangelists, for example, insist that Jesus was killed in fulfilling the law, in fulfillment of the law. Therefore there are no persons guilty of this death. It is the relation with the law that originates it. The later orthodoxy preferred to blame the Jews in order to escape the consequences of a theology critical of the law, which was completely incompatible with the aspirations of Christianity of imperial power. Cf., Hinkelammert, Franz J.: *La fe de Abraham y el Edipo Occidental*. DEI: San José, Segunda Edicion Ampliada, 1991; Hinkelammert, Franz J.: *Sacrificios humanos y sociedad occidental: Lucifer y la Bestia*. DEI: San José, 1991; Pixley, Jorge: "La violencia legal, violencia institucionalizada, la que se comete creyendo servir a Dios" in *Ribla* 18: San José, 1994.

Works Cited

Assman, Hugo and Franz J. Hinkelammert, *A Idolatria do Mercado: Ensaio sobre Economia e Teologia*, São Paulo, 1989.

Assman, Hugo, "Teologia de la liberación: Mirando hacia el frente," in *Pasos* 55 (Sept/Oct 1994).

Hinkelammert, Franz J., "Paradigmas y metamorfosis del sacrificio de vidas humanas," in Hugo Assman, ed., *Sobre idolos y sacrificios: Rene Girard con teólogos de liberacion*, San José, Costa Rica, DEI, 1991.

Popper, Karl, *the Open Society and Its Enemies*, 2 vols., Princeton: Princeton University Press, 1971.

Sorman, Guy, "Sauver le capitalisme: Le dernier combat de Milton Friedman," *Le Devoir*, April 5, 1994, Montreal, Canada.

Sung, Jung Mo, *Economia: Tema ausente en la teologia de la liberacion*, San José, Costa Rica, DEI, 1994.

2

When the Horizons
Close Upon Themselves

A Reflection on the Utopian Reason
of Qohélet

Elsa Tamez

Q ohélet is a book to be read when it would seem that the chronological times are conspiring against human beings: the horizons close upon themselves, the present is frustrating and the glorious past remains forgotten. The following article is a desperate attempt to bring out hope in times of messianic drought.

Present time: total frustration, hebel

According to the theologian and economist Franz Hinkelammert, to be hopeful for a different future is a threat to the stability of the present capitalist system that maintains that its implementation is already on its way to the perfect society (Hinkelammert 1994). It is everyone's hope; to create other hopes is to be against the only possible hope. Therefore, one needs no other expectations but to live waiting for (with respective readjustments) the promised hope. If such is the case, the reflection upon utopia is a task for those who wish to seek new realities for all.

Just like the present, Qohélet's narrated world asserts the non-novelty under the sun. All is an absurdity, an immense emptiness, a bunch of crap, "filth." He expresses this feeling of frustration with the Hebrew term *hebel.* Qohélet relativizes the commmon theology inherited from the sapient tradition, as well as the theology of the messianic promises of prophets, by confronting them with the experience of the quotidian and with the recognition of the schism. The theoretical and theological schemes do not respond to the present historical challenges. There are no messianisms in sight, neither punishment to the bad ones nor reward to the just ones.

The vision of frustration and impotence is present throughout his discourse, but in the midst of such discourse, departing from it and under the silence of God, Qohélet reflects upon concrete possibilities of escape in these times of messianic drought. In his book and from daily experience he will advise us how to survive in the best way possible the spurns of a society that is guided by the slogan, Every man for himself.

Qohélet, or Ecclesiastes, is an argumentative book. The Hebrew term *qohélet* can mean "one who is in the assembly," or "one who disputes or argues."[1] His non-narrated world, that is to say, the real world in which the text is produced, asserts the opposite of Qohélet. All is new. Scholars of the Hellenistic period maintain that an amazing and unprecedented[2] structural change took place during this period, mainly after the death of Alexander the Great and during the mandate of the Ptolomeans from Egypt, the time in which *Ecclesiastés* was written (between 280 and 230 B.C.E.). Innovations occurred in every field: in the military sciences, in the manner in which power was exerted from Alexandria, in the royal administration and its finances, in the field of coinage, in the fiscal policies in Egypt and its provinces, in technology applied to agricultural production, in large scale commerce and in the discussion of philosophical issues. It was also during this period that principles in mathematics and physics, still in use today, were formulated. The geographic and economic structures of Egypt under the Ptolomeans required a well organized and centralized administration. The Eastern idea of deifying the king was adopted by the Greeks and was put into practice in combination with Greek logic. To the absolute power of the king as possessor of the land was added Greek efficacy.

Why then does the author reject novelty?[3] There can be but a few reasons: either he was sharp and daring in his ability to discern the negative consequences that the new Hellenistic economic order would bring to the non-Greek population, or he was a xenophobic conservative, skeptical of innovation. We favor the former interpretation.

However, what concerns us here is the fact that the author cannot envision a utopia capable of organizing existence as a structure of possibility, as something different from slavery (*amal*), from constant self-censorship, from lack of solidarity, from anxiety in the face of imminent death, cannot envision a utopia capable of inciting struggle. Qohélet is not strengthened by a faith that would lead him to a praxis of transformation. The *hebeliana* atmosphere darkens his horizons. As we shall see later, the overcoming of this predicament is limited when, on the one hand, he projects his inability to relate the future to a transcendental God who acts mysteriously and who organizes the times for each thing; and on the other, when he categorically asserts that the only way out is by living intensely what is good in the present (to eat and drink merrily amidst arduous work). This way of living is by no means the realization of his utopia, since it ultimately falls within the logic of *hebel*, given that it is not accessible to every one and that it is ephemeral like adolescence and youth (11.10). But, because it is *hebel*, this stand is the most plausible one. Let us now analyze carefully his discrete utopia.

Qohélet's Hidden Utopia [4]

After Hinkelammert analyzes (avowedly realist and explicitly anti-utopian) neoliberal thought, he reaches the conclusion that even it has a hidden utopia since it refers to impossible horizons that transcend the human condition. This leads Hinkelammert to postulate that utopias exist as part of the human condition; therefore he points out that:

> No human thought could be placed outside the utopian horizon. When a thought involving a "realism without utopias" is intentionally formulated, it will reproduce non-intentionally its own utopian horizons (Hinkelammert 1993, 50).

If such is the case, our character Qohélet, despite his overwhelming pessimism cannot be anti-utopian or non-utopian, although at times he seems to be as shown in declarations such as "what's twisted cannot be straightened" (1.15, cp. 7.13).

One also needs to take into account that the text is like an interior monologue, subjective and contradictory. For instance, at one point he worships the dead and the unborn, because they do not see the great violence and injustice committed under the sun (4.2–4). He also congratulates the aborted ones over those who have lived two thousand years, working without enjoying (6.6). At a different point, however, he concludes that life is better than death for the dead will not take part in life under the sun, since they have no love, no hatred, and no envy (9.4–6). Only at the following point in the text does the word "hope" appear: "There is still hope for all those who are among the living; because it's better to be a living dog than a dead lion" (9.4). The declaration is certainly not as optimistic as "keep hope alive." In reading Qohélet one must venture on a different path to uncover his utopian horizons. One could do so from three different levels: first, from the level of implicit desires in terms of a rejection of the present; second, from the level of the utopian horizon of the explicit desire in terms of the affirmation of life as it unfolds in the realm of the quotidian; and third, from the level of the explicit faith and trust in an almighty and imponderable God who, at some juncture of history, will realize that which is impossible for humans to realize, precisely because they are humans.

Implicit Desires in Terms of a Rejection of the Present.

We identify four important desires: to know the times, to wish for justice and freedom, to wish for happiness, and to transcend death.

1) Of the desire to know the times and its impossibility.

One of the greatest frustrations of Qohélet is his inability to know the future and to understand the complexity of the present unraveling under the sun. He understands why the present of *hebel* does not fit the traditional theoretical frameworks that seek to interpret such complexity. Salvation appears to lie in knowledge; it is important to know what will happen in order to bear with this "filthy" present and organize oneself. However, despite Qohélet's efforts to understand and to know through wisdom and science, he cannot know and understand (6.12; 7.24; 8.7). Knowledge and wisdom are painful and disturbing (1.17–18). According to him, all he finds is

hebel; and he cannot understand God's purpose either in the beginning or in the end:

> He made everything beautiful in its time; and he has placed eternity
> (*olam*) in their hearts, without humans being able to reach an under-
> standing of the work God has made from the beginning until the end
> (3.11).

Eternity (*olam*) can have various significations: unlimited dura-
tion, the distant and hidden, or the sum of all concrete things, that
is, the set of historical events. The human being, then, has the
potential to understand beyond what is given. In spite of all this, it
is impossible to understand reality in all its plenitude; the work of
God surprises Qohélet and supersedes his suppositions. In 8.17 he
repeats once again that despite having carefully observed (*rah*), he
cannot fully understand reality and God's works.

The impotence of not being able to know either the times or the
purposes of divinity causes him pain; for, consequently, he cannot
organize a coherent praxis. This experience diminishes him when
he tries to overcome the obstacle to realize such praxis; and given
that no one knows the evil that can befall the earth (11.2), he floun-
ders in his search for the signals that would lead him to new path-
ways (11.1-6). Qohélet makes clear that wisdom is better than
wealth and strength, but he also recognizes that wisdom has limitations. In this regard, as a wise man, he is self-critical.

Since the narrator can neither dominate the times objectively,
nor order them rationally, he re-articulates them and translates
them beyond his consciousness: he catapults them to God's domains. Since the times transcend him, he can only assign to them
a utopian function that reasserts his human *condicio* by making
him aware of his limitations. The reliable affirmation that all happens in due time is the utopian phrase that orders life. Only by having faith in this affirmation is it possible to face and to bear the
rejected present with a certain tranquility and safety. If there is a
time to be born and to die, to embrace and not to embrace, to love
and to hate, then there should be a time to *hebel* and to non-*hebel*.
The new, denied by Qohélet, is the sign of the non-*hebel* time. This
time is utopian in as much as it happens independently from the
effort of humans. He has faith that this time will come some day,
but does not know when and how; he can identify its signs, like

clouds that filled with water herald rain (11.3), but he cannot pre-
dict the time of its arrival. Time is thus made into a structure of
possibility.

2) Of Desires of Justice and Freedom in Society

A desire for justice for the poor and oppressed is a desire that is
implicit in terms of the denied present. Society is inverted; there is
injustice rather than justice (3.16); power is in the hands of the
oppressors, the poor are oppressed, and there is no one to dry their
tears (4.1). The state does not conform to its role as administrator
of justice and social welfare (5.7) and the tyranny of the king is
unbearable and cannot be censored for he does what he pleases as
if he were God (8.3-4) and has spies everywhere (10.20).

The non-*hebel* society of Qohélet is that in which justice, liberty,
and law reign. Such is his utopia. Since it is not explicit and he does
not think it feasible, not even via anticipation, he does not state
how to attain it, or how to bring it closer through praxis. Again, by
means of the faith in the times he finds a possibility for each thing.
The structure of possibility is not provided by the times in their
chronological perspective, but by the faith in the existence of the
mature and fortunate times.

3) Of the Desire for Happiness

The desire for happiness appears explicitly in the following refrain
"there is nothing better than to eat and to drink with happiness. . . ." But, it also appears in the rejection of the present in relation to enslaving work (*amal*); It serves no purpose to work so
earnestly in order to amass wealth if the soul is defrauded from
goodness [*tob*], (4.8); or if one lives too many years without enjoying them (6.6). Happiness ought to correspond to taxing work; it
does not reject the process of working but the enslaving manner in
which it is carried out, and that its product is not enjoyed. The
enjoyment of work is the corresponding payment, it is its share
(*jeelec*). It is not money, but the feeling of joy one gets in the process
of laboring (2.10). Therefore, moderation is suggested in working.
"It's worthier to be rested with one full fist than to be fatigued after
trying to grab the wind with two fists" (4.6). What does happiness
mean exactly? Qohélet cannot define it in the above citations; he

only asserts that one ought to enjoy, probably referring to the sequential time that is lived daily, still he is not satisfied as to the actual happiness that would cover long and short times. For this reason he asks himself: "Who knows what is happiness in the life of a human being, all days in the life of his *hebel*, which pass like a shadow? For who would teach the human being what will become of him under the sun?" (6.12). In this last verse one can clearly perceive the problem of death as it puzzles Qohélet.

4) The implicit desire to transcend death.

Qohélet congratulates the dead ones and the abortive ones who are in the *Seol*, not because he wishes to be among them—we already pointed out his preference to be among the living—but because he does not know the oppressions and injustices of their world. Our character does not want to die. Although he does not express it explicitly, it enrages him that the just and the impious die, without any distinction among them (9.2–3). For Qohélet the bad ought to die, but not the good. The oppressor spends his life doing evil without being judged and at the end he simply dies. The just one spends his life doing good without acknowledgment and at the end he receives the same recompense as the bad one: death. And all the living forget. Moreover, death not only equates human beings of different conditions, but it also equates beasts to humans (3.20–21). Qohélet does not formulate possibilities of resurrection since during the third century BC resurrection rarely comes up as an issue in Judaism.

Death is a misfortune which the human being cannot prevent (cp.8.8). Qohélet describes the time of death as bad, as a time of darkness (11.8). And it is also bad that the human being cannot know the time of death's arrival: "Because the human being does not know his time; like fish imprisoned in a net, and like birds that get entangled in a rope, thus are human beings entangled in the bad time, when it suddenly befalls them" (9,12).

Since death is an unchallenged reality, neither its beyond, nor the time of its arrival is known to any human being. Qohélet accepts death and in doing so acknowledges his human condition. From this acknowledgment, he proposes two plausible alternatives: not to hurry the arrival of death with a particular practice that can cause sorrow; and to enjoy intensely this present life, mainly before the coming of old age announcing the time of irrevocable death (p.7–12.7).

Since his world is that of *hebel*, it is indispensable to know how to conduct oneself adeptly, trying to distinguish among the times. In times of repression one must "walk with cat paws." In favorable times one must enjoy and be happy, and in times of adversity one must reflect and discern (7.14). If society is inverted because the just does poorly and the bad one does well, one cannot be either too just or too bad; extremes in this inverted and repressive situation can lead to a premature death (cp. 7:16–19).

This escape is not the ideal solution. This is also sometimes classified as *hebel*, but this is the best that can be done in a given moment of daily life, in order to resist the oppressive reality and to avoid dying before it is time. It is not about cynicism or aloofness, but about historical realism in a measured and chronological time. The concept of the fear of God, which I will analyze later, will provide us with an important clue to counteract the frustrating impotence and thus be able to enjoy life sensually with freedom and without guilt.

The other plausible suggestion that attempts to beat death consists in interrupting by means of pleasure the context of *hebel*. One must accomplish this interruption before our vital energy runs out and before death, the world of darkness arrives. The context of future and eternal death, abode of the human being, is also *hebel* (11.8, cp 12.5).

Qohélet also includes advice for the young: take full advantage of the present, let yourself be carried by what your heart and your eyes dictate, protect your body from suffering (11.9–12), enjoy pleasure freely. In this time of joy he recommends remembering the Creator, before the world of the present time comes to an end (12.2) and fortitude weakens with old age (3–6), and death comes irrevocably (12.7). This pleasure must not be self-destructive or destructive to others. With this in mind Qohélet is careful to warn us that one must enjoy fully, yet knowing that God will judge all deeds (11.9). God is a beacon of limits to protect people.

Qohélet does not fear death, neither does he love it nor does he invite suicide; he conceives it as an inevitable reality which we can defeat with many days of material happiness before it arrives. Thus he mocks it now, to accept it later. Whoever does not enjoy life in the midst of so much enslaving work allows death to happen prematurely, because the opposite of death is not simply life, but life lived in all its sensuality. The faith in the fact that everything has its time—a time to be born and a time to die—is what allows him neither to fear nor to love death and to take advantage of real life in the span between birth and death.

5. The explicit viable alternative: the affirmation of a material and sensual life in daily experience

After Qohélet examines his world and objectively observes the closing of the horizons in the near future, he proposes a solution in the rejection of the present by affirming a concrete and sensual life in the very same present. He does not propose to remember the good old times and thus be happy basking in reminiscences. Neither does he propose to live now the illusion of a better future, knowing that everything has its respective time and that happiness will come at its time. This would amount to accepting the present with resignation. Its explicit alternative is to live now, in the midst of *hebel*, that which could resemble the non-*hebel*: an unfettered happiness, knowing that everything has its time and hour. This is a good and plausible solution. If the future is uncertain and the past leads to alienation, one must establish a consciousness in the present. But the present can reveal itself to consciousness as a straitjacket, given the lack of utopian horizons that are explicitly configured or the promises made to ancestors. There are few alternatives in the present: cynicism, resignation, suicide, or to live the present guided by a logic different to the one imposed by the system "of excrement," that is, of *hebel*.

Let us return to the alternative of the affirmation of the concrete life in the present, but taking into consideration the non-narrated world of Qohélet. The logic of the Hellenistic system of production is that of enslaving labor: the economic and political administration marks the rhythm of labor at a dehumanizing beat, that does not take into account the subject. Religious leaders, guardians of the temple, also mark the rhythm of events by closely following the Mosaic law and sacrificial rituals. The subject, blindly obedient to the Law, becomes objectified. It is not his consciousness that guides his steps, but the Hellenistic and Ptolomeic administration, along with the requirements of the temple's rituals. Qohélet proposes to counteract all this with a different logic, guided by the heart (con-

sciousness proper) and the eyes (what the subjects see). This logic
vindicates the subject. The best manner in which this logic guides is
not within a rational and coherent life experience (at the present
moment such is not possible); the only thing this rationality indicates is the negative character of the present: *hebel*. Therefore, the
best logic available to face hebel is the affirmation of life in the joyful eating of bread and drinking of wine, with the loved one, in the
midst of enslaving work. Such is the central content of the proverb
that is repeated six times.[5] It touches on key aspects of Qohélet's
discourse: Qohélet works, acts, examines, reflects, seeks, and
arrives at the conclusion that there is nothing better than daily
activity. In each refrain different details appear. The most nearly
complete form is the last one:

> Go, and eat your bread with joy and drink your wine with a happy
> heart; for your deeds are already pleasing to God. At all times let
> your clothes be white and never be without ointment on your head.
>
> Enjoy life with the woman you love, all the days in the life of your
> *hebel* given to you under the sun, all the days of your *hebel*; for this is
> your role (*jelec*) in life and in your work with which you toil under
> the sun
>
> All that comes to your hands let it be done in relation to your
> strengths; because in *Seol*, where you are going, there is no deed, nor
> work, nor science, nor wisdom. (9.7–10).

With this affirmation of concrete life, Qohélet, without making it
explicit, brings to bear the signals of the times innovations: the
eschatological banquet, the already known utopia of Isaiah (62.9).

Let us not be mistaken by thinking that this proposal comes from
a selfish, isolated character who cannot bear any other company
than that of the loved one. He categorically advocates unity with
others, since such communal relations endow one with strength
and help one to live a better life.

The utopia of the quotidian feast is the only possible solution for
Qohélet: to reject the present, to then accept it again in a positive
manner, affirming and living that which the present is unable to
offer: rest, joy, shared food, and to do so at a pace in which chronological time is unimportant. In this sense, it is like living eternity
within sequential time, but without taking this latter into consideration, for minutes are not counted. Here time is not gold (money)

as it is in the marketplace, not finances, the stock market, and the production of enslaving work. What matters is a full belly and the happiness of the feast. What matters are the living bodies and the worldly joy preceding eternal death. If death is the eternal abode, as he says in 12.5, life has to be lived as if it were eternal; that is to say, living exquisitely intense moments where there is no consciousness of time.

In other parts where the proverb appears (2.24–26) it is said that such disregard of time comes from God's hand. With His guidance the subject can enjoy life without feeling guilty. The Mosaic Law, as interpreted by the leaders of the temple, constantly required rituals of purification. Qohélet is guided by a different logic, as the following section of 9.7–9 makes clear: "Your deeds are no longer pleasant to God." Freedom, then, within a non-*hebel* world becomes absolute. This is only possible because life is inscribed in a joyful world characterized by shared and intersubjective happiness, not guided by the law but by a logic that tends to acknowledge the subject as independent from the law.[6]

This is the explicit utopia of Qohélet, although by denying all novelty in the times of history, he doesn't acknowledge it as such. Because it is a utopia, its full realization in history is not possible.[7] Indeed, one cannot always be in a feast, Qohélet exhorts. To dress up in white and to anoint oneself with oil means to dress for the banquet. However, this amounts to a poetic expression of his desires,[8] in a reality in which, on the one hand, foreign dominance, production, commerce, competitiveness, and war point to efficiency, leaving aside human beings, especially agricultural workers, slaves or freemen; and on the other hand, in which a temple requires sacrificial rituals for the purification and the fullfilment of the law.

It is true, however, that not everyone has the means to eat and to drink, or to enjoy life in the company of the loved one. The proposition amounts to Qohélet's desires, manifested not so much subjunctively (wishful thinking) but imperatively. For our character, the real world is *hebel* because the worker cannot enjoy his work; someone else does and that is *hebel*. Non-*hebel* means to be able to enjoy the product of one's own work. Moreover, his reflection seeks universality; he refers to everyone including the wealthy (5.19).[9] He also proposes that the rich man enjoy his wealth while he can; for either he won't know how to do it in the world of *hebel*, or a foreigner will enjoy it for him, or he will lose it in bad deals given the instability of the market. Such a life style, however, will not allow him to know the joy of daily life, or the sharing of bread. The wealthy man does not acknowledge himself as being more important than his wealth. The utopian horizon of Qohélet consists of all enjoying material life, and knowing how to do so.

The alternative joyful experience of corporal life, realized without worries, in the midst of the rigor of sequential time and the threat of demanding laws is not the proposition of a vital force simultaneously paralleled and irresponsible to the power of the dehumanizing efficiency of the Ptolomean machinery, or the sentencing of the Mosaic law's dictums. It is neither about an experience of joy that turns its back to the dehumanizing ordeals of power, nor is it an experience of joy produced by sentiments of cynical powerlessness and disinterestedness in the face of the most fragile victims of political economies. Qohélet clearly states that one ought to celebrate life with joy in the midst of enslaving work, in the midst of *hebel*. And this, we believe, is the greatest defiance to those that deny a full and dignified life to others.

This interpretation is not farfetched. In the Glyptyic art of ancient Mesopotamia, one observes funeral scenes in which the participants celebrated sacred banquets, with music, dance, drinks, and lovemaking. These actions represented the vital force challenging death, mocking it, and thus holding on to life.[10] In this sense Qohélet's proposal from the quotidian, acquires a greater signification for the economic, political, and religious macro-structure. It is then not about attempting to approach the utopia by creating a parallel community isolated from the world of *hebel*[11] and thus untouched by it. Qohélet, ultimately and perhaps unconsciously, proposes to challenge the logic of "filth" by living, in the midst of it with a logic of of "non-filth," a logic whose synthesis is to eat bread, to drink wine with happiness, and enjoy life with a beloved one.

6. The impossible alternative. The faith-trust in God Almighty

Qohélet's frustration is his powerlessness against the *hebel* of the world. The signifiers in the initial poem (1.4–11) connote the presence of a self-regulated machinery that does not admit interference. In that world, daily events are neither considered, nor do they affect the almost perfect functioning that characterizes the monotonous events of the universe. All is *hebel* and nothing is possible against it

(1.12–15). We will now try to observe the contradictory changes of Qohélet's consciousness in his understanding of the absurd events, and his theological reading, which in turn helps him read the times in order to survive well.[12]

The work of wisely examining what one does under the sun is a sad occupation that God gave humans. This wise knowledge of "madness and delirium" becomes "distress and pain" (1.17–18) because human beings cannot understand with certainty the absurdity of reality—its immense emptiness, the *hebel*. The wisdom inherited from ancient times implies all things were created beautiful by God and that He made humans as good creatures. Experience of the world, according to Qohélet, contradicts this premise. Qohélet does not understand and then universalizes his lack of understanding: All things God made are beautiful but humans cannot achieve understanding of the whole work of God, even though God implanted in their hearts the possibility of comprehending the most abstract concepts (3.11). Regardless of the efforts a human being makes to understand God's ways in history, he cannot achieve such understanding, even if he is a wise man.

Despite lacking understanding, our character continues with his theological reasoning: God made humans to be fair, but they perverted this situation (7-29). This is a step toward understanding the events of his world. But not even this step can help one understand the work of God; since God, in His omniscience, becomes responsible for all the events under the sun, then God is responsible for the miserable world of Qohélet. God is the one who has twisted the twisted: "Look onto the work of God; for who could straighten what He has twisted?" (7.13). God is responsible for the fact that some can enjoy and some cannot enjoy the product of His work. Qohélet describes this event as a great and painful malady (6.1–2).

At one particular point Qohélet's reasoning reaches its limit: God is God and a human being is a human being. God is stronger and one cannot argue with the divine. Qohélet presents this reality as a well-known and non-mysterious fact: "As to what he is, it has been some time since he had a name, it is known that he is human and that he cannot contend with the One which is more powerful than he is (6.10)."

Once this step is taken, the narrator projects his powerlessness in the face of transcendence and divinity. Curiously, once he has acknowledged his impotence, his enthusiasm is reactivated, and writing a viable history of the ideal of a joyful life now, in the midst of *hebel*, becomes possible. This indispensable step allows him to reconstruct his consciousness and to reorganize his world from a dimension outside of the urgency and the overwhelming agony of *hebel*. It is here where the notion of fear of God comes into place (5.7), a notion that Proverbs describes as "the beginning of wisdom"(12.13); and according to the appendix of our text, as "the whole of the human being" (12:9–14).[13]

The meaning of the term "fear of God" (*iara*) does not mean to be afraid of God. In Qohélet, it means to acknowledge the distance that separates humans from God (Westermann 1978, 1066). It means to acknowledge God's noumenal and extraordinary nature, a nature that overwhelms humans since it is an inscrutable, indispensable, and undecipherable enigma. God is a mystery. God establishes the limitations of humans' potential, as a mirror or a clear pond: He makes His creatures see their human nature. In this sense the acknowledgment of God as such initiates the possibility of human realization. Paradoxically, fear of God means "not to fear"; it invites quietude in the middle of disquieting practices. Fear of God is related to human behavior and to human attitudes towards life, hence, it emphasizes trust (Mussner 1983, 98). Once the limitations of humans are acknowledged, consciousness moves within the margins of the possible; since God will take care of the impossible, even through His subjects. All is in front of God (9.1).

Powerlessness launches humans to the dimension of faith. At the same time faith gives humans energy to go on living. Qohélet as we mentioned, re-orients the world towards the non-*hebel* by assigning the appropriate times to God. If the time of *hebel* neutralizes or paralyzes, faith that everything has its time and its hour becomes liberating. God manages the times, and he who fears Him, he who acknowledges his own limitations, will do well. This is the force of faith, although it is not experienced in the now of the present. Qohélet has faith that God will act with fairness in the appropriate time (3.17–18; 8.12–13).

At this point, Qohélet makes his alternative explicit: affirming concrete life in the joy of eating bread, drinking wine, and enjoying life with the loved one. There is not irresponsibility nor is there indifference in the face of events of exploitation under the sun. There is a move for life because one rests under the grace of God, even in the midst of enslaving labor and its anti-human logic.

Trans. Pedro Lange Churión

Notes

1. For Graham Ogden the one who "argues" is a more appropriate translation (Neh. 5.7), *Qohélet*, 1987, p. 27.

2. M. Rostovtzef, *Histoire Economique et sociale du mode hellénistique*, 1989; Martin Hegel, *Judaism and Hellenism*, 1974, pp. 6–57; M. Rostovzeff, *A History of the Ancient World*, 1963, pp.258–300; Helmut Koester, *Introducción al Nuevo Testamento, Historia, Cultura y Religión de la Epoca Helenística e Historia y Literatura del Cristianismo Primitivo*, 1988, pp. 73–345; Stephen de Jong, "Quítate de mi sol! Eclesiastés y la Tecnocracia Helenística", *Ribla* (1992) n. 11.

3. It is believed that Qohélet is an aristocratic sage.

4. For this analysis we will use Franz Hinkelammert's basic categories as fundamentally presented in his book *Crítica de la razón utópica, 1984*; and in "El cautiverio de la utopía: Las utopías conservadoras del capitalismo actual, el neoliberalismo y la dialéctica de las alternativas" in *Pasos* (1993) n.50.

5. Cf. 2. 24–26; 3.12–13; 3.22; 5.17–19; 8.15; y 9.7–16; in 11.9–10 the advice to the young to be happy and to live happily during their youth appears.

6. In this line we interpret the Pauline theology that consists in the justification by means of faith and not by the works of the law. The Law, absorbed by sin, alienates the consciousness of the subject and enslaves it. Faith transcends the Law and places the human being above it. Elsa Tamez, *Contra toda condena*, 1991.

7. Hinkelammert thinks of utopia as the construction of impossible worlds. Politics would be the art of the possible, oriented by the proposition of the impossible. *Crítica a la razón utópica.*

8. As Rizzante and Galazzi say, it seems like a micro-psalm of the quotidian.

9. Probably he is referring to his aristocratic contemporaries, also subjected to the domination of the Ptolomean Empire; their wealth could be confiscated at any time by the King.

10. Cf. Marvin H. Pope, *Song of Songs*, p. 210ss.

11. This is much like the Utopia of Thomas More that Vasco de Quiroga tried to create in some of the villages of the conquered land in Mexico, where the privileged ones in the utopia were those who participated in the villages, and the other indigenous people were brutally exploited, without any pronouncements being made on their defense.

12. In the text they are not ordered and there is no reason for them to be so, since it is about a struggle of consciousness itself. The order corresponds to our own re-reading.

13. It is clear that a second epilogist, who included the appendix 12.13–14, does not share the same understanding of fear of God that Qohélet has. For Qohélet fear of God has nothing to do with the fulfillment of the commandments.

Works Cited

de Jong, Stephen. 1992. "Quítate de mi sol1 Eclesiastés y la Tecnocracia Helenística," *Ribla* n. 11. (1992).

Hegel, Martin. *Judaism and Hellenism*. Philadelphia, Fortress Press, 1974.

Hinkelammert, Franz. "la lógica de la exclusión del mercado capitalista mundial y el proyecto de liberación" in *America Latina: resistir por la vida*. San Jose, DEI, 1994.

———. *Crítica de la razón utópica*. San José, DEI, 1984.

———. "El cautiverio de la utopía: Las utopías conservadoras del capitalism actual, el neoliberalismo y la dialéctica de las alternativas" in *Pasos* n. 50. (1983).

Koester, Helmut. *Introducción al Nuevo Testamento, Historia, Cultura y Religión de la Epoca Helenística y Historia y Literatura del Cristianismo Primitivo*. Salamanca, Sigueme, 1988.

Musner, Franz. *Tratado sobre lo judios*. Salamanca, Sigueme, 1983.

Ogden, Graham. *Qohélet*. Sheffield, JSOT Press, 1987.

Pope, Marvin H, *Song of Songs*, New York, Doubleday & Co., Ind., 1977.

Rostovtzef, M. *Histoire Economique et sociale du monde hellénistique*. Paris, Robert Laffont, 1989.

———. *A History of the Ancient World*, Oxford, Clarendon Press, 1963.

Tamez, Elsa. *Contra toda condena: La justificacion por la fe desde los excluidos*, San José, DEI, 1991.

Westermann, Jenni. *Diccionario Teológico Manual del Antiguo Testamento*, v 2., Madrid, Cristiandad, 1978.

3

Renewing the Option for the Poor

Gustavo Gutiérrez

First of all I would like to thank you for this invitation, which allows me to share with you some reflections on our common faith and hope.

You know well that I will not salute you with polite words. For many years El Salvador has been a very important and beloved country for Latin Americans. We carry it deep in our hearts, not only because of Monsignor Oscar Romero who convokes us this week, but also because of many others, among whom are our Jesuit friends who have worked in this university and many other anonymous persons from this Salvadoran nation.

The topic that has been selected for me, in its enunciation and in its content, is familiar and well known: "The option for the poor." I believe that the preferential option for the poor is the most important contribution to the life and reflection of the Latin American Church. If one writing and reflection of our time must remain, it is precisely this option. This reflection moves undoubtedly beyond the Latin American experience since it is clearly interwoven in the most essential aspects of the Christian message. But this message, as it has occurred with other great topics of the biblical word, seems at times if not to become opaque, at least to be pushed aside. In our days, the Latin American Church and its Christian communities have been responsible for bringing it again to the foreground.

Phenomena of this type have occurred many times in the history of Christianity. Not more than fifty years ago a book was published

that revolutionized some milieus of moral theology. It was titled—
the author was a Belgian Jesuit—*The Primacy of Charity in Moral
Theology*. The title was provoking and the work was innovating,
although it sounds familiar today. But it happens that theologians
and moralists had forgotten about the primacy of charity in the
moral behavior of Christians.

This simply shows how fundamental questions can become
eclipsed at any time. Well then, I believe that we in Latin America
have put the question of the poor and our solidarity with them
under the spotlight again. Nevertheless, and this makes us happy,
the roots of this question are quite old; they are in the Christian
message. The preferential option for the poor was welcome and it
has inspired many experiences, but has also been questioned. I
would like to begin by taking word for word the formulae *preferential option for the poor*.

1. "Poor"

Let us begin with the last word of the formulae we used in Puebla.
No one doubts that when we talk about poor we are referring to the
"real" poor. The Bible speaks of the concrete poor, of the reality of
poverty. What is the theological reflection that becomes intertwined
with this perspective of preferential option for the poor?

a) A new presence

For some decades now a new phenomenon in Latin America and
other places of the world has been put forward. It has to do with a
different presence of the poor.

In these years the poor in Latin America, traditionally absent
from the history of our peoples, become progressively present by
means of popular, peasant, and syndicalist organizations. The poor
begin to realize their poverty and to become conscious of its causes.
I am not talking about absolute beginnings but I am talking of
something which did not exist before. This will mean that this new
presence will cause the social, political, cultural, ecclesiastical, and
theological life of Latin America to change.

Physically, the poor were always there. But I am speaking of an
active presence, of a demand for their rights, and of their will to
become subjects of their own history, protagonists of their own des-

tiny. This process has not reached an end yet (for instance, we see the increasingly more important presence of ethnic groups, of the indigenous groups, of the blacks in the continent, and of women, whose presence is increasingly more important in popular sectors).

The new presence of the poor has had many repercussions. One of them was that the causes of poverty begun to be discussed. It is not enough to describe poverty, it is necessary to point with the finger, like the biblical prophets used to do, to those who are responsible for poverty, to the causes of it, such as social injustice, the social and economic mechanisms, etc. To indicate the causes was also an innovation. Before, we limited ourselves to corroborate the existence of poverty. What is new today is to speak of that which motivates poverty in order to attack it from the root.

This new presence of the poor also brought to Latin America, that word and that concept, so important for us today: solidarity. Solidarity, as you all know, comes from solid. Solidarity implies a certain solidity, something consistent that one wants to do. And, it might seem curious to you, the word "salary" also comes from solid. Therefore, those who evaporate the salary of workers also seek to evaporate social solidarity. The more solidarity there is, the more defense of the solid, the salary, the wages that are necessary to live.

b) Meaning of Poverty

The poverty to which we allude here encompasses economic, social, and political dimensions, but it is undoubtedly more than all that. In the last instance, poverty means death: unjust death, the premature death of the poor, physical death. Unfortunately, not only in Latin America do people die of ailments that medicine has defeated elsewhere. There is no justification for Cholera related deaths nowadays, but Cholera takes many victims in Peru, my country, as it takes them in other locations of the world, such as Asia, and wherever one finds poor people.

Poverty, therefore, leads to physical death, including the deaths caused by the situation of repression of a people, and cultural deaths. When a community is not taken into account, when it is rejected in one way or another, then, in a certain way, the persons that belong to that community are being eliminated. In Latin America, we have a great variety of races, cultures, and languages: if they are rejected, the people that belong to those social groups are being killed. Anthropologists usually say that culture is life; well then, if one rejects culture, one rejects life. This also happens when women are denied full human rights.

Poverty, therefore, means death. When I speak this way I am not attempting to hide its social, political, and economic dimensions. I have preferred to insist on the profound meaning of poverty in order to tell you that what ultimately constitutes the real problem is the defense of life. Thus, in the Christian communities of Latin America, one speaks frequently of the God of life, and unjust cultural and physical death is rejected, as well as any other manifestation of selfishness and sin.

What then does being poor mean? I believe that a good definition does not exist; but we can approximate it if we say that the poor are the non-persons, the "in-significant ones," the ones that don't count either for the rest of society, and—far too frequently—for the Christian churches. For instance, the poor are the ones who have to wait for a week by the door of a hospital to see the physician; the poor are the ones who have no social and economic relevance, the ones disowned by means of unfair laws; the poor are the ones who have no possibility to speak to change their predicament. The poor are the ones who constitute a despised and culturally marginalized race. At best, the poor are present in statistics, but they do not appear in society with proper names. We do not know the name of the poor. They are and remain anonymous. The poor ones are socially insignificant, but not so to God.

Today we speak of a "surplus of population" in the world. As some economists say ironically, economic mechanisms have made it possible for exploitation to be a privilege. The exploited ones can then be grateful to their master because he gives them work, given that some are not even exploitable. They are insignificant. There are those whom we call nowadays, with a term that has a cruder flavor than before, "the excluded ones" (Actually the poor have always been excluded. One has to be cautious of intellectual fashions).

But the poor ones are not only persons who lack things. The poor are human beings. The poor have a way to pass their free time, to make friends, to pray, to laugh, to think, to speak. Poverty is a world of its own. We are not denying, by any means, that the poor are part of an exploited social class, of a marginalized race, of a discriminated culture, of a gender not sufficiently appreciated. This expression aims to make us realize that there is a world of the poor, and that the commitment to it means entering this world. It not only means to be committed to a social class or a particular culture, but to enter into the world of the poor; this acion brings about something important: friendship. There is no genuine solidarity with the poor if there is no friendship with them.

c) There Will Always be Poor Among You

Allow me to allude now to an evangelical text which is at times presented as an objection to what we are saying here. It has to do with the ointment offered to Jesus by a woman in Bethany. I will allude to St. Mark's Testament for various reasons, among others because in it the name of the woman is not given. She is an anonymous woman. She pours perfume over the Lord. The disciples protest saying that such an action is a waste of money, money which should be given to the poor. The Lord responds with a phrase taken from the Old Testament: "There will always be poor among you." How many times has this phrase been used to state: why so much worrying about the poor? if the Testament says that there will always be poor, why make an effort to have even one less poor person?

However, the context in Deuteronomy from where this phrase is taken is quite clear. It appears in chapter 15; there we find three basic affirmations: "that there should not be any poor among you"; if there were, "you should not close your hand"; and, "there shall always be poor among thee." The latter is a realist affirmation. We ought to strive toward the first affirmation, namely that there not be poor among us, but if there were we know what our behavior should be. The observation: "There shall always be poor among you" means that we are between the ideal and crude reality.

Before the Lord cites Deuteronomy, he says to his disciples in defense of the woman: "Leave her alone, don't stop her, she is doing a good deed". The word good, as used in the Testament, is a Greek term that also means beautiful. Let's then read it that way: "She is doing a good and beautiful deed for me." This is a capital lesson. With the poor we must recognize two notions: the struggle for justice and solidarity with them—there is no commitment to the poor if there is no struggle against the causes of poverty—and the ability to perform altruistic acts, gestures of friendship, such as the one performed by this woman who anoints Jesus with perfume.

In friendship we consider the other as equal. One shares only with friends. What that woman did with Jesus is what we must do with the poor. It is necessary to be in solidarity with their struggles, something which you know well. But once in a while it is important to learn how to open bottles of perfume as well. Human beings are more complex than we imagine them to be.

One more detail about St. Mark's Testament. It is said that the incident occurred in Bethany. In Hebrew, the word "betania" means "house of the poor" (Bet': house, ani: poor). The Testaments are filled with symbols.

2. Preference

There are people who argue that it would be better to simply speak of "option for the poor," since preference seem to weaken the expression. I disagree. Preference reminds us of a fundamental affirmation of the biblical message: the universality of God's love that excludes no one. Only within the context of this universality can one understand preference, that is to say, "that which is given priority." The Bible speaks of God's preference for the poor. Why in the book of Genesis does God prefer Abel over Cain? Nowhere is it said that Abel is better or that Cain had behaved badly; but Abel was the youngest, the last one. God preferred the sacrifice of Abel, the more fragile one, over the sacrifice of Cain: Cain's sin was not to accept God's preference for Abel.

The rejection of preference consists of not understanding that one must combine the universality of God's love with His preference for the poor. Pope John XXIII alluded to this when he spoke of "the Church of all, and in particular the Church of the poor." As Christians we cannot say that "only the poor count." Such an attitude would not be Christian, as it would not be Christian either to pretend one loves every one when in reality one loves no one. To combine both of these aspects, universality and preference, is not an easy thing; it's a great challenge.

a) The reason for preference

But why this preference? It is not social analysis that allows us to understand poverty and that leads us to prefer the poor. Such analysis is certainly useful, but it is not enough. Human compassion is also important, but it is not the ultimate reason. If we must prefer

the poor it is because God is good. The ultimate reason of preference is the God of our faith. This affirmation commits all believers.
No one can escape from the demand of this preference for the poor.
Preference comes from the goodness of God, and from God's gratuitous love, a central notion of the evangelical message. God loved us
first, and our lives should be a response to that free initiative from
God. That is the meaning of "spiritual poverty."

The great mystics, St. John of the Cross, for instance, taught us
how a God that loves us gratuitously constitutes the center of the
spiritual life. Without contemplation, without prayer, there is no
Christian life. But without solidarity with the poor there isn't one
either. It is necessary to keep these two dimensions united.

b) To bring out of anonymity

Allow me another illustration from the Gospel; I am referring to the
episode of the hemorrhaging woman The context is important.
Jesus restores the health of the daughter of a relatively important
figure who has implored him for help A bit later Jesus comes into
contact with the sick woman who has spent all her money on doctors who could not cure her. The disciples try to open a path among
the multitude that presses around Jesus. Jesus asks: "Who has
touched me?" They tell Him: everyone is touching you so how could
you ask who has touched you? But Jesus insists, thus removing
from anonymity a poor woman, so humble and anonymous that she
does not even dare to ask him for a miracle. He brings her out of
anonymity, asks her to identify herself. He speaks to her and makes
her emerge from the masses.

Such then is the preferential option: the dismantling of anonymity to give people a name and a face. In general Jesus has opted for
the poor, but also, concretely, he has opted for people like the hem-
orrhagic woman. Do you understand what I'm trying to say? When
I affirm that Jesus favors the poor I know this woman is included,
but one must value her as a person, make her assume an identity,
she who thought of herself as worthless. To love is always to bring
someone out of anonymity. Love helps give identity to others. When
we speak of preferential love, and the love of God, preferably for the
poor, we are speaking of giving the loved ones an identity, of making them feel like people. This woman felt so worthless that she did-
n't dare speak to the master, but he makes her "appear."

3. "Option"

Let us move on to the third word, option. Allow me to refer here to some texts from the New Testament in which we find some models for the option for the poor.

a) Knowing how to look

Let's begin with the episode called the widow's obolus in Mark: "And he [Jesus] sat down opposite the treasury, and watched the multitude putting money into the treasury. Many rich people put in large sums. And a poor widow came, and put in two copper coins, which make a penny. And he called his disciples to him, and said to them, 'Truly, I say to you, this poor widow has put in more than all those who are contributing to the treasury. For they all contributed out of their abundance; but she out of her poverty has put in everything she had, her whole living" (12, 41–44; cf. Lk. 1–4).

I will not insist upon the clear and beautiful meaning of this small donation valued so much by the Lord. Rather, I would like to highlight what is said at the beginning of the text I just read: "And Jesus sat over against the treasury." The temple of Jerusalem was quite large and it had many doors; the books refer to these doors. Apparently Jesus was alone because it is said later: "and he called to his disciples." Jesus sits in front of the seat of the treasure, just where donations are deposited. Perhaps he was on top of a stone on the streets from where he simply begins to observe. I beg you to use your imagination a little and think about this Jewish young man who is in Jerusalem (a city always dangerous for him), who stops in front of the temple of his religion to observe what is happening. For how long was he there? We don't know, so let's imagine he observed for a few hours.

What does Jesus do? Something important, something in line with the option for the poor: he teaches us to see. The first thing that must be done in this option is to know how to look. Why do I use "to know"? Because there were many doors in the temple. Jesus chose to stay in front of the Treasure's coffer. Sitting by this door appeared to him important in order to understand the underlying attitudes of those who would come by to make donations. And because he knew what to see, he could say that the widow's donation was quite worthy, much more than others; that is to say, a donation which to an inadvertent observer might have no special importance is highlighted by the Lord.

Jesus teaches us how to see. He tells us in order to see one must properly choose the viewpoints. That's what he does. What we see depends on where we are placed. If in life you choose a particular place, you will see certain things; if you choose another you will see others. (For instance, if you stand by the doors of the World Bank you will see many interesting things . . .) One must have intelligence to know how to see; and thus that which appears small or insignificant becomes important. We live on a continent with immense, increasing poverty; on a continent in which there are diverse peoples, races, cultures, languages that still have not met each other; we live on a continent that is constructing its identity; on a continent where the poor appear more and more in the social, cultural, and religious scene.

We are talking about a massive reality that cannot be postponed. We know, however, that it is also possible to choose an angle that impedes seeing the reality of poverty. We must learn how to see authentically. In this case that which was considered insignificant appears in the foreground: the poor. Jesus was the first model who teaches us not only how to look, but also how to see.

b) Knowing how to listen

Let's talk about a second model: "knowing how to listen." I will refer to another text by St. Mark. We know it as the episode of the blind man of Jericho (10,46–51).

Jesus is on his way to Jerusalem. There he will be apprehended and executed; he knows it and fears it. Jericho is on the way to Jerusalem from Galilee, a province marginalized by the Jewish people; here Jesus performed most of his ministry. A blind beggar, thus someone twice poor, heard that Jesus was near. The blind man, then, began to shout (the testament states it textually): "Jesus, Son of David, have mercy on me!" He shouted many times like people who have deep needs do. People that suffer scarcity, misery , and hatred, also clamor: "Have mercy on me!"

The blind man first receives the response that many poor are given today: people attempt to silence him. There are plenty who think that if the poor don't complain, poverty would disappear; if suffering goes unnoticed, it seems to evaporate. The blind man does not heed this and cries even louder: "Son of David, have mercy on me!" Jesus stops, listens to him and says to the crowd: "call him." At the voice of the Master, the same ones that had demanded the blind man to be silent now tell him to go near Jesus. Now, they are silent. They say to the blind man: "Be hopeful, rise, he calls you." And he, throwing his garb away rises and comes to Jesus.

And what do you think the blind man could want from him whose cures have been so talked about? Although it is obvious what he wants, Jesus still asks him: "What do you want me to do for you?" It is relevant to highlight Jesus' question. The blind man is a poor man; he goes near to the Lord and the Lord takes the time to say to him: "What do you want from me?" Jesus does not impose his power and grace. Rather, he inquires because the opinion of this poor blind man is important to him. He converses with the blind man; it is a brief conversation yet a significant one.

How many times do we, as Christians and church people, not know how to ask the poor what they want? We think that we know what is best for them. Furthermore, we say: "It's not worth it to ask them," and we impose somehow our own conception of charity on them. The Lord knows how to listen: "What do you want me to do for you?" And then the blind man responds: "Raboni, Raboni [that is to say, "my Master," "my Rabbi"] that I can see." We already knew it, but in human relations we can not guess what the other person wants. It is important for that person to express himself. Jesus says to him: "Go! your faith has saved you."

Once again, the lesson is important. Jesus doesn't say to him, although it is obvious: "Go! I have saved you, I have given you sight." He says to him: "*Your* faith has saved you," that is to say, he makes this poor beggar realize that he himself has participated in his salvation and cure. "Your faith," and faith is something free, something that this man has expressed in his cry. In effect, by saying "Son of David" the blind man is manifesting his faith. When Jesus says "your faith," he implies that the man has made possible his own cure.

Of course, the Lord has made the cure possible; but at the same time there is a respect for the man's contribution. He asks the poor man what he wants; he talks with him; despite the worries that accompanied him on the way to Jerusalem where he would find death, he takes time for this man, and furthermore tells him: "You have made it, yourself, cooperating with me, you have accomplished your cure."

Jesus entered into a dialogue with this man on an equal basis. Thus, we too, if we want to serve this people, all of them, but particularly those who are in dire need, our solidarity requires that we listen to them. The dialogue, as the formation of mature persons whose faith and participation gives sense to their lives, is important.

c) Knowing how to share

I would like to move to a third point always within the option for the poor. And here I would also like to refer to a text of the Gospels. If we have talked about knowing how to see, how to listen, I would like now to insist on something else: *knowing how to share*.

Let us remember a passage that is in the four Testaments, proof of the importance this story had for the disciples of the Lord. It is the story of the breaking of the bread, a title that has never been convincing to me.[2] In effect, I would argue that the message of the text is something else.

The Lord is teaching a multitude; it's getting late, and he and his disciples are tired. Jesus sees that it is good for the disciples to rest and then decides to go to a secluded place. The Testaments present the fact with some variations. One of them tells the story beautifully. Matthew says that the Lord took a boat and sails across the so called Tiberias Sea. What do the people do? According to the Testament the people go by land, walking rapidly, so when Jesus and disciples arrived by boat, the crowd is already there (perhaps seated) in order to listen to Jesus once again. The people anticipated Jesus. And the Lord kept on teaching according to the Testament.

At one point he says: "And now what am I going to do with these people? They are so many, they have passed the day here and they have nothing to eat." Then Jesus speaks with his disciples. The dialogues, in the four Testaments have variations, but basically they consist of the following: the disciples, being practical, say that there is no way to feed these people, that Jesus should send them away so that they go to buy something in the closest town, since they (the disciples) are not able to do anything, and will need a lot of money to feed them, two hundred denarius according to John's Testament.

Upon hearing "we don't have anything to feed them with, send them away," the Lord responds: No, you feed them. And the disciples, always very practical say: "How, if we don't have anything? How are we going to do it?" This is the response that the poor know well. If they ask, they are told: there is no money (there is never money for them . . .). Suddenly, according to John's Testament, someone says timidly, almost convinced that what he is going to say won't do any good: "Here there is a little boy who has five loaves of bread and two fish"; but, it's clear, this is not enough.

Jesus says then: "bring the five loaves and two fish" and then he adds something very important, something that might pass unnoticed: "Make them lie on the grass." This is important because during Jesus' time only those people who had a certain social standing were able to eat while resting. Servants ate standing up because to eat on foot implied to eat rapidly and thus to be always ready to obey the master's orders. To ask them to sit down is a manner of declaring them free, of dignifying them. Those men and women lay down and the Testaments say that they even did it in an orderly manner, forming circles of fifty and one hundred people each.

Then, according to the text, Jesus blesses the bread in the name of the father and gives it to the disciples so that they may distribute it among the people. The disciples then become servants as they serve the bread. Interestingly enough the texts say that they gave bread and fish out of the five loaves and two fish. Our idea that the food was multiplied comes from here, but the Testaments actually say that they gave of the five fish and the two loaves of bread.

What needs to be underscored is that the Lord gave from what he and his disciples had; what, in this case, according to John, a little child had. From that small amount, he gave to all and all ate to until they were satisfied. John's Testament says furthermore that they filled up twelve baskets. Twelve is a symbolic number in the Bible; it means "all the people." There were twelve tribes of Israel; there were twelve apostles who were the pillars of the new people of God. The meaning of the twelve baskets is that if we were to follow the example of Jesus, we should feed the whole humanity. Sharing, then, will consist of giving from the twelve baskets that have remained since the time when the Lord fed the multitude. We are called upon throughout history to feed people out of those twelve baskets. We are called upon to share the bread.

The message of the episode is this: to break the bread is to share what one has. Jesus gave to them the bread of the word and also gave to them the actual bread, the bread that calms hunger, because for Jesus daily life is important. The Testaments are clear: the focus is on sharing, not on multiplying.

Three fundamental items as conclusion

1) The fundamental option for the poor is to keep alive in us the right
to dream.

It is a fact that the breach between the rich and the poor has
widened. But what is most critical is that today, the powerful of the
world and of Latin America try to rob the people of their right to a
utopia, to a dream, to the project of a just and egalitarian society.
Remember the prophet Joel. The prophet describes a terrible
predicament for the Jewish people. He says at one point: "They
were just about ready to lose happiness." If a people lose happiness,
all is finished. I believe that this is very important.

2) In line with the blessings of the mountain one should say: "Blessed are
the stubborn ones for they will have the Kingdom of God."

Today a great stubbornness is required. I do not pretend to affirm
that all obstinate people are saints, I believe that all saints are obstinate, which is not the same thing. It seems to me that in the face of
the immensity of the problems and deceptions that debilitate the
efforts of the poor to make their rights count and to achieve liberation from all that oppresses them, we need stubbornness. If someone doesn't like the expression, he/she can change it to a more
common one: fidelity. The point is to go on. We live in a compli-
cated time, but why not have hope when encounters of solidarity
like this one and like so many others in Latin America are possible?
In spite of all, we are living through one of the most passionate
moments in the history of Latin America. I also believe that the
church's presence in this continent is going through a very rich and
vital stage. I don't ignore the difficulties we find on the way, but we
are in a present filled with promises. The fulfillment of these
promises requires from us strength and even stubbornness.

3) Loving at the same time roses and justice, the beautiful and the just.

A Peruvian poet, Gonzalo Rose, important though not well known
internationally, a friend from childhood, exiled in Mexico because
of his socialist ideas, wrote a letter to his little sister in which he
tried to explain to her why he had caused his mother so much pain.

He said two things that I think are very important. The first is this: "I have, Maria Teresa, I have had to love the roses and the sea tides of June, and at the same time justice; I have had to love the beautiful and the just." This is what I wanted to remember by alluding to the passage of Bethany. The poor, let's never forget it, are also in need of gratuitous gestures from us, and of gratuitous acts among themselves, of course.

The poet added: "One day the laughter of the poor will clasp your waist." It will clasp your waist; it will fasten it; it will make itself present to you. He does not say that the suffering of the poor will clasp your waist but the laughter of the poor. I wish inded we could be clasped by the laughter and the happiness of the poor, a happiness as festive as that with which in these days we want to remember Monsignor Romero.

Translated by Pedro Lange-Churión

Notes

1. This text has been slightly altered from the talk given by the author at the UCA (Universidad Centroamericana José Siméon Cañas) of San Salvador on the twenty-third of March of 1995. The editors have retained the colloquial tone of the talk.

2. Mt. 14, 13–21; Mk. 6, 34–44; lk. 9, 12–17; Jh. 6, 1–13.

4

A Post-Christian and Postmodern Christianism*

María Clara Bingemer

W ithin the context of a modernity in crisis and its more or less immediate consequences, of change in the religious scenario of Brazil and of the world, Christianity finds itself in a difficult but also rich moment. The new forms of societies in which Christianity is inserted as a religious and communitarian project force Christians to search for a new way of comprehending their place, their identity, and their face.

This search, however, does not occur without conflicts. Problematic for some, the cause of discontent, and the source of perplexity for others, Christian identity today is not easy to interpret or to comprehend.[1] Perhaps what is unique to Christianity ever since its historical origins, is this type of "hermeneutic intrasponibility," a reposition of the self within the hermeneutic circle, which forces one to keep going forward in the attempt to define what makes up the nucleus of Christian identity. The paradoxical and indissoluble alliance between the flesh and the spirit, between the human and the divine that is brought into human reality through Jesus Christ, the Word made Flesh, left humanity with the "impossible" task of saying in words the ineffability of the divine. It is not to be admired that the hermeneutic and discursive intransponibility inaugurated there is still a source of problems and perplexity for all those who approach it.[2]

Western civilization today is confronted with a Christianity that shows a face different from the traditional one, with which this civilization could for a long time identify. It has to do with a Christianity that went through the sieve of modernity and that changed in the passage. On the one hand, to speak of modernity is to evoke the process of secularization as one of its most central characteristics—even though the secularization process signifies among other things, the "disappearance" or "occultation" of the religious in all of its denominations, including Christianity. On the other hand, precisely due to its incarnatory characteristics, that is of immersion in reality and the world, Christianity has been seen— it seems with good reason—as the only religion capable of establishing an alliance with modernity and surviving it, while realizing a new synthesis from the very crisis, which the advent of modern times breathed into its interior. Modernity is the social and cultural matrix in which the totality of relations and of social, human, and spiritual creations have taken form in the last centuries. Christianity as a historical fact and institutional voice, is inscribed within this matrix, albeit in a contradictory way.[3]

Capable of allying itself with modern society and culture, Christianity is called to rise as one of the critical instances of this same modernity. Faithful to the logic of incarnation, Christianity refuses the comfortable position of an utopian distance in relation to the crisis in which modern times and civilization are embedded and therefore, must assume its role within the world, in social reality, politics, and culture. It is an authentic presence that is at the same time lucid, engaged but not failing to be critical. To assume its place in modern society and culture without trembling does not mean to accept moral deterioration or to give up the courage of denouncing the evil of the times. It means accepting the challenge of imagining an order of things that is different from the values and ethical imperatives that serve as background to modern development and are spread through all available channels of technological society.[4]

It appears to be important to search for an understanding of all implications of the affirmation—certainly problematic for some— that the Christian project not only survives the crisis of modernity but also lives with modernity without loss of its identity. If on the one hand, Christianity as an all encompassing cultural and religious project reveals itself as anachronistic, on the other hand, it is indisputable that the Christian fact is alive and visible, even though it has a different face and is confronted with the new perspectives of the actual moment. Pushed to the margins of social life, Christianity is now a private question in the lives of individuals and does not mold society and culture as it has done before, at least not in the same way. It does not, however, cease to be present.

A large part of why Christianity finds itself in an identity crisis is probably due to the secular convention of perceiving as the foundational principle of comprehension and interpretation of reality, together with a strong ecclesiocentrism that conceives the totality of the Christian fact only as or primarily of the ecclesiastic institution. The impact of becoming conscious of the modern process entered powerfully through the doors of the church. Therefore, it is certainly not surprising that many historians, theologians, and other thinkers—Christians and non-Christians—questioned, in the middle of this century, whether Christianity was dying or fragmenting.[5]

We have arrived at the threshold of the millennium and it seems that Christianity is still alive. However, its features are very distinct from those of former times. Immersed in the crisis of modern society, Christianity is also affected by many of the interpellations hurled at society, which force it to reevaluate itself as a proposal and as a form of communication. A deep ambivalence emerges from the Christian proposal, generating a relationship with religion that cannot subscribe either to a simple refusal of modernity or to a simple acceptance of modern values (Hervieu-Leger, 16).

New Questions and New Subjects within Historical Christianity

Because of its *anthropocentric* character, modern Christianity is questioned by alternative and ecological movements unleashed by the apocalypse that threatens the planet. Christian thinking, discourse, and action in the post-conciliar phase have transferred the central axis of Christianity from the previously mentioned ecclesiocentrism to a more accentuated christocentrism, which in reflecting on the person of Jesus Christ and his project, searches for what is fundamental in Christian identity. Perhaps because of this emphasis, the anthropocentric characteristics of Christianity have been accentuated. The human being has been the center of theological and pastoral concerns of the Church, and it is in the name of human growth, development, and wholeness that the most significant Christian movements of the last decades have been formed and brought together.[6] This anthropocentrism finds its base in christology, in Jesus Christ, Lord of the Church and Redeemer of humanity (Pope John Paul II 1979).

Ecology puts into question this anthropocentric Christianity, opening up the possibility for reflection about the totality of creation, about nature, and other aspects besides the anthropological Christian proposal. The repercussions of this question cause present day Christianity to widen the reflection of its own identity beyond the anthropological prism. This new angle of reflection brings important consequences for the understanding of many aspects of Christian revelation as well as in relation to God, its central object of interest and convergent point of organization. The experience and vision of God as creator of all that exists, not only human beings, and the implications of the centrality of creation as the inaugural act of God in history, has been the constant object of study of important theologians of the Christian churches, Catholic and Protestant.[7]

Other alternative movements—the feminist movement, the black movement, all those that occupy themselves with a cause and the indigenous cultures—also touch the interior of historical Christianity, questioning its distinctly masculine institutional configuration, conceived and organized around the matrix of the white, developed European society. Allowing other voices to sound, and other subjects to be visible in the life of the Church, these movements bring to light aspects of Christianity that have not even been touched on until recently. Based on their own experiences, they reexamine antique and traditional aspects through a different angle or prism.[8]

Christianity and Inter-religious Dialogue

Another interpellation cast at Christianity today regards ecumenism and ecclesiastic dialogue. This pertains not only to intra-ecclesiastic dialogue, which refers to the different currents that occupy the interior territory of one or another Church, but also to inter-religious dialogues in which Christianity and other religions search together for points of contact and convergence in order to find common ground.[9] There is no lack of interpellations that the large non-Christian religions and new religious movements cast at the historical Christian Churches.

Often criticized that their moral values do not conform strictly to doctrinal and ethical principles of Judaism or Christianity, many of the new religious movements actually possess strict moral codes, at times more than those found in the Judeo-Christian canons. As an example, we could cite *Santo Daime*, an ecologically based religion in which it is common for members to cultivate values such as chastity and virginity. The hierarchical relationships of the movement's authorities are full of respect and consideration for the distinct degrees and positions of each member within the group.[10]

The figure of Jesus, central for Christianity, appears also within these movements but within a perspective different from the Christian tradition. His death and resurrection are questioned and consequently his divinity as well.[11] Other Christian figures such as Mary and the saints are also invoked in many of these movements but they do not carry out the roles equivalent to those of Catholicism.

The communitarian dimension is extremely strong in these movements and it is surprising to discover that new forms of the Christian search for community (the Charismatic Renewal and other experiential groups, Catholic or not) parallel them in terms of motivation (with a strong emotional charge) and expression of inter-relationships. Although these groups are accused of "alienation" by the more politically conscious and engaged currents of the historical churches, it is imperative to recognize that even though they remain within the ecclesiastic institution, they share many similar characteristics with the so called new religious movements and also have a large power of attraction and recruitment.

In certain popular circles of Latin America, including the indigenous, one perceives a continuity between popular Catholicism and rural Protestant sects regarding ritualization and the emotional components so strong in both groups. Some traditional rites are kept even after the exodus of one religious form to the other. The collective emotional element is distinctly relevant and constitutive of the religious domain.[12]

The sects constitute a separate phenomenon within this context.[13] Of a fundamentalist character, they maintain a veiled protest against traditional Christianity, particularly the Catholic Church, which they accuse of defiling the purity of the Gospel. They emphasize the eschatological principle, the millenaristic profile, and the pneumatic-spiritual principle in opposition to dogmatic predominance that—according to their interpretation—prevails in the Church. The sects today possess an enormous power of seduction and reach more and more people who participate intensively in their rituals.

With all these ambiguous aspects, one can ask if this seduction, which the sects use in greater and greater proportion even with old members of the historical Christian churches, does not represent a serious interpellation to these same churches. One can ask if the great success of these sects in the communication of their proposal and message—with all the ambiguities which they carry in terms of resources and methods used—does not have something to say to the historical Christian churches concerning the coldness of their liturgies, the excessive bureaucratization of their institutions, or the need to reexamine the emotional dimension in the communication of their proposal.[14]

The eastern religions and Islam are other religious traditions that present themselves as an instance for dialogue and as an interpellation to Christianity. Currently in the West, even within the Church, it is common to utilize techniques and elements that come from eastern religions as auxiliary for the praxis of prayer and meditation of western Christians. The fascination directed at these traditions, at these millennial schools of meditation and prayer, has been a source of rediscovery for many Christians—old and new—of the contemplative dimension of Christian life. These were apparently given less importance due to the emphasis given to the need and urgency of action and historical liberating engagement.

There exists, however, an ambiguity and risk in this process of rediscovery. By using these prayer techniques as an aid in the experience of God, one could also accept the world view and doctrinal content of these traditions which in many points diverge fundamentally from Christianity.[15]

At the bottom of all this, the great challenge, the great scandal for Christianity in the world of religious pluralism today, continues to be faith in Jesus Christ, Son of God and universal Saviour. To recognize and to proclaim the singular event of the incarnation of God, which no one had ever seen before, and notwithstanding show the historical particularity of Jesus of Nazareth, is the indisputable requirement of Christianity. This is exactly what is being questioned more and more by other religions that defend the thesis that there are other forms of mediation besides Jesus for the revelation of God. The proposal of rethinking the uniqueness of Jesus is found even in currents within Christianity.[16]

Nevertheless, the inter-religious dialogue does not cease to present hope and prospective for Christianity today. Stated concretely, it obligates Christian theology to search for a *theocentrism* and a *mystical experience* as points of departure for its discourse and to balance the *pneumatological* route with the *christological* in the attempt to think and to speak about the concept, the idea, and the experience of God.[17] In this process of true convergence with other religious confessions, searching sincerely with them to find dialogue and consensus, Christianity will perceive the immense difficulty of renouncing that which constitutes the last pillar of its identity: faith in Jesus Christ, Word of God incarnate in historical time and space who revolutionizes with his incarnation the notion of that same time and space that governs the human mind and experience. It is this new temporality that Christianity inaugurates and celebrates within history, inventing an "other" time, a liturgical time—which is nothing less than the annual recovery of sidereal time by the memory of the Incarnation of all of Jesus' life.[18]

The situation of Christianity in Brazil

In Brazil the complex and plural reality with which Christianity is confronted today has many things in common with what we have tried to describe. On the one hand, academia and the means of communication, have recognized a certain decline in interest for the Church—especially the Catholic—and its involvement in society. This occurred after the political moment in which the Brazilian Church ceased to exercise a function within the national political scenario in defense of human rights, especially during the military regime. This effort of the Church was led by the National Conference of Bishops of Brazil and found its expression in a series of events and articulations related to the theology of liberation and the notable increase in the ecclesiastic base communities.

On the other hand, it seems to point to another angle by which Christianity could search and encounter a way to be present in the lives of the Brazilian people. This can be seen especially in the attempt not only to dialogue with the children of modernity, who are characterized by revolutionary, post-marxist disillusions and who have returned to spirituality and religious experience, but also by the attempt to respond to the demand for more profound spaces and experiences of the divine mystery. This demand prevails even among the Christian militants most engaged in secularization and political transformation.[19]

In Brazil as well as in other places, it is enough to say that Christianity did not finish its historical task, but on the contrary, finds itself in a moment of extreme hope and fecundity. It appears to us that one of the characteristics of this new moment is the need to become conscious that a time for silence and discretion about one's conviction and adhesion to the Christian faith, characterized by modernity and secularization has passed and is over. The shame to announce explicitly, the need to transmit more by behavior and witness than by the word as a sign of respect to non-believers and members of other churches, no longer seem to be primordial requirements. This is a time of the non-repression of the sacred and the religious, in which the explication and proclamation of one's own convictions and experiences in this area have become a reality. This has left many Christians perplexed and bewildered with the danger that, from one day to the other, they find out that they are the latest secularized group.[20]

Within this situation, Christianity is called to turn its interests back to themes that are fundamental to the understanding of its identity and the communication of the message that it bears. More and more, certain ideas such as the logic of alterity as a regent force of Christian dynamism, the notion of transcendence proper to the Judeo-Christian revelation, and the question of universal salvation have polarized the interests of Christians. This goes for common believers, theologians, and pastors in the sense that they are at the height of the mission, which they understand as theirs within the present time.

Without a doubt, the theme of God is the most central to the circumstances in which Christianity finds itself today. If a religion defines itself above all by the divinity or superior being—one or multiple—around which it organizes its symbolic universe, its ritualistic expression, and its reflection, then in the case of Christianity, this rule applies in a unique and original manner. Before being a religion or form of organizing the sacred, Christianity is an experience. It is a human experience, lived within history, which has as its object the total other, the Transcendent, the ineffable God who becomes a fellow being, revealed in the history of a people, and in the plentitude of time, in the flesh of one man, Jesus of Nazareth.

Translated Amós Nascimento and Margaret Griesse

Notes

*Originally appeared in Maria Clara Bingemer. *Alteridade e Vulnerabilidade. A Experiência de Deus e pluralism religioso no moderno em crise* (*Alterity and Vulnerability: The Experience of God and Religious Pluralism within the Crisis of Modernity*), São Paulo: Ediciones Loyola, 1993.

1. For example, see the recent works of C. Palacio. 1989. "A identidade problemática (em torno do mal-estar cristão)," in *Perspectiva Teológica* 21, pp. 151–177 or França Miranda, 1989. *Um Homem Perplexo: O cristão na sociedade*, São Paulo: Loyola, or even D. Hervieu-Leger. *Vers un christianisme nouveau?*

2. See M. Gauchet. *Le désenchantement du monde: Une histoire politique de la religion*, Paris, Gallimard, 1985, p. 189 in which the expression "béance Herméneutique" is used to signify the challenge of Incarnation, which we freely translate as "hermeneutic intransponibility."

3. Cf. what is said about this in J. M. Mardones, *Postmodernidad y cristianismo: El desatío del fragmento*, Santamden, Sal Terrae, 1988, p. 87 and D. Hervieu-Leger, *Vers un christianisme nouveau?*, p. 319.

4. Cf., to the critique of modernity, P. Valadier, *La Iglesia en proceso. Catolicismo y sociedad moderna*, Santander, Sal Tarrae, 1990, pp. 131, 132, 137 and also J. M. Madrones, *Postmodernidad y cristianismo*, p. 122.

5. We refer to the celebrated works produced in Europe in the last decades in which the titles relate something of the contents: E. Mounier, *Feu la chrétienté*, Paris, Seuil, 1950; W. H. Van de Pol, *O fim do cristianismo convencional*, São Paulo, Herder, 1969; M. de Certeau e J. M. Domenach, *Le christianisme éclaté*, Paris, Seuil, 1974; J. Delumeau, *Le christianisme t-il mourir?*, Paris, Hachette, 1977. See also—although it has a quite different focus—the book by the American thinker J. Needleman, *Lost Christianity*, 1980, Brazilian trans. São Paulo, Martins Fontes, 1987, with the title, *Cristianismo perdido/ Uma viagem de redescoberta*, São Paulo, Martin Fontes, 1987.

6. Above all, we refer here to the movements centered on the struggle for justice, for social and political militancy, etc., as well as to the currents of theological thinking derived from them. In Latin America we think of the entire ecclesiastic mobilization that came out of the Episcopal Conference in Medellín in 1968 and the three fundamental axes that articulated a good part of the life of the Church of this continent from that time on: the struggle for justice, the articulation of the base communities, and a theological thinking based on the reality of the very poor.

7. Cf. the ever growing number of reflections about ecology that fill the world of Christian publications. We highlight two of them: J. Moltmann, *Dios en la creación*, Salamanca, Sigueme, 1985; C. Gesche, et al., *Création et salut*, Bruxelas, Publications des Facultés Universitaires Saint Louis, 1989. We cannot leave out the global tendency of the Asian Christian theology in the last years, which has given special relevance to the elements of the cosmos and creation in its reflection. Cf. above all the theological productions such as

S. Rayan, T. Balassuryia, M. Amaldoss, among others. In terms of Latin American and Brazilian works we recommend the recent book of A. Garcia Rubio, *Unidade na pluralidade* especially chapter XIV, as well as the recent publication of A. Garcia Rubio, et alii, *Reflexão cristã sobre o meio ambiente*, São Paulo, Loyola, 1992, cited in chapter I, n. 6.

8. It would be impossible to enumerate all the works of the last years on the subject of women and the questions of race and ethnicity. As an example we cite only some that deal more strictly with the relationship between modernity and Christianity: J. Cone, *A Black Theology of Liberation*, New York, Lippincott, Co., 1970; H. Assman et al., *Teología negra—Teología de la liberación*, Salamanca, Sígueme, 1974; S. Benhabib and D. Cornell (ed.) *O feminismo como crítica da modernidade*, Rio de Janeiro, Rosa dos Tempos, 1991; M. C. L. Bingemer (ed.), *O mistério de Deus na mulher*, Rio de Janeiro, 1990 and *O segredo feminino do mistério*, Petrópolis, Vozes, 1991; X. PiKaza, *La muher en las grandes religiones*, Bilbao, DDB, 1991.

9. Cf. the ever growing number of works that emerged in the last years about this particular subject. We cite only a few: H. Küng, *El cristianismo y las grandes religiones*, Madrid, Europa, 1987; C. Gesché, "Le christianisme et les autres religions," *Revue Théologique de Louvain* 19 (1988), pp. 315–341; J. Dupuis, *Jésus Christ à la recontre des religions*, Paris, Desclée, 1989.

10. Cf. the various works which appeared recently about this religious movement, from which we mention just a few: L. E. Soares, "O Sant Daime no contexto da nova consciência religiosa, *Cadernos do ab 23* (1990), pp. 265–274; R. Abreu, " doutrina do Santo Daime," *Cadernos do ab 23* (1990), pp. 253–264; M. Camurça, "Da Alternative para a sociedade a uma sociedade alternativa," *Cadernos Atualidade em Debate 1* (1990), pp. 19–36. Also Cf. the commentaries on this by J. A. Saliba, "Religious themes in the new religious movements," in *Research Project on New Religious Movements—Dossier*, Roma, FIUC, 1990, pp. 156–157.

11. On how the image of Jesus appears in the new religiosity see the book by J. Vernette, *Jésus dans la nouvelle religiosité*, Paris, Desclée, 1987 and also his more recent article with the same title, published in *Research Project on New Religious Movements—Dossier*, Roma, FIUC, 1990, pp. 245–272.

12. On experiential groups within Catholicism see M. França Miranda, *Um homen perplexo. O cristão na sociedade*, pp. 22–25. On the question of new and popular religions see F. Damen "Las sectas religiosas en los puelbos indígenas," in *Research Project on New Religious Movements—Dossier*, p. 431. See also P. Sanchis, introduction to the collection *Catolicismo no Brasil atual*, vol. I: *Modernidade e tradição*, São Paulo, Loyola, 1992, pp. 9–39.

13. We apply here the term "sect" according to the definition of Max Weber, who contrasts the concepts "sect" and "church," but we give to this term a meaning that is more convergent with the organizational visibility of those religious groups called sects that are present today in Brazil and in other parts of the world: believers in Jesus, congregated around the Bible, with rituals that are marked by affectivity, emotions, the claim to direct inspiration from the Holy Spirit that speaks through the mouth of any believer, without hierarchical rigidity. On the discussion around this concept see P. F. C. de Andrade, "Sinais dos tempos: Igreja e Seitas no Brasil," in *Perspectiva Teológica* 23 (1991), pp. 223–240, esp. pp. 224–225.

14. On this subject see R. Bergeron, "Les sectes et l'Elgise catholique," in *Research Project on New Religious Movements—Dossier*, Roma, FIUC, 1990, pp. 599–616. See also my text "A sedução do Sagrado," in *Cadernos Atualidade em debate* 1, Rio de Janeiro, 1990. See also J. Hortal's communication to the 30th General Assembly of the CNBB, Itaici, April 29 to May 8, 1992, pp. 13ff. Although it refers to Brazil, we believe it is pertinent on a wider scale. Some of the accusations that he lists of the sects on the Catholic Church are: the weight of the institution, the almost federative structure of the Catholic Church, etc. In the same way, he lists some of the motivations of those who leave the Catholic Church to join sects: deeper interpersonal relationships, the emotion of the supernatural and the search for wonders, immediate solution to afflicting problems, the privatization of religion (4–5).

15. A warning concerning this risk was made by the Congregation for the Doctrine of Faith, in the document *Carta aos Bispos de Igreja Católica acerca de alguns aspectos da meditaçNao cristã*, 1990. The difficulty with this rests especially in the consequences that these techniques have of clearing the mind. They could result in leading the believer in a direction opposite to the incarnate aspect that is central to the whole experience and comprehension of the Christian mystery and to Christian prayer and meditation.

16. Cf. for example works such as that from P. Knitter, *No other name? A critical survey of christian attitudes toward world religions*, Maryknoll, Orbis, 1985. Cf. also other writings of M. Amaldoss, R. Pannikar and others. Comments on this point are also made by J. Dupuis, "Pour une théologie du dialogue," in *Jésus Christ à la recontre des religions*, Paris, Desclée, 1989, pp. 299–313.

17. An important element in this process is, without a doubt, the document of the Pontifical Council for Inter-Religious Dialogue, *Diàlogo and Anúncio*, May 19, 1991, which is characterized by an openness of perspectives.

18. Cf. the beautiful pages on this subject written by M. Meslin, *L'expérience humaine du divin*, Paris, Cerf, 1988, pp. 146–147. See also, on the turn performed in time by the event of Christ, H. C. de Lima Vaz, "Religião e modernidade filosófica," *Sintese*18 (1991): p. 105, in which he classifies the non-philosophical civilizations as anachronistic, our philosophical civilization as diachronistic, and Christianity as catachronistic, for it recuperates and saves the fluent time. This refers to the unique and unrepeatable singularity of Christ, the permanent now, the only "modern" that does not pass.

19. Cf. the present moment, especially in the Brazilian Catholic Church, in the introduction of P. Sanchis, *Catolicismo no Brasil atual*, Rio de Janeiro, Iser, 1990, pp. 1–40. See also J. Hortal, *O que fazer diante da expansão dos grupos religiosos não-católicos?*, Oa. Assembléia Geral de Conferência Nacional dos Bispos do Brasil, Itaici, VF, pp. 9–11.

20. See the reflection by M. de Certeau, "Penser le Christianisme," in *La faiblesse de croire*, Paris, Seuil, 1987, pp. 183–226. Also H. C. de Lima Vaz, "Religião e modernidade filosófica," in *Síntese Nova Fase* 18 (1991), pp. 147–165; J. P. Rosa, "'Enfouisement" ou "visibilité"? Un débat dans l"eglise,' in *Études* 376 (1992), pp. 229–248. I tried to reflect on this in my text, *A seduão do sagrado*.

Works Cited

D. Hervieu-Leger, *Vers un christianisme nouveau?*, Paris, Cerf, 1986.
Pope John Paul II, *Redemptor hominis: The Encyclical Letter of His Holiness,
Pope John Paul II*, Boston, St. Paul Edition, 1979.

Black Masks on White Faces

Liberation Theology and the Quest for Syncretism in the Brazilian Context[1]

Josué A. Sathler

Amós Nascimento

Our contribution to the discussion on liberation theology, postmodernity, and the Americas centers on the question of syncretism in Brazil. As far as we are concerned syncretism is a central issue that needs to be studied carefully, especially when it is related to the general description of the Americas as a "melting pot." Observing the specific situation of African Americans in Brazil without losing sight of the general situation in other countries (the Caribbean, Colombia, Peru, the United States, Venezuela, etc.), we would rather speak of a "meeting plot." Even in liberation theology, which criticizes colonialism and cultural imperialism, there are many who have not yet liberated themselves from old and obsolete views concerning syncretism and inculturation. Liberation theologians should consider not only the fact that Europe once "met" the New World, but also the complex ways of interaction between cultures that still "meet" today.

The multicultural character of the American continent has been traditionally defined in slogans such as "racial democracy" in Brazil (Freyre, 1933; for a critique Fernandes 1978: 249-269), "mestizo society" in Colombia (Rodriguez 1992; Wade 1993: 29-37), "café con leche" in Venezuela (Wright 1991), and as "the melting pot" in the United States (Schlessinger 1992). Anthropologists, sociologists, and theologians call this process of encounter and interaction

95

among Natives, Europeans and Africans in the Americas called "syncretism." The *Dicionário Aurélio da Língua Portuguesa* gives the Greek origins of the term, showing how the prefix "syn" (reunion, conjunction) was linked to the predicate "Cretan" to denote the "union of the various states in Crete against a common adversary." The militant and military character of the word will become clearer when we see how the idea of syncretism was applied in the recent history of the Americas in bringing people together to fight for political independence and cultural emancipation. In philosophical and sociological terms "syncretism" has an ideological character, which implies the harmony of differences seen earlier in gnosticism or, more recently, in eclecticism. The word acquired an anthropological and sociological meaning of acculturation and *bricolage*, related to the jargon of chemistry: "Fusion of different cultural and even antagonistic elements into an unique whole that still preserves some of the original characteristics existent beforehand" (Bastide 1973). However, it is in the issue of religious syncretism where we find the most polemical discussions (Berner 1991; Boff 1982; Pieris 1986, 1994; Stewart & Shaw 1994) and the recent debate on intercultural communication (Schreiter 1985; Siller 1991; Sundermeier 1992). All these definitions apply to the Brazilian situation. But because these different aspects are sedimented in Brazilian history and are taken currently without qualification, we must review this history to see clearly the ideological assumptions hidden behind these definitions.

We begin by presenting the issue of postmodernity in liberation theology. We then give an historical analysis of syncretism in Brazil, to show how conservative ideas of miscegenation appear as a continuum in political, literary, and scientific discussions. In the third section we turn to an anthropological and sociological view of religious syncretism. In the fourth section we concentrate on the theological debate around syncretism and inculturation, showing how an obsolete and actually racist ethnological approach of the nineteenth century is still present in liberation theology. Finally, we look at this whole with the eyes of the postmodern perspective presented at the outset, showing that there is a need to consider the problems of syncretism, without falling prey to conservative assumptions that have contaminated the discussion. We conclude with a plea for tolerance and the recognition of African cultures and religions as a constitutive part of the Americas, rather than as an alien element that must be syncreticized and christianized.

The Postmodern Face of God: History and Liberation in the Americas

Let us first consider postmodernity. From the debate on postmodernity in the Anglo-American context from the 1940s up to the 1970s, postmodern and the generatives postmodernity and postmodernism, have been defined in many ways that are not always compatible with one another (Koehler 1977; Lyotard 1979; Hassan 1982). Postmodern should not be taken just in its semantics, but seen as a way of judging things, persons, events, and situations on the basis of coherent principles and usage. Therefore we need to clarify how we understand "postmodern" when we relate it to liberation theology and to the Americas. For a critique of syncretism we emphasize the adjective postmodern as it was defined in Latin America because it was the first definition used and also because it gained new connotations in the 1970s as it was used by liberation theology. In the first case, postmodern identified a literary tendency in Latin America after 1914 (Oniz 1932) that is recognized less for creating new styles and more for bringing to light the perspective of social groups that were excluded from society: anonymous artists, single mothers, African Americans, and homosexuals. This allows us to define postmodern as a way of stressing heterogeneity and plurality, by bringing up ideas and persons that are left out by dominant discourses. Later this same meaning was stressed also in liberation theology, in the principle of an "option for the poor." In 1973 Enrique Dussel was the first to apply the term to identify this new theological tendency:

> 'Theology of liberation' directs itself towards an interpretation of the voice of the oppressed to place itself in the perspective of the praxis of their liberation. It is neither a particular moment of the univocal Whole of the abstract universal theology, nor is it a equivocal or auto-explicative moment on itself. Theology of liberation is a new moment in the history of theology, an analogical moment that arises after the european, russian and north-american modernity and as a latin-american theology it comes shortly before [*antecede en poco*] the african and asiatic postmodern theology. . . . We know that we are situated beyond the european Totality that is modern and dominating, and as we put ourselves on the side of the liberation of poor people, we at the same time represent a future human being that is worldwide, postmodern and a [symbol] of liberation. (Dussel 1974, 148)

This quotation brings together many topics, but we would like to stress the self-understanding of liberation theology as postmodern, which is applied by Dussel in the introduction to his *Filosofía de la Liberación* (1977). Gustavo Gutiérrez also took up this discussion in 1977 and in his *Teología desde el Reverso de la História* (1982), in which he affirmed that liberation theology was opposed to modernity, although he rejected the term postmodern as an undialectical category. Going beyond the "limits of modern theology," liberation theology was then defined as a "theology from the underside [*reverso*] of history." This definition is also compatible with both the historical Latin American meaning of postmodern and with the principle of an option for the poor. Some authors defined a postmodern theology of liberation according to these views, emphasizing the appositional relationship between Europe and Latin America (Santa Ana 1989; Scannone 1992). As a theology that has its context in a poor continent, liberation theology can be seen as postmodern in the way it opposes the wealth of Europe (Eckholt 1994). Accordingly, postmodern is an instance that criticizes the multifarious consequences of the imperialism inaugurated by a modern global system: ethnocentrism is negated in multiculturalism; eurocentrism is replaced by polycentrism; christian fundamentalism and universalism are superseded by ecumenism; colonialism is sublated in postcolonialism (for a general view of these issues see Bhabha 1995; Metz 1984, 1987; Said 1989, 1993; Spivak 1987).

Along these lines, liberation theologians claim that the history of the Americas ought to be interpreted primarily as a history of conquest and oppression, as the history of the fatal encounter between Europe and the "New World" (Dussel 1992; Boff 1992; Hoornaert 1974; *Concilium* 26/6, 1990). This is indeed valid, since the *Conquista* was nothing else but the systematic genocide of the greater part of the native population. But another aspect of this history of oppression has been left aside. When one considers the Africans during the period of slavery, their role in the constitution of global mercantilism, their interaction with other cultures in the Americas, their situation as victims of another genocide and their stigmatization under racism, there are so many difficulties to be accounted for, that many have find it easier to neglect this issue totally or to summarize it in a few phrases. The consequence of such an analytical abstraction, is an incomplete and tendentious picture that does not do justice to the concrete situation of the poor in the Americas, since being African American and being poor is practically synony-mous.[2] We want to point to this abstraction in Brazilian history.

The Many Faces of Syncretism in Brazilian History

Brazil was a colony of Portugal from 1500 to 1822, the period in which the Natives were destroyed, poor and undesirables, were expelled from Europe to become colonists, and Africans were brought as slaves.[3] The political independence of Brazil in 1822 par-alleled the efforts for liberation of other South American countries at the beginning of the nineteenth century, but although a series of popular movements—including groups of free Africans and proletar-ians—were engaged in the revolutionary struggle for democratic ideals, the result of independence was not the same as in the revolu-tions led by Simón Bolívar in other countries. In Brazil there was the establishment of the first and only monarchy of South America under D. Pedro I. It is not surprising that the new regime mantained the slavery that brought ten times as many Africans to work in the regions once colonized by Spain and Portugal (Curtin 1969, 268). Such a contradiction between liberation movements and slavery became evident to one of the intellectuals of that time, José Boni-fácio de Andrada e Silva, who was one of the first to propose syn-cretism as a solution to this political antithesis:

> It is time to start gradually to erase the last vestiges of slavery among us, so that we are able to form a homogeneous nation within a few generations, otherwise we will never be free, respectable and happy. It is an urgent necessity that we end with so much physical and civil heterogeneity; it is an imperative, that we, from now on and wisely, combine the different and contrary elements; that we amalgamate so many different metals, so that a homogeneous and compact whole be resulted, a whole that does not fragment itself with even a little touch of any political convulsion. (quoted in Prado 1970, 144)

The idea of "fusion," taken from chemistry, was an allusion to the need for a common denominator that would reunite the ethnic groups inhabitating Brazil. The melting of these different groups into the same pot would bring about a "new race"; such a program for cultural and ethnic identity would guarantee unity and national security. But the question remained: Which model should be used?

Neither the Europeans (in this case, the Portuguese as colonizers) nor the Africans (as slaves) could be an acceptable model, for the first would be a regression to colonialism and the latter to a primitive stage. Since neither of them represented civilization or modernity, the only option left was the already destroyed native culture of the Guaranis, who had left their land in face of the European invasion and searched for "a land without evils" in the far west of the large Brazilian territory (Lanternari 1974; Queiroz 1973, 1977; Sschaden 1962). National identity was to be found then in the distant *"Indio,"* the *"bon sauvage."*

This romantization à la Rousseau is considered a high point in Brazilian literature: the Indianism [*Indigenismo*] in the poems of Gonçalves Dias and in the novels of José de Alencar, member of the conservative party and author of the trilogy *O Guarani, Ubirajara* and *Iracema*.[4] These are the forebearers not only of recent esoteric movements that try to return to a state of nature, but also of the generalized view of the *"Indio"* in liberation theology. The syncretic "Indian face of God" may be relevant in many regions of the Americas, but the mere acculturation of Pachamama by including potatoes in the liturgy, an acritical mysticism, and an ethnocentric wish for the ressurgence of the great imperialistic cultures of the past should be avoided (Dussel 1983, 34–36). In this way, eurocentrism is just replaced by an equally dangerous indiocentrism—disconnected from the idea of an ethnic polycentrism. Old times are gone and present problems remain untouched!

For these reasons, it also is important to bear in mind the historical background of the discussion on the *"Indio,"* which is not particular to Brazil, but is seen in other American countries as well, as, for example, in Mexico (Cf., Powell 1968; Raat 1971). There was a change, however, echoed by the slogan "We are not Indians, we are Brazilians" that emphasized the *"Caboclo"* or *"Mestizo"* as the genuinely Brazilian synthesis between the Native and European. This became a popular idea around 1870 that was taken up by new religious movements and sealed the end of the "Indianism" movement.

These literary movements enriched the debate on syncretism at the same time that its political significance grew impoverished. Syncretism became a topic in the aristocratic cafés and salons during the second half of the last century and progressively reached a new religious movement of the white middle class, Umbanda, to which we will return later. A political turn would occur not only due to external pressures from a new world-system that wanted the abolition of slavery for economic reasons, but also due to internal controversies in newspapers and parlamentary discussions in which a new political movement, Abolicionismo, opposed monarchy and recognized the african participation in forming the Brazilian culture. José do Patrocínio alluded to in the daily *Gazeta da Tarde* on May 5, 1887:

We have been able to fuse all races into a single native population, because portuguese colonization assimilated the savage races instead of trying to destroy them, thus preparing us to resist the devastating invasion of race prejudice (quoted in Skidmore 1974, 25)

Although the quotation shows that some abolitionists had gone beyond Indianism and Caboclism to include Africans as part of "the fusion of all races" in the Brazilian culture, it also reveals how much even a person such as Patrocínio, who was a "mulatto," was prey to the political ideology behind the talk of syncretism. Patrocínio defined Brazilian culture in terms of race, and was opposed to the experiences observed in the United States, which Patrocínio refers to indirectly in the polite term "race prejudice." This was interpreted as a warning of a civil war, if there was no "Abolition of Slavery." However, the ethical question against the economic justification of slavery itself was not articulated in all its complexity, and thus abolition was used much more as a political argument against monarchy.

Joaquim Nabuco, a representative of the liberal party in the Brazilian parliament who opposed the conservatives that supported monarchy and an important abolitionist, launched the political instrumentalization of the discussion. A disguised Eurocentric motivation hid behind his initiatives, which contradict his supposed humanitarian aims; he oriented his criticisms towards England— which pressured the Brazilian government to stop the slave trade and to abolish slavery—and argued in favour of sovereignity. He defended a process of "whitening" for Brazil, complained that the country was colonized by the Portuguese and not by the Dutch, deplored the fact that Africans had to be brought as slaves, and saw the immigration of Europeans to Brazil as the only alternative for the beginning of a civilizing process that would lead to a genuine Brazilian. The abolition of slavery was just a means to an end: "What we visualize is not the emancipation of the slave, but the emancipation of the nation" (Nabuco, 1883).

With the talk about "emancipation" we hear the echo of democratic and liberationist ideals that contradicted to the factual maintenance of slavery. The Abolition of Slavery in 1888 was the condition for the establishment of the Brazilian Republic in 1889 without a civil war, but with a *coup d'état*. Due to the fact that this process was led by the positivism of the military academy (that represented the bourgeoisie and not the aristocracy), there was practically no change in the situation of Brazilians of African ancestry (ex-slaves who became the poor).

Under the positivistic view of scientific syncretism (Ortiz 1985, 13) the debate on national identity this time was not about people and nations—the locus of egalitarian republicanism—but reduced to "race." The tools of the new sciences understood syncretism in the more objective terms of "racial miscegenation" between the red Natives, the black Africans, and the white Europeans. With such colorful images—still present in schoolbooks at the time of the military dictatorship between 1964 and 1980—the idea of a melting process was transformed into a myth. As Mário de Andrade defined and ridicularized it (1927) and Roberto da Matta recently repeated (1981), at the beginning of the twentieth century Brazilians were put to sleep with the "fable of the three races."

Moreover, let us not forget the military meaning of syncretism. Between 1870 and 1930, under the leadership of military positivism, there was the installation of scientific academies, museums, research institutes, and hospitals that concentrated their interest on the "racial question" and impregnated the Brazilian society with specific bodies of knowledge. Disciplines at the turn of the century such as phrenology, eugenics, antropometry, craniology, and ethnology followed Darwinistic determinism and, while establishing a hierarchy of the races, tried to arrive at the synthesis of "racial perfectability" (Schwarcz 1993, 43–66).[5] The Brazilian philosopher Sílvio Romero spread this idea in his defense of ethnic and cultural syncretism. We select two of his polemic affirmations: "All Brazilians are mestizos, if not in their blood, for sure in their ideas" and "The Brazilian people are mestizo and there is no sense in discussing if this is good or bad; it is so and that is enough" (Romero, 1882, 85, 149).[6]

It is useless to search for any trace of egalitarianism or acceptance of Africans in the defense of syncretism by these movements. Unfortunately the fable of the three races was not only an unfulfilled dream, it was, and still is a nightmare spread and synthesized by positivistic scientificism. The inclusion of Africans in the "melting pot" of the Brazilian cultural fabric is instrumental to the assimilation of this "race" in a progressive process of degeneration that led to its whitening (Cf. Skidmore 1974, 173ff.).[7]

The function of positivism was to institutionalize racism as a doctrine. There are some "selective affinities" between colonial and conservative tendencies that have always advocated syncretism; affinities that are seen in other American countries as well, as they reduce the issue of syncretism to a dilemma: either a systematic abstraction and segregation of African Americans or their assimilation as a constitutive part of the main culture through whitening. Whether it be *mestizage*, cosmic race, harmony of races, or racial miscegenation, there is always the assumption that a pure type will be the organic result of such a mixture. The result of such a mixture is an acceptable "whiter" ethnic group that, by definition, excludes Natives and Africans. If one talks about syncretism and leaves this problem unquestioned, the whole is accepted as a given. This is precisely the case when one takes religious syncretism into account. Even in newer movements for inculturation and ecumenism, this ideological heritage and its variables remain untouched.

Holy Wars: Brazilian Religions Facing Religious Syncretism

Despite the long history of this concept of Greek origins and its practical application in Brazil, syncretism is considered today especially in a religious context. The turn to the issue of religious syncretism in this century is due not only to the development of missionary techniques of evangelization (Harnack 1915), but is also due to anthropological approaches. Although the coining of a more specific term such as religious syncretism gives the impression of a change of orientation, there is a continuity that allows us to link very recent trends with the old views mentioned above. The anthropological approach at the beginning of the century to African culture served as a transition from ethnology to the more recent sociological debate on religious syncretism. Parallel to this we can see the historical relationship of the Brazilian Catholic Church to the African slaves and their religions. Among the many groups, clans and civilizations that came from West Africa to Brazil (Iorubá, Mandinga, Bantu, etc.), the Iorubás were able to maintain their religion of the Orishas unified in a movement (Candomblé) that had its origins in the nineteenth century (Bastide 1985; Verger 1981). As Candomblé influenced other groups a new Afro-Brazilian religion came about: Umbanda, the result of syncretism between Candomblé, native religions, Catholicism and Spiritism (Birman 1983).

The anthropological interest in Afro-Brazilian Studies is contemporary with the abolition of slavery in Brazil in 1888 and gained more and more relevance in the twentieth century, reaching a wide public in the 1960s. The physician Nina Rodrigues initiated an ethnological study about the presence of Africans and of the iorubá religion in Brazil ("Candomblé"). Although it has limitation, his book *Os Africanos no Brasil* (published posthumously in 1906) is a source of data. His ideological presumptions are obvious from the beginning, as he approvingly quotes Sílvio Romero:

> It is a shame for the Brazilian science that we have not consecrated our effort to the study of African languages and religions. We see men, such as Bleek, to insert themselves decades and decades in the middle of Africa, just to study the language and collect some *myths*, and we, who have this material in our own house, who have Africa in our *kitchens*, the Americas in our *forests* and Europe in our *salons*, we have not produced anything in this area. It is a disgrace! (Rodrigues 1988, xv)

Under the influence of positivism, Nina Rodrigues was the first to research the interaction between African and Christian religions, but he understood it in the same neuropathological terms that he used to define the "criminality of Negroes" at the end of the nineteenth century. Observing how the "most underdeveloped Negroes" used the saints of Popular Catholicism to disguise their "fetish cults" and polytheistic beliefs—and comparing them to the "Methodist howlers" in the United States —Rodrigues warned against the inefficiency of evangelization and alerted the Church of the dangers of syncretism (1988:255ff.). Others (including Arthur Ramos (1940), Paulo Barreto, Oscar Freire, Edison Carneiro (1948) and even Mário de Andrade (1963; 1976)) followed his initiative and did historiographical and ethnographic research in the communities of ex-slaves that still existed at the beginning of the century. Notwithstanding, there was an anthropological turn represented by the studies of Gilberto Freyre, to which foreign researchers, such as the U.S. Americans Melville Herskovits (1941) and Donald Pierson (1945) and the French Pierre Verger and Roger Bastide contributed.

In 1933, in *Casa Grande & Senzala*, Freyre reconstructed the different aspects of the Brazilian culture (food, health, climate, etc.) to see how they came to a synthesis in the "conciliation of the races." Although he emphasized the "sexual ethics" that allowed such a mestizage and led to the "racial democratization of the country," he also included religious syncretism, which was viewed in terms of the African and Arabian origins of the Jesuit method of catechizing: the use of liturgy, feasts, and dances (Freyre 1933, 54, 87). On this basis he inferred that "Catholicism was really the cement of our unity" (30). Although he saw the African influence in Brazil with sympathy, his cultural analysis was elitist and did not address the problems of Brazilian society. A whole generation of Marxist sociologists thus questioned and criticized the idea of "racial democracy," and studied the situation of African Americans in a class society (Cardoso 1962; Thales de Azevedo 1966; Moura 1977; Ianni 1978; Nascimento 1978; Fernandes 1985). More relevant to the issue of religious syncretism in relation to class structures is Roger Bastide, who performed a sociological inversion of the anthropological tendency and influenced newer studies, including those in orthodox and liberation theologies.

Bastide elaborated a map of religious syncretism in Brazil. Even though his analyses and terminology are over fifty years old, no other researcher has taken on such an overarching project. In one of his first studies of religion, developed in accordance with Durkheim, Hübert, and Mauss (l'école sociologique française), Bastide defended the thesis of a "religious evolution" that has the "law of syncretism" as one of its moments: "Religions develop themselves by means of a progressive synthesis that corresponds to the crescent unification of groups, which are bond by religious spirituality" (1990, 134). Later he applied this to Brazilian religions. His definition of Catholicism is relevant on two points:

(1) He goes beyond the differentiation between portuguese and brazilian Catholicism and contextualizes what he calls "two brazilian Catholicisms": the white Manorial Catholicism of the elites and the black Popular Catholicism of the poor (1985:157ff.); (2) He defines Candomblé beyond this framework, seeing it not as a difuse movement, but as a "non-Christian" traditional religion on its own, that is at the same time "non-syncretic." It has its roots in the ioruba culture and, though adapted to the brazilian situation, it remains coherent to its original principles (1985, 359ff.).

Following the first point we can describe two positions within the Brazilian Catholic Church today: the official institutional theology and liberation theology with its "option for the poor." Church historians and theologians of both tendencies have followed Bastide's position as they defined syncretism within Popular Catholicism (Hoornaert 1974, 23ff.) as a problem of contextualization. Official theology and liberation theology see a double challenge in Popular Catholicism: at the same time it distances itself from the "official white Catholicism," Popular Catholicism approximates itself to religions of African influence such as Umbanda and Candomblé. The definition of these religious forms, as given by Bastide and taken up by catholic theologians, is also relevant: (1) Candomblé is a "non-syncretic" religion in relationship to Christianism and therefore, it is a "non-christian" religion; (2) Umbanda is a "non-christian and syncretic" religion that appropriated christian elements, in a "confused religious practice" (Bastide 1973, 187ff.; Cintra 1985, 155; Boff 1982, 167–8). Popular Catholicism is a "christian syncretism" (Bastide 1985, 237).

Popular Catholicism has been influenced by African religions and is confronted by the institutional Church that still represents "the white Catholicism of the elites." Yet we are impelled to ask: Does liberation theology represent a "black Catholicism" (in Bastide's sense) that is coherent with the option for the poor? We have reasons to suspect that there is little difference between these two tendencies when the issue is syncretism and the relationship of the Church to the African cultural influence in the past and to the present situation of African Americans as a constitutive part of poorer classes.

This leads us to Bastide's consideration of African religions. Starting with Nina Rodrigues's observation that there was a relationship between Catholic saints and the African gods, Bastide proposed a "sociology of the civilizatory interpenetration" (1985). According to Bastide, the slaves who came from different ethnic groups developed "analogies" between their beliefs and respective cults through "functional equivalencies" that were brought together in Candomblé. Such equivalencies are found also between Iorubá gods and Catholic saints. For Bastide, however, even the parallel between the goddess Iemanjá and Santa Maria did not represent a syncretism—in the strict and original sense of the word—since there was no "synthesis" or identity, but only similarity (1978, 183–191). The saints were simply "white masks" consciously placed over the "black faces" to dissimulate the truly African character of the cult and, therefore, to protect it from policial repression. Candomblé should be understood then as a conscious cultural resistance of a minority (1985, 229, 361), similar to that of Black Islam (1985, 203ff.).

In fact, with the abolition of slavery, African Americans constituted the *Lumpenproletariat* in Brazilian society and found the only possibility of social and cultural integration in their original religious communities and *terreiros*, or "Houses of Candomblé." To answer the question on how the Houses of Candomblé kept their religion alive despite the evangelization of Africans and African Americans by Catholicism, Bastide refers to social facts, such as the intense exchange between the cities in northeastern Brazil and the west coast of Africa (Dahomey, Benin, Nigeria), admitting that these are not a sufficient explanation (1985, 233; cf., Verger 1957; 1968). Other reasons are to be found in the formation of "Brotherhoods of Blacks" during the eighteenth century, which turned into centers of resistance against the monarchic regime and slavery, and later in a movement of "return to the origins" around the 1930s, which advocated stronger ties with Africa (Bastide 1985, 166).

We agree with Bastide's view of Candomblé as a form of cultural resistance that allowed the slaves to appropriate and to transform elements of the Catholic religion of their owners, but we would add another fact: the internal structure of Candomblé allows for the addition and assimilation of new deities.[8] Polytheism, trance, possession, and sacrificial rites are not just particularities that differentiate Candomblé from Christianism, but are also flexible forms of religious life that allow for the integration of other elements. Is this a form of syncretism? Because Bastide leaves this question untouched and emphasizes syncretism as an offensive movement of assimilation of other cultures by the Catholic Church, he concludes that there is a religious syncretism of African and christian elements in Brazil, but that this cannot be applied to Candomblé, since it resists syncretism with the Catholic Church. On this basis he arrived at the definition of two characteristics of the african religions in Brazil, syncretism and synthesis, which he defines as follows: (1) *Syncretism* is the progressive process of evolution and constitution of a new religion. This process can be questioned, however, by a movement of resistance, as in the case of Candomblé, which refused to be syncretic (1985, 359); (2) *Synthesis* is a state in which a religion emerges. This results in the conscious amalgamation of previous religious elements into a new system that did not exist before—as in the case of Umbanda, which brings a native mysticism, African rituals, and christian doctrines together (Bastide 1985, 440; Ortiz 1991, 16; 1989, 91).

Umbanda has been considered a religion that is genuinely

Brazilian, the final result of a syncretism (*bricolage*) that has its roots in new religious movements of the nineteenth century. Although in the 1950s Bastide saw it as a religion that was still in the process of syncretism, today Umbanda is seen as a Brazilian religion, as a synthetic religion that did not exist before in any other place (Ortiz 1975; 1991, 16; 1989, 90ff.).

The word *Umbanda* comes originally from the Kimbundo language (Angola) and was used to describe religious objects and the religious leader (also called *Kimbanda*). In Brazil it was applied from the 1930s on to denote a new religious system of great appeal to the middle class, which synthesized native, African, and European elements. From the native culture it appropriated Herbalism and the heroic image of Caboclo; from the Africans it took the ritual elements of Candomblé; and from Europe it absorbed Allan Kardec's Spiritism and Catholicism (Kloppenburg 1961; Birman 1983).

Since we can now take the discusion on the native, African, and European religious elements for granted, we need to give some details about Spiritism, so as to have a basic comprehension of the synthesis performed in Umbanda. Originating in France under the guidance of Allan Kardec, Spiritism appeared in Brazil in the 1860s, propagating mysticism and healing through mediumistic powers, communication with dead persons, reincarnation, and telepathy (Kloppenburg 1960). Spiritism also maintained centers that provided spiritual care and social charity. These elements were taken in Umbanda and mixed with rituals, sacrifices, gods, and objects seen before in Native, African, and European religions. In this process Umbanda came to be considered a Brazilian religion *par excellence*. Due to its character, Umbanda actualized the nativist ideas of syncretism seen in the nineteenth century, and due to its crescent appeal, it challenged both the resistance of Candomblé (which turned to Africa) and the universalist character of Catholicism.

We should keep in mind that in the discussion on syncretism in Brazil there is a racist *Leitmotiv* that guides the different discourses: the alleged synthesis between Natives, Africans, and Europeans that results in the whitening of Natives and Africans. These same categories applied to the idea of religious syncretism. In this last case the various native religions, the African Candomblé, and the European Christianism and Spiritism were supposed to have their synthesis in a truly Brazilian religion: Umbanda. At this point we have then four different religions which, together with Islam, other forms of Christianism (Protestantism, Pentecostalism), other traditional religions (Buddhism, Judaism, etc.), and new religious movements, make up what may be defined as the brazilian religious market (Bourdieu 1974).[9] It is also in this context of competition and "holy wars" for the religious market that the recent discussions on evangelization, syncretism, and inculturation within the Catholic Church in Brazil must be understood.

Inculturation and the Syncretic Face of God in Catholicism

Without losing sight of the whole spectrum developed thus far and concentrating our attention upon that population that is both African American and poor, we will turn our interest to Catholicism in Brazil, asking how the Catholic Church sees the issue of syncretism. The two positions we saw above, official (institutional) theology and liberation theology, seem to have an uneasy relationship with what is called "Afro-Brazilian Religions," reflected not only in their concrete offensive strategy against African religions in their pastoral theology [prática pastoral], but also in the abstraction from African Americans in their theological speculations.

Let us start by considering the discourse of the official theology. That the mission was the right hand of European colonization is an unquestionable fact (Dussel 1974; Hoornaert 1984, 157ff.). Therefore we can spare many unnecessary details and recall when Nina Rodrigues adverted the Catholic Church at the end of the last century that the alleged conversion of Africans in Brazil was only a "catechetic illusion" (1935, 199). As the slaves turned back to Candomblé and as Catholics later turned to Umbanda and Pentecostalism, the efficiency of the catechese and evangelization was put into question. As a matter of fact the theological discussions on syncretism within the Catholic Church from the 1950s on have to be seen as a theoretical answer to this concrete situation of religious competition.

In the documents of the Second Vatican Council the Church's new atittude towards non-christian religions is seen primarily in its relation to Judaism and in the question of acculturation of alien liturgical and theological elements. According to the doctrine of the semina Verbi, non-christian religions were accepted as "historic-cultural facts, social and institutional expressions of people's religious consciousness" that bring in themselves the seeds that can germinate when exposed to the christian message (Vatican II 1992; Cintra 1985, 126). Therefore, ". . . in their basic and authentic elements and as expressions of the religious capacities and moral laws that are inscripted in people's hearts," these religions can be considered as *previous ways* ordained by God that lead to salvation (*Ad Gentes*, c. 2,3). This represented a new interest of the Church in the "dialogue of cultures."

As the Synod of Bishops gathered in Rome in 1974, bishops from Asia and Africa brought up the problem of inculturation and indigenization, that is, the question of the "penetration of the gospel into the core of different world cultures" (Angrosino 1994). Theologically, this was understood as a Christian "incarnation" in each social and cultural reality (Cintra 1985, 135).[10] In Brazil this discussion centered on the relationship of the Catholic Church with African religions, following a controversy that goes back to the beginning of this century. Therefore, the decree *Ad Gentes* and the message *Africae terrarum* (from December 7, 1965) are more relevant for the Brazilian case (cf. Cintra 1985, 114ff.). One must bear in mind, however, the resolutions of the Latin American Council of Bishops in Medellín (CELAM 1968), of the General Conference of the Latin-American Bishops in Puebla (Puebla 1979) and in Santo Domingo (1992), and those of the National Conference of Brazilian Bishops (CNBB), which, according to their hierarchical competence, interpreted and contextualized the documents elaborated in Rome (Kloppenburg 1968, 406). In 1985, in *Candomblé e Umbanda*, Raimundo Cintra summarized the main points of the old controversy between the Church and the Afro-Brazilian religions (for a first view see Kloppenburg 1961) and gave some suggestions for action in face of the problem of syncretism.

The fact that Cintra begins with Sílvio Romero and repeats at length the same quote with which Nina Rodrigues started his book a century ago is symptomatic. Like many other theologians who discuss syncretism and inculturation according to Rome's orientation, Cintra takes up the doctrine of the *semina Verbi* and tries to establish an existential "dialogue of cultures" in the Brazilian context (1985, 127, 133). However, he centers his attention on African cults and reduces their variety to a "basic common structure," with the assumption that "in all those people there is a *monotheistic conception of God*" (1985, 138). As we mentioned already, polytheism, trance and possession in Kardecism, Spiritism, Umbanda, and Candomblé touch the neuralgic point of Christian theology. Their ritual experiences are unacceptable for Catholicism, since they represent irrationality, artificiality, unscientific practices such as homoeopathy, and a mere catharsis for individuals under the stress of belonging to a lower class. So Cintra concludes pragmatically: members of the Catholic Church who have been attracted to these religions must be instructed and warned by Church leaders about the "physical, psychic, moral and spiritual inconveniences" of attending these cults (1985, 154–155).

At the end, Cintra wants to provide the Church with tools to react to the growing appeal of Afro-Brazilian religions, insisting that the christian nucleus cannot be changed and that the transcendence of the Church cannot be given up.[11] However, in doing this he in fact hinders any attempt at a "dialogue of cultures." It is important to note that Cintra himself is not open for a dialogue even within the Catholic Church: he does not take CELAM, Puebla and CNBB into account, neither does he quote the previous discussion of syncretism by theologians such as Leonardo Boff, nor does he recognize the particularities of the African religions.

Another author, Pedro Iwashita, complemented his views with more sophisticated arguments, also leaving liberation theology aside, in a study about the syncretism between the Iorubá goddess Iemanjá and Santa Maria. Following the orientations of mariological documents and the analytical psychology of C. G. Jung, he analyses the psychological characteristics of both objects of veneration and recognizes that there are many feminine elements in Iemanjá that are not present in Maria. For this reason he sees the need to explore the more human and anthropological characteristics of Maria, without changing the dogmas (Iwashita 1987, 253ff.). This would lead then to a "contextualized marial spirituality" and thus fulfill the lack of mysticism and ritual in the liturgy (1987, 341–349). As a result, he concludes that Catholics would not search for alternatives elsewhere.

Now it is necessary to consider how liberation theology, as an alternative position to the official view, sees syncretism and inculturation. To give a summary definition of liberation theology we will leave aside the praxis of the Basic Ecclesiastic Communities (CEBs —Comunidades Eclesiais de Base), although they are an important element in the reaction of the Catholic Church to the advance of Umbanda and Pentecostalism in Brazil from the 1950s on. This is a complex issue, especially concerning the separation between the progressive political orientation of the CEBs and that of other religious movements within Popular Catholicism. We remain at the theoretical level and concentrate on the fact that Latin American theologians took up and at the same time influenced the praxis of the CEBs, functioning as "organic intellectuals" (Gramsci) who articulated—also at the institutional level of CELAM and CNBB—the need for a contextualized Church in Latin America that does not remove itself from social and political issues. It is in this context that the question of syncretism gains relevance, but now with another word. Because the name syncretism acquired a negative meaning, the Latin American documents follow the guidelines of Rome and liberation theologians speak now of inculturation and indigenization (cf. Marzal 1985; Beozzo 1986; Scannone 1991; Suess 1994).

We concentrate our attention upon Leonardo Boff, not only because he is a Brazilian liberation theologian who became a symbol as a victim of the same persecution once made against Galileo after challenging the ecclesiastic institution; but also because of his "plea for a syncretism" (1982, 145–171). Even though he acknowledged the word's negative connotation, he tried to rehabilitate syncretism as the intrinsic nature of the Catholic Church. According to Boff, syncretism is the life process and legitimation of a religion. Like any organism, a religion dies if it does not nourish itself by incorporating alien elements and "digesting" them in a process of preserving what is useful and compatible with its identity while rejecting and puting aside [*colocando prá fora*] what cannot be digested. Such metaphors of biology bring Boff closer to the traditional discussions on syncretism at the beginning of the century.

As one reads his theological terminology one must account for the defense of plurality, the avoidance of censorship, and the attempt at a dialogue with the official theology. Amidst all this, there is a clear line. He wants a true syncretism that is opposed to many types of pathological syncretisms that must be rejected, since they imply a loss of identity, loss of history (continuity in the discontinuity of time), "exemption from ethical commitment and social responsibility," and inability to "witness universality in a particular manifestation." A Christian experience that defines itself as Catholic, claims Boff, must be open to universality without choosing previously in which culture it must be incarnated (1982, 188, 191–2).[12] Therefore, syncretism is understood in the traditional terms of mission and conversion. Just after the conversion, the process of syncretism begins, when habits and traditions of the people are taken, insofar as they "contribute to the glory of the Creator." So Boff concludes, that in this way a true syncretism is originated, which has the christian identity as its "substantial nucleus."

Yet, although Boff tries to speak of a "dialogue of cultures," he finally holds on to a substantive universalism, for Christianity comes from the top and follows the same logic of conversion proper to neo-colonialism—that is criticized by many liberation theologians (Dussel 1978, 47-53; Pieris 1986, 79–91 and 1994; Schreiter 1985 and 1994; Castillo 1994). When Catholicism is converted instead of converting the other, as when Candomblé accommodated Catholic elements without losing its own identity, Boff maintains that this is a false or pathological syncretism. He affirms indeed that Candomblé cannot be interpreted within the "intra-systemic" realms of Christianity, but only within the historical horizon of universal salvation. It is an anonymous Christianism, a previous phase of the "Christian event." This justifies an assymetric "missionary position" in which "the whole *iorubá* wealth can be compatible with the Christian faith" (1982: 186, 187). With an apparent openness to other cultures, Boff actually confirms the official *loci theologici*: the Catholic Church is the only instance for an authentic culture and religion and the only way to liberate the poor people from their oppression in Latin America and grant eternal salvation (cf. Morandé 1982). This is similar to other theologians who define Latin America as a "barroque continent" (Eckholt 1994) with a Catholic original identity.

Some recent debates with members of Candomblé show not only that the problem of the Catholic Church with Afro-Brazilian religions remains, but also that the official theology and liberation theology hold a common position, although they are opposed to each other. In 1990 the Institute for the Articulation of Afro-Brazilian Religions (INARAB) protested against the offensive of the Catholic evangelization towards Candomblé, for some African-American Catholic priests performed the mass with the inculturation of traditional *Iorubá* clothes, acceptable rites of Candomblé, offerings of food, dance, and Iorubá words. According to newspapers, there was an authorization of the Pope for such an initiative (*O Dia,* March 11, 1990; *Jornal do Comércio,* March 25; *Diário de Pernambuco,* March 23; *Correio da Bahia,* March 30). However, in an interview, Bishop D. Lucas Moreira Mendes explained that this was against Church law, since there was only a request from the CNBB that the Vatican authorize the initiative of preliminary studies on Afro-Brazilian rites

(*Jornal do Brasil,* April 4). The controversy did not stay on the question about the legality of these liturgies, since the INARAB accused these initiatives as a form of offensive evangelizing towards other religions (Candomblé, Umbanda, and Pentecostalism). The Church appropriated sacred elements of Candomblé, took them out of their context, and turned them into mere folklore. Confirming what he had written in 1981 in his plea for syncretism, Boff said that the Church is itself a fruit of syncretism, and that it was a mistake by the members of Candomblé to treat their religion as a "fossil" instead of acknowledging syncretism—they should give up their beliefs! Moreover, he joined forces with Bishop D. Estevão Bittencourt and affirmed that only "healthy" elements of Candomblé should be taken by the Church (*Folha de São Paulo,* April 9, 1990).

With all this data we can now answer the two questions asked earlier. How is the Catholic Church inserted in the discussion about syncretism? For both official and liberation theology, syncretism or inculturation is the appropriation of external elements taken from other cultures without losing the universality of the christian identity. Fighting for its share in the "religious market," the Church admits syncretism and considers itself as a "true syncretism," but rejects some practices of Candomblé and Umbanda, such as polytheism, trance and possession, considering them as pathology—in the same way that Nina Rodrigues once described African cults. Does liberation theology represent a Black Catholicism? Or put in another way: Can liberation theology consider the African-American culture in a dialogue? In his plea for a syncretism, Boff maintains an offensive position towards the Afro-Brazilian religions; he reduces their social elements to psychopathologies and acknowledges their members as underdeveloped subjects that need a true, universal, psychic, social, and religious salvation, which can be given only in the Catholic Church. So he comes close to the orthodoxy.

Unmasking Ideology and Power: Syncretism in a Postmodern Face

We started with liberation theology, considering its position as postmodern, insofar as it criticizes the status quo and negates ethnocentrism by means of multiculturalism, replaces Eurocentrism with polycentrism, supersedes Christian dogmatic universalism and fundamentalism with ecumenism, and sublates colonialism in a postcolonialism. All these slogans are good reasons to accept the view of liberation theology as postmodern and to relate it to our critique of the ideology of syncretism, since the denunciation of discovery, *Conquista*, and proselytizing evangelization of the Americas made by liberation theology are compatible with a rejection of the forms of oppression used against African Americans, who make up the majority of the poor in Brazil (Asett 1986). However, as we reconstructed history from an African American perspective, we came to results that contradict the view of liberation theology as postmodern, since the ideology of syncretism is left unquestioned and accepted by liberation theologians.

In the Brazilian society at large African American and members of Candomblé were and still are seen as "primitives, diabolic, and savage" and their acceptance was conditioned by their assimilation grounded on political syncretism. Cultural syncretism appropriates values, extracting them from their context (cf. Shohat & Stam 1994); scientific syncretism proposed a process of "whitening" in racial miscegenation; and religious syncretism demands the "Christianizing" of African Americans as a condition to recognize them as persons. In all these cases there is a systematic rejection of the African and African-American element as constitutive of Brazilian multiculturalism, ethnic diversity, and religious plurality. The great problem of all these views, as they try to understand Brazil and the Americas, is their inability to conceive simultaneously Native, European, and African cultures, without reducing them to something else that is, at the end, white, European, Catholic (Christian)—the Brazilian complement of the WASP ideology in the United States. Due to all this, these different discourses contradict a postmodern perspective, since they collaborate in the maintenance of the hegemony of one group over another and stress the reduction of differences.

Syncretism, understood in the postmodern perspective presented at the outset, which stresses multiculturalism, polycentrism, ecumenism, and postcolonialism, is something unavoidable, since it occurs when cultures meet each other (Cf. Sundermeier 1992; Stewart & Shaw 1994). But it does not occur abstractly, for it also implies a relationship of power that maintains asymmetry: aggressor and victim or domination and resistance (Bastide 1985; Foucault 1977). Insofar as one person or group does not have the right to decide which elements it takes or it gives in a situation of cultural interaction and exchange, this person or group is at the bottom and can be defined as victim, as excluded, or as the weaker part on which another alien discourse is imposed in its totality (Foucault 1971). Assimilation is imposed. All this can be seen in the

different forms of poverty, since they are a result of this relationship of power. In face of this situation we cannot maintain a neutral
position as a distant observer, but we must contextualize and define
our own positioning in the process of syncretism by means of self-
reference (Feldtkeller 1992). With liberation theology, we must say
that a postmodern perspective is reached when we put ourseves on
the side of the poor and excluded by recognizing that they come to
the surface anyway and express themselves, revealing the resistance
against syncretism.

We have shown this relationship of power in the Brazilian context and pointed to a holy war between groups that fight for the
religious market. As a way to resist the colonialist methods of catechese and to maintain their own identity, many Africans and
Brazilians of African ancestry turned to Candomblé. In this religion
there was a "return to Africa," more precisely a turn to Nigeria and
to the Iorubá culture, since it was in those traditional values that
they found a legitimate and authentic representation of their social
and cultural reality. This led to a purism that was challenged by a
newer religion, Umbanda, which claimed to represent an authentic
Brazilian synthesis and syncretism, since it assimilated not only
Candomblé and Catholicism, but also other native and European
religious elements. The growth of Umbanda by means of its acceptance by ex-Catholics of the middle class affected Catholicism. For
Catholicism, in turn, the growth of these religions confirmed that
there was a "catechetic illusion" after five centuries of missionary
work. The alternative seen in the Catholic theology was to search
for a form of syncretism similar to that of Umbanda, which could
be theologically acceptable. Such a strategy demands not only theological debates, but also practical actions. It is obvious that the
universalist position of the Church remains at the top, as it is challenged by Umbanda, which is in a middle position, while Candomblé is at the bottom and receives the pressure of the whole.
According to the double task of holding fast to the option for the
poor and of acknowledging a variety of discourses that are
excluded, there is then only one coherent position to take: to recognize that African Americans and members of Candomblé have valid
forms of culture and religion and have been victims of the oppression based on a racist ideology.

Nevertheless, liberation theology still supports the ideology of
syncretism seen in Brazilian history, which is valid also for the
whole of the Americas in the many projects of assimilation. Many

problems arise. First, liberation theology did not embrace multiculturalism, but followed the official view in reducing the dialogue of
cultures to syncretism and inculturation of Natives justified as
Indigenization, although there is no talk of Africanization. There
are many groups that live and meet each other in the Brazilian context now, but they are forgotten. Second, liberation theology
remained bound to a Eurocentric ethnic view elaborated in Rome,
although this theology holds fast to the claim that it represents the
Latin American periphery. African-Brazilian religions are rejected
due to the presumed psychic pathologies of their members, since
they admit transe, possession and sacrificial rites. Third, it affirmed
Catholicism in its universalism as a principle that is inseminated in
other "underdeveloped" cultures, thus contradicting both ecumenism and their own view that African religions are pathological.
There is no recognition of religious plurality in Brazil, but a
defence of the Church monopoly of the religious market. Fourth, it
accepted a change of name from mission to evangelization and
inculturation without practically questioning the new catechism
that goes back to the times of colonialism, although this critique
was nominally expressed timidly by some theologians (cf. Castillo
1994). The most striking point over all is the contradiction between
an option for the poor and excluded, and the concurrent exclusion
of African Americans' culture and religion, which lies behind each
of these four points mentioned above.

Liberation theology as a whole has neither taken the side of
African Americans as the majority of the poor, excluded, and discriminated, nor tried to see their movements of resistance and religion as equal partners in a dialogue of cultures and religions.
Without a recognition and correction of this contradiction, liberation theology leaves untouched a whole tradition of conservative
thought and action that systematically negates multiculturalism,
polycentrism, ecumenism, and postcolonialism. Therefore, without
a recognition and correction of this contradiction, liberation theology runs the risk of remaining in a position that is neither historically relevant, nor postmodern, nor liberating.

Notes

1. We would like to acknowledge our debt to Margaret Griesse for her
valuable comments on this text.
2. Going beyond such early stigmatized descriptions such as Savage and

Indian, as well as Creole, Negro, Black, or Mulatto (the mixture between a horse and an ass that results in an hybrid "mule"), we adopt the terms "Native Americans" and "African Americans" with their political connotations. This could be seen as a vitious pleonasm, if one accepts the ideology of miscegenation or of melting pot. Because we want to criticize this ideology we emphasize the particularity of oppressed groups.

3. The deportation of those living in European cities to the Americas was justified by Thomas Roberth Malthus at the end of the eighteenth century in his *Essay on the Principles of Population as it Affects the Future Improvement of Society* and has been reactualized in the recent discussions on immigration and overpopulation.

4. In Alencar's *O Guarani*, the strong and beautiful Peri is the ideal partner for the blond daughter of a Brazilian landowner of European origins. In *Iracema*, his portrait of the central Indian character has had so much influence that today the name Iracema is still a synonym for pretty woman. It should be noted as well that the Tupi name "Iracema" is an anagram of the word "America."

5. This utopia of a "perfect race" complements what liberation theologian Franz Hinkelammert criticized as the conservative doctrine of "cosmic mimesis" and "perfect plausibility" (1984, 47–52) at the economic and political level, and rests on the same metaphysical assumptions behind the positivistic "social engineering." The relation of this issue to slavery in the Americas is a topic that liberation theology still needs to consider.

6. These ideas have parallels beyond the Brazilian boundaries, as for example in Argentina—where José Ingenieros defended an ethnic cleansing—and in Mexico—where the hybrid inheritance of the Malinche was defined in terms of a proud "cosmic race" by the philosopher José Vasconcelos. Therefore, despite their defence of something purely Latin American, there is a need to be cautious with these thinkers and recognize that they remained tied to the prejudices of their time. Although their positions may represent a critique of Eurocentrism, they still maintain a hierarchical view of the "races" proper of positivism.

7. In the United States, the ideology of the "melting pot" was characterized not by miscegenation, but by segregation. However, the process of assimilation and "whitening" was proposed also in the United States as a solution to the "Negro Problem" (Myrdal 1944, Ch. 3; McDaniel 1995).

8. For a sociological and political interpretation of this characteristic of the Iorubá religion and society in West Africa see Apter 1992.

9. One must see the inner divisions of Popular Catholicism (CEBs, *romarias, folias de reis*, etc.) and at the same time see how other new religious movements (Umbanda and Pentecostalism) displace Popular Catholicism.

10. For a recent discussion on inculturation, including cases of other Latin-American countries cfr. a series of articles in *Concilium* 30/1 and 30/6 (1994) and Peter (1995).

11. On this basis he suggests some attitudes that the Church must have in face of "Candomblé and other specifically african cults": confrontation with these religions must be avoided; these cults must be treated as "valid ways to God"; their authentic values can be assimilated through inculturation or indi-

genization (in which the Benedictin Order could be of help); the communitarian experience in Candomblé could be accepted, since it is similar to that of earlier Christianity; concerning syncretism, it is a "matter of fact" that must be taken into consideration; but trance and possession must be avoided, since they represent a psychic problem in the pagan religions that should be studied (1985, 147–150).

12. A true syncretism occurs when the Christian identity is maintained amidst the processes of changes "occurred during the incarnation of the Church in other cultures and contexts" according to two criteria: (1) the balance between pathologies of syncretism; and (2) the identification of true and false syncretisms. Moreover, there are two intrinsic pathologies of syncretism (1982, 184–185): (1) "Religion without faith" (the reduction of rites and norms to a magic experience); and (2) "Faith without religion" (the maintenance of a purism that destroys the "salvation's mystery" and the sentimental dimension). A true syncretism must "preserve the transcendence" (1982, 185) and proclaim the *evangelium*. With this formula Boff tries to reveal the pathologies in the Church and in the "Afro-Brazilian religions" and to propose criteria for the identification of the christian identity. These criteria are centralized in the "salvific mystery of the divine revelation in the man Jesus Christ" and based on the Scriptures, on the Tradition of the Church, on the decisions of the episcopal Synods, and on the prophetic and Jesuit Tradition that defends the Freedom and the spontaneity of the human being in face of the cultural universe.

Works Cited

Andrade, M. 1927. *Macunaíma. O Herói sem Nenhum Caráter.* São Paulo: EDUSP, [1989, Critical Edition].

———. 1963. *Música de Feitiçaria no Brasil.* São Paulo: Martins.

———. 1976. *O Turista Aprendiz.* São Paulo: Duas Cidades.

Angrosino, M. 1994. "The Culture Concept and the Mission of the Roman Catholic Church." In *American Anthropologist 96/4.*

Apter, A. 1992. *Black Critics & Kings: The Hermeneutics of Power in Yoruba Society.* Chicago: The University of Chicago Press.

ASETT (Associacao Ecumenica de Teologos do Terceiro Mundo) 1986. *Identidade Negra e Religiao: Consulta sobre Cultura Negra e Teologia na America Latina.* CEDI/Edicoes Liberdade.

Bahbha, H. 1993. *The Location of Culture.* London: Routledge.

Bastide, R. 1973. *Estudos Afro-Brasileiros: Perspectiva,* São Paulo.

———. 1985. *As Religiões Africanas no Brasil.* São Paulo: Pioneira.

———. 1990. *Elementos de Sociologia Religiosa. Cadernos de Pós-Graduação.* São Bernardo do Campo.

Beozzo, O. 1986. "Visão indígena da conquista e da evangelização." In CNBB/CIMI (Ed.) *Inculturação e Libertação.* Paulinas, São Paulo.

Berner, U. 1991. "Synkretismus und Inkulturation." In H. P. Siller (1991, 130–144).

Boff, L. 1982. *Iglesia: Carisma y Poder.* Santander: Sal Terrae.

————. 1992. *América Latina: Da Conquista à Evangelização*. São Paulo: Atica.

————. 1990. *Conquista. Concilium* 26/6.

Bourdieu, P. 1974. *A Economia das rocas Simbólicas*. São Paulo: Perspectiva.

Cardoso, F. H. 1962. *Capitalismo e Escravidão*. Difusão Européia do Livro, São Paulo.

Carneiro, E. 1948. *Candomblés da Bahia*. Publ. do Museu do Estado. Nr. 8, Bahia.

Castillo, J. 1994. "Christentum und Inkulturation in Lateinamerika." In *Concilium* 30/1.

Cintra, R. 1985. *Candomblé e Umbanda*. Sao Paulo: Ediçoes Paulinas.

Curtin, P. D. 1969. *The Atlantic Slave Trade: a Census*. Madison: University of Wisconsin Press.

Dicionário Aurélio da Língua Portuguesa. 1986. Rio de Janeiro: Nova Frontiera. 2nd ed.

Dussel, Enrique 1974. *Historia de la Iglesia en América Latina*. Barcelona: Nova Terra, 3.ed.

————. 1978. *Desintegración de la Cristiandad colonial y Liberación. Perspectiva Latinoamericana*. Salamanca: Sígueme.

————. 1983. *Introducción General a la Historia de la Iglesia en América Latina*. Salamanca: Sígueme.

————. 1989. *Filosofía de la Liberación*. México: Contraste, [1977]. 4th ed.

————. 1990. "The Real Motives for the Conquest." In *Concilium* 26/6.

Eckholt, M. 1994. "Schwierige Identitätssuche. Die lateinamerikanische Diskussion über Moderne und Postmoderne." In *Herder Korrespondenz* 7.

Feldtkeller, A. 1992. "Der Synkretismus-Begriff im Rahmen einer Theorie von Verhältnisbestimmungen zwischen Religionen." In *Evangelische Theologie* 52/3.

Fernandes, F. 1978. *A Integração dos Negros na sociedade de Classes*. Vol. 1. Sao Paulo: Editora Atica.

Foucault, M. 1971. *L'ordre du discours*. Paris: Gallimard.

————. 1977. *Michel Foucault: Microfisica del Potere*. Eunaudi, Turin. (Ed. P. Pasqualino & A. Fontana).

Freyre, Gilberto. 1987. *Casa Grande & Senzala*. Rio de Janeiro: José Olympio Editora, 25th ed.

Gutiérrez, G. 1979. *La Fuerza Histórica de los Pobres*. Salamanca: Sígueme.

Harnack, A. 1915. *Die Mission und Ausbreitung des Christentums*. Leipzig: Heinrichs.

Hassan, I. 1982. *The Dismemberment of Orpheus: Towards a Postmodern Literature*. Madison: University of Wisconsin Press, 2nd. ed.

Herskovits, M. 1958. *The Myth of the Negro Past*. Boston: Beacon.

Hinkelammert, F. 1984. *Crítica a la Razón Utópica*. San José: DEI.

Hoornaert, E. 1984. *História da Igreja no Brasil*. Vol. 2. Petropolis: Vozes/Paulinas.

Ianni, O. 1978. *Escravidão e Racismo*. São Paulo: Atica.

Iwashita, P. 1987. *Maria no Contexto da Religiosidade Popular Brasileira.Análise religiosa e psicológica do sincretismo entre Maria e Iemanjá, na perspectiva de C.G. Jung*. [Doctoral Dissertation] Université de Freibourg/Suisse.

Kloppenburg, B. 1960. *O Espiritismo no Brasil.* Petrópolis: Vozes.

———. 1961. *A Umbanda no Brasil.* Petrópolis: Vozes.

———. 1968. "Ensaio para uma nova posição pastoral frente à Umbanda." In *Revista Eclesiástica Brasileira* 28, 404–417.

Koehler, M. 1977."Postmodenrismus: Ein Begriffsgeschichtlicher Überblick". In *Amerikastudien* 22.

Lanternari, V. 1974. *As Religiões dos Oprimidos.* São Paulo: Perspectiva.

Lyotard, J.-F. 1979. *La condition postmoderne.* Paris: Minuit.

Marzaal, M. 1985. "Análisis antropologico del Sincretismo Latinoamericano." In *La Antigua.*

Mata, R. da. 1981. *Relativizando.* Petrópolis: Vozes.

McDaniel, A. 1995. "The Dynamic of Racial Composition in the United States." In *Daedalus,* Winter (Special Issue: "An American Dilemma Revisited").

Metz, J. B. 1984. "Theologie im Angesicht und vor dem Ende der Moderne." In *Concilium* 17/1.

———. 1987. "Im Aufbruch zu einer kulturell polyzentrischen Weltkirche." In *Zukunftsfähigkeit.* Hrsg. von Metz & Kaufmann. Freiburg: Herder.

———, Schillebeex (eds.) 1989. *Concilium: World Catechism or Inculturation.* Edinburgh: T. & T. Clark, .

Morandé, P. 1982. *Synkretismus und offizielles Christentum in Lateinamerika.* Muenchen: Fink.

Moura, C. 1977. *O Negro: De Bom Escravo a Mal Cidadão?,* Rio de Janeiro.

Myrdal, G. 1944. *An American Dilemma: The Negro Problem and Modern Democracy.* New York: Harper & Brothers.

Nabuco, Joaquim. 1883. *O Abolicionismo.* Londres.

Nascimento, Amós, 1978. *O Genocídio do Negro Brasileiro.* Rio de Janeiro: Paz e Terra.

Oniz, F. 1934. *Antología de la Poesía Española y Hispanoamericana.*

Ortiz, R. 1975. "Du Sincretisme a la Synthese: Umbanda une Religion Bresilienne." In *Archives de Sciences Sociales des Religions,* 40, Paris.

———. 1985. Cultura Brasileira e Identidade Nacional. Editora Brasiliense, Sao Paulo.

———. 1989. "Ogun and the Umbandist Religion." In *Africas Ogun, Old World and New.* Ed. by Sandra T. Barnes. Bloomington: Indiana Univ. Press.

———. 1991. *A Morte Branca do Feiticeiro Negro.* Sao Paulo: Editora Brasiliense, 2nd ed.

Peter, A. 1995. "Inkulturation, kontextuelle Theologie, Befreiung." In Fornet-Betancourt, R., ed., *Für Enrique Dussel. Aus Anlaß seines 60. Geburtstages.* Aachen: Augustinus Buchhandlung.

Pieris, A. 1986. *Theologie der Befreiung in Asien. Christentum im Kontext der Armut und der Religionen.* Freiburg: Herder.

———. 1994. "Universalität und Inkulturation in unterschiedlichen theologischen Denkmodellen." In *Concilium* 30/6.

Pierson, D. 1945. *Brancos e Pretos na Bahia,* Brasiliana, Comp. Editora Nacional.

Powell, T. G. 1968. "Mexican Intellectuals and the Indian Question: 1876–1911." In *Hispanic American Historical Review* XLVIII/1.

Prado, Jr, Caio. 1970. *Historia Econômica do Brasil.* Sao Paulo: Brasiliense.

Queiroz, M. I. 1973. "O Mito da Terra sem Males, uma Utopia Guarani?" In *Revista Católica de Cultura* LXVII/1.

―――. 1977. *O Messianismo no Brasil e no Mundo*. Alfa-Omega, São Paulo.

Raat, W. 1971. "Los intelectuales, el positivismo y la lucha indígena." In *Historia Mexicana* XX.

Ramos, A. 1940. *O Negro Brasileiro*. Edit. Univ. de Brasilia/Cia Edit. Nacional, S. P.

Rodrigues, N. 1935. *O Animismo Fetichista dos Negros Baianos*. Civ. Brasileira, Rio de Janeiro.

―――. 1988. *Os Africanos no Brasil*. Edit. Univ. de Brasilia/Cia Edit. Nacional, S. P., 7th ed.

Rodriguez, J. A. 1992. "Afro-Colombia Denied." In *Report on the Americas* 25/4: 28-31.

Romero, S. 1882. *O Naturalismo em Literatura*. São Paulo: Lucta.

Said, E. 1989. "Representing the Colonized: Anthropology's Interlocutors." In *Critical Inquiry* 15.

―――. 1993. *Culture and Imperialism*. New York: Alfred Knopf.

Santa Ana, J. 1989. "Teologia e Modernidade." In *Estudos de Religião* 6. São Bernardo do Campo.

Scannone, J. C. 1991. "Kulturelles Mestizentum, Volkskatholizismus und Synkretismus." In H. P. Siller (1991:106–116).

―――, et al. 1992. "Die Moderne." In *Concilium* 28/6.

Schaden, E. 1962. *Aspectos Fundamentais da Cultura Guarani*. São Paulo: Dif. Européia do Livro.

Schlesinger, A. 1992. *The Disuniting of America*. New York: W.W. Norton.

Schreiter, R. 1985. *Constructing Local Theologies*. London: SCM.

―――. 1994. "Inkulturation des Glaubens oder Identifikation mit der Kultur?" In *Concilium* 30/1.

Schwarcz, L. M. 1993. *O Espetáculo das Raças.* Sao Paulo: Cia das Letras.

Siller, H. P. 1991 *Suchbewegungen* Wiss. Buchges. Darmstadt.

Skidmore, Th. 1974. *Black into White: Race and Nationality in Brazilian Thought*. New York: Oxford University Press.

Spivak, G. 1987. *In Other Worlds: Essays in Cultural Politics,* New York: Methuen.

Sundermeier, Th., et al. 1992. "Syncretismus und Inkulturation." In *Evangelische Theologie* 52/3.

Thales, de Azevedo, 1966. *Cultura e Situação Racial no Brasil*. Rio de Janeiro: Civ. Brasileira.

Vatican II. 1992. *Vatican Council II: The Conciliar and Postconciliar Documents*. Costello, Northport, NY. Rev. ed. [Austin Flannery, ed.].

Verger, P. 1968. *Flux et Reflux de la traiete des Negres entre le Golfe de Benin et Bahia, du XVII au XIX siecle*. Paris: Mouton.

―――. 1981. *Orixás: Deuses Iorubás na Africa e no Novo Mundo*. Salvador: Corrupio.

Wade, Peter. 1993. *Blackness and Race Mixture: The Dynamic of Racial Identity in Colombia*. Baltimore: The John Hopkins Univ. Press.

Wright, W. R. 1991. *Café con Leche: Race, Class, and National Images in Venezuela*. Austin: University of Texas Press.

Part II

Crossing Borders
Remapping the Sacred/Secular

6

Section Introduction: Dancing with Chaos

Reflections on Power, Contingency, and Social Change

Sharon D. Welch

Hopes for improving society are in a state of flux today. Many social activists are questioning the myths of cultural progress, institutional change, and political reform. The dynamics of political change are hardly clear-cut. Institutional reform rarely follows a pattern of smooth transition from identifying forms of injustice, to mobilizing people to public action, to dismantling those institutional structures, and to then replacing them with just structures managed by fair-minded people. The journey to fundamental social change is far more circuitous.

Patricia Williams, in her work the *Alchemy of Race and Rights* (1991), weighs the failures and successes of rights discourse in the United States. She debunks popular misconceptions, such as the notion that civil rights have resulted from the application of absolute truths to changing situations, or that this country has experienced a steady progression of expanding rights. Williams describes instead a complex historical struggle in which imperfectly articulated and framed rights are applied sporadically and unevenly to alleviate and to challenge injustice.

Social activism is often grounded in the hope that things will improve in the future, that our work, though partial, will not be in vain, that our children will have more freedom, more justice, more peace. As Williams demonstrates, however, gains in civil liberties are not so easily won, and once established may be eroded. Living with power, courage, and joy in the face of ongoing political struggles is a challenge. It requires a "politics of meaning," to use Michael Lerner's phrase, that is not dependent on progress or definitive victories.

The moral vocabulary of the political right attempts to address the crisis of U.S. society, and its message can be seductive in times of uncertainty. The Right's discourse rests on sharp dichotomies, a clear delineation of us against them, of right versus wrong, of good versus bad. Reserving the language of righteousness for itself, the Right questions the integrity of groups that hold divergent views. Success requires eliminating and excluding those who challenge the "rightness" of its vision, the coherence or viability of its strategies.

Self-righteousness and scapegoating have not been foreign to the political left either, of course. The identity of the Left has been honed all too often on dualistic divisions of oppressors and oppressed, sold-out reformers and pure revolutionaries. Political and moral absolutism is dangerous wherever it exists. While it is relatively easy to mobilize political energy under the guise of righteousness and scapegoating, indignation alone cannot sustain a prolonged movement of political struggle.

As a feminist theologian, I have argued for the importance of women's voices and experiences. As a liberation theologian, I have supported the "preferential option for the poor," the necessity of including the perspectives and insights of those marginalized by a social system. But while these theologies criticized the dualistic logic that excludes most of humanity, they often merely reverse the division of humanity into legitimate and illegitimate knowers and actors.

Much of liberation theology equates epistemic inclusion with epistemic privilege. Women, the oppressed, the marginalized, and the exploited are assumed to be somehow more moral, less culpable, less subject to the abuse of power than those in positions of dominance. But the truth is we are as partial, as petty, as subject to error, betrayal, and cruelty as those currently in power.

Postmodern theories and analyses of social change provide fresh perspectives for social movements. Such theories claim our experiences should be included in understanding social systems not because we are superior, but because we are human. Furthermore, our contributions will be unique since it is easier to see the costs of a social system from the bottom. A critical analysis needs our perspective, not because it is complete or free of distortion, but because it is a key piece in understanding the contours of social reality.

Postmodernism does not interpret the misuses and abuses of power the marginalized perform as either accidental or incidental, nor frame them as mere remnants of internalized oppression. To the contrary, a postmodern analysis recognizes that epistemic inclusion does not require or presume closure, purity, definitive insights, or the final word. It takes seriously the open-ended nature of social activism, recognizing that political action has unintended consequences. For example, debates that occur as a result of our mistakes—such as when homophobic stereotypes are replicated in the effort to challenge homophobia—actually can move a group forward. Postmodern theory aims to acknowledge the conflicts, contradictions, and surprises that attend social action.

The solution to the crisis of political theory is not the abdication of power, but an exercise of power that co-exists with an ironic awareness of our limits and our potential for error and harm. That means moving beyond a logic of dualism and constructing new vocabularies for social analysis that are capable of creating group cohesion and motivating political action without demonizing our opponents or ignoring our mistakes. The goal is a theology and politics of liberation fueled not by protest alone but by an inspiration to reimagine and to refashion existing social systems and institutions. Our theories must propel us to take the risks that are necessary for sustained social struggle.

Works Cited

Williams, Patricia J. (1991). *The Alchemy of Race and Rights*, Cambridge: Cambridge University Press.

7

Writing for Liberation
Prison Testimonials from El Salvador

Lois Ann Lorentzen

All you, are part of the game
interrogators, detectives, officials,
class, agents, prison guards, administrators,
doctors, infirmary workers,
and also the builders . . .
All sustain this hell.
which isn't from Dante.
some are more dangerous, others indifferent
but, all play, the victim is my people.
(Díaz 1988, 167)[1]

Salvadoran political prisoner Nidia Díaz writes "combat" poetry from her prison cell as counterhegemonic ideology. The prison context makes alternative resistance strategies necessary, yielding texts that articulate a powerful counterdiscourse to that offered by the state through its prison apparatus.

This paper explores texts emerging from prisons in El Salvador to explore resistance literature's contribution to theology, critical theory, and liberative practices. Prison testimonials, both strategies of resistance in themselves as well as accounts of resistance strategies, are the primary foci. As postmodern texts, the writings demystify the hegemonic history represented by the prison. As liberation theology they provide strategies of autonomy and emancipation. I realize that these discursive strategies are currently the site of contestation. Whereas others (Lyotard, Baudrillard, Foucault) might question the possibility of creating strategies of autonomy and emancipation in relation to hegemonic discourse and structures, I suggest that they are reconcilable strategies. Although I will conclude that the insights of postmodern analyses provide challenging and needed criticisms of theologies of liberation, I do not despair of the possibilities of emancipatory narratives.

Women's *testimonios* are the primary foci of this article. *Las cárceles clandestinas de El Salvador* (El Salvador's Secret Prisons) tells the story of the capture, torture, and imprisonment of Ana Guadalupe Martínez by the Salvadoran army in 1976. Her account of seven months in a "secret" National Guard prison was first published in Mexico and distributed clandestinely in El Salvador. *Nunca Estuve Sola* (I was never alone) by Nidia Díaz tells of 190 days in prison after her April 1985 capture by a United States' military advisor. Both are examples of the *testimonio* or testimonial genre.

The *testimonio* developed out of Latin America's history of military dictatorships. Anyone wishing to study popular resistance in El Salvador must study *testimonios*. The *testimonio*, often told by the actual protagonist or witness, chronicles a life episode such as imprisonment. The narrator is generally not a professional writer, and may even be illiterate. Often an intermediary records, interviews, transcribes, or edits the *testimonio*. The protagonist claims to speak for or in the name of a group. Ana Guadalupe Martínez, for example, says her story was repeated thousands of times in the decade after her imprisonment (Martínez 1992, 454). And Nidia Díaz states, in an interview, "Although I was physically alone and disadvantaged, tortured, wounded, I had the conviction that I was part of a collective force" (Ueltzen 1993, 65).

These *testimonios* do not claim to be postmodern texts. Neither are the "authors" self consciously writing liberation theology. Why then, do I use them as examples of an intersection between postmodern and liberation strategies? Although I will later devote considerable time to exploring both liberation and postmodern strategies at work in the *testimonio* genre, let me make a few initial justifications here.

Liberation theology's link to *testimonio* is the easier case to make. Nearly every Salvadoran woman I know who has been imprisoned considers radical Catholicism, or liberation theology, an important part of her lineage. Ex-comandante Rebeca Palacios claims that "most women of the front come from religious sectors as part of the 'boom' of liberation theology" (Ueltzen 1994, 4). Nidia Díaz worked with Catholic Student Youth and was influenced by both Paolo Freire and liberation theology. The Committee of Mothers and Relatives of Prisoners, the Disappeared, and the Politically Assassinated of El Salvador, (COMADRES), was a direct outgrowth of liberation theology. The group, founded in 1977 under the direct oversight of the Archdiocese of San Salvador and Archbishop Romero, maintained close ties to Christian base communities. Alicia, of COMADRES, says, "Most of us at this time were from Christian base communities . . . Monsignor Romero would read our public letters out loud in his Sunday homily in the Cathedral so that the COMADRES became known nationally" (Schirmer 1993, 36).

Although Martínez's *Cárceles clandestinas* is not about liberation theology, per se, she begins and ends her book by placing it in the context of liberation history. Martínez dedicates her book, in part, to ". . . catholic priests, Rutilio Grande, Alfonso Navarro Oviedo and various members of the brave progressive Church of El Salvador which the dictator brutally assassinates" (Martínez 1992, 13) and the epilogue honors Romero as "our Bishop martyr." The book ends by recounting lessons learned from Ignacio Ellacuria, one of the six Jesuits assassinated at the University of Central America. *Cárceles clandestinas'* final sentence reads, "Ignacio is a martyr of the negotiated revolution in El Salvador, together with his brothers and the two women, who for us signify the innocent people martyred in this long transformation process" (1992, 456).

Opposition movement women and the texts they write are part of the history of liberation theology in El Salvador. Many women describe liberation theology and involvement in Christian base communities as a life transformation that led them to resistance, and in many cases, to prison.

The case for considering *testimonios* postmodern texts is harder to make. Without engaging in the "unthinking repudiations or mindless approbations" of which the authors of *The Postmodern Bible* accuse some critics of postmodern theories, let me note a few problems (Bible and Culture Collective 1995, 9) postmodernity presents. In *Literature and Politics in the Central American Revolution*, John

Beverly and Marc Zimmerman discuss the problem of applying postmodernism to groups that haven't gone through the phase of modernity (1990, xii). The Salvadoran literary critic George Yúdice claims that revolutionary literature is actually an expression of resistance to postmodern trends in literature and to the ". . . collusion with capitalist logic in the penetration of Third World culture" (Yúdice quoted in Beverly and Zimmerman 1990, 117). Postmodern North American fashions and television programs such as MTV give "credence to the idea that postmodernism may be a new form of cultural imperialism" (Beverly and Zimmerman 1990, xii).[2]

Cynicism exists among some Central American political and literary theorists about using language imported from Europe and North America to describe Southern realities. As Neil Larsen notes, "Long before French poststructuralist criticism had been imported to the United States literature departments, artists and writers were already 'appropriating' images and 'decentering' the subject . . . to recuperate now a long tradition of experimentation with the uncritical use of european poststructuralism is unnecessary" (Larsen in introduction to Hicks 1991, xxvii). Salvadoran friends who are movement leaders, politicians, writers, and academics are painfully aware of their ongoing struggle to create a language that is not subservient to a colonized past and present. Using European and North American terms, whether they be feminism, postmodernism, or deep ecology, often is undesirable, even when the terms may describe and/or illuminate local realities.

I have no interest in using conceptual tools offered by postmodern theories without consent. It is important to listen carefully to debates in El Salvador concerning language. Yet, I will argue, as Beverly and Zimmerman finally conclude, that Salvadoran resistance literature is part of what is now commonly called "postmodernism of resistance" in that it both collapses the distance between elite and popular culture, challenges the "great narrative" of western progress, and generates a new postcolonial narrative of historical space and destiny. They write, "We want to posit Central American revolutionary literature as in effect involved in and constructed out of a dialectic of oppressor and oppressed, negotiating between the opposing terms of its dichotomies: literature/oral narrative and song, metropolitan/national, European/Creole, ladino or mestizo/indigenous, elite/popular, urban/rural, and intellectual/manual work (Beverly and Zimmerman 1990, xiii).

Testimonio records the prisoner/oppressor dialectic. In so doing, it calls existing power structures, symbolized by the prison, into question and furthers social transformation. As ideological criticism, *testimonio* may indeed find, as the authors of *The Postmodern Bible* hope, ". . . a home today in the postmodern context" given that they share "concerns for the margins—the margins of discourse, the marginal of society" (Bible and Culture Collective 1995, 303, 305).

Why is it important that we consider these texts, and by extension, other texts of resistance as postmodern writings? Dwight N. Hopkins neatly synthesizes my willingness to use conceptual tools of some postmodern theories. He writes:

> A second approach [to postmodernism] is the irruption of the poor against all that the negativity of modernity has brought, e.g., capitalism, imperialism, intensification of sexism and racism, Reason and Theology and Religion when used to justify modernity. In that sense, liberation theologies have emerged as postmodern realities. What is new about postmodernity is not that the poor have not been struggling against the meta-discourses and structures, etc., but that, because of the post-world war global configuration, the poor have burst upon the world scene like a prairie fire and have forced their presence against worldwide power structures. As always, we academics have, correctly so, reacted to the power of people, and have created theories of the postmodern which we hope will clarify things a little better in order to have social transformation for people who are dying. . . . How can we use the tools of the academy to help (in some small way) the poor free themselves in this new global configuration called post-modernity which the poor has forced upon us academics? (Hopkins 1995)

Postmodern analyses risk becoming the new discourse of the elite, the language of the academy, and forgetting the initial impetuses for this new global configuration. *Testimonios* emerge from the conditions of postmodernity and articulate those conditions. Analyzing the texts as both liberation and postmodern recognizes the multiple loci of struggle—within the academy as well as on the streets.

Prison Strategies and Counter Strategies

Early in *Cárceles clandestinas*, Martínez gives a brief history of political interrogation in El Salvador. Imprisonment and disappearance of political prisoners generally resulted in death for the captured. As the need for information grew however, political police refined their techniques in hopes of demoralizing prisoners and forcing them to collaborate (Martínez 23). Martínez's *testimonio* narrates her imprisonment and looks at the combination of methods used in prison, and prisoners' counterstrategies. We will first look at strategies and counterstrategies within the prison, looking later at the characteristics of *cárceles* as *testimonio*.

Salvadoran prisons employed a variety of well-known strategies to demoralize their inmates. Nidia Díaz experienced total sleep deprivation for weeks. Martínez went for three weeks without eating and when her food finally appeared, it was often accompanied by cockroaches. The prisoners depended on their torturers for all basic needs including food. As Kaminsky notes, ". . . in the experience of arrest and internment in a prison, power is stripped from the victim and invested in the interrogators . . . the victim depends on them for all of life's necessities, food, clothing, shelter . . . the torturers exercise power over the victim's body in the functions of sleep, elimination, movement, sight, speech . . . they have power of life and death" (1993, 56).

The interrogators consciously manipulated this dependency, calling themselves the only hope and family for the prisoners. To Martínez they said, "here we are the only ones who can do something for you" (Martínez, 101). To Díaz, ". . . we know that the FMLN is not going to help you. Only we are able to help you. From now on, we are your mother, your father, your husband, your child. We are your world, know it. . . . We will help you" (Díaz, 43). Díaz, in an interview says of her experience, "I understood that the first objective of my interrogators was for me to feel alone and to feel that they alone were my mother, father, and brother" (Ueltzen, 69). As Harlow notes, one of the purposes of the actual isolation, coupled with the constant reminder of solitude, is ". . . isolation of opposition leadership from its base of popular support in the larger community"(19).

Sensory deprivation exacerbates the sense of isolation. Both Díaz and Martínez wore the famous *capucha* or hood throughout their internment. Martínez's permanently closed eyes developed serious infections. Silence was an additional part of the violence used to demoralize the captured. Speech itself became an offense, and as Kaminsky notes, "under these conditions language is a highly val-

ued commodity . . . for the victim to put the experience of disappearance and torture into language is to exercise a form of control
over that experience . . . this articulation is not a private affair"
(56–57). When Martínez was finally able to speak with other political prisoners she noted, ". . . at times the only thing that distinguished us from animals was the possibility of talking .among
ourselves" (Martínez, 128). Her captors even offered her a television
program, hoping to exploit her need to speak. But refusing to speak
to one's interrogators, thus controlling one's discourse, became an
important resistance strategy. As Martínez notes several times,
"Quien habla, colabora" (who speaks, collaborates) (Martínez, 116).

Skilled at physical torture, interrogators beat prisoners with fists,
boots, wooden paddles, whips, chairs, etc. Martínez describes electricity as the worst torture. Probes were placed on different parts of
her body, including in her vagina, water was splashed on her and
she was shocked. She writes, "what is it possible to say about people who can discharge electricity in this way on a human body?"
(Martínez, 115). Observing and/or hearing the violence inflicted on
others was another common strategy. Martínez writes, ". . . how
many times did I hear the shouts of pain of some patriot who suffered indescribable torments at the hands of the same ones who
were in that moment torturing me" (Martínez, 112).

In addition to physical violence and discomforts, the interrogators waged psychological warfare as well. With Díaz, they success-
fully made her feel guilty, nearly convincing her that papers she
carried caused her companions to fall. Traitors were flaunted
before the prisoners. Martínez was confronted by Valle, the col-
league who turned her in to the National Guard. She admits to
being demoralized by his defection and the [alleged] betrayals of
others. Torturers also exaggerated internal conflicts within the
resistance movement. Guards, many of whom were members of the
death squads, enjoyed congregating outside prisoners' doors to discuss which leaders had been killed or defeated (Martínez, 91).

This psychological war was waged, according to Díaz, to "alter
the emotional direction of the prisoner" and the most effective
aspect was the prisoner's conscious destabilizing. Physical aggres-
sion and terror were altered with apparent calm. The hatred of the
interrogator reversed and he become someone ". . . who offers a
friendly hand, who speaks in a paternal tone . . . the man who only
wants the best for you" (Díaz, 81). Martínez's primary interrogator

became her savior who "rescued" her from electrical torture. She writes, "each time the door opened, you wonder what torture the interrogators would think of next" (Martínez, 51). Interrogators regularly stripped prisoners. Of the month she spent without clothes, Martínez writes ". . . being without clothes leaves you feeling disempowered, feeling unprotected and more exposed to whatever abuse they want at that moment" (51).

Prisoners developed counterstrategies to physical violence, sensory deprivation, and psychological warfare. Díaz and Martínez both employed counterinterrogation strategy. Although prisoners would generally refuse to answer questions, some would interrogate the interrogators. Díaz was repeatedly asked who she was. The interrogators would ask, "You are Maria Marta Valladares?" to which she would respond "Who do you think?" They asked, "How are you" to which she would answer "How do you want me to be?" (Díaz, 54). Martínez's captors were also obsessed with forcing her to say her name. Interrogators persistently told her they knew her name and she should say it aloud. Martínez asked again and again, "Why do you want me to say it?"

Interrogating and counterinterrogating exposes the battle for information and "truth" waged within the walls of the political prison. Harlow notes, "the interrogators waged a different discursive battle in the attempt to extract information from the prisoners and to introduce destructive disinformation" (1992, 172). The torturers used personal information as part of their psychological warfare, showing Martínez documents about the movement, including a file on her with pictures and descriptions of how she walked and combed her hair (40). Prisoners, however, waged a counter discursive battle through watching and witnessing. As Harlow notes, "the witnessing of torture by the tortured yields another kind of information that is the testimony of the political prisoner who survives" (26). A COMADRE tells the story of being tortured, beaten, raped, shocked, and of being thrown naked in a dark room. As she felt around the room she detected shattered bones and picked up a human finger. Her mother writes "But what she saw in that room and what they did to her is to witness what goes on in the military garrisons" ("Alicia" quoted in Thomson, 42).

Martínez describes how she and Ana Gilman listened to telephone conversations and peered through a little hole in the door to see who was walking by. As listeners, watchers, and witnesses, they were, as

Harlow puts it, "'semiologists' of the prison system, whose collective discursive strategies of resistance served as a continuous renovation of the circuits of communication" (172). Díaz not only witnessed the torture of others, but upon hearing violence, shouted for the torturers to be quiet, claiming torture "is not allowed here" (Díaz 225).

Prisons, as battlegrounds over information and knowledge, become training grounds for resistance. Marbel tells an interviewer, ". . . before I was captured, I hadn't participated in any organization, but the experience of being a political prisoner soon changes your mind. Through COPPES (a prisoners' organization) I learned a lot about the political situation of our country" (Thomson, 107). Harlow writes, ". . . penal institutions as part of a state's coercive apparatus of physical detention and ideological containment, provide the critical space within which, indeed out of which, alternative social and political practices of counterhegemonic resistance movements are schooled. . . . Prison education, unlike much university instruction professed in the Western academy, functions to undermine the very walls and premises that contain it" (5, 23).

The act of writing and creating becomes subversive within the prison. Díaz wrote poetry and drew. Her poem, "Playing the Blind Chicken," refers to a children's game in which all are blindfolded. The drawing illustrating the poem depicts a woman facing the "players" who are blindfolded. This reversal, in poem and drawing depicts her captors as the blind, imprisoned players of a destructive game. A drawing of Díaz and her interrogators is another reversal. A blindfolded, wounded woman stands erect as flying demons surround her, but don't touch her.

Bonds developed among prisoners and those remembered with loved ones outside the prison walls sustained captives. Díaz writes in order to ". . . record those days, to see my pain alive, which is yours" and claims she learned to survive in the enemies' jails through hearing ". . . the voices of a people who sing better than I" (Díaz 162, 167). Martínez's prison friendship with Lil Milagro Ramirez led to the development of new tactical strategies of the resistance movement (Martínez, 285). Yet, all friendships and emotions remained imprisoned. Díaz writes, "One can't manifest anything personal to your captors and interrogators." Clandestine emotions and a "camouflaged" heart were necessary resistance strategies (Díaz, 8). The most common response to all interrogations was "Yo no se nada" (I know nothing). Yes, I act like the dumb woman, the *puta* (whore) you want me to be, and in so doing I resist.

Gender and Prison

Sexual violence, notes Martínez, was the "primary way women suffered" (51). Sexual assaults, gang rape, mutilations, and the constant threat of rape were methods used against women political prisoners. As Harlow notes, ". . . the sexual violence unleashed against women political prisoners is seen as the key in controlling them" (170). Martínez concurs that constant references to rape and sexual abuse were the most demoralizing aspect of imprisonment (51).

Martínez was kept naked with her head covered during most interrogations. On many occasions she heard other prisoners being raped. Captured COMADRES often watched guards rape fellow COMADRES. Most women were addressed as *puta* (whore). During her first interview, Martínez's captors commented, *"Bonita esta puta"* (this whore is pretty). Controlling and repressing the bodies of women political prisoners clearly was central to interrogation strategy. Kaminsky notes that these strategies reverse the insight of North American feminists that the personal is the political: "the political is the personal . . . the official and unofficial structures of power and authority of the state get expressed in our day-to-day experience." Of Argentina in the 1970s she writes, "national politics was played out on the field of the body in the form of physical and psychological torture, and life was indivisible from politics" (50). The same statement could be made of El Salvador in the 1980s as state policies were played out on the bodies of prisoners.

Women political prisoners, in addition to being seen as especially vulnerable sexually, were perceived in light of gendered family roles. Threats against prisoners' children and other family members were made repeatedly. Harlow notes that interrogators' "particular stratagems practiced against their women victims" included ". . . the suggestion that their children too will be made to suffer for the 'subversive' activities of their mothers, who, according to the militarized patriarchal customs of the society, do not know their proper place as women in the home" (162). She concludes that "family as a contested sociopolitical institution is thus central to the issue of political detention" (233).

Women political prisoners found themselves in a unique position to pose a counterdiscourse to the family language of the state. Interrogators asked Díaz, "Where does your family live?" She responded, "Go to the front, there is my family" (35). Martínez writes, "How would they be able to understand the friendship and love that one is able to feel for her compañeros" (103). Within the prison setting, women articulated new conceptions of family.

COMADRES most clearly demonstrates the reorganization of the traditional family brought about by the prison experience. Many of Ilopango's (the women's prison) political prisoners were there due to their participation in COMADRES (or accusations of participation). Women often entered the political/public arena because of their family roles. COMADRES cofounder Raquel Garcia became involved when her fifteen-year-old son was captured in 1980. Death squads killed two nephews in 1985.

COMADRES at one point, visited all the jails and military barracks in El Salvador, inquiring about young people who had "disappeared." Schirmer reports that, "In every place the soldiers would tell them, 'They haven't been captured, they aren't here. We don't know anything [about it]'" (1993, 37). The state claimed that the children never existed, that these mothers never had children. The COMADRES battle was one of "seeking to know who claims the truth about the disappearance of their relatives" (Schirmer, 31).

In the process of battling with the state over truth claims, these peasant women gained knowledge of national and international law, protest and resistance strategies, and public relations. As COMADRE Alicia notes, ". . . now there are COMADRES who can't read or write but who can debate the socks off a lawyer about international law and war" (Alicia quoted by Schirmer, 30). According to Schirmer they have also ". . . come to question the acceptance of violence against women, and have made a theoretical leap: they have connected their experience and analysis of political violence (disappearance and torture) to personal violence against women (rape and battering) (31). As Mercedes Canas notes, ". . . the same type of torture that was practiced in the secret prisons was practiced by men in their homes" (Ueltzen 1993, 154).

The prison experience, whether their own, or that of their relatives, politicized motherhood. A COMADRE mother became a truth seeker, subversive, threat to the state, political analyst and strategist, and eventually one who challenged traditional patriarchal family structures.

Testimonio as Liberation Text

Testimonios not only chronicle resistance strategies within the prison, they also self consciously serve as part of a larger revolutionary struggle. As René Cruz writes of *Cárceles clandestinas*, ". . . the book is an initial effort to write the history of our revolution from the trenches of combat" (Martínez, 21). *Testimonio*, the "dominant contemporary form of narrative in Central America," serves, Beverly and Zimmerman note, as a "cultural aspect of the overall struggle for hegemony linked to the impulse to displace or overthrow both elites and elite cultural modes" (172). The purpose of *testimonio* coincides with that of theologies of liberation. The word itself suggests witnessing as a religious term.

The narrators place themselves self consciously within a liberation lineage. Martínez later finds it significant that her clandestine book was encouraged by Ignacio Ellacuria and Ignacio Martín Baro and eventually published by the Jesuit University of Central America. The agendas of liberation theology and *testimonio* coincide concretely in an urgently expressed need for the taking of sides. They both serve as ideological criticisms clearly on behalf of the "most oppressed." For liberation theologians, such as the Jesuit Jon Sobrino, faith commitment is expressed in praxis, or struggle with and for the poor. God is seen, quite literally, in the faces of the poor and the oppressed. Jesus may be symbolized as a *campesino* (peasant) struggling for land, or as Archbishop Oscar Romero who was killed for his criticisms of the Salvadoran government and military. The stations of the cross adorning the chapel walls at the Jesuit University of Central America depict peasants being tortured and/or killed. These "suffering servants" are the focal point of the liberation gospel. One's faith commitment is judged by how one stands vis à vis the poor.

Testimonio and liberation theology share the same subject and struggle to bring this subject to visibility. Leonardo Boff writes that liberation theology "starts from a definite practice of liberation focused on the poor themselves as subjects of change" (1995, 123). *Testimonio* records the voice of a subject we are meant to experience as a real person, who also stands for a group as its speaking subject. It is, as Beverly and Zimmerman claim, "the mark of a desire not to be silenced or defeated, to impose oneself on an institution of power like literature from the position of the excluded or the marginal" (175). That which is repressed, that which is forbidden, that which was literally imprisoned, claims a voice through *testimonio*. The significance of the liberation-oriented, University of Central America's press publishing *Cárceles clandestinas* was, to Martínez, that "it wasn't a pamphlet, it was a reality, la UCA publishes reality" (Ueltzen, 67).

The texts play with the concept of "presence" in Central American political practice. I have often participated in political and/or religious events in which names of victims of repression are called out. We, the audience, respond by saying, *"presente."* Those who have died are not only remembered but are present with us. In *Cárceles clandestinas*, Martínez interviews other prisoners, some of whom were later killed. Martínez self consciously presents herself and other victims. Their presence becomes a "political claim which declares the existence of the individual not as a coherent psychological subject but as a potent political subject" and is "claimed in a situation in which some dominant force deliberately denies it" according to Kaminsky (25). The victims, present in the text, are also seen as present in the continued action of others. As a Salvadoran refugee puts it,

> Monsignor Romero first said things that no one else was brave
> enough to say. We couldn't say those things. Who would believe us?
> Who would care? So he said those things and when he did, he said
> he was speaking for those without a voice. Now Monsignor is dead
> and can no longer raise his voice for us, but you see, we are changed.
> We have found our voice. (Interviewed by Thompson, 1995, 115)

Similarly, as Beverly and Zimmerman note, *testimonio* cannot affirm a self that is "separated from a group or class situation, marked by marginalization and oppression and struggle" (177). The narrator has taken sides and is part of an ongoing social struggle. And, just as the protagonist remains involved in social struggle, the reader is called to praxis. Kaminsky writes, "Taking testimonial writing seriously, which means paying attention to its call for action in society, means a return to the concrete" (54).

The praxis demanded by both theologies of liberation and *testimonio* is social transformation. The Christian and the church are called to change unjust social and economic structures. Jesuits consistently denounced the structural violence and injustice witnessed in El Salvador. The popular church in El Salvador provided the ideological critique and motivation which helped radicalize many Salvadorans, including the COMADRES and Martínez.

History is contested ground for both *testimonio* and theologies of liberation. *Testimonios* use the prison experience to articulate the dominant history, which is then challenged by a counterhistory of revolutionary struggle. The *testimonio* view of history, capitalism, and imperialism is remarkably similar to that found in theologies of liberation. Leonardo Boff writes, "The same logic that destroyed the 'witness cultures' of Latin America in the sixteenth century has continued its devastating course to the present. . . . Today in the name of modernity, Latin American governments are bringing the logic of domination up to date through the grandiose schemes of multinational corporations from Japan, Germany, Italy, and the United States. The cost of this and of a foreign debt that cannot be repaid is more and yet more deaths" (1995, 101–2). René Cruz's prologue to *Cárceles Clandestinas* similarly places the text in the context of global capitalism and North American imperialism's role in "sustaining the edifice of exploitation and dependency of America" (Martínez, 17).

The narrating of this history occurs in very concrete ways in *testimonio*. Díaz knew her captor was a Yankee when she saw his blond hair, athletic body, and RayBan glasses: "This Yankee was a symbol of Reagan, he was one of the 300 advisors in El Salvador" (Díaz 15). When her interrogators asked her, "Where do the arms come from?" she answered, "From the United States. Reagan sends them to you" (40). In a later interview Díaz says, "I knew that I fought against the United States" (Ueltzen, 69). The blond captor stands for Reagan who stands for the United States as the embodiment of the "metanarrative of modernity" and the history of dominance thrust on El Salvador.

When Martínez was released from prison, her former jailers and torturers became her bodyguards, charged with insuring her safe release. She reflects on the irony of this asking, "what power changed their roles like this? The only power which came from being members of the class that held the political and economic power of the country" (Martínez, 321). She further notes that the political police, horrible as they were, were merely a means of repressive control against the popular movement, an "instrument of the dominant classes . . . in almost all parts of the world they are used . . . above all in Latin America, where the Imperialist Yankee" encourages repressive control (Martínez, 363). The political police, like the prisoners themselves, are represented as mere pawns in the grand history of domination and dependence.

Testimonios, however, spend more time articulating the counterhistory of revolutionary struggle than the history of dominance.

This understanding mirrors the liberation perspective of the one "real history" which consists of

> . . . the defense of the rights of the poor, punishment of the oppressors, a life free from the fear of being enslaved by others, the liberation of the oppressed. Peace, justice, love, and freedom are not private realities; they are not only internal attitudes. They are social realities, implying a historical liberation. (Brown cited in Tilley 1995, 126)

Díaz views her book as a "small piece of the prolonged history of the fight of the Salvadoran people" (Díaz, 9). Prison provides a story, within which larger revolutionary history is told. As Harlow writes, "texts written out of political detention" are an "important dimension of the history and theory of organized struggle and dialogue between political detainee and the state's prison apparatus" (178). Díaz's references to Reagan demonstrate that "the most ordinary of daily encounters between victim and victimizer managed by the prison apparatus and its routines are remodulated into a historical struggle" (Harlow, 16).

Both Martínez and Díaz self consciously place their texts in the line of prison narratives and revolutionary struggle. Martínez begins her *testimonio* with a reference to Cayetano Carpio's 1952 prison narrative, *Secuestro y Capucha* (11). Díaz writes that she remembered the earlier prison books *Secuestro y Capucha* and *Las Cárceles Clandestinas* while in prison (46). This linear historical progress reflects an attempt to articulate an alternative national narrative of social struggle, "leading to some kind of socialist salvation" (Beverly and Zimmerman, 116).

Testimonios as liberation texts share a common lineage, are on the side of the "most oppressed," call the reader to praxis, demand social transformation, bring the poor to visibility as political subjects, and articulate the "real" history of engaged struggle over and against the "metanarrative" of the history of domination.

Testimonio as Postmodern Text

As noted earlier, considering *testimonios* as postmodern texts is a trickier proposition than claiming a liberation status for them. I will briefly sketch ways in which these agendas coincide.

Testimonios challenge conventional notions of authorship and consequently of a "professional discursive practice that legitimates the production and dissemination of knowledge in one form at the expense of another," as the writers of *The Postmodern Bible* write (Bible and Culture Collective, 1995, 16). The narrator is generally not a professional writer or an intellectual. Producing the text often involves recording by an interlocutor such as a journalist, writer, or activist. The "author" is erased, to be replaced by the narrator, who in turns "stands" for a group, and a compiler. Although the recorder may be of a different class background, she depends on the collective subject for the story. Thus, as Beverly and Zimmerman note, "control of representation does not just flow one way" and "these are important contradictions, which have to do with testimonio's location at the center of the dialectic of oppressor and oppressed in the postcolonial world" (176). Removing the author in *testimonio*, also challenges the class distinctions and cultural elitism signified by the "great writer." Was the text, *Nunca Estuve Sola* "written" by Maria López Vigil who recorded Díaz's oral account, by Díaz who spoke the words, or by the Salvadoran people who are, according to Díaz, the "subject" of the book?

The powerful subject of *testimonio* is simultaneously centered *and* decentered. The "I" in Díaz's title is a collective "I". In an interview Díaz says, "I was a product of others," moving attention away from Díaz as literal narrator (Ueltzen, 66). She begins her oral account by demystifying herself as narrator/author saying, "I didn't have the revelation of a saint, nor the art of a diviner, nor the presentiment of a witch, or the imagination of a magician, so didn't know I would be captured" (Díaz 11).

Testimonio asks the reader to consider the power of the speaking subject, who is a real, not a fictional, subject, but who is also a collective and decentered subject. Kaminsky writes that this move involves "the reader's recognition of the text as a form of practice, connected to existing ideological formations in a combination of resistance and complicity, and it is a reminder of the responsibility that we as readers, critics, and political actors have in addressing these texts" (26).

Testimonio shares an understanding with postmodern thinkers that discursive strategy is not only important but both reflects and *is* real power. Díaz's book is primarily accounts of dialogues between prisoner and captors. Harlow writes that "each of these discursive modalities in turn contributes within the narrative to the political detainee's own examination of the necessary reconstruction of an oppositional political stance within the extreme structural constraints imposed by incarceration" (176). The text both records discursive strategies and is itself a "counterhegemonic cultural production" that serves as "counterdialogue that contributes to the establishment of a multidimensional activist front whose very sociopolitical articulations constitute the alternative cultural narrative against which the military government has launched its predatory attack" (Harlow 163). Those who would normally be denied access to literary production enter forcefully through *testimonio*, waging discursive and "real" battle.

Testimonio also clearly shares the postmodern suspicion of the "grand narratives" of western progress. The master narratives of modernity acted out, in this case through the Salvadoran prison apparatus, are both named and challenged by the writing of a counterhistory. Yet, it is the very nature of this challenge that may disqualify *testimonios* from being considered postmodern texts. As part of their challenge, the texts reflect a firm belief in the metanarrative of political emancipation from oppression. Such a counterhistory becomes another grand narrative. Beverly and Zimmerman write that testimonial writings are "postmodernisms of resistance" and challenge metanarratives of modernity by generating a "new postcolonial noneurocentric narrative of historical space and destiny" (xii).

Jean-Francois Lyotard cautions us however, against such "politics of redemption," writing that the "grand narratives of emancipation . . . have lost their intelligibility and their substance" (1993, 169). The alternative revolutionary history offered by the *testimonios* is a thoroughly modern project for Lyotard. He writes:

> The presumption of the moderns, of Christianity, Enlightenment, Marxism, has always been that another voice is stifled in the discourse of "reality" and that it is a question of putting a true hero (the creature of God, the reasonable citizen, or the enfranchised proletarian) back in his position as subject, wrongfully usurped by the impostor. What we called "depoliticization" twenty-five years ago was in fact the announcement of the erasure of this great figure of the alternative, and at the same time, that of the great founding legitimacies. This is more or less what I have tried to designate, clumsily, by the term 'postmodern.' (Lyotard 1993, 169)

Testimonio then shares with much postmodernist thought the "radical task" of deconstructing "apparent truths," dismantling "dominant ideas and cultural forms," and undermining "closed systems of thought" (Wolf 1990, 85). It decenters the subject, erases the author, and challenges the hegemonic history embodied in the prison apparatus. In posing an alternative history of revolutionary struggle it may, as Lyotard suggests, supplant one grand narrative with another. Does this leave us with irreconcilable contradictions between theologies of liberation and postmodern thought?

Lyotard's suspicion of emancipatory histories need not lead to political inaction anymore than Foucault's ideas of the pervasiveness of power necessitate political paralysis. Rather, caution is given to those who might hope for utopian "salvations" of any form, be they socialist or liberationist. Any emancipatory narrative adopted for political aims and goals must, of necessity, be a provisional narrative, a narrative open to questioning, and aiming at proximate goals. We cannot live or act without narrative, yet it may be possible to conceive of metanarratives as endlessly open, fluid, rather than as static and reified. To retreat from the endless opening and questioning of narrative is to reify and thus to face the dangers suggested by Lyotard. In postwar El Salvador, women of the popular movement are struggling against the Communist Party and other members of the left over land rights. The revolutionary metanarrative of the poor struggling against the rich has not proven overly helpful in this internal debate over justice.

Reified metanarratives, even if emancipatory, contradict a hermeneutic of suspicion. The challenge postmodern thought poses to theologies of liberation is to apply the hermeneutic of suspicion to themselves as well as to the enemy. This can only strengthen emancipatory strategies. The dangerous "game" played by the many actors Díaz identifies in her "Blindfold Chicken" poem warns of the high price of subjugation and any and all forms of totalizing. As texts of liberation, postmodernity, and resistance, *testimonios* demand a dismantling of prison in its multiple forms.

Notes

1. All translations by Lois Ann Lorentzen.
2. For an excellent, sophisticated analysis of MTV, from the perspective of postmodern theories and political economy, see Andrew Goodwin 1992.

Works Cited

Algería, Claribel and Flakoll, D. J. 1993. *No me agarran viva: La mujer salvadorena en la lucha*. San Salvador, El Salvador: UCA Editores.

Arac, Jonathan, ed. 1986. *Postmodernism and Politics*. Minneapolis: University of Minnesota Press.

Beverly, John and Zimmerman, Marc. 1990. *Literature and Politics in the Central American Revolution*. Austin: University of Texas Press.

The Bible and Culture Collective. 1995. *The Postmodern Bible*. New Haven: Yale University Press.

Boff, Leonardo. 1995. *Ecology and Liberation: A New Paradigm*. Maryknoll, NY: Orbis Books.

Callari, Antonio, Cullenberg, Stephen and Biewener, Carole, eds. 1995. *Marxism in the Postmodern Age: Confronting the New World Order*. New York: Guilford Press.

Cooey, Paula M. 1994. *Religious Imagination and the Body: A Feminist Analysis*. New York: Oxford University Press.

Díaz, Nidia. 1993. *Nunca Estuve Sola*. San Salvador, El Salvador: UCA Editores.

Goodwin, Andrew. 1992. *Dancing in the Distraction Factory: Music Television and Popular Culture*. Minneapolis: University of Minnesota Press.

Harlow, Barbara. 1992. *Barred: Women, Writing and Political Detention*. Hanover: Wesleyan University Press.

Hicks, Emily D. 1991. *Border Writing: The Multidimensional Text*. Minneapolis: University of Minnesota Press.

Hopkins, Dwight N. 1995. Unpublished letter.

Kaminsky, Amy K. *Reading the Body Politic: Feminist Criticism and Latin American Women Writers*. Minneapolis: University of Minnesota Press.

Larsen, Neil. 1991. Foreword to Hicks, Emily D. *Border Writing: The Multidimensional Text*. Minneapolis: University of Minnesota Press.

Lyotard, Jean-Francois. 1993. *Political Writings*. Minneapolis: University of Minnesota Press.

Martínez, Ana Guadalupe. 1992. *Las cárceles clandestinas de El Salvador*. San Salvador, El Salvador: UCA Editores.

Pottenger, John R. 1989. *The Political Theory of Liberation Theology: Toward a Reconvergence of Social Values and Social Science*. Albany, NY: State University of New York Press.

Rodríguez, Guadalupe. 1994. *Marianela*. San Salvador, El Salvador: Editorial Guayampopo.

Schirmer, Jennifer. 1993. "The Seeking of Truth and the Gendering of Consciousness: The COMADRES of El Salvador and the CIBAVUGYA Widows of Guatemala," in Radcliffe, Sarah A. and Sallie Westwood, eds. *'Viva': Women and Popular Protest in Latin America*. London: Routledge.

Sobrino, Jon, S. J. 1985. *Christology at the Crossroads: A Latin American Approach*. Maryknoll, NY: Orbis Books.

Thompson, Martha. 1995. "Repopulated Communities in El Salvador," in Sinclair, Minor, ed. *The New Politics of Survival: Grassroots Movements in Central America*. New York: Monthly Review Press.

Thomson, Marilyn. 1986. *Women of El Salvador: The Price of Freedom*. London: Zed Books.

Tilley, Terrence W. with Morris, C. Bradley. 1995. "Gustavo Gutiérrez and Praxis in Christian Communities," in Tilley, Terrence, ed. *Postmodern Theologies: The Challenge of Religious Diversity*. Maryknoll, NY: Orbis Books.

Ueltzen, Stefan. 1993. *Como Salvadorena Que Soy: Entrevistas con mujeres en la lucha*. San Salvador, El Salvador: Editorial Sombrero Azul.

Wolf, Janet. 1990. *Feminine Sentences: Essays on Women and Culture*. Berkeley: University of California Press.

8

Charting (dis)Courses of Liberation

David Batstone

The quest for a hermeneutic obsesses intellectual life at the turn of the century. What one says is much less significant than why, where, or how one says it. Perhaps this debate over the site and legitimation of knowledge is the defining cognitive characteristic of the postmodern condition.

The tempest is such, however, that even the presumption of a postmodern condition is suspect. The postmodern critique confronts universal or totalizing foundations, noting their own variability and specificity of location, thereby splitting them. Thus, its representations are fragmented, making a univocal "condition" a contradiction in terms.

Therein lies postmodernity's continuity (yet also its tension) with another important philosophical movement that has emerged in the second half of the twentieth century, liberation theology. Theologies of liberation posit heterological grounding and critical decentering as a resource and an inspiration for people seeking social and political freedom. Its hermeneutic promises access to interlocuters historically excluded from the production of knowledge. Voices from the margins of social power aim to critically analyze rational constructs so as to unmask their material interests and to bring them to historical accountability.

Postmodernity and liberation theology are essentially neo-modernist movements, sophisticated elaborations of ideology critique within a post-colonial and post-industrial global order. Modernism also delegitimated established authorities and their social constructs, while supporting independent avenues for rational critique and legitimation. In his seminal essay "What Is Enlightenment?" Kant boldly called for "immature" thinkers to examine closely the cognitive formulas of state officials and the clergy so as to cultivate their own insights about the material interests of the commonwealth. His motto for the new age was, "Have courage to use your *own* understanding" (Kant 1970, 55–57).

Kant, of course, was a cultural idealist. He was convinced that "after many revolutions, with all their transforming effects . . . a universal cosmopolitan existence will at last be realized as the matrix within which all the original capacities of the human race may develop." He did not pretend that a philosophy of history might supersede the empirical unfolding of history itself, but did believe that rational ideals nonetheless contribute to furthering the cause of freedom (Kant 51, 53). His hope represents a composite of ensuing modernist constructs of history and utopian visions of how world events must unfold if they are to conform to truly rational ends.

Postmodernity and theologies of liberation respond quite differently to this legacy, a tension that emerges most dramatically in the realm of political ideology. Much of liberation theology is built on utopian discourses of emancipation and revolution. Postmodernism, by and large, renders such meta-narratives obsolete, arguing that marginal ideologies of critique still mirror centers of domination and are built on the same totalizing foundations. Liberation theologians, in turn, are apt to consider postmodernism as "toothless in the face of oppression" (Gilkey 1985, 728). They are adamant that the moral force of philosophy is, in the spirit of Marx, not to interpret the world but to change it.

The implications of this conflict for systems of interpretation and communication are complex and move across academic disciplines. Emancipation is a house with many windows. To look into a house through only one window yields a limited perception of its spatial relations.

So we best signify emancipation in material culture through multiple representations of existing power relations and their transitions. Critical rationality is indeed a useful lens for understanding the patterns that link theoretical constructs and social events. But a clearer view of material culture comes into focus when we place critical rationality in a perceptual field shared by other ways of knowing, most notably testimony, aesthetics, intuition, wisdom, and imagination.

The challenge to traverse these domains of knowledge, or, better yet, to integrate them within a perceptual field, inspires the artistic impulse to map their cultural representations. The purpose of this cartography is to chart a course toward a postmodern hermeneutics of liberation.

The representations hang together by a thread of imagination, not by irreducible logic. The cartographer informed by postmodernity operates self-consciously within the limits of his or her own subjectivity. The cartographer informed by liberation theology pays special attention to those who live on the outer borders of rationalized systems of power.

Oppression

I worked in community development in Central America for more than ten years under the auspices of Central American Mission Partners (CAMP). CAMP is a network of religious communities and political organizations that provides start-up capital and training workshops in popular education and appropriate technology. Since most of the fertile land in Central America is reserved for cash crops like coffee, sugar cane, and cotton, *campesinos* are forced typically to till soil-depleted hillsides. For that reason our strategic center is an experimental farm in rural El Salvador where *campesinos* observed and practiced organic farming techniques particularly suitable for these environmental conditions. Our methods aimed to prevent soil erosion and to reduce reliance on expensive, fertilizer-based agricultural methods.

During my first stay in El Salvador I visited a rural agricultural cooperative. My two work companions were Salvadorans, an organizer of community economic projects and a literacy trainer, both members of the popular movement to end oligarchical rule in their country. One day I casually asked the literacy worker if she came from an indigenous community, as her facial features led me to believe. I realized immediately that I had said something offensive; she became extremely embarrassed, while the *mestizo* community organizer broke out in laughter.

"Look, it's obvious I've done something stupid," I confessed. "Could you please explain to me what it was?"

"It's an insult to tell someone they look *indígena*," explained the *mestizo*, still grinning from ear to ear. Confused, I asked why. "Everyone knows that *indígenas* are ugly." He stated it as a matter of fact. The literacy trainer, whom I learned was indigenous, dutifully shook her head in agreement.

The complexities of cultural oppression that mark the Americas are hinted at in this anecdote. The experience was my first hint that social transformation in El Salvador would require more than simply overthrowing "fourteen families" and their hired guns, or even the more ambitious political project of autonomy from the empire. My analysis of power relations, heretofore circumscribed in terms of state, relations of production, and class struggle, were insufficient for individualizing techniques of domination.

Alienation in the Americas runs deep. Ideologies that neatly divide social space into oppositional polarities are limited in their capacity to yield that depth. The mechanisms of domination and exploitation produce complex and circular relations which are not reducible to deterministic forms of subjection and subjectivity. An appreciation for material culture is not achieved merely through the construction of a general theory, but by close consideration of the connections between forms of experience and their relations to power and to knowledge.

The Cartographer

The *subject* is at present deeply distrusted in scholarly conversations on knowledge. The critique is generally directed at the self-contained, self-determined subject who was the source and instrument of knowledge in the modern European tradition. This Self assumed unmediated access to universal reason and absolute justice.

The autonomous subject of modern Europe extended itself into social reality as an imperial Self. It had license to define the world of the stranger, for the subject's rationality was a gateway to universal reason and its understanding of justice was absolute justice. But this subject construct failed to appreciate four interrelated limitations regarding subjectivity: (1) the identification of the person whose experiences were being considered; (2) the realization that knowledge is inescapably an instrument of power exercised in social space; (3) an analysis of whose interests were being served in the interpretation of knowledge; and (4) a suspicion of the purity and transparency of knowledge.

A constantly changing political economy, the pace of which has quickened since the Second World War, made the univocity of the Self increasingly untenable. As a result of the extension of capital that arrived with colonialism and the rationalization of labor that evolved with industrialization, subjects relationally linked by economic and social activity (producers and consumers) proliferated. Many voices made a claim on experience. Religio-political movements of liberation in Latin America are prime examples of colonized people who clamor for economic and social rights as "subjects of their own history" (Gutiérrez 1983).

Even within dominant centers of cultural production it is now accepted that no event of consciousness or prediscursive experience may serve as an uninterpreted source of knowledge. The subject and its self-representation through language, art, and media are cultural products born of relational difference.

Cartography

car•tog•ra•phy: the *art* or *science* of making maps.
(Websters, 1993, 344).

There are many ways to read a map, an insight often ignored when your sole aim is to get to your destination. To identify what is missing, the gaps between the spaces, is often more important than that which is actually displayed. After all, any map is the product of a joust [Aristotle's *agon* (1970)] to name, to arrange and to frame relational space.

The archaeological remnants of the joust are revealed and hidden dialectically in the delineation of borders. Consider the last two centuries of charting the Mexico/U.S. border. A current map does not reveal that California was until 1848 in the full possession of Mexico. Nor does it tell the tale of the political manipulations that led to a shift in that border, a history apparently invisible to those who today so fervently apply laws of citizenship. What a current U.S./Mexico map does reveal, and hide, is the product of a joust.

Drawing borders is always arbitrary, not in the heuristic sense of a capricious choice, but insofar as it indicates an act of judgment. Rarely do these judgments stem from consensual agreements among knowing subjects, except on odd occasions or in specialized subcultures (cf. Habermas 1975; 1981). But judgments are delivered in a specific history, which is the reason why the capacity to read borders is a necessary tool for strategic movement, even when the judgments do not seem judicious. A Mexican farm laborer who crosses the Rio Grande to look for work, for instance, knows that borders matter. The judgments of history always exact their cost.

Denotative markings on a map therefore are not isomorphic reproductions of material relations. The cartographer presumes axes of polarity around which sites rotate, a center from which other sites appear distant or near, borders that arbitrarily separate. Cartography is a creative art.

Prescriptive markings on a map, however, cannot escape the symbolic field that "as-signs" them value. The cartographer fixes the sites on a map following carefully established rules of protocol and measurement. Cartography is an exact science.

Science

"Whoever determines what technologies mean will control not merely the technology market but thought itself."
—Sandy Stone in *Wired* (Stryker, 1996, 135)

Jean François Lyotard argued persuasively in his influential report on "the postmodern condition" (1984) that the pragmatics of science functionally rely on a consensual method of legitimation. Scientific knowledge is a set of truth-claims that have proven before a tribunal of credible peers their capacity to explain reality. "Not every consensus is a sign of truth," Lyotard notes, "but it is presumed that the truth of a statement necessarily draws a consensus" (24).

Knowledge so constructed effectively contributes to the rationalization of material culture. The verification (or falsification) of scientific knowledge demands that any new statement about a referent contradicts and refutes previously approved statements that purport to explain the referent's reality (26). Science thus utilizes a language of referents that does not permit plurality or inconsistency, except in temporary moments of crisis. It predicates a knowing that is both denotative and universal.

These mechanics of legitimation are not limited to the natural sciences, for they mark borders as well in the province of ideology. Ideology arranges into a coherent system the signifying practices and relations that human beings perform as social subjects (Althusser, 1969). Though ideology is not wholly empirical, it nevertheless aims to explain reality in ways that are verifiable and non-contradictory. The verification is pragmatically dialectical: "Not: I can prove something because reality is the way I say it is. But: as long as I can produce proof, it is permissible to think that reality is the way I say it is" (Lyotard 24).

The primary function of rationalized knowledge is the creation of more intelligent systems of efficiency and technique. These systems, in turn, enhance performativity in the relations that exist within material culture. Human civilization is both the progenitor and the product of such rationalizations.

The "scientific method" did not debut with the sixteenth century rising of the sun in Europe. It is a way of knowing that has always co-existed with, though certainly subordinate to, other forms of knowledge grounded in custom, authority, and revelation.

Performativity as the primary imperative in the production of knowledge is unique to the modern era in the countries of the North Atlantic, however. A greater fluidity and extension of capital circulation ensured that increased efficiency of activity would yield greater surplus value (Harvey 1975). In effect, knowledge translated into technology became a valuable (valuated) commodity of exchange. With the gradual eclipse of traditional forms of knowledge, the demand to deliver empirical proof either to legitimate or to deligitimate technical knowledge became paramount.

The objective, of course, is to control or to condition the context. The truth of any statement, be it denotative or prescriptive, is measured largely by its capacity to explain Reality, since the defining of such is a valuable investment in the operational capacity of information. Wealth and privilege accrue to those who have the capacity to define the system of normalized human activity (cf. Microsoft since the 1980s). The discourse of legitimation is ultimately a discourse of power.

Performativity as a criterion of truthfulness applies to ethical, legal, and political ideologies as much as it does to more technical fields of scientific knowledge. Lyotard provides one example of how performativity informs the modernist discourse of political justice: "The probability that an order would be pronounced just was said to increase its chances of being implemented, which would in turn increase with the performance capability of the prescriber" (46).

Given the importance of mastering Reality, it is no wonder that ideology became such a highly valued weapon in the geo-political wars of the twentieth century.

Art

"Remember, the world's a messy place . . . maybe art really is then the art of adaptation."
                                                    —Jennifer Keeler-Milne (1994, 2)

What is commonly coined "the secularization of modern society" is in pragmatic terms the devaluation of mythic and narrative forms of knowledge in favor of truths legitimated by their mastery of material culture. This transition was posed by modernist intellectuals as an epic battle pitting rationality against superstition. "We think we ought to believe because our forefathers believed," wrote Sigmund Freud in his treatise on the wish-fulfilling delusions of mythic cultures, "but these ancestors of ours were far more ignorant than we are. They believed in things we could not possibly accept today" (1961, 33).

The formation of the modern psyche owes, in reality, more to the mechanics and centralized bureaucracies of industrial production than to a pyrrhic triumph over mythic knowledge. The hegemony of linear modes of perception was essential for the construction of a society that relied on the capacity to calculate human activity, an observation correctly made by Max Weber (1958). In the wake of empirical (data-based) measurement, alternative modes of consciousness that frame identity through the interplay of enchanted spirits, imaginative aesthetics, and mythical archetypes were bound to appear cognitively inferior. Empirical measurement assures competence, of course, not wisdom or aesthetics.

Many cultural critics now ironically claim that the scientific method masks the mythic character of its own legitimation. Referents which are assumed to exist in necessary relation are actually ordered by rule-prescribed narratives which cannot be *proven* to correspond to Reality.

Jean Baudrillard, for instance, seriously doubts the capacity of analytical theory to uncover deep structures or latent meanings of Reality. His critique is not a nihilistic denial of Reality per se, but a suspicion that there is no way around or beyond Its "surface." He deems critical theories that purport to do so exercises in self-referentiality. The legitimation of knowledge has more to do with the mechanics of an interpretive system than its actual explanation of Reality.

Baudrillard's epistemology is not entirely consistent. At times he appears to argue that the simulated relationship between Reality and Its referents is a recent phenomenon brought on by consumer propaganda, communication networks, and information technology. He implies that prior to the industrial revolution objects and their representations were related in "a natural law of value" (1983, 83). The referent only disappeared as a meaningful representation of the real in a post-industrial world dominated by simulacra (1988, 21, 50).

Yet, elsewhere Baudrillard argues that there has never been a time when language and other cultural products served as direct representations of social experience. Perception, he argues, is ever formed "symbolically, magically, irrationally" (1983, 68, 73).

Since he is prone to such contradictions, it is easy to discount Baudrillard wholesale. Yet perhaps more forcefully than any other contemporary thinker he has raised the problematic of the "fatal and enigmatic bias in the order of things" (Baudrillard 1990, 10). Baudrillard forces us to see that our interpretive systems are immersed in the *agon* of cultural relations from which there is no escape. The knowledge that provides us with a map of material culture is itself a contribution to the ongoing reconstitution of its geography.

Material culture is not universally perceptible—a pragmatic fact of life in the globalized, post-industrial society (Batstone 1996). The "nature" of an object is contingent on where and when the subject finds it, and for what purpose it is desired. Objects do take on functional identities, of course, but these identities are a product of the subject's interaction with them. The plurality of subject identities in turn are a product of those interactions.

The aesthetic thus plays an integral role in the process of knowing. Imagination works with reason to position cultural representations within a symbolic field of meaning. That is how Carl Jung presented his (quasi)empirical studies of alchemy (1967), self-consciously beginning and ending the work with Mercury, the god of fictions and of fabrications, the trickster of deceptions and of the sleight-of-hand. Jung was convinced of the value and limitations of multiple forms of knowledge. Knowledge is *both* cognitive and affective, a product of critical reason and of the imagination, the province of science and of art.

The demands of Reality (the judgments of history) necessitate a "poetic activity" of endless reinterpretation (Rorty 1979, 359). "Necessitate" in this sense does not presuppose an ontological teleology (*àla* Hegel), but rather is grounded in the collective testimony of human survival and of adaptation. What we experience by chance or intrusion inexorably presents itself with a materiality and a history. The ways we rearrange, recontextualize, and represent our sensual impressions of that materiality is contingent upon our capacity to adapt to what we and our ancestors have already experienced (Keeler-Milne, 2).

Work

"People have to do with what they have, and everyday life is the art of making do."

—Michel de Certeau (1993, 25)

Sebastiâo Salgado recently exhibited his photographic essays, starkly entitled "Workers," in major museums around the world. The Brazilian photographer had traveled the globe documenting the labor of men and women who, for the sake of their own survival, work arduously with their hands.

One of the unforgettable photographs in the exhibit dramatizes the cost of human life in the gold mines of Serra Pelada in Brazil. A mass of humanity grovels in the mud of a strip mine, their task to carry loads of dirt out of the chasm. Heavy sacks on their back, the workers make their way up steep trails to the top, their skin and tattered clothes slowly turning to clay. Uniformed soldiers with rifles ready are visible amidst the crowd. At the bottom of the mine, tools are raised, men preparing to strike deep into the dark earth. The scene rivals the most chilling images of Dante's hell.

Salgado's words hang poignantly next to his own images:

These photographs tell the story of an era. The images offer a visual archaeology of a time that history knows as the Industrial Revolution. . . .

Concepts of production and efficiency are changing, and, with them the nature of work. The highly industrialized world is racing ahead and stumbling over the future. . . .

The developed word produces only for those who can consume—approximately one-fifth of all people. The remaining four-fifths . . . have transferred so many of their resources and wealth to the prosperous world that they have no way of achieving equality. . . .

The destiny of men and women is to create a new world, to reveal a new life, to remember that there exists a frontier for everything, except dreams. In this way, they adapt, resist, believe, and survive.

History is above all a succession of challenges, of repetitions, of perservances. It is an endless cycle of oppressions, humiliations, and disasters, but also a testament to man's ability to survive. In history, there are no solitary dreams; one dreamer breathes life into the next.

Every relationship of power implies a potential strategy for struggle, but that confrontation has as its limit the stable mechanisms through which the necessary conduct for survival, like work, is regulated and ordered. Resistance, while always colonized by power and inscribed within it, is not wholly determined by it. Power and resistance are bound by their sociality.

(dis)Courses of Liberation

For the last three decades Latin American revolutionaries have put their faith in an emancipation narrative that would transcend, or at least subvert, the social conditions in which they lived. Many of them joined the revolution after a period of popular education in base Christian communities through which they became acutely aware of the root causes of their cultural dislocation (Pearce 1986; Berryman 1984; Batstone 1991). A theology of liberation was born.

The God of liberation theology is a Redeemer who intervenes in history to free the poor from social and political oppression. Just as God once had delivered the Hebrew people out of slavery in Egypt, God will liberate the poor today from bondage. Members of Latin American base communities committed themselves to this process, divinely inspired to create an era of justice when weapons of war would be turned into machetes, when every family would own their own *parcela* of fertile land, and when no one would be threatened with state repression. The kingdom of God, it seemed, was at hand.

More than a few revolutionaries abandoned their religious moorings, however, and replaced them with a secular version of millenarianism, the marxian vision of a classless society. (In many base communities, images of the kingdom of God and of the classless society were one and the same.) Debunking religious categories, these secular revolutionaries invested their faith in material forces that were moving history inexorably, even if dialectically, toward liberation.

Some of us laugh now when we recall the weekly updates on *coyuntura* that members of our network would receive from revolutionary vanguards. A *coyuntura* is an analysis of present social conditions, often presented as a dialectical moment in a historical process. The messages we received usually were confident that today's *coyuntura* represented a movement forward in the liberation struggle. Sustaining regular conversations about the social location of the community was indeed an invaluable resource in the development of our critical consciousness; but it was quite a stretch at times to put every event at the service of the revolutionary ideal.

Years later these romantic readings of history have yielded not only humor, but a serious critique of political ideology. My experiences instilled in me a suspicion of any discourse that offers up one Paradise for another, either by romanticizing the past or by fabricating the future.

Much of our contemporary political language relies on binary rules of grammar. Before a justifiable appeal for cultural action can be made, it is practically axiomatic that one reconstruct a moment of purity when dislocation did not exist, at least in the form or to the degree it presently exists. Circumscribing this space will produce, ostensibly, an awareness of our own dislocation and move our imagination to recreate some semblance of a past social order.

Alternative forms of political discourse promise redemption in a world that is yet to come. Though here in this place life is dislocated, there is a place that will break into history and transform what we have here into an entirely new place.

This political discourse has its theological counterpart. The coincidence of the political and the theological should come as no surprise; after all, theological discourse is responding to the same material culture that finds expression in political discourse. Mark C. Taylor claims they often share the same grammatical rules around standards:

> Throughout human history, gold is not so much sign as the transcendental signified that is supposed to ground the meaning and value of other signs. . . . God functions in a semiotic system in the same way that gold functions in the economic system. The go(l)d standard is the base upon which everything rests. When this foundation crumbles or becomes inaccessible, signs are left to float freely on a sea that has no shores (1994, 607).

Religion's primary concern is to explicate the human relationship to the transcendent. Still, all patterns of grammar in a semiotic system, the theological included, reflect a semantic context of valuation. The word "God," for instance, does not identify the existence of a spiritual being in a way that is self-disclosing, for an encounter with "God" cannot be contained in any language system. The way one speaks of such an encounter will be understood by reference to other terms that are placed in a grammatical link to "God" vocabulary.

Pivotal to the "God-centric" discourse of modernist theology is a vocabulary of good and evil that is grammatically linked to a creation-redemption pattern. God loves good and hates evil; more specifically, evil is the negation of a relationship with God. "In the beginning" the material culture was good and existed in perfect harmony with God. But the introduction of evil into the world disfigured this perfection. The intrusion of evil into Paradise separated the material culture from God, a situation that universally conditioned the existential structures of the human being in the form of bondage.

What was originally of value to God, the good, is now in need of revaluing. Redemption is God's act that transfigures the disfigured. It is an interruption of divine space from outside material culture that restores it to its original goodness. In the act of redemption "there is a new creation."

The foundational myth of the creation-redemption pattern is the Garden of Eden story. In the Garden there is no knowledge of good and evil; Adam and Eve do not know the taste of its fruit. The image of the divine is male and female, made of one flesh, without awareness of its difference. So, too, the divine and human are free of differentiation; the Creator and the created casually walk through the Garden in "the cool of the day."

Once Adam and Eve eat of the tree of the knowledge of good and evil, their departure from the Garden is imperative. They undergo "dis-location," for good cannot share space with evil. Shame occasions their realization of differentiation; they hide from God and from each other.

Since there is no place outside the Garden that is free of the differentiations of history, emancipation from bondage (redemption) can only occur in the realm of ideal. Modernist discourse sought to reconcile this contradiction through its valuation of "time," time past (the Garden) or time future (heaven), both of which are bound by eternity. Time so constructed has no organic link to place. The forthcoming (future) and the antecedent (past) are not contingent on the horizon of the present.

But this temporal orientation is by no means universal, a critique depicted exceptionally well in the movie *Black Robe*. The film relates the awkward and often tragic relationships that evolved (or more to the point, failed to evolve) between North American Indians and the French Jesuits who came to bring them redemption. The Huron tribe is convinced that the clock is the god of the foreigners since it tells them what to do and when to do it. In one of the more poignant scenes in the movie, the Hurons are brought to the mission chapel where they sit down patiently, turn away from the altar, and face the clock. They wait in reverent silence for the cuckoo god to arrive and to announce the next sacred hour. Time is the transcendent arriving from beyond history.

The European missionaries, for their part, are frustrated with their inability to communicate to these "primitives" a world of eternal destiny autonomous from their tribal arrangements. The Hurons cannot grasp the simple attraction of immortality, that is, a place where time has no end.

If we were to read the Garden of Eden story through the eyes of the Hurons, with grammatical boundaries set by the symbolics of cultural space, the mythic thrust of the story would change dramatically. Lived relations are then the pattern around which the vocabulary of the story gains its semantic valuation. The sexual, spiritual, and ethical differentiations that are signified in the Garden story are then inevitable, perhaps even necessary, judgments of history. The vocabulary of good and evil signify the high costs of those differentiations. Identifying the unity of force that lies behind the differentiations is to tap into the mystery of transcendence.

The much maligned serpent is the mythic key to this reinterpretation of the Garden story for several reasons. First, it is noteworthy that in many sacred traditions the serpent is a symbol for the primal relation of opposites, life and death. The serpent sheds its skin once its use has been exhausted; the death of its own being yields forth its life. A second way that the serpent represents the vulnerability of living is in its mode of survival. The snake's body is one long digestive canal that is fed by eating other life. This disturbing image of relationality shakes existence down to its primal core. The survival of life demands feeding off itself. Finally, the snake, which usually kills not by overcoming its victim but by injecting the victim with its venom, represents the fear of internalizing the forces of destruction. Sociality implies inevitable infection.

A theological or political language dominated by binary rules of grammar masks the terrifying relationality of Reality. It splits off the differentiations, creating the illusion of spaces of non-differentiation. They are called utopia, literally, no place, because they image a space where the elements of life are not implicated by their other(s). Utopia so produces a false consciousness of unity.

Michel Foucault noted that utopia is in fact a mirror image of a cultural system in inverted analogy to itself:

> In the mirror, I see myself there where I am not, in an unreal, virtual space that opens up behind the surface; I am over there, there where I am not, a sort of shadow that gives my own visibility to myself, that enables me to see myself there where I am absent. . . . (1986, 24)

Perhaps therein lies the creative possibilities of the human imagination. The mind spins images that give visibility to the place where I am not, yet where I want to be. Surely, out of this womb is born a critical consciousness of lived relations in material culture.

But it produces a false consciousness when it leads me to identify with the place where I am not, so that the place where I actually am becomes the illusion. That is what makes me most suspicious of a cultural grammar of ideals, whether it uses religious or political vocabulary. It asks me to move within a space where I am absent.

Hope

How much ideological charlatanism is passed on with the justification, "We have to give the masses some hope"? Hope is "just another word with nothing left to lose."

Modernity's hope is rooted deeply in the apocalyptic tradition of the semitic religions (though mainstream Judaism, following the disaster at Masada, deemed it too costly a cultural strategy). Apocalyptic utopia, or hope, mediates between reason and passion; it gives reason its *raison d'être* and passion its *á toutes fines utiles*. Utopia arrives from beyond history to move and to transform it. The history to which it refers is, of course, a string of shattered dreams.

Hope can be conceived otherwise. The hope that grows in oneself and in one's community signifies a deep trust that is earned, the confidence in the wisdom that got us here so far, and a sensitivity that our actions simply do not pass away, but contribute to an ongoing inheritance. Hope *in* our reason and passion.

Salvadoran novelist Manlio Argueta so refashions the ground of hope via his *campesina* character, Lupe:

> [José would tell me] hope is the sustenance of fools. I had never believed him. I understand what he's getting at, but I don't take him literally. Hope also nourishes us. Not the hope of fools. The other kind. Hope, when everything is clear. Awareness. (1983, 144–5)

A Political Cartography of the Americas at the Dawn of the Twenty-First Century

> "[In America] only what is produced or manifested has meaning; for us in Europe, only what can be thought or concealed has meaning."
> —Jean Baudrillard (1988a, 84)

To be involved in grassroots political work in Central America during the 1980s was to be swept up in the power of ideas. Our activities were fueled by the revolutionary hope that the organization of the masses would lead to the overthrow of oppressive economic and political structures. To watch those hopes crushed a decade later was a harsh lesson that political and economic systems do not rise and fall with ideas, however enthusiastic belief in them may be.

The fate of the popular movement in El Salvador is in many ways emblematic of the failure of revolutionary movements during the twentieth century. Perhaps nowhere else in modern history had a population of poor people been so effectively organized for their own political solutions. But after ten years of civil war, the revolutionary party was soundly trounced in national elections by leaders of the business-military elite, the very group whose death squads had carried out nearly 75,000 civilian assassinations. In the sardonic words of one Salvadoran guerrilla leader, "We fought ten years for 25 percent [of the vote]" (Batstone 1995, 18).

In the mid-1990s I held a series of discussions with members of religious and political organizations from El Salvador, Guatemala, and Nicaragua. Many of those present had worked for over three decades to change the social conditions in Central America. They spoke of the ambiguities of their struggle, the forces of resistance they encountered, and the terrible toll of human lives. Perhaps most painful was an admission that few of their expectations for social reform had been met. What they gained was their own political voice and a realization of the power of marginal communities, united. Such achievements are not to be lightly regarded.

There was little doubt in their minds where the struggle now was headed. "We lift up our heads and see a fast-moving train coming toward us from the North," lamented one activist. "The name of that train is the new world economic order, and there is nothing we can do to get off the tracks and out of its way."

The language of open markets is the *lingua franca* of cultural life in the Americas at the gateway of the twenty-first century. The centers of political power preach the gospel of the market. It is a religion of choice. The market gives citizen-consumers the rights and rituals to adopt or to reject commodities, whether products or politicians.

There is much to lament about these material conditions, but it is essential to know how we got here. Systems of political economy do not drop like manna from heaven nor do they emerge from ideological convictions, even from those of a dominant social group. They happen *in* history because they came *out of* a history. Freud's appreciation for culture was particularly attuned to this inheritance of material relations:

> [Culture] includes, on the one hand all the knowledge and capacity that men have acquired in order to control the forces of nature and its wealth for the satisfaction of human needs, and, on the other hand, all the regulations necessary in order to adjust the relations of men to one another and especially the distribution of the available wealth. (1961, 6)

We are stuck on this present course because it came out of a past and it is taking us to a future. Survival requires learning how to decipher the log book that charts the course of this fast-moving train. At least then those who are lying on the tracks have a fighting chance to adjust to its cargo.

The market economy arose out of a world of oppression with a promise to more efficiently allocate resources and distribute goods. We now know how coldly efficient the market can be. But as enormous as its costs are, the market did not introduce dislocation into history. Contrary to many leftist political theologies, capitalism is not the original sin.

Economic forces have dislocated human communities through-out history. We are still learning more about the impressive achieve-ments of the "classic period" of the Maya empire that gathered near Tikal and other urban centers around the third century, C.E. A dis-turbing truth erodes away the majesty of their social organization, however. Brutal repression surely was required to amass such a large concentration of capital in an urban center. Who built those enormous temples and royal burial tombs? It is not likely that an agrarian people would voluntarily uproot themselves so that they could drain their life blood lifting heavy stones out of reverence for royalty and priesthood.

Jumping eras on this continent, the Mayan people in the fifteenth century were not exactly grateful to the Aztec empire for exacting massacres and forcing them into slavery. Nor do we have a record of field workers singing the praises of the U.S. plantation economy; we do have a blues tradition in this country that tells the story. The qualifier golden does not come to mind when referring to the age of industrialization either, except for those few industrialists who really did get the gold. The only reward most workers received was long hours in a mine or in a factory.

These sweeping historical judgments might be taken as a precur-sor for arguing that social conditions are better today than they were in the past, or that history is progressively moving toward more humane and just conditions. I think not, but it makes little difference whether one argues that the conditions of human life have advanced or deteriorated, for it does not change today's mate-rial conditions. Perhaps that appears glib, if not cynical, but the rel-ativity of such historical judgments became quite clear to me when I was working in Central America.

In the late 1980s I paid a visit to a village in rural Nicaragua with a member of the National Assembly for the Sandinista party. I was there to represent CAMP in the donation of building supplies that would be used to add a classroom onto the community school. Nearly everyone from the village came out to mark the event. The Sandinista official was seizing on the opportunity to hold a general town meeting and to create some good will for the party. Once the meeting started, he probably wished he had not come.

The local residents were quite vocal about their dissatisfaction with the dismal economic conditions. The women in particular were upset about the scarcity of food in the market and the high prices for what was there, a situation they had endured for many years. The Sandinista official reminded them that sacrifices were necessary to keep the revolution alive. That was the only cue an elderly woman needed. She immediately stood up and announced, "I don't care about your revolution if I can't get rice and beans. Life was better in this village during the time of Somoza." A sea of heads bobbed up and down in agreement.

I witnessed enough of these encounters in Nicaragua not to be surprised when the Sandinista party lost the ensuing elections. Revolutionary ideology was no match for rice and beans. It matters little that it is possible to demonstrate that this crisis was the very intention of U.S. military-political operation to destabilize support for the Sandinista government. Ideas do not make the political and economic interests of the empire disappear, either. *Campesina* women know that all too well; they are not foolish to worry where their rice and beans are going to come from next.

The empire has not disappeared for the last seventeen centuries in the Americas, and it will not any time soon. When in the mid-1990s Mayan Indians organized a rebellion in Chiapas, Mexico, New York's Chase Manhattan Bank secretly called on the Mexican government to crush the Zapatista insurgency. "While Chiapas, in our opinion, does not pose a fundamental threat to Mexican political stability, it is perceived so by many in the investment community," warned an internal bank memo (Silverstein and Cockburn 1995, 28). The threat was not about territory this time, since international financiers are not at the moment so interested in fixed sites for investment as they are in the free movement of capital. (Virtual reality is not just a computer game!) It was to the Zapatistas' credit that they foresaw the reach of empire and built alliances that effectively could counterbalance the pressures on their government to destroy them militarily.

Resistance will rise up to meet each and every attempt to change lived relations. Claiming that does not imply that all forms of repression equal. The tools of repression available to military and economic centers of power in a global economy may quite likely pass well beyond anything yet seen in human history. One could also argue that new stages of capital advancement require a "dislocation" of workers that exceeds any other movement of resources in history. Like it or not, that is what history has brought us.

Culture is not a creation of something out of nothing; that only happens in the Garden. "I did not create this Here . . . but this Here is what I've got to respond to," are the blues laid down by Bill Smith:

No longer do the false hopes of democracy/revolution/ develop-
ment/consumption let me off the hook. I am really Here and it
doesn't go away. I cannot dream it away/ sleep it away/cry it
away/smoke it away/drink it away/ eat it away/buy it away/love it
away . . . I do not know why Here was made this way but as long as
I live Here, to be truly alive, I have to accept and acknowledge all of
this pain and despair that makes Here Here. This is the 'awe-full-
ness' of my freedom. Here is where I must confront the reality of my
being and all that which would deny me the awareness of the task or
the means to accomplish it. (1993, 160–1)

Whatever you may doubt in this age of uncertainty, trust in the
capacity of capital to reproduce itself. To acknowledge this reality is
to merely recognize what it takes to be awake at this moment in
history.

Awareness means making decisions that are conscious of the
options that are set before us and where they are most likely to lead.
It means charting how knowledge is distributed and how to access
it. It means learning the ideas, skills, and strategies that permit success in a given location. It means learning how to use the resources
of local communities to establish leverage against more dominant
forces. It means intentionally creating the kinds of community that
will allow us to live with dignity. It means learning how to take care
of people, not just people learning to take care of themselves.

No revolutionary ideology can rival the value of an evolving intelligence that is fueled by critical reason, wisdom, and imagination.

Works Cited

Althusser, Louis (1969). *For Marx*. New York: Pantheon Books.

Argueta, Manlio (1983). *One Day of Life*. New York: Vintage Books.

Aristotle (1958). *Topica et Sophistici Elenchi*. W. D. Ross, ed. Oxford: Oxford
University Press.

Batstone, David (1996). "Transcendence and Material Culture," in Dwight
Hopkins and Sheila Davaney, eds., *Changing Conversations: Religious
Reflection and Cultural Analysis*. New York: Routledge.

Batstone, David (1995). "What's Left of the Left in Latin America." *San Francisco Bay Guardian* 29/19.

Batstone, David (1991). *From Conquest to Struggle: Jesus of Nazareth in Latin
America*. Albany: SUNY Press.

Baudrillard, Jean (1983). *Simulations*. New York: Semiotext(e).

Baudrillard, Jean (1988a). *America*. New York: Verso.

Baudrillard, Jean (1988b). *The Evil Demon of Images*. Sydney: Power Institute Publications, No. 3.

Baudrillard, Jean (1990). *Fatal Strategies*. London: Semiotext(e).

Berryman, Philip (1984). *The Religious Roots of Rebellion: Christians in Central American Revolutions*. Maryknoll: Orbis Press.

de Certeau, Michel (1994). *The Practice of Everyday Life*. Berkeley: University of California Press.

Freud, Sigmund (1961). *The Future of an Illusion*. James Strachey, trans. and ed. New York: W.W. Norton & Co.

Foucault, Michel (1986). "Of Other Spaces," *Diacritics* 16/1.

Gilkey, Langdon (1985). "Events, Meanings, and the Current Tasks of Theology." *Journal of the American Academy of Religion* 53/3.

Gutiérrez, Gustavo (1983). *The Power of the Poor in History*. Maryknoll: Orbis Press.

Habermas, Jürgen (1975). *Legitimation Crisis*. Boston: Beacon.

Habermas, Jürgen (1981). *Zur Rekonstruktion des Historischen Materialismus*. Frankfurt: Suhrkamp Verlag.

Harvey, David (1975). "The Geography of Capitalist Accumulation: A Reconstruction of Marxian Theory." *Antipode*, Vol. 7.

Jung, Carl (1967). *Works: Alchemical Studies*, Vol. 13, Princeton: Princeton University Press.

Kant, Immanuel (1970). *Kant: Political Writings*. Hans Reiss, eds., Cambridge: Cambridge University Press.

Keeler-Milne, Jennifer (1994). *Art and Everyday Life*, unpublished manuscript.

Lyotard, Jean-François (1984). *The Postmodern Condition: A Report on Knowledge*. Minneapolis: University of Minneapolis Press.

Pearce, Jenny (1986). *Promised Land: Peasant Rebellion in Chalatenango, El Salvador*. London: Latin American Bureau.

Rorty, Richard (1979). *Philosophy and the Mirror of Nature*. Princeton: Princeton University of Press.

Silverstein, Ken, and Alexander Cockburn (1995). "Major U.S. Bank Urges Zapatista Wipe-Out: A Litmus Test for Mexico's Stability," *Counterpunch* 2/3.

Smith, Bill (1993). "Locating My Theology in Sacred Places," in David Batstone, ed., *New Visions for the Americas*. Minneapolis: Fortress Press.

Stryker, Susan (1996). "Sex and Death among the Cyborgs," *Wired* 4/5.

Taylor, Mark C. (1994). "Discrediting God," *Journal of the American Academy of Religion* 62/2.

Weber, Max (1958). *The Protestant Ethic and the Spirit of Capitalism*. New York: Chs. Scribners.

Webster's Third New International Dictionary (1993). Springfield, MA: Merriam-Webster, Inc.

9

Vodou Resistance/Vodou Hope
Forging a Postmodernism That Liberates

Mark McClain Taylor

It must come from the poor—a rebellion of the spirit that reaffirms their intrinsic human worth based upon who they are rather than what they possess.

—Mumia Abu-Jamal (1994)

The crisis of the American poor, and of the world's disinherited generally, poses severe tests to all discourse, not least to the "postmodern" discourses now playing in many North American settings. I argue here that if users of postmodern discourses wish to contribute to the liberation of the poor, they must position their language of carnival, difference, and otherness in relation to an ethos of the poor's own resistance.

The pillaging of the American poor is the context for my reflections on postmodernism, since I believe postmodernism often serves as a smokescreen for exploitative initiatives within the global market. Its discourse is in many respects a co-optation of the arts of struggle, exemplified by its absorption of a vodou-inspired slave resistance. This essay is an effort to re-position postmodern discourse through an engagement with vodou resistance and vodou hope.

Economic Apartheid and Its Challenge to Postmodernism

I see New York as a symbolic city. These buildings are our concrete
prisons piled up like Babel. A satanic technology surrounds us. What
we see is apparatus, not humanity.
                              —Neighborhood poet to Kozol (1995)

While it is true that more of the world's regions have entered the
global market, and developing nations report "growth" in their
economies, the ranks of the poor are burgeoning, consigned to a
sprawling, global slum.

World income distribution is one of the most obvious indicators
of this trend. The contrast of the "trilateral North" (Europe, United
States, Japan) to the rest of the world is startling. Only 17% of the
world's population resides in the trilateral north, yet it pulls in a
hefty 82% of the world's income. By 1988, the per capita income
for the rich countries of Europe, the United States, and Japan was
23.4 times greater than that for all the rest of the world (Brouwer
1993a, 84).

Wealth also tends to flow *from* the South *to* the North, at the expense of the South (Dunkerly 1988, 203-4). As Eduardo Galeano
noted long ago, Latin America has open veins, through which its
energy ebbs out and to the North (Galeano 1973). Contrary to advocates of the global market, who still claim that the gap between rich
and poor is shrinking (Fukuyama 1995: 353), a broad array of ana-
lysts use the language of "global apartheid" (Kohler 1982; Makhijani 1991, 1992; George 1991; Schelling 1992; and Falk, Kim, and
Mendlovitz 1982). Arjun Makhijani eloquently states the conclusion
reached by many:

> The structure of the world economy is in its most essential ways like
> that of apartheid in South Africa. . . . In global apartheid, the hunger,
> the desires, the tears and the joys of those who are dispossessed do
> not register as parts of the economic system. (Makhijani 1992, x)

Apartheid is increasingly replicated within the borders of the
United States as well. The democratization of wealth was never
intended by the framers of U.S. government, of course. (Tushnet
1982, 219–36). Moreover, the country's ongoing inability to resolve
economic inequalities threatens its democratic project.

A tiny one-half of one percent of the U.S. population owns 33% of its total net wealth (Brouwer 1993b, 2–4). In terms of the most powerful kinds of assets to control, "economic assets" (corporate bonds and stocks, privately owned business assets, large trust funds and investment portfolios), that same tiny elite owns 56% of the wealth (4–5).

The largest owners of capital have long been able to maintain their control of that wealth through networks of cross-generational inheritance and cronyism. Other forces have been unleashed since the waning days of the Carter presidency, and subsequently fueled by the economic policies of the Reagan and Bush tenures, that accelerated the growth of this elite. Taxation, for instance, has become increasingly regressive. The wealthy pay increasingly fewer taxes on their disparately large holdings (Peschman 1986). Deregulation of commerce, banking, and industry has greased the tracks for corporate mergers and makes corrupt practices like the Savings & Loan debacle inevitable.

Military spending is another key dynamic powering the creation of economic apartheid. Between 1979 and 1991, spending on education plummeted by 18%, while military spending skyrocketed by 154% (Brouwer 1993b, 20–22; De Grasse 1983). Military spending in that period was the single greatest contributor to the double-deficit (trade deficit and budget debt) that continues to burden the U.S. populace.

With these kinds of dynamics at work, it is little wonder that U.S. culture approximates its own apartheid structure. *The New York Times* recently reported on a two-year international study, which found the United States displaying the largest gap between the rich and the poor among all industrialized nations. Its rich make more than double the median income; its poor receive only thirty-five percent of the median (Bradisher 1995, D-2).

An imperial corporate culture in the United States has attained an almost unrivaled capacity to accumulate, to concentrate, and to manipulate wealth. By the mid-1980s the large corporations checked in with a remarkable increase in economic power. The top 100 corporations in the United States controlled in 1966 approximately 44% of total U.S. assets. By 1984, that figure had grown to 61.2% of total assets (Brouwer 1993b, 15–16). With this kind of power, corporations can command the use of computer and transportation technology, making possible an extraordinary global flexibility, especially evident in their ability to race to a Haiti, a Guatemala, or an Indonesia to find the lowest paid workers.

The power and interests of the corporate elite even extends to the shaping of peoples' diverse cultural lives. Perhaps the most striking example of this is corporate investment in prisons and prison labor. Prisons are currently one of the largest growth industries in the United States. We now have an extensive prison archipelago in this country, increasingly and disproportionally filled with the poor and peoples of color. A million and a half people are behind bars and, when those on parole and probation are counted, a total of 3.5 million or more are involved in the prison system (Stratton 1995, 8).

Corporations not only make money from prison-building transactions, and ever-refined equipment production, but also from a larger pool of cheap labor in the prisons. Flexible and powerful corporations, racing south of the U.S. border for Haitian or Guatemalan women's cheap labor ($.30/hour or lower), can race back into the U.S. and get the work for the same or lower wage costs (Parenti 1996, 12). In fact, since 1990, thirty states have legalized the contracting out of prison labor to private companies, such as Dell, I.B.M., Honda, John's Meats, Texas Instruments, Toys R Us (Parenti 1996, 11).

As the U.S. organizes itself to maintain these rituals of confinement, the entire society becomes, as Foucault noted long ago, a "carceral" one (1979, 295–97). Security consciousness becomes everyone's concern, not only in and around prisons, but on the streets, in the homes, at the shopping mall, in the municipal building (Davis 1992, 221–57).

Neoliberalism's Postmodern Face

The economic crisis—the worst we have experienced in this century—is hidden under the euphemism of a beautiful anarchy. . . .
—Martin Hopenhayn (1995)

To understand postmodernism's relation to the crisis of the American poor, it is important to identify "neoliberalism," a vision and practice that animates the crisis (Sherman 1992, 6–8; Hopenhayn 1995, 98).

Neoliberalism is a late development of capitalism that deploys "flexible modes of accumulation" (Harvey 1989, 189–97). In a global space marked by enormous flexibility, centers of capital accumulation are able to move toward locations where wage labor is cheapest, and also make profits by mere changes in the currencies in which they hold their wealth. Neoliberalism therefore grafts belief in human development and progress onto intense market initiatives and capitalist offensives.

Postmodernism often functions to provide an enchanting human face to this complex process of capital extraction. Martin Hopenhayn's essay, "Postmodernism and Neoliberalism," summarizes the ways in which postmodern cultural traits are "cofunctional" with market offensives. I highlight three of these modes of cofunction.

First, postmodernism's exaltation of diversity inspires a kind of "ludic individualism" that is crucial for the deregulated environment that capital needs in order to move in and out of, and across, borders. When diversity is continually celebrated, analyses of structural dynamics of disparity, of routine exploitation and suffering tend to fall out of a people's roster of concerns (Hopenhayn 1995, 98–99).

Second, postmodernism has frequently championed a critique of "vanguard" movements of liberation and their discourse as naive, "totalizing" modernisms. "Critique of the vanguard" typically supports a postmodern neoliberalism that resists a focused transformational function in the political realm, and serves elite owners of capital who often resist being identified and named as such. Even modest state planning and intervention, which would limit the free reign of capital accumulation on behalf of local communities of the poor, are rendered suspect (99, 100).

Third, and closely related to the above two tendencies, is the propensity for postmodern image-making, with its supporting technologies, to portray structural heterogeneity (which often may be a case of oppression) as healthy diversity. In doing so, not only can cases of structural violation be hidden, they can be seen as a simple difference to be observed (100).

In these and other ways, postmodern discourses serve as a smokescreen to mask the continually flexible mode of exploitative patterns of accumulation. Hopenhayn eloquently sums up the ways in which postmodernism's language employs euphemisms that prevent grappling with the exploitations against which the poor struggle today.

It is more attractive to talk about diversity than the market, about desire than the maximization of profits, about play than conflict, about personal creativity than the private appropriation of the economic surplus, about global communication and interaction than the strategies of transnational companies to promote their goods and services. (100)

Perhaps there is no better example of the way postmodern discourse generates euphemisms to conceal neoliberalism's exploiting ways than the functioning of the Benetton corporation. The Benetton Group SPA is an Italian textile company named after its founder and managing director, Luciano Benetton. The company is a franchise of clothing manufacturing and marketing. It offers products that are contemporary in style, and aimed at the up-market, affluent wearers of informal clothing. Its stores are global, located throughout Asia, Europe, and the United States. The company is heralded in business schools as what professors and financial reporters call "a model way to do business in the era of global competition," and a "quintessential model of postmodern managerial flexibility" (Belussi 1987: 10–11).

Benetton's explicit advertising ideology displays many of the postmodern virtues. It is ludic, playful, striking. It dares new images, continually juxtaposing unexpected visions (such as high-fashion boys and girls, death-bed scenes, black and white babies kissing, and colored condoms). It invites a diverse feasting of the eyes on a globe of multicultural people and experiences. The message circulates: "Diversity is being celebrated and is a positive way to create wealth and bring the world together."

But two crucial factors are hidden. First, Benetton's ability to create wealth is not based simply on a flexible and innovative marketing strategy and a corresponding embrace of diversity. It is based rather in large part upon the Benetton family's roots in a tradition of entrepreneurship in Italy. From that tradition came the funding necessary to establish the "propulsive core" of the company, i.e., its sophisticated computer technology that was necessary for continual adaptation to world fashion trends. Benetton, at least in its early days, also had its first investments enhanced by protectionist policies implemented in wealthy countries (Belussi 1987, 10–11).

The second hidden factor is that the great "flexibility" of Benetton is also strikingly dependent upon piece-work labor, using family-based, sub-contractors that hire women to work in their homes or in small shops that lack union organization. These sub-contractors do 40% of Benetton's knitting and perform 60% of its garment assembly (Enloe 1989, 156).

Neoliberalism's flexible mode of accumulation, at least in the case of Benetton, entails using women workers, many of whom are often already performing uncompensated labor in their homes as they care for other workers, for children, and for the aged. In addition, they do not receive the employee benefits and rights that typically attend union organization. Furthermore, labor practices undercut the work opportunities of unionized labor in other sectors. Behind the facade of "postmodern managerial flexibility," then, dwells the exploitative ways that nurture the global slum.

Cynthia Enloe describes well the world often hidden behind the neoliberal advertisers who exploit the postmodern euphemisms:

> The eighteen year-old woman has become the essential though unequal partner of the banker in his glass and chrome office in London and Chicago. The risk-taking banker needs the conscientious seamstress to hold his world together. The politicians and his technocratic advisor need the seamstress to keep the banker and his home government pacified. (Enloe, 1989, 160–61)

Postmodernism as Co-opted Slave Resistance

> The slaves kept their mysteries, their *vodun*, and their mysteries kept them.
>
> —Michael Ventura (1985)

Postmodernism compounds its tendency to obscure exploitation with a penchant for co-opting the strategies of those who drastically need to resist such exploitation. More particularly, postmodern play, and its ludic and moving critical poses, drink from spaces marked by vodou music and culture that once were forged by slave communities in the Americas. Awareness of this oft-obscured historical connection prepares the way for the re-connection of ludic postmodernism to vodou struggles for cultural liberation.

The historical connections are brought to light by making three key moves that explore different aspects of the matrix from which postmodernism has grown to its present forms.

The first move is suggested by Andreas Huyssen's research that what is called postmodernism today is rooted in a U.S. avant-garde movement that positioned itself critically against domesticated forms of high modernity (Huyssen 1990). This avant-garde movement challenged not all forms of modernism, but that kind which in the late fifties resulted in a liberal-conservative consensus that was ". . . turned into a propaganda weapon in the cultural-political arsenal of Cold War anti-communism" (243).

Cornel West has embellished Huyssen's point, noting that U.S. culture in this period failed to exploit the full subversive potential of modernist giants in literature and architecture: "Only in America was modernism diluted and domesticated into an artistic armpiece of the 'vital center' . . . "(West 1988: 168). Postmodernism, then, is traced to a critical movement against this diluted modernism.

Neither Huyssen nor West mention the connections of Latin American literary developments to what Huyssen calls a "prehistory" of the postmodern. Latin American poets and novelists at the turn of the twentieth century had occasionally used the term, *postmodernismo*, while Latin American novels (such as those of Borges, Garcia Márquez, Cortázar, and Fuentes, among others) contested the hierarchies of Euroamerican modernism (Hassan 1987, 85–86; Beverly 1995, 223–24). This heritage signals the need to examine also, as some Latin American postmodernists now do, the Amerindian contributions to postmodernist sensibilities, since Amerindians especially had a stake in contesting compromises with modernist structures (Beverly 1995, 55–64).

The second move is to note another point where Cornel West has developed Huyssen's mapping of postmodernism. West claims that the context within which the avant-gardist critiques of modernity developed were notably marked by African-American artistic traditions, notably jazz, blues, and rhythm-and-blues. In a mass consumer society African-Americans became "exemplary embodiments of otherness, difference, and transgression" (West 1988, 169).

This phenomenon surely has a relation to the distorted collective psyche of racist white cultures. But it is also true that black musicians provided a crucial, positive stimulus for developing critiques of high culture by using artistic eclecticism, play, mocking, posing, and performance—all traits dear to the postmodern sensibility today. West rightly interprets such black artistic production, especially in music, as reinforcing the black freedom movement which in the fifties inaugurated new spurts of anti-Establishment activity.

Jazz historian John Lincoln Collier writes that Gillespie, Parker, Coltrane, and other black artists could dress "like Westchester County stock-brokers," or could wear the horned-rimmed glasses and berets standard with the Bohemian artists and intellectuals, or, as Gillespie and Parker did, could affect a British accent—all this, in order to play with and transgress boundaries of Europeanized traditions (Collier 1993, 213). West rightly cautions that this does not make such black artists the first postmodernists or *the* source of American postmodernism. It does remedy silences, however, that have blocked full understanding of postmodernism.

A mapping of the postmodern that perpetuates silence about African-American resistance, while at the same time appropriating many of the strategies of their resistance, is lamentable on two counts. First, it strengthens that kind of postmodernism, which, in its current neoliberalist versions, renders invisible those who suffer from structural, social disparity. Second, it denies to postmodern agents and movements themselves a real power of resistance that is best found at the heart of an ethos of struggle. When play, performance, and transgressing boundaries are embraced only to strike a pose of "postmodern cool," they are usually bereft of effective powers of resistance.

The "play" in black artists' work was often a result of critical elements in their music which, as in Parker's "Now's the Time," were deeply rooted in black slave culture (Collier 1993, 217). To be silent about those roots is to place them in another cultural space where they function against the very people who forged them. Such co-optation is a theft; although, perhaps it is more in the category of *attempted* robbery since hegemonic cultures have *not* been completely successful in depriving struggling peoples of these strategic resources.

The third move evokes some of the most creative African slave traditions in the Americas, driving home postmodernism's co-optive connection to slave resistance.

The powerful work of Black musicians that fed the matrix of postmodernism's American "prehistory" is rooted in West African culture, as it flourished especially in New Orleans. Its vodou musical culture bears analogies to many of the so-called "postmodern traits," but in the form of a celebrative resistance to the disenfranchisement of African peoples in America.

Vodou comes from the word *vodun*, meaning "mysteries" and refers to speaking by African deities, particularly in Abomey, Africa (Ventura 1985, 111). It involves a music and a dance in which body and spirit inseparably commingle to nurture endurance and struggle throughout the slaves' centuries-long ordeal.

The number of Africans imported to Haiti and the Dominican Republic were enormous—864,000 in the eighteenth century alone

—and their mortality rate was high (Hunt 1988, 9,15). New Orleans, along with areas throughout the Mississippi River valley, was the place to which many slaves from Saint Domingue, "Haiti," fled and migrated (Hunt 44). Vodou thrived in these slave conditions, sustaining communities once they were transported to the mainland. It especially thrived in "Black creole" culture that had such a remarkable influence on American music (Collier 1993, 193–95).

In terms of music and spiritually, New Orleans was the mainline to Africa, and Haitians in particular embodied this connection. Ethnomusicologist Richard A. Waterman stresses that Haiti was one of the places in the Americas where "African religious music has persisted almost unchanged and African influence upon secular music has been strong" (Collier, 194–95).

While much that was original from West Africa was preserved, in the context of American slavery the music and spirituality of vodou was distilled and re-distilled in ways that released its power anew. Ventura ably characterizes this power:

> Vodou is the African aesthetic shattered and then desperately put back together. More than simply "put back together," it has been recreated to serve its people under the shattering impact of slavery and poverty. Vodou is not so much Africa *in* the New World as it is Africa meeting the New World, absorbing it and being absorbed by it, and *re-forming* the ancient metaphysics according to what it now had to face (1985, 113).

The impact of music and spirituality shattered and, even today, continues shattering the racism that disinherits people in the Americas, recreating a people's life, reforming it, absorbing the New World and being absorbed by it.

This complex mode of resistance is one to which a postmodern critic today might resonate. It contains motion, play, and shifting, while avoiding simple oppositional postures. It makes all the difference in the world, however, that these motions and postures occur amid a shattered world and within an ethos of struggle. Disconnecting the ludic motions and postures from the context of struggle is both to gloss the struggle and to defang the resistance. Silencing black music's contribution to postmodernism's "prehistory" in 1960s America further neglects vodou's powerful resistance to slavery and to disenfranchisement.

Postmodernism for Liberation

Postmodern culture with its decentered subject can be the space
where ties are severed or it can provide the occasion for new and
varied forms of bonding.

—bell hooks (1992)

Identifying the co-optive feature of postmodern discourse is not a
precursor to rejecting the discourse. On the contrary, the identification helps to clarify the primary condition under which postmodernists' ludic play might actually serve liberating struggle. Being
positioned in such an ethos requires of postmodern thinkers more
than simply assuming that their avant-gardism is liberating for the
poor. It also requires more than the ad hoc or occasional advocacy
of oppressed peoples. To enter an *ethos* of struggle is to enter into a
communal ethos with a vodou aesthetic.

The deconstructionist writings of Jacques Derrida are a prominent example of the way postmodern thinkers implicitly acknowledge the need to struggle for liberation of oppressed peoples.
Especially in his article, "Force of Law: The 'Mystical Foundation of
Authority'," Derrida makes a fascinating shift in political orientation
(Derrida 1992). The bulk of the essay, which interrogates an essay by
Walter Benjamin, links a notion of justice with deconstruction itself,
its oscillation, its movement, its playing amid difference. Derrida
also makes many postmodern moves, nodding approvingly in the
direction of "ghost," "ruin," and even "sovereign violence."

In the postscriptum, however, Derrida finds "intolerable" a possible interpretation that would make violence, especially acts like the
Holocaust (the "Final Solution"), somehow necessary or expiatory,
as an "indecipherable signature of the just and violent anger of
God." Derrida, pulled toward struggle, writes:

> . . . This text [Benjamin's], despite all its polysemic mobility and all
> its resources for reversal, seems to me finally to resemble too closely,
> to the point of specular fascination and vertigo, the very thing
> against which one *must* act and think, do and speak, that with which
> one *must* break (perhaps, perhaps). (1992, 62)

Not only the Holocaust, but other oppressions also haunt Derrida's postmodern project.

> No justice . . . seems possible or thinkable without the principle of
> some *responsibility* . . . before the ghosts of those who are not yet
> born or who are already dead, be they victims of wars, political or
> other kinds of violence, nationalist, racist, colonialist, sexist, or
> other kinds of exterminations, victims of the oppressions of capital-
> ist imperialism or any of the forms of totalitarianism. (1994, xix)

Derrida's texts implicitly acknowledge the importance of entering
into an ethos of liberating struggle for oppressed peoples, without
which the deconstructive sensibility becomes complicit in horror.

But such acknowledgments function only as ineffective lament
unless one takes steps toward an ethos of struggle. At least three
very important challenges are implicit in commitment to such a
struggle.

1. *Entering this ethos will mean, first of all, that postmoderns
accommodate themselves to more informal communication networks
than postmodern thinkers, especially academics, have usually employed.* The book, the professional essay, even the Internet and computer lists are conduits of postmodern discourse, but more is
required for liberating struggle.

Postmodernism demands more respect and participation in the
"informal media." Leaflet distribution, newsletter dissemination,
neighborhood visitation, group networking in disenfranchised communities, rally and union-hall speech-making, banner displaying
and carrying, and radio journalism—these practices have been the
staple of working peoples and grassroots movements for some time.
Participating in this informal media does *not* entail a rejectionist
posture regarding books, journals, and computers. But the latter
are insufficient forms of communication given transnational capital's domination of the infrastructure of those media and the role of
privilege in gaining access to them.

Postmodernists need not create something out of nothing. The
resourcefulness of grassroots communities of struggle is already in
motion. To enter an ethos of liberating struggle, then, will mean
entering the worlds where the poor are already in struggle using
such modes of communication.

Alternative newspapers and radio outlets are also vital channels.
Radio has always played a crucial role in uniting and keeping peoples of struggle together, and is an essential form of resistance communication in the United States. Outlets like Pacifica Radio[1], which

is almost completely free of corporate sponsorship and impact, can generate whole new sensibilities on crucial issues. Pacifica Radio played a key role, for example, in mobilizing public opinion against the GAP textile corporation when it publicized the North American tour of two El Salvadoran women from a GAP factory in their country where human rights abuse and wage exploitation were daily realities. GAP felt enormous pressure from people and finally consented to the installation of independent human rights monitors in their plants.[2]

2. *Positioning postmodernism in an ethos of struggle will require a deliberate cultivation of a "sense of place" and its implications for the production of discourse.* Most postmodern discourse in North America (unless one is speaking of popular culture media as discourse) flourishes in the halls of academe, especially at the conferences held in hotel convention centers.

Whatever subversive potential there may be in the "left postmodernism" of these settings, the dominant system is able to contain and to neutralize subversive critique when it only "plays" in those settings. Even if it launches some "deviant" critique of "the system," those critiques rarely connect with the movements necessary to challenge that system. Moreover, the hotel, the convention center, the academic hall, are all places that are increasingly difficult for people of struggle to enter. They are physically "carceral," walling out the poor and walling in the privileged and powerful.

The particular spaces that need inhabiting today are the streets; not the streets in general, but those streets that seriously contest tendencies of the powerful. In 1995, for example, scholars of the American Academy of Religion moved out onto the sidewalks and streets outside their host convention center in Philadelphia to register their opposition to the death penalty, and particularly to the execution of the award-winning journalist on Pennsylvania's death row, Mumia Abu-Jamal. Out-of-town academics joined local organizers and professionals on the sidewalks, held a press conference, and marched in protest to the Philadelphia office of the District Attorney—one notorious for pursuing the death penalty. Many of those participating work in liberation philosophy and theology, as well as in postmodern discourse and theory. Many also presented papers within the walls of the convention center.

Such actions transgress boundaries and play in a way that is much more transformative than the postmodern-speak of the convention papers that pun and pose verbally for forty-five minutes in a hotel conference room. State executions will not be prevented by rhetoric that does not venture to speak and to act in new spaces, beyond those which the system routinely allows.

3. *A postmodernism that enters an ethos of liberating struggle will need to embrace genres consonant with that struggle.* Postmodern discourse has blurred boundaries between high and low art-forms and discourses, pioneered studies in pop culture, and embraced the televised image and the computer screen. Though these ventures already experiment with varying genres, they do not in themselves constitute an entry into an ethos of liberating struggle.

Postmodern theorists need to embrace the root cultural practices of the black musical traditions that helped created 1960s-avant-garde postmodernism. *More importantly, postmodern thinkers need to enter into, or strike solidarity with, communities in which vodou aesthetics of practice and spirit are already being deployed with liberating effect.*

Since so much of the music of the U.S. is indebted to vodou practice and spirit (jazz, blues, gospel, rhythm-and-blues, rock 'n roll, reggae, rap), close interaction with communities of struggle using any of those musical genres may be helpful. There is a special gain, however, in an explicit embrace of those communities of struggle linked to and employing the music and dance of vodou. Postmoderns committed to play and to the deviant should be delighted to do so, if for no other reason than that U.S. culture, from Hollywood to street talk, has so routinely maligned and marginalized vodou as "spooky, black magic, sorcery" (Brown 1991, ix).

Hardly another culture on U.S. soil offers such complexity, such play amid difference and juxtaposition, such vitality and such indefatigable resistance, as does vodou. Robert Farris Thompson, in his splendid book *Flash of the Spirit*, finds a "spiritualized militancy" dwelling in vodou (Thompson 1983, 180). Along with other scholars, he emphasizes that though vodou practices are spiritualized, they are inextricably bound to the bodily and the practical, and as such foment cultures of resistance (Murphy 1994, 11–14; Deren 1953, 62).

French colonizers feared vodou as a danger to their power. The 1791 Haitian revolution, when slaves rose up to drive the powerful French armies of Napoleon off their Island, reportedly started in a vodou ceremony. Mederic Louis Moreau de St. Mery, following a trip to the Island, warned the colonizers, "Nothing is more dangerous . . . than this cult of Vaudaux. It can be made into a terrible weapon—this extravagant idea that the ministers of this alleged god know all and can do anything" (Murphy 1994, 11).

Years later, when the United States Marines were occupying Haiti from 1915 to 1934, vodou was identified again as "an alarming plot" (Murphy, 13). In a second U.S. occupation initiated in October, 1993, Haitian vodou communities were just as resistant against the presence of U.S. troops and other external powers, such as the International Monetary Fund and the World Bank.

Perhaps most exemplary of the ongoing power of Haitian vodou is the music and dance embodied by the world music group from Haiti, Boukman Eksperyans (Santoro, 1995). Lead vocalist Lolo Beaubrun and his family of musicians and dancers do performances that are at once reverent praise songs and incendiary calls to political action. The groups offers a startling plurality of religious sensibilities (including images of Jesus, Krishna, Buddha, the Taino, Mohammed, and various Haitian and African figures, like Damballah, Gran Bwa, Zili, Samba, Wangol, et al.). Their rhythms, syncopation, melodies, and dance steps are also extremely varied, fully embracing of play.

Whether through musical polyphony, rhythmic complexity, or religious plurality, however, the always announced goal of Boukman Eksperyans is revolution. Life and vitality—that which moves in the people's body and spirit—is working and being worked in the music and dance, as this selection of the group's lyrics exemplifies:

> The day has arrived for us to make a revolution,
> for us to stop copying other nations.
> For a long time they were telling us how to live.
> The day we revolt, this will all stop.
> The day has arrived for us to leave Babylon. (Beaubrun and
> Beaubrun, 1995)

Following the 1791 revolt inspired by priest Boukman and led by General Toussaint Louverture, France's confidence about controlling its lands in the Americas was so shaken that it ceded the largest land mass ever received by the United States government, the Louisiana purchase (O'Reilly 1995, 21-22). The tiny Caribbean thereafter loomed as a threat to the U.S., diplomatically shunned and isolated, the last to benefit from social or military actions, and indeed the victim of nearly every imaginable onslaught by the larger powers of its hemisphere (Farmer 1994, 55–257).

Has Haiti been driven down so low, relegated to the bottom of the American hemisphere because it is the most feared? Is it known deep in the neoliberal's consciousness that Haiti, because it holds a subversively diverse Africaness, possesses a force that could galvanize a revolutionary threat?

The ludic play of some postmoderns might find renewal in reconnecting to liberating Haitian genre of vodou. Embracing its music, dance, and spirit is not a solitary strategy for liberating struggle. It *is* a significant one, however, since it represents a return to neglected roots of avant-garde postmodernism in the United States. Vodou is also a place where stubborn and renewing hope persists among the poor, from "the basement of Babylon" (Abu-Jamal 1996). Given the forces that today create the global slum, that is no small contribution.

Notes

1. For information about Pacifica outlets throughout the nation, write Pacifica Program Service, 3729 Cahuenga Blvd., North Hollywood, CA 90068.

2. Details on this campaign and its final settlement are available from the National Labor Committee Education Fund in Support of Worker & Human Rights in Central America. 15 Union Square. New York, NY 10003.

Works Cited

Abu-Jamal, Mumia. 1994. "War Waged Against the Poor." Radio address accepted, then quashed, by National Public Radio. Printed in *Connexions* (September 1995): 6–7. AMAJ Newsletter. Princeton: Academics for Mumia Abu-Jamal.

———.1995a. *Live from Death Row*. Reading, MA: Addison-Wesley.

———.1996. "Babylon's Basement." Column #269. Internet: Mumia@aol.com.

Baptiste, Clemente. 1996. "Armegeddon Soon Come: Fugees Even the Score." *The Source: The Magazine of Hip-Hop Music, Culture & Politics* (March 1996): 62–65.

Barent, Richard J., and Cavanaugh, John. 1994. *Global Dreams: Imperial Corporations and the New World Order*. New York:Simon and Schuster.

Bartzell, E. Digby. 1958. *Philadelphia Gentleman: The Making of a National Upper Class*. New York: Free Press.

Beaubrun, Daniel, and Beaubrun, Jr., Theodore "Lolo." 1995. "The Day We Revolt"/"Jou Nou Revolte." On the Compact Disc, *Dangerous Crossroads/ Kalfou Danjere*. New York: Mango.

Belussi, Fiorenza. 1987. *Benetton: Information Technology in Productions and Distribution—A Case Study of the Innovative Potential of Traditional Sectors*. SPRU Occasional Paper Series, No. 25. Brighton: Science Policy Research Unit of the University of Sussex.

Beverly, John, Oviedo, José, and Aronna, Michael. Editors. 1995. *The Postmodernism Debate in Latin America*. London and Durham: Duke University Press.

Bradsher, Keith. 1995. "Widest Gap in Incomes? Research Points to the U.S." *The New York Times*. October 27.

Brouwer, Steve. 1993a. *Conquest and Capitalism, 1492–1992*. Carlisle, PA.: Big Picture Books.

———. 1993b. *Sharing the Pie: A Disturbing Picture of the U.S. Economy*. Carlisle, PA: Big Picture Books.

Brown, Karen McCarthy. 1991. *Mama Lola: A Vodou Priestess in Brooklyn*. Berkeley: University of California Press.

Coker, Cheo Hodari. 1996. "All for One. *Vibe* (March 1996): 71.

Collier, John Lincoln. 1993. *Jazz: The American Theme Song*. New York: Oxford University Press.

Davis, Mike. 1992. *City of Quartz: Excavating the Future in Los Angeles*. New York: Vintage.

De Grasse, Robert. 1983. *Military Expansion, Economic Decline*. New York: M. E. Sharpe.

Deren, Maya. 1953. *Divine Horsemen: The Living Gods of Haiti*. New York: Thames and Hudson.

Derrida, Jacques. 1992. "Force of Law: The 'Mystical Foundation of Authority'." In Drucilla Cornell, Michel Rosenfeld, David Gray Carlson, eds. *Deconstruction and the Possibility of Justice*. London and New York: Routledge.

———.1994. *Specters of Marx: The State of the Debt, the Work of Mourning, & the New International*. Translated by Peggy Kamuf. London and New York: Routledge.

Dunkerly, James. 1988. *Power in the Isthmus: A Political History of Modern Central America*. New York: Verso.

Dussel, Enrique. 1995. *The Invention of the Americas: Exlipse of "the Other" and the Myth of Modernity*. Translated by Michael D. Barber. New York: Continuum.

Enloe, Cynthia. 1989. *Bananas, Beaches and Bases: Making Feminist Sense of International Politics*. Berkeley: University of California Press.

Falk, Richard. 1992. "Economic Aspects of Global Civilization: The Unmet Challenges of World Poverty." *World Order Studies Program Occasional Paper*. No. 22. Princeton, NJ: Center of International Studies.

Falk, Richard, Kim, Samuuel S., and Mendlovitz, Saul H. 1982. *Toward a Just World Order*. Boulder, CO: Westview.

Farmer, Paul. 1994. *The Uses of Haiti*. Monroe, MA: Common Courage Press.

Folbre, Nancy. 1987. *A Field Guide to the U.S. Economy: 160 Graphic Keys to How the System Works*. New York: Pantheon.

Foucault, Michel. 1979. *Discipline and Punish*. Trans. Alan Sheridan. New York: Vintage Books.

Fukuyama, Francis. 1995. *Trust: The Social Virtues & the Creation of Prosperity*. New York: The Free Press.

Galeano, Eduardo. 1973. *Open Veins of Latin America: Five Centuries of the Pillage of a Continent*. New York: Monthly Review Press.

George, Susan. 1991. "Some Future Dimensions in International Relations: The Debt Question." Paper presented at 90th Anniversary Nobel Jubilee Symposium, December 8.

Harris, Leonard. 1995. "Postmodernism and Utopia: An Unholy Alliance." In Fred Lee Hord (Mzee Lasana Okpara) and Jonathan Scott Lee, eds. *I Am Because We Are: Readings in Black Philosophy*. Amherst, MA: University of Massachusetts Press, 1995.

Harvey, David. 1989. *The Condition of Postmodernity: An Enquiry into the Origins of Cultural Change*. London: Basil Blackwell.

Hassan, Ihab. 1987. *The Postmodern Turn: Essays in Postmodern Theory and Culture*. Columbus: Ohio State University Press.

hooks, bell. 1992. *Black Looks: Race and Representation*. Boston: South End Press.

Hopenhayn, Martin. 1995. "Postmodernism and Neoliberalism." In John Beverly, Jose Oviedo, and Michael Aronna, eds. *The Postmodernism Debate in Latin America*. Durham and London: Duke University Press.

Hunt, Alfred N. 1988. *Haiti's Influence on Antebellum America*. Baton Rouge: Louisiana State Press.

Huyssen, Andreas. 1990. "Mapping the Postmodern." In Linda J. Nicholson, ed. *Feminism/Postmodernism*. New York: Routledge.

Kozol, Jonathan. 1995. *Amazing Grace: The Lives of Children and the Conscience of a Nation*. New York: Crown Publishers.

Lewis, Charles. 1996. *The Buying of the President*. New York: Avon Books.

Lyotard, J. 1985. *The Postmodern Condition*. Minneapolis: University of Minnesota Press.

Makhijani, Arjun. 1992. *From Global Capitalism to Economic Justice: An Inquiry into the Elimination of Systemic Poverty, Violence and Environmental Destruction in the World Economy*. New York: Apex.

Murphy, Joseph W. 1994. *Working the Spirit: Ceremonies of the African Diaspora*. Boston: Beacon.

Nelson, Havelock. 1996. "The Rap." *Request*. (March 1996): 65.

O'Reilly, Kenneth. 1995. *Nixon's Piano: Presidents and Racial Politics from Washington to Clinton*. New York: The Free Press.

Parenti, Christian. 1996. "Making Prison Pay: Business Finds the Cheapest Labor of All." *The Nation*. Vol. 262, No. 4., January 29.

Peschman, Joseph. 1986. *Who Paid the Taxes? 1960–1985*. Washington, D.C.: Brookings Institute.

Phillips, Kevin. 1990. *The Politics of Rich and Poor: Wealth and the American Electorate in the Reagan Aftermath*. New York: Harper Perennial.

Santoro, Gene. 1995. "Boukman Eksperyans." *The Nation* (May 29, 1995): 769–772.

Schelling, T. C. 1992. "Rethinking the Dimensions of National Security: The Global Dimension." In Graham Allison and Gregory F. Treverton, eds.

Rethinking America's Security: Beyond Cold War to New World Order. New York: W.W. Norton.

Sherman, Amy L. *Preferential Option: A Christian and Neoliberal Strategy for Latin America's Poor*. Washington, D.C.: The Institute on Religion and Democracy, 1992.

Smith, Hedrik. 1988. *The Power Game: How Washington Works*. New York: Random House.

Stovall, Natasha. 1996. "Rhymers of the Gods." *The Village Voice*. Vol. xli. No. 10. March 5, 1996.

Stratton, Richard. "Prisonland America." *Prison Life* (December 1995): 8–9.

Tate, Greg. 1996. "Prodigal Dawta." *Vibe* (March 1996): 48.

Thompson, Robert Farris. 1983. *The Flash of Spirit: African and African-American Art and Philosophy*. New York: Random House.

Tushnet, Mark. 1990. "The Politics of Constitutional Law." In David Kairys, ed. *The Politics of Law: A Progressive Critique*. Revised edition. New York: Pantheon Books.

Ventura, Michael. 1985. *Shadow Dancing in the USA*. New York: St. Martin's Press.

Waldman, Michael. 1990. *Who Robbed America? A Citizen's Guide to the Savings and Loan Scandal*. New York: Random House.

West, Cornel. 1988. *Prophetic Fragments*. Grand Rapids, MI: W. B. Eerdmans.

Wilkins, Roger. 1970. "A Black Man at the Gridiron Club." *Washington Post*. March 26. Opinions and editorial page.

10

William Apess
A Pequot and a Methodist under the Sign of Modernity

Robert Allen Warrior

For better or worse, discussion that directly engages the conditionalities of modernity and postmodernity has not occupied much space in contemporary Native American criticism. Though many Native critics have deployed arguments and critical frameworks that obviously draw on the work of poststructuralist and postmodern critics, little work exists that posits Native writings and Native history as existing within the complexities of the modern and the postmodern condition (Vizenor 1989; Blaeser 1990).

In my own work on the process of recovering the work of Native intellectual writing, much of the challenge has been to establish, first, that something that can be read as a tradition exists and, second, that a constitutive element of that tradition is its historicity. This is a departure from many of the critical norms of contemporary scholarly work insofar as I have embraced rather than rejected the notion of Native writing and existence as participating in the grand cosmopolitan struggle of modernity (Warrior 1994; Cook-Lynn 1991).

I have taken the reluctance of Native critics to place the work of Native writers firmly within the boundaries of modernity as an overly cautious attempt to insure that readers of Native texts acknowledge the differences between Native worldviews and non-

Native worldviews (Sarris 1993; Blaeser 1990). In many ways, this neglect of the impact of modernity on contemporary Native existence has been a reaction against simplistic thinking and theorizing that pronounces Natives living under the sign of modernity as always already assimilated subjects. The benefits of such critical strategies are that the premodern, precolonial realities of Native peoples can be reconstructed, legitimized, and presented as alternatives to modern realities.

That is important work. Just as important, though, is criticism and history that places Native realities in the crucible of modernity, different in important ways from other realities in the same crucible, but existing side by side nonetheless. What follows is a modest attempt to demonstrate three ways in which one Native intellectual, Pequot writer and Methodist minister William Apess, did his intellectual work precisely as a modern subject.

These three categories—Pequot writer, Methodist minister, and modern subject—provide the beginning point for understanding Apess's work. First, his work clearly reflects his own past and present as a Pequot, one of the many tribes that were in the way of the Puritan conquest of New England. Second, I show how Apess's position in the Methodist movement clearly indicates his modern subjectivity. Finally, I show how the period in which Apess worked, the same period in which the United States government was force-marching American Natives from the southeast and Ohio River Valley to Indian Territory, is a definitive outgrowth of the politics of modern colonialism. In conclusion, I will offer some thoughts as to where this analysis of Apess and modernity is headed; specifically, I will suggest that a developing theoretical construct that I call the *rhetoric of ancientness and novelty* can bring fresh critical light to the struggle Native intellectuals face in representing the struggles of Native groups to retain their own visions of tribalism in the process of becoming tribal nations.

William Apess, Pequot

William Apess, a Pequot writer and Methodist minister whose writings and speeches appeared in the 1830s in the northeastern United States, is a remarkable figure in American Indian history who is only now taking his place as a major Native and American intellectual of the nineteenth century (Gustafson 1994; Ashwill 199x).

Apess is one of a number of Native Christian converts who predominate in the early periods of North American Native intellectual
written work. Like Samson Occam before him and William Copway
after him, Apess sought to use Christian rhetoric to better the lot of
Native people (O'Connell 1992; Copway. 1850).

Given that William Apess was never enough of a public figure
during his life to warrant any yet-known collection of archival
materials on his life and times, his writings provide the foundation
upon which he is considered. Between 1829 and 1836, he published
five major works. The first was *A Son of the Forest*, an autobiogra-
phy. In 1831, he published a sermon about what he believed was a
connection between North American Indians and the ten lost tribes
of Israel. In 1833, he produced *The Experiences of Five Christian
Indians of the Pequot Tribe*, a collection of pietistic accounts of conversions that are also critiques of the racism of white Christians
(O'Connell 1992).

In 1835 Apess published a part-narrative, part-anthology of press
accounts of a revolt of Mashpee Indians in Massachusetts, a revolt
he helped to organize. The Mashpee revolt of 1833 was prompted
by overseers who were systematically robbing the Mashpees of their
lands and resources. The action garnered attention in the local
press, in Boston, and even in limited ways in the national press
(O'Connell 1992).

Apess's final publication was the text of an oration he gave at the
Odeon Theater in Boston on two occasions in 1836. In the sermon,
Apess argues that the greatest American figure of all time was the
seventeenth-century Wampanoag leader Metacom, or King Philip,
who waged war with the growing settler nation. That war ended in
devastating loss for the Wampanoags and for the other Native
nations in the northeast, a devastation that Apess inherited over a
century later (O'Connell 1992).

The most complete record of the life of William Apess is his own
autobiographical writing, especially *A Son of the Forest*. In that
work, Apess offers a detailed account of his troubled life that began
in 1798 in Colrain, Massachusetts. By the time he was three years
old, his parents, both of whom he claimed were Native, split up and
young William went to live with his grandparents.

The situation with his grandparents was also troubled, and local
authorities placed Apess under indenture with local white families.
These families, although using Apess for labor, undertook his education and his religious instruction. William ran away several

times, but was caught and returned each time. Around age eleven, he began, on his own, to attend Methodist meetings rather than the services of the more mainstream denominations the families he lived with attended (O'Connell 1992).

Thus Apess became an early case of a Native young person adopted or fostered out to white parents. To some, this experience of foster care would no doubt signal the point at which Apess began to shed his Native skin and began the process of assimilating the values of New England culture. Such an interpretation ignores the fact that the experience of being adopted or fostered out remains an all too common experience of tens of thousands of Indians in the years since Apess and is therefore a constituent element of an American Indian history that seeks to include the widest range of experiences of Native people.

Any assumption that Apess began to lose a sense of his tribal identity would also be wrong, though, because of what it meant to be a Pequot person in the late eighteenth and early nineteenth centuries. The fact is, no matter how long Apess would have spent among other Pequots while growing up, he would have had access only to a social, religious, and political culture in chronic crisis.

The process of peopling New England with settlers of European origin was a brutal one for the Pequots (Jennings 1975; Tinker 1993). The Pequots were introduced to modernity over the course of the process. Even though the Puritans retained much of a medieval mindset, their actions are evidence of how the transition to modernity in North America.

The Puritans were among the first to wage genocidal war against the indigenous people of what would become the United States. In 1637, less than twenty years after arriving in what would become Massachusetts and accepting the hand of friendship offered by the Indian people of the northeast, settlers launched a surprise attack upon an unsuspecting village of Pequots at the site of what is now Mystic, Connecticut (Jennings 1975; Noley 1991; O'Connell 1992; Tinker 1993).

The village was not the stronghold of the Pequots. Rather, it was mainly comprised of women, children, and elderly people. Various versions exist as to the reason for the massacre, but undoubtedly much of the motivation lay in the desire for people in the trading companies for more land and for a stable political landscape. John Mason, a Puritan leader of the attack, had purely tactical reasons for leading the attack on the minor village. By massacring those in

the village, he hoped to demoralize the main force of Pequot soldiers downriver (Jennings 1975).

The attackers surrounded the village, set fire to it, and killed
Pequot people who attempted to escape the flames. Warriors from
the Naragansett tribe, a traditional rival of the Pequots and allies of
the Puritans who would soon meet a similar fate at their hands,
withdrew from the main attacking force when they realized what
Mason planned.

Over four hundred Pequots—that's one hundred more than were
killed in the massacre at Wounded Knee a century ago—died in the
attack. Captain John Underhill, another Puritan leader of the
attack, justified the killing of women and children with the word
"Scripture declareth women and children must perish with their
parents. . . . We had sufficient light from the word of God for our
proceedings" (Jennings 1975).

This type of dubious use of scripture for justification would go on
to define the ways in which the Pequots, Naragansetts, Mohegans,
and other tribal nations interacted with the settlers. A significant
number of settlers believed that what they were doing in New
England was a divinely ordained parallel to the Israelites taking
possession of the Promised Land. One of the places Apess lived, in
fact, was named New Canaan.

New England as New Canaan needed its Canaanites, Amelkites,
and other ites. The Pequots, Naragansetts, Wampanoags, Mohegans, and others served that function, and ended up losing nearly
every part of their identity. By the end of King Philip's War, named
for the Wampanoag leader who fought desperately but unsuccess-
fully against the colonists, the Native population declined by 5800
from 70,000 to 12,000. As Francis Jennings has argued, those who
came to people New England, rather than coming into virgin land,
occupied widowed land (Jennings 1975).

One hundred and sixty years after the massacre at Mystic,
William Apess was born. Let me posit a parallel situation: imagine a
Lakota person born today. As he or she grows up, he or she will be
told about the massacre at Wounded Knee in 1890, since all Lakota
are tied to it by history and by blood.

One hundred and six years later, the memories of that atrocity
remain and probably will remain fifty years from now, when the
distances between the dissolution of the Pequot and Apess and the
massacre at Wounded Knee and the young Lakota equal each other.
During those one hundred and sixty years since Mystic, the Pequots

and other Natives of the northeast cobbled out an existence from whatever they could at the desperate margins of New England. Apess was a Pequot at a low point in the group's history.

Unwelcome in New England's white institutions except as laborers and servants, the Pequot represented the underside of what many believed was a history foreordaind by God (O'Connell 1992). Native men were especially vulnerable to violent deaths, and often fell prey to the lures of whisky-traders who offered an anesthesia for their pain and *ressentiment*. Those who chose work often ended up as skilled laborers in the burgeoning whaling industry, a life that kept them at sea for years at a time. Men of African descent, who faced a similar dearth of woman in the northeast, increasingly intermarried with Native women (many of whom they met while working as domestic or agricultural laborers).

Thus, those who might be disappointed in Apess's lack of knowledge of Pequot traditional culture should be clear that it was historical agents like John Underhill and John Mason, not those who inherited that awful legacy 160 years later, who were most responsible. And those who would rue Apess's lack of authenticty or of a richly detailed Pequot traditional system of ceremonies, social structures, and crafts ought instead to celebrate the sheer survival of the Pequots.

Pequot William Apess was a survivor of a horrific, modern past, who eventually became a Methodist minister and advocate for justice. At his most trenchant, he was a formidable critic of the carnage of colonization. As he says in one of his essays, "If black or red skins or any other skin of color is disgraceful to God, it appears that he has disgraced himself a great deal—for he has made fifteen colored people to one white and placed them here upon this earth" (O'Connell, 157). From there, he continues,

Now let me ask you, white man, if it is a disgrace for to eat, drink, and sleep with the image of God, or sit, or walk and talk with them. Or have you the folly to think that the white man, being one of fifteen or sixteen, are the only beloved images of God? Assemble all nations together in your imagination, and then let the whites be seated among them, and then let us look for the white, and I doubt not it would be hard finding them; for to the rest of the nations, they are still but a handful. Now suppose these skins were put together, and each skin had its national crimes written upon it—which skin do you think would have the greatest? (O'Connell 1992, 157)

Anyone seeking an assimilated, cowering William Apess champi-
oning the ways of white America will be hard pressed to find him.

Instead, Apess's voice defiantly reminds the New England sophis-
ticates exactly what the history of their region had been. While
plenty of those New Englanders were happy to look with compas-
sionate eyes upon the remnant of Pequots living by the rivers of
Connecticut, Apess sought to provide those same people with a history that would offer some context to their station. As his essay continues,

> I will ask one question more. Can you charge the Indian with rob-
> bing a nation almost of their whole continent, and murdering the
> women and children, then depriving the remainder of their lawful
> rights, that nature and God require them to have? And to cap the cli-
> max, rob another nation to till their grounds and welter out their
> days under the lash with hunger and fatigue under the scorching
> rays of a burning sun? I should look at all the skins, and I know that
> when I cast my eye upon that white skin, and if I saw those crimes
> written upon it, I should enter my protest against it immediately and
> cleave to that which is more honorable. And I can tell you that I am
> satisfied with the manner of my creation, fully—whether others are
> or not. (Apess 1992, 157)

Apess, then, protests not just present injustice, but contextualizes
his protest in a history that many in New England were more than
happy to forget.

Perhaps the latest battle of history and irony has been won by
Apess. Today, descendants of those people barely scraping by on the
riverbanks of New England have become perhaps the most famous
operators of casinoes in the world. These same people who were at a
degrading nadir in 1800 have managed to persist for 190 more years
and have again begun to reassemble themselves and prosper selling
the ultimate consumer economy diversion—casino gambling.

Apess and Methodism

There is a long-standing dispute as to the origins of Methodism in
what is now the United States. Some believe the John Street
Methodist Church in New York City was first. Others contend that
Baltimore was the font of North American Methodism (Richey

1991). Regardless of birthplace, Methodism was a backwater region in the northeast in Apess's time. This isn't to say that evangelical religion had no impact in the region; Methodism enjoyed success there, but clearly the impulses and initiatives of the consolidating denomination were coming from the South.

Importantly, much of the success of Methodism, in England and in the North American English colonies, was due to its response to the conditions modernity was imposing on vulnerable classes of people (Hempton 1996; Schneider 1993). John Wesley self-consciously pitched his message to working class people in England. In North America, Methodists reached out to slaves and to poor whites.

Methodists in the new republic of the United States did not begin working in a systematic fashion with American Indian nations until the second decade of the nineteenth century (Noley 1991). And William Apess single-handedly brought Methodism to the Pequots. Apess's ministry does not then represent a Methodist priority, but rather, that his work was what he made of it.

Apess became a Methodist in an ambiguous time for Methodism in North America. The cleverness of Methodism in England had always been its ability to adapt to the strict denominational regimen of England and to the state church. In North America, the messages inherent in the theology logically led to a theology of radical egalitarianism. In its extreme forms in the eighteenth century, Methodism demanded the fraternity of others across class, racial, and gender lines. The acceptance of that fraternity among white elites was ambiguous and uncomfortable, but the sheer fact of groups of poor people and wealthy people, white people, black people, and Native people meeting together in feasts of love is a striking response to the various injustices of the colonization and settlement of North America.

Apess was baptized in 1818. At age 31, he sought ordination and was denied by the main arm of the Methodists. After their rejection, he accepted a place with the "republican" Protestant Methodists (O'Connell 1992). While the majority wing of the church, that which followed the lights of Thomas Asbury, focused on moralism and piety, the republican wing sought to incorporate religious identity and political identity by trying to change those structures in American society that were unjust (Richey 1991).

Clearly, the Methodism that accepted Apess and the one that he espoused was falling further and further away from its early ideals.

The reason for the shift, as most commentators contend, was that living out the demanding ideals of egalitarianism severely limited the allure of the Methodist message to the broadest base of whites. In order for the church to grow both numerically and financially, the message had to appeal to people who owned slaves and tenements. Also, in the time during and after the Second Great Awakening, which began at the turn of the century, evangelical Christians in the new republic developed a highly individual, experiential polity in which political questions of the relationship of the church to the nation were subsumed (Richey 1991; Pelikan 1989).

That is not to say that Apess espoused a message outside the boundaries of Methodism. As Russell Richey argues, American Methodism has traditionally spoken in four languages: the popular or evangelical, in which the pietism and devotion of the broad base of Methodists expressed themselves; the Wesleyan, in which Methodists questioned the necessity of a continuing relationship to the mother church; the episcopal, in which the church's leadership revealed its origins in the Church of England; and the republican, in which the church sought direct engagement with national politics. While one or another of the languages may predominate in a certain period, Richey argues that all have a valid place within the Methodist tradition (Richey 1991).

Apess spoke a combination of the popular and republican languages of Methodism. His own conversion and devotional life, as well as those of the other Native people he wrote about, were central to him. But he also spoke in unwavering terms about the persistence of racism in the church and in society, using scripture as his guide.

As with African-American Methodist contemporaries David Walker and Maria Stewart, the politically and socially engaged aspects of the Christian gospel were central to Apess (Houchins 1988). All three deployed the republican language of Methodism, a language that offered a public theology clearly devoid of the American Christian triumphalism of various expressions of Calvinism (Richey 1991).

In general, the Calvinist approach to the politics of North America posited the complicity, indeed the authorship, of the Christian god in the history of the continent. Methodism offered an alternative in which something other than destiny and necessity had caused things to be the way they were. Methodism, in its most egalitarian forms, sought to address the oppression of those whose lives were laid waste by the march of American history.

Certainly Apess was able to embrace this alternative, oppositional rhetoric which the modern movement of Methodist generated internally. But it wasn't only the politics that attracted African-Americans and American Indians to Methodism. No doubt the emphasis on the creation of community in the form of love feasts, conferences, and camp meetings was appealing. So also was the opportunity to understand worship as involving the body and the singing voice. For groups of disenfranchised poor people, Methodism offered hope for a reconstituted present. Insofar as William Apess could hear good news in the gospel, his ears welcomed the message. It had been a long time, after all, since his ears or other Pequot ears had heard much good news.

Apess in the Removal Period

The period of legislated Indian Removal from 1830–40 was perhaps the single most disastrous period of the execution of federal Indian policy in the history of the nation. Over the course of that decade, 46,000 people were force-marched 1,500 miles from their homes, often in the wintertime to already occupied lands in what was then Indian Territory (Prucha 1984). Soldiers along the way raped the young women, ignored the sick, and let the dead fall in their tracks. The Cherokees are the people most associated with the Trail of Tears, but they were only one among many tribal nations who now carry the harrowing, multitudinous stories of removal through the ages (Weaver 1996).

The details of those stories are beyond the scope of this essay, but I do want to make some observations. First, the very phenomenon of equating removal with the Cherokees and losing the sense of geographical, tribal, and numerical immensity of Indian Removal has allowed the most simplistic images of removal to exist in the popular mind. Important salient features of the forced marches to Indian Territory, such as the multiple routes, the fact that much of the land the refugees passed through was populated by whites (thus defying the idea that removal was necessitated by the arrival of the frontier to the borders of Native communities), that all of the removed groups included in their ranks elites educated western style who could advocate in English (both verbally and in the written word) white military and political leaders have given way to a generalized picture of helpless primitives in tatters being driven across pathless land to unknown destinations (Rogin 1987).

That simplified image denies to Native history the many ways in which the history of removal was part of a complex set of ideologies of movement and migration in nineteenth-century America. Methodism, with its itinerant preachers and camp meetings, was one part of the complex. As William Freehling argues, antebellum America was obsessed with dealing with social, political, religious, interpersonal, and other problems through the act of migrating. He writes,

> Antebellum ethnic groups, when faced with white Anglo-Saxon males' political drives to remove them and/or Americanize them, always debated the same two countervailing strategies. Southerners debated coming out from Washington, D.C., or staying inside the capital city and seeking to dominate it. Women debated coming out from the home, as Grimké advocated, or staying inside the household and seeking to moralize the men, as Beecher advocated. Denigrated groups in the North debated between staying inside Wasp communities and fighting for their distinctive identity or leaving and establishing their own communities. Of those who moved away to be free, the Mormons are the most obvious. But the antebellum landscape was dotted with the self-exiled and their ethnically pure communities: the transcendentalists' Brook Farm, the Owenites' New Harmony, the Shakers' twenty colonies in eight states, John Humphrey Noyes' Oneida, the midwestern Irish, Norwegian, and German towns. (Freehling 1994, 153)

Make no mistake. Native Removal was a coercive act that carried with it next to none of the voluntarism of any of these examples. And the alternative to removal, as I will discuss in a later section of this essay, was not remaining, but extinction.

But Native Removal happened in an era in which the idea of packing up and moving everything to a new place was not absurd. Indeed, as Freehling points out, Indian Removal would come to serve as an exemplar to those seeking to recolonize black slaves to Africa. If Native people could be moved so efficiently in a decade, what was to stop the same process for people of African descent (Freehling 1994)?

All of the southeastern tribal nations who became the victims of removal had already accepted themselves as subjects of the modern condition. Like the one nation and the many states around them, these native nations may not yet have established their boundaries, but they were all in the process of consolidating themselves as peoples. They certainly didn't understand themselves as necessary victims of someone else's plans for their place (Womack 1995).

What did no doubt seem necessary to the citizens of these tribal nations was that they would have to undergo a process of modernization through which they would develop institutions and social structures to confront the new realities of existing alongside a settler nation. In the cases of the Creeks, Cherokee, Chickasaws, and Choctaws in the southeast, that process was moving along with varying rates of success. The other major group, the Seminoles, were making their own highly modern response to the situation—all-out defensive warfare to protect their territory from colonization (Noley 1991).

Modernity was an undeniable reality for the tribal nations of the southeast and the Ohio valley. Compounding the problems tribal nations have faced in such situations, the two options offered by the dominators were extinction, which had been an effective if horrific tool in Puritan New England, or removal.

Furthermore, unlike today, where the vagaries of federal Indian policy work themselves out with next to no one in the mainstream of American political life noticing, the removal of Natives to Indian Territory in the nineteenth century occured in full sight of the American public. The debates in print, in public forums, in Congress, and in parlors and salons were highly charged. Every self-respecting public intellectual or political leader from Thomas Jefferson to Ralph Waldo Emerson had a detailed position on the Indian Question. As much as the peculiar institution of chattel slavery threatened the purported ideals of ascendant American democracy, so did the question of Indian removal (Maddox 1991).

But as Lucy Maddox has argued, after the Indian Question was answered with the Removal Act and most of the Native peoples east of the Mississippi ended up in Indian Territory, the question itself and the history it spawned could be removed from the national consciousness and to some extent the historical record in just a few generations (Maddox 1991). And, almost as if to demonstrate the capacity of modern society to avoid its own history, the battles over land and politics between settlers and Natives on the Plains and in the Far West by and large happened at a convenient remove from centers of population, allowing a gap between experience and interpretation that both the Puritans of colonial New England and the liberals of Andrew Jackson's removal era could have only wished for.

Conclusion: The Rhetoric of Ancientness and Novelty

Having made this case for understanding the work of William Apess in the contexts of the history of modernity and colonization in the forms of Pequot decimation, Methodism, and the history of removal, let me now suggest some of the directions future scholarship on Apess and the era might proceed.

First, Apess being not only Pequot (a mirror of the horrors of the Puritan legacy), but a Methodist (an advocate of non-triumphalist egalitarianism) in the period of removal is fortuitous. Who better to emerge as a major critic not only of removal policy, but of the hypocrisy of white New Englanders in failing to acknowledge either their own historical treatment of Native peoples or their failure to recognize that in their own midst Native peoples were living in chronic poverty? Two centuries may have passed, but Apess could recall the massacre at Mystic and remind New Englanders that it wasn't only white Georgians who were capable of crimes against humanity.

That argument from history, of course, was one that would have been made whether Apess did so or not. The Puritan past of the region was a matter of controversy during Apess's time. How to escape from the benchmark of character established in the seventeenth century was a conundrum. The Saints of Plymouth, Massachusetts, and Connecticut who demanded that their history was sacred history became the embarassing agents of history called to account for their actions.

In the end, every syllable Emerson wrote on the subject is available while only the published books of Apess remain to tell us what he, a direct descendant of those on the underside of history, thought of the "Indian Question." Beyond the obvious facts of station and positionality of the two, I would suggest that Apess came face to face with a problem that continues to plague Native writers: the work of writers of tribal nations is considered to represent a timeless reality (for which I use the term *ancient* since it suggests something different than just old), and at the same time as something that is only now accessible to a non-tribal audience (as in, "look, even Indians are writing books these days—they're so up to date!").

This barrier is a structure of attitude and reference, a predetermined, incomplete framework that provides the foundation for understanding phenomena and sensations (Said 1993). Indian knowledge was regarded somehow timeless, something to know because of its intricate relationship to its place. And Indian knowledge, also, was offered in a form never offered before. The novelty of it all is as important of it ancientness. And the danger of both sides is of losing the historicity of the modern crucible of experience in which the transaction took place.

That, to me, seems the ripest area of further engagement with the life and work of William Apess: his almost over-determined subjectivity and the way in which his subjectivity subverts the usual, accustomed categories of who and what Indians are. Much of that work remains undone.

The shape of that work will have to confront in serious ways the manner in which modernity has been able to manage its own history through selective amnesia and shallow interpretations of complex historical processes. Insofar as William Apess projects himself out of that history as a reminder in his time as well as ours of the awful human price paid by those on the underside of modernity, we are able to glimpse and to grasp the shape of our own liberation, even if that liberation lives in generations yet to come.

Works Cited

Ashwill, Gary. (199x). "Savagism and Its Discontents: James Fenimore Cooper and His Native American Contemporaries." *American Transcendental Quarterly* 8/3, 1994, 211–27.

Blaeser, Kimberley. (1990). "Gerald Vizenor: Writing—In the Oral Tradition." Ph.D. dissertation, University of Notre Dame, South Bend, Indiana.

Cook-Lynn, Elizabeth. (1991). "The Radical Conscience in American Indian Studies." *Wicazo Sa Review* 7 (1, Fall): 1–8.

Copway, George. (1850). *The Traditional History and Characteristic Sketches of the Ojibway Nation*. London: Gelpin.

Cronon, William. (1983). *Changes in the Land; Indians, Colonists, and the Ecology of New England*. New York: Hill and Wang.

Freehling, William W. (1994). *The Reintegration of American History; Slavery and the Civil War*. New York: Oxford University Press.

Gustafson, Sandra. (1994). "Nations of Israelites: Prophecy and Cultural Autonomy in the Writings of William Apess." *Religion and Literature* 26/1, 31–53.

Hempton, David. (1996). *The Religion of Hope; Methodism and Popular Religion c. 1750–1900*. New York: Routledge.

Houchins, Sue, ed. (1988). *Spiritual Narratives*. New York: Oxford University Press.

Jennings, Francis. (1975). *The Invasion of America; Indians, Colonists, and the Cant of Conquest*. New York: Norton.

Maddox, Lucy. (1991). *Removals; Nineteenth Century American Literature and the Politics of Indian Affairs*. New York: Oxford University Press.

Noley, Homer. (1991). *The First White Frost; Native Americans and United Methodism*. Nashville, TN: Abingdon Press.

O'Connell, Barry. (1992) *On Our Own Ground; The Complete Writings of William Apess, A Pequot*. Amherst: University of Massachusetts Press.

Pelikan, Jaroslav. (1989). *Christian Doctrine and Modern Culture (Since 1700)*, Volume 5, *The History of Christian Doctrine; A History of the Development of Doctrine*. Chicago: University of Chicago Press.

Prucha, Francis Paul. (1984). *The Great Father; The United States Government and the Indians*. Lincoln: University of Nebraska Press.

Richey, Russell E. (1991). *Early American Methodism*. Bloomington, Indiana University Press.

Rogin, Michael. (1987). "Liberal Society and the Indian Question," in *Ronald Reagan, The Movie and Other Episodes in Political Demonology*. Michael Rogin, ed. Berkeley: University of California Press.

Said, Edward W. (1993). *Culture and Imperialism*. New York: Knopf.

Sarris, Greg. (1993). *Keeping Slug Woman Alive: A Holistic Approach to American Indian Texts*. Berkeley: University of California Press.

Schneider, A. Gregory. (1993). *The Way of the Cross Leads Home; The Domestication of American Methodism*. Bloomington: Indiana University Press.

Tinker, George E. (1993). *Missionary Conquest; The Gospel and Native American Cultural Genocide*. Minneapolis: Fortress Press.

Vizenor, Gerald. (1989). *Narrative Chance; Postmodern Discourse on American Indian Literatures*. Albuquerque, University of New Mexico Press.

Warrior, Robert A. (1994) *Tribal Secrets; Recovering American Indian Intellectual Traditions*. Minneapolis: University of Minnesota Press.

Weaver, Jace G. (1996). "That the People Might Live." Ph.D. dissertation, Union Theological Seminary, New York, New York.

Womack, Craig. (1995). "A Creek National History." Ph.D. dissertation, University of Oklahoma, Norman, Oklahoma.

Part III

Postmodern Praxes
and Liberation Theories

11

Postmodernity, Black Theology of Liberation and the U.S.A.
Michel Foucault and James H. Cone

Dwight N. Hopkins

I would like to engage a critical conversation between post-modernity and liberation theology by comparing and contrast-ing two representatives of both intellectual developments: Michel Foucault signifying postmodernity thought and James H. Cone marking liberation theology in the Americas. To achieve such a crit-ical interchange, first I present an interpretation of postmodernity and black theology of liberation, next an examination of both men's contributions, followed by a critique of each; and then a possible way of synthesizing their strengths.

Postmodernity and Black Theology

Postmodern thought (as exemplified primarily by European and Euro-American intellectuals) and black theology of liberation (as represented mainly by African-American thinkers) are, in one sense, heirs of the European Enlightenment's discursive and non-discur-sive practices, but heirs with fundamental differences.

The European Enlightenment accompanied the ascendancy of modernity, and a firmer grasp of postmodernity follows a brief out-line of the basic planks of modernity. Modernity indicates the centrality of the autonomous, meaning-giving individual. Human beings are the subjects of history, a unitary history, inevitably developing through social progress to emancipation. Critical reason and objective science are the crucial tools required for humans to become free from the bondage of Christianity, superstitions, and nature. In fact, religion is relegated to the private sphere and churches are separated from the state. European capitalism assumes ascendancy over feudalism; bureaucratism and centralization become signs of the economy and the state apparatus. Bodies of knowledge are organized into discrete disciplines where language operates as a neutral medium that represents the world and various essences. Another hallmark of modernity is the stress on foundations, universal knowledge, and metanarratives—whether in science, nature, biology, social relations, or religion.

Postmodernity in contrast to the modernity project argues for a collapse of metanarratives and foundations; instead, one discovers multiple positions or positionalities, pluralities of discourses, micro-realities, relativity, diverse truths, multiple centers, pragmatic methodologies, divergent histories, interdisciplinarity, located knowledges, contextuality, historicity, and particular struggles of resistance. Binary oppositions collapse between science and literature, science and ideology, fact and fiction, reason and intuition, high art and popular art. One does not have an essence but a social production of identities. Instead of salvation of humanity by objective science, one encounters science as humanly created and steeped in power and domination. And the unitary march of progressive history is detoured by the eruption of subjugated knowledges and practices that short circuit linearity with disjuncture. In a word, the subject, for postmodernity, has been or is being decentered; objective scientific metadiscourses become fragmented.[1]

Black theology likewise is somewhat of an heir to the European Enlightenment, more particularly a victimized heir of the theological and practical residue manifested in the offspring of Europe, that is, Euro-America.[2] While Euro-Americans with power fashioned their own form of Enlightenment in the so-called New World of North America through synthesizing reason, science, and religious "chosen people" God-talk in a multileveled manifest destiny, African Americans experienced the brutal bottom of the Enlightenment's effects. The separation of church and state in the founding of the American republic meant, for enslaved blacks, that both state and church were united in maintaining the chattel condition. The praise of scientific discovery and objectivity for whites played out as biological experiments on the natural inferiority of blacks. While philosophy supposedly correlated universal meaning via juxtaposing knowledge and the world, in the case of African Americans, philosophy became an epistemological tool for rendering black skin intellectually subhuman or even possibly akin to the orangutan.[3]

The Western modern condition for African Americans translated into a metanarrative of white superiority, cogently signified in the adage that a black person (whether slave or free) had no rights that a white man was bound to respect. What was universal, as European modernity crossed the Atlantic and became Euro-America, was that ebony people suffered a deleterious asymmetry on a hierarchical scale biologically, theologically, noetically, and culturally. Black slaves knew intuitively that the supposed neutrality of language, trumpeted by the European Enlightenment, could get you killed. What a slave said or did not say vis-à-vis the dominant colonial and subsequent American masters was a matter of life and death. Thus while Europe and Euro-America hailed the rise of modern sensibilities, enlightened epistemologies, and capitalist democracy, Africans and African Americans were already suffering and enduring characteristics of what intellectuals and cultural workers today call postmodernity—such as decentered subjects, multiple locatedness, particularized struggles, no discrepancy between scientific and fictionalized discourse, an impression of the affective and the scientific, the sensuousness of the body and the intellect, and so forth. Perhaps what is new about postmodernity on the contemporary scene for African Americans is that sectors of the dominant population are now encountering the "post" condition and ramifications of their own created modernity project. The Enlightenment's rationalism smashed the illusions that pre-eighteenth century orthodoxy maintained through self-delusion in religion. Post-modernity is the recognition (especially with the crucial insights of the masters of suspicion of Marx's reason and economics, Freud's reason and desire, and Nietzsche's reason and the will to power; and the trenchant critiques of black, feminist, Native American, Hispanic-Latino, Asian-American and Pacific Island, and Lesbian/Gay theologies) that Enlightenment reason is another form of illusory salvation. Reason, science, and language are not clear and neutral media of progress, but are riddled with ambiguity, ide-

ology, and power. Hence the turn to postmodernity is a disillusionment with a disillusionment.

Shaking the Foundations

The turn toward postmodern thought by (primarily some) white
Americans and Europeans of the intellectual stratum and a black
theology of liberation by certain African-American theologians and
church members originates from both overlapping and divergent
social bases.

A major incentive for the rise of postmodern discourses is World
War II and fascism, for here two stellar pillars began to shake: the
sacredness of science and the inevitability of human progress.
Furthermore, the rule of Stalin and the Soviet Union's invasion of
other socialist countries in the late 1950s drove a wedge further in
the camp of those who saw Marxism as a unitary metanarrative of
secular human salvation. For Europe, particularly Britain, the second world war relegated European allies to a lesser tier status, as
the USA emerged as the undisputed leader of the bourgeois democratic world with increased consumerism and subsequently a 1973
structural economic shift, and a service-information based economy ensuing. In France, the May 1968 student-labor-civic upris-
ings, moreover, exacerbated faults in the modern philosophical
project: shaking up allegiances to phenomenology, existentialism,
and structuralism. Fundamentally in the U.S.A., the massive national resistances, initiated on a countrywide basis by the civil
rights and black power movements, but accompanied by the feroc-
ity of the anti-Vietnam war voices, brown berets, red power, Asian
American community-student groups, grey panthers, feminist articulations, and lesbian and gay protests impacted forever the intellectual modernity claim of a unitary speaking subject.

The social basis for the emergence of contemporary black theology finds its roots likewise in the conflagration of World War II.
However, African Americans perceived this war pragmatically
through the lens of a localized self-interest. If black bodies were
being mobilized to subvert the brown shirted blitzkrieg abroad,
then the patriotic stratagems of democracy, the fight against racial
genocide, and the supremacy of the American way of life were
expected to be duplicated at home when African-American service
men and women returned to Georgia, Alabama, New York, Boston,

Chicago, and Oakland. The expectation and the hope of a new world order, for black people, began at home. African Americans did not perceive the collective evil of one race over against another race as novel (for the indelible memory of 75 to 100 million African deaths in the European and North American slave trade would not let them forget). The newness was the global and domestic rhetoric of freedom that could provide possibly a fissure for self-enhancement from a Jim Crow status. In addition, inspiration arose out of the emergent cracks of decolonization—India (1947), Ghana (1957), and African independence (1960).

More pointedly, black theology arose out of some black church leaders' responses to the massive 1950s and 1960s civil rights and black power movements in which, symbolically, Martin Luther King, Jr. challenged American Christian churches to delineate their identity by fighting for the least in society and Malcolm X berated the Negro community about the African identity of their unique existence.

This schematic outline of postmodern thought and black theology and their social bases suggests that postmodernity operates on, at least, two levels. One is the whole cultural critique against the modern, that is to say, in architecture, the museum discussions, the deconstruction/post-structuralism discourse, methodological debates over whether or not metatheory is over, accenting micro-analytic theories, concerns about the subject or the lack of the subject, the body as a site of contestation, celebration of the playful in carnivalesque, and so forth. This is one creative trajectory in postmodern thought. A second approach to postmodern thought is the eruption of the poor against all the negativity that modernity has brought, that is to say, monopoly capitalism, imperialism, intensification of racism, sexism, classism, homophobia, (etc.), and the use of reason and religion to legitimate harmful progress of modernity. What is new about postmodernity is not that the poor have not been struggling against the meta-discourses and structures, but that, due to the post-World War II global reconfigurations, the poor have burst upon the world scene like an earthquake shaking the foundations of North American and European hegemony and supremacy. As always, academics have reacted to the power of people and social configurations, and have synthesized theories of postmodernity that one hopes will clarify and transform personal and systemic social relations. In this sense, black theology and other liberation theologies have surfaced as postmodern realities, multiply located with the cultural and political interests of the voiceless but with access to cultural and political resources of the academy, linked to the church and community, while grafted onto dominant intellectual conversations.

Michel Foucault the Philosopher and James H. Cone the Prophet

Though Michel Foucault and James H. Cone both wrote during the postmodern condition, each approached his particular intellectual passion from distinct stances. Foucault was a philosopher whose life long academic quest was to destroy the Enlightenment notion of the subject in order to provide novel ways of thinking about subjectivity, knowledge, and power. Cone is a prophet whose vocation is to speak the truth to power in order that poor people might participate in establishing a new society of liberation, justice, and full humanity on earth.[4]

From *Madness and Civilization* (1965) to *The History of Sexuality, Volume 3: The Care of the Self* (1988), Foucault unleashes a veritable philosophical war against the idea of a sovereign subject—a massive intellectual assault dispersed through four phases of his public career.[5] The first phase is circumscribed by the publication of *Madness and Civilization* whose central thread demolished, from Foucault's notion, the transcendent subject who deployed reason and science to ascertain and to forge universal truth. On the contrary, argued Foucault, the idea that humanity evolves automatically to a higher state through dominating nature via science was a sham because (1) in order to progress the rational subject had to create mad people. Hence insanity was not natural or biological but culturally induced, a socio-historical construct. And (2) not only is the state of madness a created reality, moreover, the so-called rational subject is a fiction who oppresses the mad by alienating them through elaborate classification procedures that fail to recognize the positivity of madness. A pre-existing essence of madness did not exist and, in parallel fashion, neither did a universal reason grasped by a meaning-generating subject exist. Each historical period, with accompanying diverse cultural, political, and moral sensibilities, treats and creates madness differently.

Unlike phase one where Foucault situates social institutions historically and the discourse of professionals in these historized institutions (both discourse and institutions constitute the subject as object), in his second philosophical phase, Foucault examines the subject while suspending an interrogation of institutional analysis. At this philosophical juncture, designated as the archaeological moment, Foucault is concerned with how certain ideas and knowledges are legitimated and others excluded or relegated to lower rungs in discursive hierarchies. Central to the archaeological method is the episteme—a way of thinking in specific eras that allows certain knowledges to appear. Furthermore, rules govern the possibility of thought. Discursive formations are relatively autonomous from social institutions. But more importantly for Foucault's project is the fact that discursive formations are arbitrary and fragmentary lacking rational direction by the human subject. The subject does not produce meaning.

In the third stage, his genealogical approach, Foucault focuses on how discourses are used or the role they play in society.[6] The condition of possibility for discursive formation is power located in nondiscursive social relations. And this power is not the centralized power of Marxism but a microtechnologies of power spread throughout society.[7] Power is determined by and constitutes the social realm. Power, here, is no longer a totalizing hermetic force of repression only. Now for Foucault power is negative and positive; the point at which power is most repressive leaves space for resistance by the subject.

And in his final stage, and for my project one of his most important, Foucault engages the subject in the ethics of the self. Particularly in the last two volumes of *The History of Sexuality*, he elaborates further how power can be positively utilized by the subject both for individual transformation and for altering exterior constraints.[8]

A turn to James H. Cone the prophet shows various accents at different times during his quest for a new reality for the marginalized and locked out voices of society. With his first publication, *Black Theology and Black Power* (1969) marking stage one of his prophetic career, Cone deconstructs white supremacy in Christian theology, church, and America. He opposes racism in the white power structure of the American political system, church, and theology and exposes how whites with privilege use religion and theology to justify the maintenance of white rule over black life. The need, consequently, for a black theology derives from the imperative of the daily black struggle for survival and freedom.[9] The white supremacist power structure has stripped African Americans of power, therefore, black people need power for self-determination and self-identity.

In a similar vein, asserts Cone, the gospel message of Jesus Christ centers on liberation of the oppressed who dwell in a victimization by systemic evils. Indeed the heart of Cone's systematic theology, which establishes his project as a black Christian theology of liberation, hinges on the central norm of Jesus Christ liberator of oppressed humanity.[10] Because Jesus is for the oppressed and because African Americans are oppressed, then Jesus must be the black Christ who provides the necessary soul for black liberation. Moreover, the gathering of the faithful, the believers of Jesus, must be where the oppressed are because Jesus is already there suffering with the lowly and engaging in their efforts toward freedom and justice. In sum, the first stage of Cone's public voice demarcated liberation of the poor and black power as essential correlations of Christian doctrines, especially, themes of liberation, Christology, and ecclesiology.

Phase two sees Cone attempting to deepen not only the content of Christian doctrinal claims, but veering toward a thorough and radical reconstruction of black theology itself. Not only does the thematic content of liberation have to be inserted into Christian theology, but for an explicit black theology, the form of the theology has to be thoroughly African American. Phase two, then, reveals Cone turning away from European and Euro-American sources and their concomitant thought structures and turning toward plumbing the depths of black sources which his *Spirituals and the Blues* and *God of the Oppressed* underscore.[11] Christian theology has to be made authentic by positioning liberation as the normative stance and likewise the rhythm and mood of a black theology has to be ensconced in black life and culture. For Cone, a two-part move liberates both content and form.

Phase three finds Cone broadening his prophetic black theology of liberation to the condemnation of monopoly capitalism, sexism, and imperialism. His basic theological query is: how can black theology call itself a liberation theology when it is either silent on, indirectly supportive of, or actively engaged in oppressing workers, women (especially African American women), and the global third world?[12]

His final stage shows a prophetic black theology more deeply delving into African American sources in order to make a black theology of liberation a more public theology. Cone's groundbreaking text *Martin & Malcolm & America: A Dream Or A Nightmare* argues that the social movement of the poor, embedded in their culture, acts as the primary datum of thought, feeling, and passion for a full and new humanity on earth. And this datum and movement are universal for the construction of any theology in the American context. This stage finds Cone pressing the claim that theology is critical public discourse—it is liberation God-talk confronting society, church, and the academy.[13]

Critique of the Philosopher and the Prophet

In a sense Foucault the philosopher and Cone the prophet complement one another in their critiques—that is to say, when we critique the shortcomings of one thinker, we can possibly find a corrective in the critique of the other.

If one begins with the notion of power, we find Cone's strength in grasping the subtleties of macro-structures of domination, oppression, and discrimination, while Foucault accentuates micro-dimensionalities of power. For Cone, power is the systemic conglomeration of macro privileges monopolized by whites in the U.S.A. It is centralized in the hands of a small group of white monopoly capitalist families whose aim is to ensure that whatever happens in the United States, their profits will increase and the control of the majority of the country's wealth will remain in their hands. Race supremacy of white people is, likewise, not the arbitrary aberration of one or two ill meaning whites. On the contrary, it is not a question of white Americans' heart, but the central issue of systemic white power. To change the heart is fruitless unless the system of white racism crumbles simultaneously. Hence for Cone, the construction of a black theology of liberation necessitates macro-structural analyses.

Power for Foucault, in radical contrast, detests Marxist political economy as another form of the European Enlightenment's bankrupt attempt to correlate an exact relation between the subject and the consciousness of the subject, a subject at the center of a naturally progressing history geared toward emancipation guaranteed by science. Power is not centralized in a class or elite stratum. Power, Foucault argues, resides in a dispersal of networks that are behind, beside, and underneath the political economy of the bourgeoisie and the state apparatus. What happens when the bourgeoisie is replaced by the proletariat if these micro-dispersals of power that are shot through every fibre of society—micro-powers such as those manifested in family, kinship, knowledge, sexuality, etc.—are not interrogated? Marxism, claims Foucault, does not attend to micro exigencies of power because power is a network or field possessed by no one class or sector of society. Power resides throughout society and within all classes.[14]

In addition to a complementary critique of Foucault and Cone over power, we can apply a similar approach to their treatment or lack of one toward culture and race. Foucault, despite his perceptive archaeological and genealogical insights and his crucial interpretations of subjugated knowledges and the fissures in normative historical claims, still appears to be overdetermined in his analysis by Eurocentrism, that is, a provincial lens of the world from the perspective and privileged concerns of Europe (and Euro-America). One must ask Foucault: how can he not understand that the formation of the European identity and history directly intertwines with Europe's disruption and underdevelopment of Africa? Moreover, though one could argue the extent of their presence, there were Afro-French citizens during Foucault's life time, whose very existence called into question the lack of non-white racial and cultural sources in Foucault's philosophical analytic. It is Foucault's white blind spot that terribly undermines his entire intellectual endeavor.

As a corrective, Cone enters his prophetic posture through African American culture initially in his career. But through the race issue, he soon discovers that not only do black folk enjoy the particularity of culture, but other American communities and theologies of liberation operate out of the specificity of their own cultures. Culture, at this juncture, suggests a total way of life of survival and resistance, undergirded by a vivacious spirituality of difference. The positive and problematic cultures of difference discovered by Cone subsequently were sites occupied by women, lesbian, and gay communities. However, a possible weakness of Cone's prophetic vocation is lack of sufficient attention to those sectors of the white community who do not have wealth or, in large sections, do not even have jobs. How does a black Christian theology of liberation relate to poor and working class white Americans?

Methodology, a third area of criticism, undergoes a radical differentiation between the two men, particularly methodology cast as the viability of metanarratives or macro analytical discourses. Here too, Foucault's strengths and weaknesses complement the opposite concerns of Cone and vice versa. From the perspective of the U.S.A, it is not a question of either-or, relative to the macro-micro debate, but the necessity of both-and. Cone stands on firm ground in his cogent exegesis of racial political economy: the American wealth and race configurations are major texts of exploitation and discrimination. The sheer display of wealth and racial disparities in North America indicates, even on a cursory level, the lethal presence of grand structural asymmetries at play. What Foucault adds are insights of micro-technologies of power, subtle, almost invisible, regions of apparent impenetrable contestations of power and lack of power. Yes, one dissects and deconstructs mega-systems. But one also excavates the pervasive presence of power in such social areas as pleasure and sexuality, geography and depth, space and time, laughter and sadness, the body and spirit, family and kinship, knowledge constructs and information content, etc.

A fourth and final knowledge of critique resides in the realm of telos—the ultimate end goal of human endeavors. Foucault, detesting philosophically any Enlightenment assertion of a rational subject moving to a preordained or more progressive linear reality, abhors the idea of telos, whether anchored in scientific discovery, natural law, intellectual capacity, or religious metaphysics. What in human history dictates the assertion of telos? Where is the proof? In contrast, Foucault proclaims, history is arbitrary, fragmented, and overwhelmed by reversals, unpredictability, and, indeed, retrogression. Why does humanity need a vision of a telos? In this critique of the Enlightenment and its heirs, from Marxism to liberalism to modern Christianity, Foucault undermines the dominant discursive and non-discursive formations of Europe and Euro-America, formations that have denoted the underside of historical meanings as dis-Enlightened Africans, black Americans, people of color, and the Third World. In other words, Foucault's break up of the white world's imperialistic and triumphalistic march through history teleologically culminating in a haven populated and controlled primarily by Europeans and Euro-Americans engenders space for the eruption of subjugated knowledges. A break in the dominating telos facilitates the methodological tack toward new narratives of struggle.

Yet Cone, more grounded in the perspective of poor and working class people, appreciates the necessity and assertion of telos, in his

case a specifically Christian one. Telos helps the downtrodden to
hold on in the absurdity of a world gone mad with cut-throat com-
petitions in the economy, the popular culture, family, personal relations, and the church. If the locked out voices did not have a telos
that promised that though evil might last through the night, joy
comes in the morning (paraphrasing an old African-American teleological faith claim), then people without power, whether racial, gender, sexual, class, may as well go insane. It was easy for Foucault to
dispense with telos, not only because of the deleterious effects of
Enlightenment teleologies, but also because Foucault, despite his
marginalized gayness, still had enough money from his family's
wealth and elite educational status to not feel the effects of financial, gender, or racial uncertainties—conditions of possibility
engendering hope for, faith in, and the necessity of a liberating telos
constituted by a new space and identity on earth and/or beyond.

Integrated Lessons for Theology

How does the Foucault and Cone interchange, marking one slice of
the liberation theologies, postmodernity, and the Americas confluence, instruct us about the method of constructive liberation theologies, the thrust of my own creative and interpretive project?

Liberation theology is grounded, if not in anything else, in a commitment to those least in any society; and for a black theology of
liberation, those least are poor and working class people. The
macro-analysis of Cone astutely informs us so, with critical tools,
namely, a flexible and fluid Marxism. It is the liberation thrust that
distinguishes a general African-American religious studies or the
phrase black theology from a black theology of liberation. Put differently the phrase black theology by itself and the terms African-
American religious studies will have a tendency toward reformism;
while a black theology of liberation structurally attaches its analysis to enabling the least in society. Foucault's de-emphasis of mega-
investigation, perhaps adequate for the French context, would
detour black theology of liberation and other liberation theologies
away from the issues of the concentration of wealth in the hands of
a North American few. A holistic analysis serves as the first ingredi-
ent in a constructive black theology of liberation.

Yet, although de-emphasizing his macro-analytical creativity,
Foucault's insights on micro-power dispersals can complement

Cone's macro-contributions. Constructive black theology of liberation must acknowledge and take into account the presence of power
alongside, behind, and below the monopoly capitalist political
economy in America. How does power operate in diverse avenues
in civic society, in personal love relationships, in the family, inside
the church, in the politics of laughter and fun, etc.? What if the
larger systemic arrangements and personnel changed but the
micro-power configurations remained the same? Is this really what
the gospel is all about? What is at stake is that new and radical
social relationships must sweep through every sphere, sector, seg-
ment, and shell of North America. Liberation is holistic, integrative,
and comprehensive.

Language, a third piece in a constructive black theology of liberation, is exceedingly important. As a postmodernist, Foucault helps
us to see that language is not neutral but is saturated with biased
positionalities, maneuvering and assertive distinct voices. Theological language is not objective, or neutral, a transparent transmission
of God's will to the human domain. The person or community of
faith, on the contrary, which speaks or writes is already overdetermined by the social and personal traditional constructs of human
interaction. The oral and the aural suffer a priori. Thus a black theology of liberation, with Foucault's caveat, must submit any language of God-talk to the question: how does this language aid in the
conditions of possibility for poor and working class emancipation?

Furthermore, deepening the requirements of language within the
contours of a black theology of liberation, Cone's work indicates the
need for multivocality, grounded primarily in black talk about God.
In the first phase of his prophetic intellectual vocation, Cone engaged traditional theological God-talk by exhibiting his grasp of academic languages, both traditional doctrinal categories and the form
of presentation. This was one way of speaking. In his second phase,
we perceive his attempt "to write his way back home" to the black
church and to the black community. Here his content of faith claims
and rhythm of presentation reflect deeply the need to speak black
about God. Language embodies contested spaces of the speaker and
the context of the spoken; it does not simply reflect passively.

Accompanying macro, micro, and linguistic analyses, culture is
paramount in a black theology of liberation. Here Cone, unlike
Foucault, proves key. Culture is a foundational glue which, often on
the surface, surpasses the impact of the political. In fact, however,

culture is constructed out of competing forces within society and, therefore, is never transcendent to power relations and political programs.[15] Furthermore, culture in the North American context is a porous location infused with racial texts of signification. In the United States, one cannot talk of culture seriously without at the same time experiencing race. Just as Du Bois named the problem of the twentieth century as the color line, perhaps a large part of Cone's prophetic theological legacy will be his relentless pursuit of racial liberation here on earth. Culture, specifically the negative and liberating dimensions of racialized culture, has been not only a controversial and volatile reality in the broader society and church, it has and remains a blind spot and a stumbling block and a scandal within diverse liberation theologies today. Race and culture matter; therefore the liberation motif of all liberation theologies have to, among other things, ask the question: How does my liberation theology deal with racism and racial difference straightforwardly? If race is not a factor in theology, then one would be hard put to argue that such a theology is fully Christian or a liberation God-talk.

Finally, we claim that the type of liberation theology and postmodernity conversation and practice in the Americas worth its focus on the least in society has faith in and is possessed by a spirituality of social transformation. This spirituality bears witness to an ultimate Spirit and ancestral spirits that everyday enable us to have both structural and personal compassion for ourselves and others, especially for those in society who cannot determine their own selves (that is, the space around them) and their own identities (that is, the names of their own choice).

Notes

1. Texts on postmodern and modern discursive and material practices abound. Brief suggestions are: Hans Bertens, *The Idea of the Postmodern: A History* (New York: Routledge, 1995); Barbara Adams and Stuart Allan, eds., *Theorizing Culture: An Interdisciplinary Critique After Postmodernism* (London: University College London Press, 1995); Steven Seidman, *Contested Knowledge: Social Theory in the Postmodern Era* (Oxford: Blackwell, 1994); Anthony Giddens, *Modernity and Self-Identity: Self and Society in the Late Modern Age* (Stanford, Ca: Stanford University Press, 1991); David Harvey, *The Condition of Postmodernity* (Oxford: Blackwell, 1990); and Alan M. Olson, "Postmodernity and Faith," in *Journal of The American Academy of Religion*, spring 1990, volume lviii, number one.

2. The whole claim here is that black theology is a mixture or confluence

of retained, fragmentary west African traditional religious reflexes and a radically reinterpreted Christianity introduced by European slavers and Euro-American Christian pro-slavery advocates. Both the negative and positive as well as the reconfigured Christianity exist in African American churches and other faith communities and, thus, in black theology itself. Because theology is self-conscious and critical, understandably it is both a critique of and product of, partially, European and Euro-American Enlightenment sensibilities. Specifically, the American experiment of the Puritans and other founders the U.S.A. hail from the modernity impulse in human history. The Enlightenment accompanied the rise of modern capitalism, which signified a specific marker for racial differentiation, primarily a hierarchy and asymmetry. Therefore the "black" in black theology is a reclaiming or refueling of positive and revolutionary content into a former negative Enlightenment category. And the "theology" part in black theology, a Greek term in origin, implies black folk's appropriation of a European discourse, though with an African-American difference. The treatment of the African retentions in black theology demands another essay.

3. For analyses on race and modernity, see Paul Gilroy, *The Black Atlantic: Modernity and Double Consciousness* (Cambridge, MA.: Harvard University Press, 1993); David Theo Goldberg, *Racist Culture: Philosophy and the Politics of Meaning* (Oxford: Blackwell, 1993); and Ali Rattansi and Sallie Westwood, eds., *Racism, Modernity, and Identity* (Oxford: Polity Press, 1994).

4. For intellectual biographies, see David R. Shumway, *Michel Foucault* (Charlottesville, VA: University of Virginia Press, 1992); David Macey, *The Lives of Michel Foucault: A Biography* (New York: Pantheon Books, 1993); Didier Eribon, *Michel Foucault* (Cambridge, MA: Harvard University Press, 1991); James E. Miller, *The Passion of Michel Foucault* (New York: Simon & Schuster, 1993); Rufus Burrow, Jr., *James H. Cone and Black Liberation Theology* (Jefferson, North Carolina: McFarland & Co., Inc., Publishers, 1994); and James H. Cone, *My Soul Looks Back* (Maryknoll, N.Y.: Orbis Books, 1986).

5. See, for a sampling, his introduction to *The Archaeology of Knowledge and The Discourse on Language* (New York: Barnes and Noble Books, 1993) where he opposes the traditional notion of the sovereign subject in history with his revisionist concept of decentering the subject. Also review his foreword to *The Order of Things: An Archaeology of the Human Sciences* (New York: Vintage, 1994).

6. See both his "Two Lectures," in Colin Gordon, ed., *Power/Knowledge: Selected Interviews & Other Writings, 1972–1977 by Michel Foucault* (New York: Pantheon, 1980), p. 80ff; and his "Nietzsche, Genealogy, History," in Donald F. Bouchard, ed., *Language, Counter-Memory, Practice: Selected Essays and Interviews by Michel Foucault* (Ithaca, N.Y.: Cornell University Press, 1977), pp. 139–164.

7. See the interview with Foucault in "Prison Talk," (especially pages 51ff) found in Colin Gordon, ed., *Power/Knowledge: Selected Interviews, 1972–1977* (New York: Pantheon Books, 1980).

8. Foucault speaks of the individual exercising "rights," "power," "authority," "liberty," in *The History of Sexuality, Volume 2: The Use of Pleasure* (New York: Vintage, 1990), p. 23.

9. See especially his definition of "black power," in *Black Theology and Black Power, 20th Anniversary Edition* (New York: Harper & Row, 1989), pp. 5–8.

10. This theological doctrine marks the singular consistency throughout Cone's existential, intellectual, and theological journey. See *Black Theology and Black Power*, p. 35; his chapter 6 in *A Black Theology of Liberation: Twentieth Anniversary Edition* (Maryknoll, N.Y.: Orbis Books, 1990); and his chapter 6 in *God of The Oppressed* (New York: HarperCollins, 1975).

11. Noting his over usage of European and Euro-American white male theologians in his previous development of black theology, Cone writes in *Spirituals and the Blues*: "I want to examine the spirituals and the blues as cultural expressions of black people, having prime significance for their community", p. 3. At issue is Cone's struggle with the following logic: politically if liberation is to arrive, then black folk must rely on their own power (an accent privileged more in his first two texts); and culturally, if black folk are to achieve full humanity, then they must delve into the depths (self-beauty appreciation) of their gorgeous black selves (culture as the right of self-identity, since God has created blackness as aesthetically appealing and sacred).

12. Review his 1977 lecture "Black Theology and the Black Church: Where Do We Go From Here?" in James H. Cone & Gayraud S. Wilmore, eds., *Black Theology: A Documentary History, Volume One: 1966–1979* (Maryknoll, N.Y.: Orbis Books, 1993), pp. 266–275.

13. See my guest editor's introductory essay and the various articles of response to Cone's *Martin & Malcolm & America* in *Union Seminary Quarterly Review*, volume 48, numbers 1–2, 1994 (a theological journal of Union Theological Seminary, New York). The essays first were presented as papers at the American Academy of Religion and both the event of the presentations and the fact of the journal attest to Cone's impact in the public arena. In the sense of David Tracy's three publics, Cone's text has impacted and received readership in the academy, in the church, and in the broader society; witness the acclamation his book received by the *New York Times*, *The New York Review of Books*, and as indicated by its sale in black, mainstream, academic, and popular bookstores. A couple of other black religious books have garnered wide acclaim; but no one has dispersed across publics a text explicitly on the sources of black theology like Cone's text.

14. Though Foucault introduces the micro-technologies of power, he is not unaware of the multiple manifestations of the dimensions of potency. He posits four technologies in total—of economics, of language, of micro realities, and of the self's ability to be pro-active and transformative. See Luther Martin, Huck Gutman, & Patrick Hutton, eds., *Technologies of the Self: A Seminar with Michel Foucault* (Amherst, MA.: University of Mass. Press, 1988), pp. 17–18.

15. For an excellent piece pondering the culture-politics dynamic, see Edward P. Antonio's chapter in Dwight N. Hopkins & Sheila Greeve Davaney, eds., *Changing Conversations: Religious Reflection and Cultural Analysis* (New York: Routledge, 1996).

Works Cited

Cone, James H. (1969). *Black Theology and Black Power*. New York: Seabury Press.

———. (1970). *A Black Theology of Liberation*. New York: Seabury Press,.

———. (1972). *Spirituals and the Blues*. New York: Seabury Press.

———. (1975). *God of the Oppressed*. New York: Seabury Press.

———. (1991). *Martin & Malcolm & America: A Dream or a Nightmare?* Maryknoll, N.Y.: Orbis Books.

Foucault, Michel. (1965). *Madness and Civilization: A History of Sanity in the Age of Reason*. New York: Vintage, 1988.

———. (1988). *The History of Sexuality: The Care of the Self, volume 3*. New York: Vintage.

———. (1990). *The History of Sexuality: The Use of Pleasure, volume 2*. New York: Vintage.

———. (1994). *The Order of Things: An Archaeology of the Human Sciences*. New York: Vintage.

———. (1994). *The Birth of the Clinic: An Archaeology of Medical Perception*. New York: Vintage.

———. (1995). *Discipline and Punish: The Birth of the Prison*. New York: Vintage.

Hopkins, Dwight N. (1993). *Shoes That Fit Our Feet: Sources for a Constructive Black Theology*. Maryknoll, N.Y.: Orbis Books.

———, and Sheila Greeve Davaney, editors. (1996). *Changing Conversations: Religious Reflection & Cultural Analysis*. New York: Routledge.

12

Interruptions
Critical Theory and Political Theology
Between Modernity and Postmodernity

Edmund Arens

W hy deal with philosophical and theological positions that are neither liberationist nor postmodern nor American in a book on liberation theologies, postmodernity, and the Americas? At least three reasons could be given to do so: first, political theology can be seen as a critical ally of liberation theology. To some extent it has not only been a European counterpart of Latin American liberation thinking but, referring to (neo)marxist theory formation and linking it to the liberative resources of biblical religion, it can be regarded as a predecessor of liberation theology. Some of the earlier political theologians maintain that its claims have made it necessary for political theology to redefine itself as and join liberation theology. Critical theory has also been a major outcome of Western marxism thoroughly critical of oppressive tendencies of modernity, and precisely for this reason has been regarded at least in some respects as one of the sources of postmodernism. Finally, both critical theory and political theology have been developed alongside and continue to engage in critical discourse with different strains of North and Latin American thinking. The effort to learn from each other can be seen for example in the ongoing conversation and confrontation between both the theology and philosophy of liberation, on the one hand, and of discourse ethics, on the other, an enterprise that is systematically relevant for the future self-understanding and orientation of both of them. This is true notwithstanding the fact that these two conceptions may differ about the issues of how to analyze and how to overcome the contradictions of modernity, or how to reach transformative praxis.

The contributions that critical theory and political theology have to offer as critical reflections of and interventions into modern society will unfold in four steps. First of all, I will address the question of which critical theory and which political theology ought to be the subject of the following investigation. Second, some of the major concerns that have characterized critical theory, despite its different phases, will be presented. In a third step, political theology as it has been elaborated in dialogue with critical theory, will be touched. Finally, I will turn to the critique of modernity and of postmodernity that both endeavors have put forward. I will try to show the reach and relevance of immanent critique that includes a proposal in view of the question of how to situate critical theory and political theology between modernity and postmodernity.

1. Which Critical Theory? Which Political Theology?

The term "critical theory", especially when used in American literature covers a whole variety of approaches including French post-structuralist thinkers like Jean-François Lyotard, Jacques Derrida and Michel Foucault, as well as the representatives of the Frankfurt School. However, when I deal with critical theory I refer to the project created by the members of the Frankfurt Institute for Social Research, generally known as the Frankfurt School (Held 1980; Benhabib 1986; Ingram 1990; Rasmussen 1995). More than a dozen scholars representing different disciplines contributed to it. These include: the philosopher and sociologist Max Horkheimer, who in 1931 became the director of the Institute for Social Research, and the philosopher, sociologist, and musicologist Theodor W. Adorno. Other members were the economist Friedrich Pollock, the psychoanalyst and social psychologist Erich Fromm, the philosopher Herbert Marcuse, the political scientist Franz Neumann, the historian of literature Leo Löwenthal, the economists Karl August Wittfogel and Franz Borkenau and the literary critic Walter Benjamin. All these people can be called the first generation of critical theory; it had been productive from the thirties to the sixties of this century. Most of their seminal works first appeared in the *Zeitschrift für Sozialforschung,* which was published from 1932 till 1941 (Schmidt 1980). A common characteristic of all the members of the first generation of the Frankfurt School was decisive for their self-understanding, theory formation, and fate. All of them were Jews. All of them had to leave their native country during the time of Fascism; most of them survived in American exile, except Walter Benjamin, who in 1940 on his flight from the Nazis committed suicide. Benjamin for the whole time of his life was forced to remain on the fringes of academic scholarship. Nevertheless, he made an important contribution to the academy and to his Jewish heritage by seeking to unite historical materialism and theology in his messianic conception of history (Wolin 1982; Handelmann 1991).

There is a second generation of critical theory as well. Its leading figure undoubtedly is Jürgen Habermas. Others who work in this tradition include: Alfred Schmidt, Albrecht Wellmer, Helmut Dubiel et al. None of them is Jewish. But just as the first generation had been engaged in an integrated critical theory of society, of the individual and of history, so are they. The theoretical endeavor of both generations could be briefly characterized by three common traits:

First of all, critical theory is critical of idealism, rejecting both the conceptions of pure reason and of pure theory; it rejects any idealistic conception and reconciliation of essence and being, or any dichotomy between theory and praxis; it is materialistic reflection upon concrete praxis and theory formation that is rooted in praxis and that has the practical intent to change the present conditions.

Second, critical theory is critical of positivism, rejecting any myth of the given, or the positivistic attitude of concentrating on what is the case; it asks for an analysis of the historical, social, political, and economic conditions that have led to the present state of affairs and it criticizes the given conditions both from a historical and a utopian perspective.

Third, critical theory is critical of capitalism. It attempts to analyze the contradictions and consequences of late capitalism from a historical-materialist point of view; it attempts to overcome capitalism by liberation and emancipation which pushes forward the project of enlightenment on a social-political level (Held 1980: 24ff).

When I speak about political theology I refer to a number of theologians—mainly German—who in the sixties started to develop this kind of theological thinking, which they called political theology. Its most prominent representatives are the reformed theologian Jürgen Moltmann, the Lutheran scholar Dorothee Sölle, and the Catholic Johann Baptist Metz. Jürgen Moltmann, who is rooted in Hegel's thought, in the early sixties discovered the marxist philosophy of hope of Ernst Bloch from which he was inspired toward his theology of hope (Moltmann 1967, 1974, 1990; Bauckham 1987; A. Rasmussen 1995). Although his approach in the course of the last decades has been elaborated in several volumes covering the whole realm of systematic theology, Ernst Bloch has remained Moltmann's outstanding conversation partner up through his recent eschatology (Moltmann 1995). Dorothee Sölle has her roots in the liberal theology of secularization from which she came to her political-theological conception by attacking the existentialist reduction of Christian faith and theology. In the meanwhile she considers herself as a liberation theologian involved in the project of a feminist liberation theology for the First World (Solle 1971, 1990a, 1990b). Johann Baptist Metz was a student of Karl Rahner, who counted as one of the founding fathers of "modern," that is Post Vatican II, Catholic theology. Metz superseded Rahner's transcendental theology and in critical conversation and dispute with him, Metz unfolded his conception of political theology, which he first worked out in his influential book *Theology of the World* and later on, with a different accent in his *Faith in History and Society* (Metz 1969, 1979).

Political theology, of course, is not only done in Germany. In North America Gregory Baum, Charles Davis, Matthew Lamb, and Rudolf Siebert, among others, are considered political theologians (Baum 1987, 1995; Davis 1980; Lamb 1982; Siebert 1985; Chopp 1986). Parallel to critical theory, political theology can be characterized by three traits: First of all, political theology is critical of idealism; it rejects any conception of theology as pure thinking, pure knowledge, as metaphysics, ontology or contemplative theory of God, Creation, Salvation etc.; instead it considers itself as rooted in concrete Christian faith praxis, and as a critical theory of such praxis.

Second, political theology is critical of positivism, neither accepting Christianity and the church as given, nor positivistically relating to some organizational or doctrinal status quo. Instead of taking resort to revelational, doctrinal, or ecclesial positivism and thus becoming a legitimating discourse of the given ecclesial reality, it critically reflects upon its own origins, functions, and possible (mis)uses. It criticizes both church and society with the practical intent to change them in the light of the Gospel in view of its eschatologically grounded and directed options for equality, justice, and salvation or liberation.

Third, it may be an exaggeration to call political theology critical of capitalism. In fact, political theology has been developed both in conversation and in dispute with Marxism; it has adopted the marxist critique of domination and its ideology critique. The aim of political theology is to analyze the church in a critical way and to reflect on its contribution to the transformation of society, that is how to turn it from an institution supporting and baptizing the status quo into an agency which in view of the subversive memory and inspiring hope of the Christian message contributes to overcoming the present unjust order.

2. Concerns of Critical Theory

The critical theory of the Frankfurt School was a collective enterprise of scholars organized around the Frankfurt Institute of Social Research. This institute, according to Max Horkheimer, should be involved in an interdisciplinary research program. It set itself the goal of developing a "theory of the historical development of the present epoch" (Horkheimer 1932, 2). As Horkheimer pointed out in his inaugural address as the director of the institute in 1931, critical theory was to examine the relationships "between the economic life of society, the psychic development of the individual, and the changes in various sectors of culture in the narrower sense" (Horkheimer 1931, 3). In other words, it intended to grasp the links between the contradictions of society and the pathologies of individuals in a way that would be in contrast to pure, contemplative "traditional theory." Instead, it would reflect upon its own origin and interest, include a critical analysis of society with the intent of changing its organizational structure and praxis.

In view of the rise of new authoritarian movements in Europe, on the one hand, the division of the working class into a social-democratic and, on the other hand, a communist movement, and finally in the face of the development of a new mass culture, critical theory arrived at its major concerns. One was to understand how

the authoritarian structures of society were converted into intrapsychic mechanisms in such a way that even "dissatisfaction and rebellion serve to strengthen the prevailing order" (Horkheimer). One helpful development was the integration of Marxist social theory along with Freud's psychoanalysis into a social-psychological approach that permitted the clarification of the hidden psychic and social structures" (Peukert 1983, 195-217; Dubiel 1985). These two conceptions for example are integrated in a paradigmatic manner in the studies on "Authority and the Family." (Horkheimer 1972)

But this interdisciplinary approach changed during the thirties. Given the destruction of the German workers' movement by Fascism, which in fact had been supported by the vast majority of the German people, given the perversion of Marxism into Stalinistic terror in the Soviet Union, and given the persecution of the Jews by Nazi Germany, ending in the "final solution," the annihilation of millions of Jews in the Nazi extermination camps, Horkheimer and Adorno were confronted with the question of "why humanity, instead of attaining a truly human condition, is sinking into a new kind of barbarism" (Horkheimer and Adorno 1971, 1). Fascism, Stalinism and the absence of revolutionary praxis forced the repesentatives of critical theory to reframe their analysis and their critique in much more radical terms. This critique was made even more pressing by experiences with the contradictions in highly industrialized American society in the United States, where most of the members of the Institute of Social Research found refuge. In the American emigration what Adorno called the "united front of monopoly and technology" (Adorno 1978, 58) became most visible. Consequently, the effects that this united front had in industrialized mass culture had to be studied.

The experiences critical theory faced can be termed historical boundary experiences. In the light of them, "what had been called reason, spirit or enlightenment in the history of the West came under the suspicion of being simply the will to self-assertion and domination, which, in the end, inevitably turned into the will to destroy others and consequently oneself" (Peukert 1983, 201). Such experiences gave rise to the thoroughly negative shape of their critique undercutting any kind of optimism in terms of a "progressive" philosophy of history, thus expelling every belief in progress. The negative shape of this second phase of critical theory is most evident in Horkheimer's and Adorno's famous book *Dialectic of Enlightenment* (Horkheimer and Adorno 1972) as well as in their additional works, such as Horkheimer's *Eclipse of Reason* and

Adorno's *Minima Moralia* up to his *Negative Dialectics* (Horkheimer 1974; Adorno 1974, 1973). From this perspective, the critique became an extensive, all-inclusive critique of ideology, domination, and deception.

According to Horkheimer and Adorno, "the notion of the human being as a person of rationality by which the whole of humanity justifies its existence is destroyed by the progress of modern industrialized society" (Horkheiemer and Adorno 1971, 183). This dialectic of enlightenment turns enlightenment itself into its opposite—deception and insanity. The most radical thesis of critical theory states that this insanity is an integral part of the very conception of rationality itself. Reason is essentially the reason of domination; domination and knowledge go hand and hand; reason and domination are one and the same.

Thus Horkheimer and Adorno's understanding of critical theory, which had started from an interdisciplinary research program oriented toward praxis, in the face of Auschwitz and the Gulags ended up in resignation and despair. They no longer saw any hope for practical change. At the end of his life Adorno recognized some kind of escape from the all-inclusive structures of domination and deception only in works of art, or aesthetic experience. And at the end of his life, the historical materialist Horkheimer turned to religion and asserted that hope could only be found in religion, thus causing a tremendous outcry in his agnostic or atheist followers. Both Adorno and Horkheimer abandoned their theoretical endeavor by taking resort either in negative aesthetics or in metaphysical pessimism.

Jürgen Habermas is the leading representative of the second generation of critical theory.[1] He can be seen as the philosopher and sociologist, who in the tradition of the Frankfurt School, has taken up and further developed its interdisciplinary research program in the most comprehensive way (McCarthy 1978; Roderick 1986; Benhabib 1986). Habermas shares the early Frankfurt School's basic concern for a critical theory of contemporary society that combines social-scientific research and philosophical reflection. Yet he also profoundly corrects critical theory. Chief among his corrections is a fundamental shift away from a paradigm oriented toward the philosophy of consciousness to a paradigm conceived within the framework of the philosophy of language. In Habermas's view Horkheimer and Adorno remain bound to the former paradigm, whereas the latter allows the development of a theory of communicative action. Habermas's theory formation is woven into a widely cast theoretical net in which, taking his orientation from the model of the reconstructive sciences, he seeks from one angle after another to elaborate a comprehensive theory of communicative action. It comprises an integrated theory of the subject and of intersubjectivity, a theory of society and of history. On the basis of his theory of communicative action, Habermas explores the dimensions in which communicative action occurs on the level of the individual subject, on the level of society, and on the level of history. As far as social theory is concerned, Habermas intends to present a theory of the foundations of the social sciences as well as a reconstruction of the fundamental constituents of society. From this, he intends to develop a critical theory of society that integrates existing marxist, functionalist, and interactionist theory components. He does so via a critical analysis of the major social-theoretical conceptions of the nineteenth and twentieth centuries: from Marx by way of Durkheim, Max Weber, George Herbert Mead, Talcott Parsons to Horkheimer and Adorno (Habermas 1984, 1987).

Habermas's theory of the subject is designed to root the formation of the subject in intersubjectivity; it contains a theory of the unfolding of the subject's cognitive competence, linguistic competence, and interactive competence. Habermas also pursues the development of a broadly anchored theory of history as a theory of social evolution by reconstructing historical materialism (Habermas 1979). His theory of history leads to a theory of modernity, in which he defends modernity as an unfinished project against its postmodern despisers. In dispute with the thinkers of postmodernity Habermas specifies the location of philosophy in the age of postmetaphysical thinking (Habermas 1987, 1992a).

One of Habermas's major concerns during the last few years has been the development of discourse ethics on the basis of which he has arrived at his discourse theory of law and of democracy. The latter two unfold the political and institutional implications and consequences of discourse ethics and integrate it into a political ethics (Habermas 1990, 1993, 1992b).

The center of Habermas's many-sided theoretical endeavour is his theory of communicative action, or a universal pragmatics, which reconstructs the basic categories and concepts of human action. Within the wider context of Habermas's work this reconstruction of basic concepts is designed to provide the conceptual tools and the normative criteria by which actual patterns of communication and action can be measured (Arens 1994). According to him, the early representatives of critical theory failed to inquire into these criteria because their concept of rationality had been essentially instrumental.

In Horkheimer and Adorno's work, Habermas notices "the impasse of a critique which in a way abandons the claim to theoretical cognition" (Habermas 1981). He overcomes this impasse by introducing a fundamental distinction into the concept of praxis and rationality, the distinction between instrumental and communicative rationality, and the distinction between instrumental and communicative action. From the latter perspective, instrumental action and rationality can be both measured and criticized.

Along this line, he distinguishes his concepts of lifeworld and system. Whereas the first is constituted and governed by communicative action, the latter is ruled by systemic mechanisms of power and money, which obey an instrumental logic. Habermas's practical interest is to uncover and to criticize what he calls the systemic colonization of the lifeworld; he wants to inspire communicative praxis and to mobilize what I would like to call communicative counter-power against that colonization (Arens 1988, 18–20).

3. Political Theology in Dialogue With Critical Theory

Within political theology there are two conceptions that have been worked out both in discourse and in dispute with the critical theory of the Frankfurt School. On the one hand, there is the political theology of Johann Baptist Metz, for whom Adorno and especially Walter Benjamin have become most inspiring and guiding. On the other hand, there is the conception of Metz's former collaborator Helmut Peukert, for whom Jürgen Habermas is the primary conversation partner. I call Metz's approach apocalyptic political theology, and name Peukert's version communicative political theology.

Every critical political theology is a post-enlightenment theory, that is to say, it is an approach that takes modernity seriously and that aims at constructing a critical reflection upon Christian faith on the conditions of the modern history of freedom and emancipation. It has been the starting point of Metz to bring the "archaic" Catholic church and its premodern neo-scholastic theology into critical contact with enlightenment and emancipation and to make use of the latter to introduce reform processes in both church and society. Metz's *Theology of the World* intended to take the secularized world seriously, and to criticize the separation of the church from "wordly" affairs. Against any post-enlightenment depolitization and privatization of Christian faith, however, he pointed out its public, political dimension. According to Metz, Christian faith in the face of the eschatological kingdom of God and in memory of Jesus had to be critical of any social-political order. The church had to become an institution of socio-critical freedom.

Whereas Metz's early political theology has been rather optimistic, relating itself mainly in a positive way to enlightenment and emancipation, in the course of the seventies he distanced himself from this conception. He began to realize a break between emancipation and redemption, stressing the non-identity of Christian faith and theology and elaborating it as a dangerous and subversive memory of Jesus' passion, death, and resurrection. In his *Faith in History and Society* Metz articulates the dialectic of enlightenment very sharply; he unveils any history of progress as the history of the winners, which he confronts with the continuing history of suffering. Following Walter Benjamin's *Theses on the Philosophy of History* (Benjamin 1969), he emphazises that religion must neither adopt nor legitimate any evolutionary conception of history and time, but must understand itself as apocalyptic interruption. "The shortest definition of religion," Metz states in his own "Untimely Theses on Apocalyptics," is "interruption" (Metz 1979, 150). That is the reason why theology should not adopt a hermeneutics of universal history but must build upon one of danger. Such a "hermeneutics of danger" (John 1991, 12–80; John 1996)[2] realizes the pathological tendencies that are inherent in modern society and becomes critical of the loss of both memory and hope, which go together with insensitivity of guilt and consumerism. Thus Metz's critique of a church having adopted a kind of "bourgeois religion" (Metz 1981) and of a society having regained interest in legitimatory religion in terms of civil religion without God has even grown sharper over the years (Metz and Peters 1991). It has become increasingly negative; being based upon subversive memory and prophetic critique including that hope that derives from God's presence within the midst of the history of suffering, it no longer aims at or works out any "progressive" utopia.

Metz's political theology in the course of its elaboration has realized the Jewishness of Christianity as essential for its survival as a messianic religion. His theology is done in view of the history of Christians' treatement of the Jews. It is a theology after Auschwitz recognizing the annihilation of millions of Jews not only as the culmination of human history of suffering but at the same time as an event that no history of salvation can pass by. After Auschwitz theology can no longer be conceived as pure, contemplative theory; it is fundamentally practical. It is critical of any universal history that must be unmasked as the history of the winners. Contrary to that, a theology pushing the history of the victims into its focus replaces the categories of metaphysical or transcendental reflection, namely reason and argumentation, with those of remembrance, narration, and solidarity. Christian faith, asserts Metz, "is a praxis in history and society, which comprehends itself as hope in solidarity for Jesus' God as the God of the living and dead, who calls all the people to be subjects in the presence of him" (Metz 1979, 70).

Metz's theology, on the one hand, is a challenging, timely, and rhetorically brilliant enterprise. It always sticks to actual social and ecclesial developments and confronts them with the Biblical message of a disturbing, intervening, interrupting God. This kind of political theology is most often done in short and sharp articulated essays. On the other hand, the question must be raised whether or not what Habermas noticed about the first generation of critical theory and its "impasse of a critique which in a way abandons the claim to theoretical cognition" may apply to Metz as well. At least some scholars maintain that Metz's conception implies "a quasi-fideistic exclusion of thinking and of giving reasons for religious contexts of communication" (Schlochtern 1978, 188).

Helmut Peukert has tried to establish and to justify political theology as a critical theological theory of communicative praxis. He does so both in discourse and in dispute with the twentieth-century philosophies of science and action and especially in discourse and dispute with the critical theory of the Frankfurt School. In his book *Science, Action and Fundamental Theology* (Peukert 1984; McCarthy 1986, 23-40) Peukert explicates the conception and status of political-theological theory as reflection upon praxis. He thus moves "toward a theology of communicative action." Passing through the discussion within the relevant philosophies of science he demonstrates that this discussion regards communicative action as the basis of scientific rationality. He points out that the questions of the philosophies of science and the theories of action converge in a theory of communicative action, as Habermas has developed it. At the same time Peukert makes clear that within Habermas's theory there is an elementary aporia. This aporia can be traced from his working out equality, reciprocity, and solidarity as the normative core of communication and interaction without being able to comprehend them as unlimited. With recourse to a famous debate between Max Horkheimer and Walter Benjamin in the thirties about the openness of history and the status of the victims of history including the possibility of solidarity with the dead (Peukert 1984, 206ff), Peukert asks, how solidarity with those who have been annihilated because of their communicative action in solidarity can be conceived. He asks:

> Can we simply exclude the question of a reality to which communicative action in solidarity is directed? Precisely at this point, does not the theory of communicative action pose the question of the reality that is the subject matter of theology, the question of a reality witnessed for the other in the face of his death by acting in solidarity with him?" (Peukert, 214)

Peukert develops his conception of a communicative political theology out of these aporias with two theses. The first is "that Judeo-Christian tradition is concerned with the reality experienced in the foundational and limit experiences of communicative action and with the modes of communicative action still possible in response to these experiences." The second thesis asserts "that a fundamental theology can and must be developed as a theory of this communicative action approaching death in anamnestic solidarity and of the reality experienced and disclosed in it" (Peukert, 215).

We can consider Peukert's approach to political theology as a critical theological theory of communicative praxis. In accordance with early critical theory it is thoroughly interdisciplinary oriented; with Benjamin it stresses the need for universal solidarity and it takes up Habermas's endeavor to reconstruct critical theory on the basis of a theory of communicative action from a theological perspective. Peukert thus laid the foundations of political theology in terms of a political-theological theory that would include a critical theological theory of the individual, of society, and of history.

Unfortunately, Peukert has not been able to pursue his theological project systematically, but indeed he has made some additional significant contributions e.g. to a critical theory of religion (Peukert

1982, 76–102) and he has unfolded the character of biblical religion and of political theology as communicative enterprises, which are directed against past and present systems of power accumulation (Peukert 1992, 43–65).

I have tried to elaborate Peukert's approach to a communicative political theology by making use of Habermas's theory of communicative action in order to explain Jesus' communicative praxis by analyzing his parables as communicative actions in which he brings up the kingdom of God, where he discloses his understanding of reality and his orientation of action in view of his addressees with whom he intends to come to an understanding (Arens 1982, 1995). From the point of view of a communicative political theology Jesus' theology proves to be political: both communicative and critical, oriented against domination and toward universal solidarity and communication. Continuing the work "toward a theology of communicative action," I have also tried to explore the basic structure of Christian faith praxis by pointing out elementary actions of faith. I consider the actions of witnessing and confessing as basic forms of faith praxis and I have tried to demonstrate their relevance and their communal, critical, and political impact (Arens 1989, 1994a). Christian communicative praxis from my perspective is basically Christopraxis including the praxis of solidarity, of suffering, and of both prophetic denounciation of evil and annunciation of new life and comprehensive communication, or the domination free dominion of God.

Arguing with Habermas's theory of communicative rationality and his understanding of religion, I have tried to show that Habermas's theory is both a challenge to political theology and at the same time has to be challenged by political theology because of its merely functionalist understanding of religion, and its evolutionist conception of history that both gives up the categories of memory and of utopia, of anamnestic solidarity and of radical hope (Arens 1991, 145–200).

The encounter, dialogue, and dispute between critical theory and political theology is still underway. In the course of the last few years, Habermas published two important essays, which for the first time take up the challenge of theology and respond to it in public. One deals with Peukert's critique; it is called "Transcendence from Within, Transcendence in this World" (Habermas 1992c, 226–259). The other was given as an address on the occasion of Metz's retirement from his chair at the University of Münster. The title is: "Israel und Athen oder: Wem gehört die anamnetische Vernunft?"(Habermas 1994, 51–64)[3] Both essays defend the postmetaphysical concept of communicative reason; both show at the same time that Habermas more and more realizes that biblical religion bears and preserves resources that communicative reason must not neglect, although it has to transform them by means of philosophical thinking. If he thus admits the lasting relevance of religion, he nevertheless is still far away from the insight of early critical theory, an insight that Adorno expressed in a letter to Benjamin. In this letter he wrote that "a restoration of theology, or better a radicalization of the dialectic into the very glowing core of theology would at the same time have to mean an utmost intensification of the social-dialectical, indeed economic, motifs."[4]

4. Critique of Modernity and of Postmodernity

Critical theory in any of its stages has been profoundly critical of modernity. The early Frankfurt School, above all Horkheimer and Adorno, saw modernity as the accomplished reign of instrumental reason having demonstrated its destructive potential and power on a horrible scale culminating in Auschwitz. Their critique of modern enlightened reason that was perverted into domination implies at the same time a thorough critique of "remorseless progress" (Horkheimer and Adorno 1971, 183) leading from the subjugation of nature to that of human beings. The latter is performed in the social oppression of the class-society of modern capitalism, even if this domination hides behind the reduction of people to agents and promoters of the exchange of commodities.

The elementary critique of modernity as domination in view of which only art or aesthetics may offer a realm of "reconciliation" has made some postmodernists think of the critical theorists as their allies or precursors. Lyotard for example remarks that reading Adorno today "one perceives how much in his own thinking he anticipated that of postmodernity, although he often had reservations against it if he not rejected it" (Lyotard 1985, 87), namely for political reasons as Lyotard thinks. Wolfgang Welsch and Albrecht Wellmer too bring Adorno close to Lyotard, while Welsch admits: "Adorno dreams of redemption and by doing so he remains modern" (Welsch 1991, 179; Wellmer 1985, 58ff). And Tomoko Masuzawa calls Benjamin "a postmodern theorist avant la lettre" (Masuzawa 1993, 16; Welsch 1991, 179).

But, in fact, it is questionable whether Adorno and Horkheimer or Benjamin ever imagined or advocated any possibility to transgress modernity in a postmodern way. The former two forbade any "post"-thinking, which according to them would not have escaped the grip of identity thinking, even if it proclaimed to be most open toward diversity, otherness, or pluralism. Indeed, they proposed to stick to immanent negative critique regardless of how desperate it turned out. In the midst of negativity they dialectically deciphered a moment that postmodernist will count as a residue of modern "grand récits": the idea—which is indeed to be differentiated from a "dream" (Welsch)—of ultimate "redemption." As Adorno puts it in the final paragraph of *Minima Moralia*: "The only philosophy which can be responsibly practiced in the face of despair is the attempt to contemplate all things as they would present themselves from the standpoint of redemption" (Adorno 1978, 247; Zamora 1995).

Habermas, for his part, is an articulate critic of postmodernity and an eloquent defender of the project of modernity, which he regards as both unexhausted and unfinished. At the same time he critizes the modernity in which he recognizes a one-sided, partial, and fragmented establishment of modern rationalization. He forcefully uncovers the capitalistic modernization of society as leading to the systemic colonization of the lifeworld by the systems of power and money. To be sure, he rejects those (neo)conservative approaches that buy into capitalistic modernization but want to avoid its devastating consequences for the lifeworld. Insofar as from his point of view postmodern thinking is part of a project aimed at getting beyond cultural modernity by getting rid of the modern differentiation of rationality he detects it as conservative. Over against the postmodern, he sees a "young conservative" or "neoconservative" (Habermas 1990a) turn or return to aesthetics and partly at least to religion or religiosity. Habermas maintains that the enlargement and institutional strengthening of communicative rationality by means of discursive processes and structures is the cornerstone of the culturally productive continuation and amelioration of modernity. Whether or not religion can play an effective part in this continuation remains to be seen; this question could be dealt with in a critical theory of religion, which in fact is a project that Habermas will have to address. To be sure, he more and more comes to acknowledge the semantic resources of religion, but he still neglects its prophetic and public-political potential. (Habermas 1992, 1994; Siebert 1985; Hewitt 1995; Cassanova 1994)

One contribution Judaeo-Christian tradition has to offer to a critical self-reflection may be the insistence on the anamnestic constitution of reason and on anamnestic solidarity. (Metz 1989, 733–739; Peukert 1992) This indeed sheds light on the victims of history and makes clear that modernity has not at all put an end to victimization but, on the contrary, has enlarged both the numbers and the quality of victimization. By claiming universal justice, universal solidarity, and the recognition of the others as others (Arens 1995a), political theology "in the face of and at the end of modernity" (Metz 1984, 14–18) affirms that the universality that the enlightenment had in view must not be abandoned but that it must be adequately brought up, namely as precisely the taking into account of the universality of suffering that has to be addressed, denounced, and overcome.

Metz's political theology not only strongly critiques modernity and particularly modern science and humanities which, according to him, have both effectively abolished not only God but the human subject as well. The terminology of this apocalyptical political theology referring to narration, interruption, polycentrism, and otherness looks close to postmodern concepts, and Metz's essayistic style sometimes sounds rather postmodernist. Nevertheless, Metz is an energetic critic of the postmodern farewell to the subject; he denounces the postmodernist "cultural carnival" that does not counteract the "normative deafness of our lifeworld" (Metz 1994a, 91); and for theological reasons he rejects its aesthetic return to religion or religiosity, which he confronts with the challenging and promising God of the Bible. His political theology, however apocalyptical and interruptive it may be, is to be understood as an immanent critique of modernity that aims at rescuing the endangered or even abolished subject, which sticks to biblical monotheism and repudiates the postmodernist praise of polytheism or better "polymythism" (Metz 1990, 170–186), which appeals to the passionate practical following of Christ instead of taking resort to aesthetizised religious myths and practices, and finally a theology that underlines the universality of suffering, of remembrance, and of hope in a future for all.

Peukert, in turn, also pleads for a critical and self-critical continuation of the project of modernity. For him, both modernity and theology are endangered by the continuously expanding mechanisms of power accumulation. By making critical use of communicative and religious ressources those mechanisms have to be unmasked and resisted. A central cultural task for Peukert lies in the development of a communicative world of action and interaction. From his perspective, a theory of modernity

> notwithstanding its "deconstructive" orientations has the task to contribute in a constructive way toward the development of a new form of a democratic "constitution" of modern societies. For that purpose, scientific, political, and moral processes of learning have to be made permanent and revisable in their form. Such a "reflective constitutionalism" oriented at transformative praxis would become the core of a theory of democracy. At the same time it could be a new place of dialogue among philosophy, theory of society and theology. (Peukert 1992a, 465–471; Tilley 1995, 5–16)

Political theology on the whole takes the path of immanent critique, correction, and transformation of modernity while recognizing the potentials of modernity as ambivalent, both dominative-destructive and communicative-liberative. The reach of this kind of immanent critique is however controversial. Whether modernity has the critical, self-corrective, and liberative potentials or forces within itself or whether it has to be transgressed if not into post-modernity maybe into what Enrique Dussel calls "transmodernity" (Dussel 1994, 1996) remains a disputed question between political and liberation theology.

Nevertheless, political theology is an enriching and challenging partner of conversation for liberation thinking. Both are able to and should learn from each other. In view of the present decline of socialism in which alternatives to capitalistic modernization seem to have vanished, in view of the accelerating globalization of capitalism and its refined structures of dominative, exploitative, and unjust exchange based primarily on the access to technological means of communication, in view of the erosion of civil democratic societies by excessive individualism and consumerism, and with regard to a highly problematic appeal to either aestheticized or—in the case of fundamentalism—to reified religion, political theology relating itself to and keeping in dialogue with critical theory remains a relevant theological enterprise. It is important because it reflects on and tries to reach for a praxis of resistance to dehumanizing structures of power and domination, because it underlines remembrance and solidarity with the victims, and the longing for justice for all, which indeed are constitutive biblical, theological, and Christian claims because it is directed at transformative action in which a communicative and a liberative orientation are dialectically related to each other and may even coincide.

Notes

1. That Habermas can be counted among the critical theorists at all is however fiercely contradicted by some orthodox adherents of Horkheimer and Adorno; cf. G. Bolte (ed.), *Unkritische Theorie. Gegen Habermas* (Lüneburg: Dietrich zu Klampen Verlag 1989).
2. The term has been introduced by Metz's former student O. John.
3. An English translation of Habermas' article is contained in this volume.
4. Letter, Th. W. Adorno to W. Benjamin, August 2, 1935, quoted from S. Buck-Morss, *The Origin of Negative Dialectics* (New York: Free Press 1977) p. 117.

References

Adorno, Th.W. 1951; 1978. *Minima Moralia*. Frankfurt: Suhrkamp.

———. 1973. *Negative Dialectics*, trans. E. B. Ashton. New York: Seabury Press.

———. 1974. *Minima Moralia*, trans. E. Jephcott. London: New Left Books.

Arens, E. 1982. *Kommunikative Handlungen. Die paradigmatische Bedeutung der Gleichnisse Jesu fur eine Handlungstheorie*. Dusseldorf: Patmos.

———. 1988. "Communication as counter-power in the struggle for democracy." *Media Development* 35, no. 1: 18–20.

———. 1989. *Bezeugen und Bekennen. Elementare Handlungen des Glaubens*. Dusseldorf: Patmos.

———. 1991. "Kommunikative Rationalitat und Religion. Die Theorie des kommunikativen Handelns als Herausforderung politischer Theologie." In *Erinnerung, Befreiung, Solidaritat. Benjamin, Marcuse, Habermas und die politishce Theologie*. E. Arens, O. John, and P. Rottlander, eds. Dusseldorf: Patmos.

———. ed. 1994a. *Gottersrede—Glaubenspraxis. Perspektiven theologischer Handlungstheorie*. Darmstadt: Wissenschaftliche Buchgesellschaft.

———. 1994. *The Logic of Pragmatic Thinking: From Peirce to Habermas*. Atlantic Highlands, NJ: Humanities Press.

———. 1995. *Christopraxis: A Theology of Action*, trans. J. Hoffmeyer. Minneapolis, NM: Fortress Press.

———. ed. 1995a. *Anerkennung der Anderen. Eine theologische Grunddimension interkultureller Kommunikation*. Freiburg: Herder.

Bauckham, R. 1987. *Moltmann: Messianic Theology in the Making*. Basingstoke.

Baum, G. 1987. *Theology and Society*. Mahwah, NJ: Paulist Press.

———. 1995. *Essays in Critical Theology*. Kansas City, Kansas: Sheed and Ward.

Benhabib, S. 1986. *Critique, Norm, and Utopia: A Study of the Foundations of Critical Theory*. New York: Columbia University Press.

Benjamin, W. 1969. "Theses on the Philosophy of History." In *Illuminations*, ed. and intro. H. Arendt, trans. H. Zohn. New York: Schocken.

Bolte, G. ed. 1989. *Unkritische Theorie. Gegen Habermas*. Luneburg: Dietrich zu Klampen Verlag.

Buck-Morss, S. 1977. *The Origin of Negative Dialectics*. New York: Free Press.

Casanova, J. 1994. *Public Religions in the Modern World*. Chicago: University of Chicago Press.

Chopp, R. 1986. *The Praxis of Suffering: An Interpretation of Liberation and Political Theologies*. Maryknoll, NY: Orbis Books.

Davis, C. 1980. *Theology and Political Society*. Cambridge: Cambridge University Press.

Dubiel, H. 1985. *Theory and Politics: Studies in the Development of Critical Theory*, trans. B. Gregg. Cambridge, MA: MIT Press.

Dussel, E. 1994. *El Encubrimiento del Otro: Hacia el origen del mito de la modernidad*. Mexico: Editorial Cambio XXI.

———. 1996. *The Underside of Modernity*, trans. and ed. E. Mendieta. Atlantic Highlands, NJ: Humanities Press.

Habermas, J. 1979. *Communication and the Evolution of Society*, trans. T. McCarthy. Boston: Beacon Press.

———. 1981. *Theorie des kommunikativen Handelns*. Frankfurt: Suhrkamp.

———. 1984/87. *Theory of Communicative Action*, 2 Vols., trans. T. McCarthy. Cambridge, MA: MIT Press.

———. 1987. *The Philosophical Discourse of Modernity*, trans. F. Lawrence. Cambridge, MA: MIT Press.

———. 1990. *Moral Consciousness and Communicative Action*, trans. C. Lenhardt and W. S. Nicholson. Cambridge, MA: MIT Press.

———. 1990a. "Modernity: An Unfinished Project." In *Critical Theory: The Essential Readings*. New York: Paragon House.

———. 1992a. *Postmetaphysical Thinking*, trans. W. M. Hohengarten. Cambridge, MA.

———. 1992b. *Faktizitat und Geltung*. Frankfurt: Suhrkamp.

———. 1992c. "Transcendence from Within, Transcendence in this World." In *Habermas, Modernity, and Public Theology*. D. S. Browning and F. Schussler Fiorenza, eds. New York: Crossroad.

———. 1993. *Justification and Application: Remarks on Discourse Ethics*, trans. C. Cronin. Cambridge, MA: MIT Press.

———. 1994. "Israel und Athen oder: Wem gehort die anamnetische Vernunft?" In *Diagnosen zur Zeit*. J. B. Metz et al., eds. Dusseldorf: Patmos.

Handelmann, S. A. 1991. *Fragments of Redemption: Jewish Thought and Literary Theory in Benjamin, Scholem, and Levinas*. Bloomington, IN: Indiana University Press.

Held, D. 1980. *Introduction to Critical Theory: Horkheimer to Habermas*. London: Hutchinson.

Hewitt, M. A. 1995. *Critical Theory of Religion: A Feminist Analysis*. Minneapolis, MN: Fortress Press.

Horkheimer, M. 1931. "Die gegenwartige Lage der Sozialphilosophie und die

Aufgabe eines Instituts fur Sozialforschung." *Frankfurter Universitats-reden* XXXVII, Frankfurt, 3.

———. 1932. "Vorwort." *Zeitschrift fur Sozialforschung* 1: 2.

———. 1972. "Authority and the Family." In *Critical Theory*. M. Horkheimer, ed. New York: Herder and Herder; first published 1936.

———. 1974. *Eclipse of Reason*. New York: Seabury Press.

_____ and Th.W. Adorno. 1971. *Dialektik der Aufklarung*. Frankfurt: S. Fischer.

——— and Th.W. Adorno. 1972. *Dialectic of Enlightenment*, trans. J. Cumming. New York: Herder and Herder; first published 1947.

Ingram, D. 1990. *Critical Theory and Philosophy*. New York: Paragon House.

John, O. 1991. "Fortschrittskritik und Erinnerung. Walter Benjamin, ein Zeuge der Gefahr." In *Erinnerung, Befreiung, Solidaritat. Benjamin, Marcuse, Habermas und die politische Theologie*. E. Arens, O. John, and P. Rottlander, eds. Dusseldorf: Patmos.

———. 1996. "*. . .Und dieser Feind hat zu siegen nicht aufgehort.*" *Die Bedeutung Walter Benjamins fur eine Theologie nach Auschwitz*. Munster and Hamburg: LIT Verlag.

Lamb, M. L. 1982. *Solidarity with Victims*. New York: Crossroad.

Lyotard, J. F. 1985. "Rasche Bemerkung zur Frage der Postmoderne." In *Grabmal des Intellektuellen*. P. Engelmann, ed. Graz and Wien: Bohlau.

Masuzawa, T. 1993. *In Search of Dreamtime: The Quest for the Origin of Religion*. Chicago: University of Chicago Press.

Metz, J. B. 1969. *Theology of the World*, trans. W. Glen-Doepel. New York: Herder and Herder.

_____. 1979. *Faith in History and Society: Toward a Practical Fundamental Theology*, trans. D. Smith. New York: Crossroad.

———. 1981. *The Emergent Church: The Future of Christianity in a Post-Bourgeois World*, trans. P. Mann. London: SCM Press.

———. 1984. "Theologie im Angesicht und vor dem Ende der Moderne." In *Concilium* 20:14–18.

———. 1989. "Anamnetische Vernunft." In *Zwischenbetrachtungen im Prozeb der Aufklarung*. A. Honneth et al., eds. Frankfurt: Suhrkamp.

———. 1990. "Theologie versus Polymythie. Kleine Apologie des biblischen Monotheismus." In *Einheit und Vielheit*. O. Marquard, ed. Hamburg: Meiner.

———. 1994a. "Gotteskrise. Versuch zur 'geistigen Situation der Zeit'." In *Diagnosen zur Zeit*. Metz et al. Dusseldorf: Patmos.

——— and T. R. Peters. 1991. *Gottespassion*. Freiburg: Herder.

——— et al., 1994. *Diagnosen zur Zeit*. Dusseldorf: Patmos.

McCarthy, T. 1978. *The Critical Theory of Jurgen Habermas*. Cambridge, MA: MIT Press.

———. 1986. "Philosophical Foundations of Critical Theory: Kant, Peukert, and the Frankfurt School." In *Civil Religion and Political Theology*. L. S. Rouner, ed. Notre Dame, IN: University of Notre Dame Press.

Moltmann, J. 1967. *Theology of Hope*, trans. J.W. Leitch. London: SCM Press.

———. 1974. *The Crucified God*, trans. R. A. Wilson and J. Bowden. London: SCM Press.

———. 1990. *The Way of Jesus Christ*, trans. M. Kohl. London: SCM Press.

————. 1995. *Das Kommen Gottes. Christliche Eschatologie*. Guterloh: Kaiser/ Gutersloher Verlagshaus.

Peukert, H. 1982. "Kontingenzerfahrung und Identitatsfindung. Bemerk-ungen Zu einer Theorie der Religion und zur Analytik religios dimension-ierter Lernprozesse." In *Erfahrung, Glaube und Moral*. J. Blank and G. Hasenhuttl, eds. Dusseldorf: Patmos.

————. 1983. "Kritische Theorie und Padagogik." *Zeitschrift fur Padagogik*, 30: 195–217.

————. 1984. *Science, Action, and Fundamental Theology: Toward a Theology of Communicative Action*, trans. J. Bohman. Cambridge, MA: MIT Press.

————. 1992. "Enlightenment and Theology as Unfinished Projects." In *Habermas, Modernity, and Public Theology*. D. S. Browning and F. Schuss-ler Fiorenza, eds. New York: Crossroad.

————. 1992a. "Philosophische Kritik der Moderne." In *Concilium* 28. C. Geffre and J. P. Jossua, eds.

Rasmussen, A. 1995. *The Church as Polis: From Political Theology to Theolog-ical Politics as Exemplified by Jurgen Moltmann and Stanley Hauerwas*. Notre Dame, IN: University of Notre Dame Press.

Rasmussen, D., ed. 1995. *The Handbook of Critical Theory*. Cambridge, MA.: Blackwell.

Roderick, R. 1986. *Habermas and the Foundations of Critical Theory*. London: Macmillan.

Schlochtern, J. Meyer zu. 1978. *Sprache—Glaube—Erfahrung*. Frankfurt, Bern, Las Vegas: Peter Lang.

Schmidt, A., ed. 1980. *Zeitschrift fur Sozialforschung* 9 vols. Munich: Deutscher Taschenbuchverlag.

Siebert, R. J. 1985. *The Critical Theory of Religion: The Frankfurt School*. Berlin/New York/Amsterdam: Peter Lang.

Solle, D. 1971. *Political Theology*. Philadelphia, PA: Fortress Press.

————. 1990a. *Thinking About God*. Philadelphia, PA: Fortress Press.

————. 1990b. *The Window of Vulnerability: A Political Spirituality*, trans. L. M. Maloney. Minneapolis, MN: Fortress.

Tilley, T. W. 1995. *Postmodern Theologies. The Challenge of Religious Diver-sity*. Maryknoll, NY: Orbis Books.

Wellmer, A. 1985. *Zur Dialektik von Moderne und Postmoderne. Vernunftkritik nach Adorno*. Frankfurt: Suhrkamp.

Welsch, W. 1991. *Unsere postmoderne Moderne*. Weinheim: VCH Verlags-gesellschaft.

Wolin, R. 1982. *Walter Benjamin: An Aesthetic of Redempion*. New York: Columbia University Press.

Zamora, J. A. 1995. *Krise—Kritik—Erinnerung. Ein politisch-theologischer Versuch uber das Denken Adornos im Horizont der Krise der Moderne*. Munster and Hamburg: LIT Verlag.

13

Israel and Athens, or to Whom Does Anamnestic Reason Belong?
On Unity in Multicultural Diversity

Jürgen Habermas

Johann Baptist Metz's way of thinking fascinates me because, overlooking certain distances, I recognize our common intentions. The fact that someone who, from a philosophical perspective adopts the position of methodical atheism asks the same questions as the theologians is even less astonishing than the parallelism of the answers. In attempting to clarify these parallelisms, I would like to demonstrate my gratitude to the contemporary theologian.

Metz once illustrated with his own life history the factum of the contemporaneity of the non-contemporaneous [*Gleichzeitigkeit des Ungleichzeitigen*], which confronts us today in the multicultural kaleidoscope of a de-centered global society:

> I come from a small Bavarian city profoundly catholic. Coming from there, one comes from very far. It is not as if one had been born fifty years ago (or sixty five), but in some point at the margins of the dawn of the middle ages. It took me a great effort to discover things that others, that "society," as it seems, had long ago already discovered [...] : democracy in everyday politics, for instance, the dealings with a diffused public sphere, rules of game of conflict even in the family life, etc. Much appeared strange and, in reality, it always continued being strange. (Metz 1981, 13)

Against the background of these experiences, Metz has opposed a defensive position of the pre-modern Catholic church and has advocated a productive participation in the processes of the bourgeois and post-bourgeois enlightenment. The biblical vision of salvation includes not only the redemption from individual guilt but the collective liberation from situations of misery and oppression as well (which, therefore, together with the mystical element, also contains a political element). The eschatological march towards salvation of those who suffer unjustly enters into contact with the impulses of the history of freedom in the European modernity.

In the same way, the consequences of the insensibility before the emancipatory potential of this history are as grave as the blindness before the dialectic of the Enlightenment. The barbaric reversal of its own mirror remained hidden for too long to the Enlightenment; under the light of its universalistic pretensions it deceived itself about the particularistic nucleus of its Western origins. This inveterate rationalism has become the silent violence of a capitalistic civilization of global reach that assimilates alien cultures, forgetting its own traditions. Christianity, which believed it could use this civilization as an "innocent catalyst for the universal propagation of its hope," and the church, which believed it could send its missionaries following the footsteps of the European colonizers, uwillingly participated in this dialectic of disenchantment and loss of memory. This explains the diagnosis that Metz presents of theology and the practical demand with which he confronts his church.

The diagnostic says: through the philosophical reason of Greek origin, a Hellenized Christianity has become so distanced from its own origin in the spirit of Israel that theology has become insensitive before the cry of suffering and before the demand for universal justice (Metz 1981 and Kuschel 1990, 23 ff.). The demand is that: the eurocentric church that emerged from the soil of Hellenism must overcome its mono-cultural self-understanding and, taking into account its original Judaic context, develop itself into a culturally polycentric universal church (Metz 1981).

Israel vs. Athens

Metz does not tire of claiming for Christianity the inheritance of Israel. With the provocative formulation that "Jesus was not a Christian, but a Jew," Metz not only opposed Christian anti-semitism, but also called to account the *ecclesia triumphans* for its victorious, profoundly questionable, attitude before a shut down and humiliated synagogue. This formulation opposes above all the apathy of a theology that appears not to have been affected by Auschwitz (Kuschel 1990 and Metz 1981). This critique obeys a practical-existential impulse. But it also means that a Hellenized Christianity, when rejecting its Judaic origin, has separated itself from the source of anamnestic reason and has become the expression of an erratic and idealistic reason, incapacitated for memory and historical remembrance. Understanding Christianity in an "Augustinian" fashion as a synthesis of reason and faith—reason deriving from Athens and faith from Israel—sunders in two the spirit of Christianity (Metz 1991, 189). Against the division of labor between philosophical reason and religious faith, Metz insists on the rational content of the tradition of Israel; he conceives of the force of historical remembrance as an element of reason: "This anamnestic reason resists forgetting, even the forgetting of the forgetting that nests in every simple historization of the past" (Metz 1992, 24). From this point of view the philosophy with Greek roots appears as the administrator of Ratio, of the forces of understanding that is made to reason only through the linkage with the memory that remits us to Moses and his promise. In this sense, a theology that, departing from its Hellenistic alienation by returning to its own origins has, before philosophy, the last word: "[this theology] appeals to the indissoluble nexus between Ratio and Memoria (expressed in late modern terms: to the grounding of communicative reason in anamnestic reason)" (Metz 1992, 24).

If we contemplate this pronouncement in a philosophical counter-light, it is more than the relation of grounding that suggests contradictions. The sketch of a philosophical tradition that is not exhausted in Platonism, but which in the course of history has appropriated the Judeo-Christian tradition and, through the inheritance of Israel, been shaken to the depths of its Greek roots, also appears too superficial. Philosophical idealism from Saint Augustine to Hegel, going through Saint Aquinas, has produced a synthesis in which the God who confronts Job has been transformed into the God of the philosophers. But the history of philosophy is not only the history of Platonism, but also of the protest against it. We can conceive of these protests, whether they appeared under the sign of nominalism or empiricism, of individualism or existentialism, of negativism or historical materialism, as attempts to rescue the semantic potential of the salvific thought in the universe of the grounding speech. With this potential, practical intuitions that in themselves are foreign to ontological thought and to the transformations undergone at the hands of the theory of knowledge and the philosophy of language have penetrated philosophy.

Metz gathers these non-Greek themes in the *one* focus of the act of remembrance (*Eingedenkens*). He understands the force of remembrance in Freud's sense, as the analytic force of the "making conscious," and in Benjamin's sense, as the mystical force of a retroactive reconciliation. Remembrance saves from ruin that which we do not want to lose and that, nevertheless, finds itself in the greatest of dangers. This religious concept of "salvation" undoubtedly exceeds the horizon of that which philosophy can make plausible under the conditions of post-metaphysical thinking. But departing from the concept of salvific remembrance, opens the field of experiences and religious motives that made themselves heard long before the doors of philosophical idealism opened, until they were finally taken seriously and, from within, planted uncertainty in a reason directed in principle only to the cosmos. But not everything remained in disquiet. In the course of an evolution that leads from the intellectual contemplation of the cosmos to a linguistically incarnated reason, passing through the self-reflexivity of a knowing subject, the Greek Logos has been transformed. Today, it no longer centers only on the cognitive relation with the world—on beings as beings, on the knowing of knowing, or on the meaning of sentences that can be true or false. What has also unfolded within philosophy, making possible that argumentative reason be receptive to the practical experiences of historically existing yet threatened identities of beings, is the idea of an alliance of the people of God and of a justice that is imposed on a history of suffering. It is the idea of an alliance that links freedom and solidarity in the horizon of an undamaged intersubjectivity.

Without this filtering of genuinely Jewish and Christian ideas into Greek metaphysics, we could not have constituted the modern network of concepts that converge in a concept of reason that is simultaneously communicative and historically situated. I mean the concept of subjective freedom and the demand for equal respect for all, including and precisely for the foreign in its particularity and difference. I mean the concept of autonomy, of a self-constraint of the will by virtue of a moral reasoning that is contingent on relations of reciprocal acknowledgement. I mean the concept of a socialized subject that is individualized in the course of its life and that as an unsubstitutible individual is at the same time member of a community, who can only carry out an authentic life in solidarity with others. I mean the concept of liberation, as much in the sense of emancipation from denigrating conditions as in the sense of an utopian project of a fulfilling life-form. The irruption of historical thinking into philosophy has finally encouraged the understanding of the "deferred" character of vital time; it has made us aware of the narrative structure of the history in which we find ourselves involved and of the contingent character of all that happens to us. To that also belongs the awareness of the fallibility of the human mind and the contingency of the condition under which it continues to still maintain unconditional claims.

The tension between the spirit of Athens and the inheritance of Israel has had profound consequence in philosophy as well as in theology. But if philosophical thinking is not resolved simply in the synthetic labour of the idealism that led to the paleochristianity of the West—conceived ecclessiatically—to be thought in theological terms, then the critique of Hellenized Christianity can not direct itself against argumentative reason "per se," nor against the impersonal reason of the philosophers as such. Anamnesis and narrative can also offer reasons and insofar give impulse to the philosophical discourse, although they do not decide its march. Although profane reason remains skeptical before the mystical causality of an act of remembrance inspired in salvific terms and does not offer any credence to the mere promise of restitution, it is not necessary that philosophers leave only to the hands of theologians that which Metz calls "anamnestic reason." I would like to clarify this by referring to two questions that for Metz are of special interest in theological terms or for ecclesiastical politics.

The Problem of Theodicy

The question of the salvation of those who suffer unjustly is perhaps the most important in maintaining the discourse about God. Metz rebels decidedly against a Platonizing weakening of this question which, after Auschwitz, formulates itself to Christians with greater radicalness than ever (Metz 1984, 382–389). It was once again the means of reflection of the Greek tradition that distinguished between a redemptive God and a creator God of the Old Testament, who was thus exonerated from the responsibility for the barbarities of a sinful humanity. God himself could not be implicated in his creation "stricken with suffering." Against this idealistic mitigation of suffering, Metz evokes a "culture of the regret [*Kultur des Vermissens*]," a culture of remembrance that keeps alive, without a false need of consolation, the existential restlessness proper to the vehement interpellation to God, stimulating with that an eschatologically fueled hope in a future that, although in stasis, almost reaches reality (Metz 1992, 15–34). According to the Nietzchean doctrine of the eternal return, the biblical hope in the future cannot founder in the element of an eternity understood in Greek terms (Theunissen 1991, 368).

Even for this protest, which reaches to the farthest depths of religious experience, there is a parallelism in that subterranean current of the philosophical thinking that, before the Neoplatonic attempt to establish a gradation between the good and the true, insists on the positivity and in the unique sense of the negative. Just as it occurs with theology, which leads to its extreme ends in eschatology, the philosophical tradition—from Jakob Böhme through Baader, Schelling, and Hegel to Bloch and Adorno—hopes to transform the experience of negativity of the existing into the propelling dialectical force of a reflection that must break with the dominion of the past over the future. Since philosophy does not depart from the premise of a God that is omnipotent and just, it becomes clear that it cannot redeem a "culture of regret"—or a sense for all that has been pillaged or has been the object of dispossession—basing itself in the question of theodicy. In any event, today philosophy has less to do with the idealist glorification of a reality in need of redemption than with the indifference before a world reduced empiristically to a figure without contours and totally deaf to the normative.

The fronts have inverted. Today's historicism is an empiricism of a second level that denies seriousness to the validity claim of universalist character that stands behind every affirmation and negation of the subject who takes a position, a validity claim that although is always held "here and now," in a local context, overflows all merely provincial criteria. If a paradigm or a world view has the same value as the next, if different discourses codify in their own way everything that can be true or false, good or bad, then the normative dimension that allows us to identify the characteristics of a human life damaged, adulterated, and without dignity, and thus to experience it as a privation, is liquidated. For this reason, before the historicist forgetfulness of forgetfulness itself, philosophy also takes recourse to the force of anamnesis. But now it is argumentative reason itself, which, in the deepest layers of its pragmatic presuppositions, discloses the conditions for the appellation of an unconditional sense and, with that, maintains open the dimension of the validity claims that transcend the social spaces and historical time. In this fashion it opens a rift in the normality of a inner worldly happening that lacks all promissory characteristics—a normativity that in another way would remain sealed shut before any experience of *absence* of solidarity and justice. Evidently, this philosophy, which incorporates the idea of the alliance in the concept of a communicative reason historically situated, cannot offer any firm hope; it finds itself under the sign of a transcendence from within and must content itself with the grounded exhortation to a skeptical resistance, not defeatist, but rather, "against the idols and demons of a world that scorns the human being."

That the relationship between philosophy and theology once again varies in terms of an ecclessiatical politics and history concerns Metz the most. Here philosophy not only tries, as in the question of theodicy, to appropriate the semantic potentials that have been preserved in the religious tradition, but can aid a theology that must clarify the self-understanding of Christianity and the church with respect to the pluralism of cultures and world views (Metz 1984, 14 ff.).

The Universal Polycentric Church

Since Vatican II, the church finds itself faced with the double task of: internally, opening itself to the multiplicity of cultures in which Christian Catholism has taken root; and, externally, searching for a dialogue with the religions of non-Christian origins that does not evade the confrontation or persist with a defensive apologetic. The same problem is formulated in both directions: how to maintain the identity of the Christian church in the cultural multiplicity of its voices? And, how can the Christian doctrine maintain the authenticity of its quest for truth in the discursive dispute with competing world views? Metz offers suggestive answers. The church, which reflects on the limits of its Eurocentric history in order to harmonize the Christian doctrine with the original hermeneutical situation of non-Western cultures, cannot depart from the "idea of an ahistorical Christianity, situated above cultures and ethnically innocent," instead it ought to have in mind as much the history of its theological origins as its institutional complicity with the history of European colonialism. A Christianity, which in a dialogue with other religions, adopts a reflexive position with respect to its own truth claim cannot be satisfied with a "pluralism without mutual relationships or merely condescending"; rather it must abide firmly, without monopolizing and renouncing every means of power, by the universal validity of its offer of salvation (Metz 1987, 93–115).

With that the polycentric church appears to adopt almost an exemplary function for the political coming to terms with multiculturalism. In its internal relations it appears a commendable model for a democratic state of law that wishes to do justice to the different forms of life of a multicultural society; and in its external relationships a church of this type could be taken as a model for a community of peoples that regulate its international relations on the basis of reciprocal acknowledgement. However, looked at closely, matters work in reverse. It is the idea of the polycentric church that, in turn, feeds on the convictions of an European enlightenment and its political philosophy.

Metz himself refers affirmatively to the bequest of a rational, enlightened, natural law illustrated in hermeneutical terms beyond its eurocentric limits. Europe is the:

> political and cultural home of a universalism which in essence is strictly anti-eurocentric. . . . Certainly, the universalism of the Enlightenment, with its quest after freedom and justice, was only universal in the semantic sense at the beginning and, its concrete process of execution, has remained particularist even to this day. However, it established a new political and hermeneutical culture that aims at the acknowledgement of the inherent freedom of the subject and the dignity of all human beings. This universalism of human rights, developed in the European traditions, cannot renounce to cultural alterity. Through it is assured that cultural pluralism does not simply disintegrate into vague relativism and that the postulated culture of sensibility maintains its capacity to be true. (Metz 1992)

Christianity can not expect for its conceptions of the history of salvation and of the order of creation—impregnated with ethical contents—an universal acknowledgement *in the same sense* that a procedural theory of law and morality does with respect to human rights and the principles of the state of the rule of law that it purports to ground, basing itself on the concept of procedural justice (Rawls 1971 and Habermas 1992). For this reason Metz himself understands the universality of the offer of salvation as an "invitation" directed to everyone and not as that universal claim of rational acceptability with which, for instance, rational natural law is presented. Even the polycentric universal church remains, in modern societies, *one* community of interpretation among many, where each one articulates its own conception of salvation, and its own idea of an accomplished life, and that debate among themselves on the interpretation of justice, solidarity, and liberation from misery and humiliation. The church must internalize this external point of view and appropriate it as a view directed at itself. To this end, it makes use of the ideas developed in the European Enlightenment, precisely those ideas that must prevail as much in democratic multicultural societies as in the relations of acknowledgment—structured in terms of human rights—between the peoples and cultures of this world.

The fundamental rights and principles of the state of the rule of law constitute, in multicultural societies, the points of crystallization for a political culture that includes all citizens, this political culture is, in turn, the foundation for an egalitarian co-existence of different groups and sub-cultures, each possessing their own origin and identity. The *uncoupling between these two levels of integration* is the presupposition that the majority culture no longer exercises the power to define the common political culture, but rather it submits and open itself to an exchange, free of coercion, with the minority cultures. A comparable situation is that which exists inside the universal polycentric church: in it a common Christian self-understanding must form that stops coinciding with the historically determined Western traditions that represent merely the background against which such traditions take note of their limitations and eurocentric specificity.

But, with respect to its relation with other religions, from Catholic Christianity another type of hermeneutical self-reflection is demanded. Here analogy with a Western world bent on maintaining a de-centered and open attitude towards learning with non-western cultures breaks down. For that, we presuppose as a common basis certain human rights that presumably enjoy a general and rationally motivated acknowledgment. However, in the dialogic debate between religious and metaphysical views of the world a common conception is lacking of the good that would serve as equivalent to that common legal-moral basis. This dispute must be resolved with full reflexive consciousness that all involved parties move in the same universe of discourse and respect one another as cooperative participants in the search for the ethical-existential truth. For that, a culture of acknowledgment is required whose first principles are derived from the secularized world of the universalism of morality as rational natural law. Thus, in this question, it is the philosophical spirit of the political illustration that offers to theology concepts that allow it to explain the sense of a march towards a polycentric church. I do not say this for the simple haste of wanting to have the reason, but because such political philosophy is marked by the idea of the alliance at least as deeply as it is by the idea of the polis. For this reason I also invoke a biblical inheritance, to which Metz appeals when he reminds the contemporary church that "in the name of its mission" it "search for freedom and justice for all" and that it be guided by "a culture of acknowledgment of others in their different ways of being" (Metz 1987, 118).

Trans. Eduardo Mendieta

Works Cited

Habermas, Jürgen. 1992. *Faktizit und Geltung*. Frankfurt: Suhrkamp Verlan.

———. 1992. "Kommunikativen Freiheit und negative Theolgie," in E. Angehrn, et. al. eds., *Dialektischer Negativismus*. Frankfurt: Suhrkamp Verlag.

Kuschel, K. J., ed. 1990. *Dorothee Sölle und Johann Baptist Metz im Gespräch*. Stuttgarkreuzt.

Metz, Johann Baptist 1992. "Anamnestic Reason: A Theologian's Remarks on the Crisis in the *Geistewissenschafter*" in Axel Honneth, Thomas McCarthy, Claus Ofe, and Albrecht Wellmer, eds. *Cultural-Political Interventions in the Unfinished Project of Enlightenment*, trans. Barbara Fultner. Cambridge: The MIT Press.

———. 1992. "Die Rede von Gott angesichts der Leidensgeschichte der Welt," *Stimmen der Zeit*, 5.

———. 1992. *Perspetkiven eines multikulturellen Christentum*. Manuscript.

———. 1986. "Im Aufbruch zu einer kulturell polyzentrischen Welkirche," in *Zeitschrift für Missionwissenschaft un Religionwissenschaft* vol 70, No. 2–3 (1986).

———. 1984. "Im Angesicht der Juden. christiliche Theologie nach Auschwitz," in *Concilium*, 20.

———. 1984. "Theologie im Angesicht und vor dem Ende der Moderne," in *Concilium*, 20.

———. 1981. *The Emergent Church: The Future of Christianity in a Postbourgeoise World* trans. Peter Mann. New York: Crossroad.

———. 1981. *Unterbrechungen*. Güterlosher Verlaghaus Mohr.

Rawls, John. 1971. *A Theory of Justice*. Cambridge: Harvard University Press.

Theunissen, M. 1991. *Negative Theologie der Zeit*. Frankfurt: Suhrkamp Verlag.

14

From Christendom to Polycentric Oikonumé
Modernity, Postmodernity,
and Liberation Theology[1]

Eduardo Mendieta

The debate concerning Modernity is not without its consequences for theology in general and liberation theologies in
particular. But what are these consequences? More is at stake than
whether we assent to or disagree about the current status of
Modernity: Is it a period that has not yet begun? Or is it already dod-
dering or on its deathbed? Chronology and historiography are the
least of the problems here.[2] The debate concerns a crisis that has
been expressed in terms of the end of metaphysics, the myth of universal history, and the death of Man (sic.).[3] Underlying these "ends-
of," obsolescences, debunkings, abandonments, exhaustions, etc., is
the question of the identity and "self-affirmation" of our culture. For
without its philosophy of the subject, its metaphysics of presence, its
ontological history, its glorification of progress, and its sacrificial
dialectic,[4] how could the West differentiate itself from other cultures
and assert itself to be the pinacle of culture and history? The identity
of Western culture(s) is at stake. This is not without its consequences for the Judeo-Christian tradition, the most integral factor of
this identity. Even a quick glance at the "sources" of contemporary
Western culture reveals a profound and convoluted history of imbri-
cation and intertwining between the Judeo-Christian ethos and our
current self-identity. For instance, the narcissistic self originated in

the romantic, expressivistic self, which in turn had its sources invariably in Luther, Cortés, Boethius, Augustine, and Paul.[5] Or take the myth of the frontier, so integral to the identity of the (North as well as South) American, as Slotkin and Frederick Jackson Turner have so well demonstrated[6]; a myth intricately implicated with the myth of manifest destiny, both of which can be traced back to the fundamental Christian notions of exile, expulsion, and the "perennial" search and construction of paradise, the heavenly city, the utopia of the lost Eden.[7] We could also trace the concept of progress, whether technological or moral, to the Christian God who is eternal, all benevolent, and always revealing Himself progressively, gradually in and through history. So when the postmoderns proclaim the end of metaphysics and of history, and the death of Man, to a large extent they are also pronouncing a death sentence, or proclaiming the death, of the Judeo-Christian tradition. Liberation theologies are no less affected by this, not just because they see themselves as rescuing and transformating the best of the Judeo-Christian tradition, and thus its theology, but also because their means of transmutation, transformation, renewal, and rescue of this tradition resemble in many significant ways the claims and presuppositions of the postmodern challenge.

In the following *Vorbemerkungen* (preliminary considerations), I would like to begin to reflect on the links and differences between the "Judeo-Christian" tradition and the latest of its maladies, postmodernism. I would like to pursue these links in terms of the centrality of time, the temporal, and space, the spatial, in both. Indeed, the matrix that holds together the edifice of Modernity, and by phylogeny postmodernity, has as its most important coefficients space and time.[8] In the second half of this essay I will focus on liberation theology with this same framework in the background. As my title intimates, the transformation from "Christendom to Polycentric Oikonumé" reflects the same transformation that is encapsulated by the crises of Modernity and the instauration of a postmodern *mundus*. The crises can be grasped summarily under the rubric of an uncoupling of time and space from the Imperial geopolitical and historical projects of Christendom and Europe.[9]

Exile, Redemption, and Salvation: The Annihilation of Time

The German romantic poet Novalis defined philosophy as "essentially a homesickness—the universal impulse to be at home in the world" (Novalis 1959: 379).[10] With this aphorism Novalis captured the foundational experience of the Christian. The Christian is never at home in the world, not just because she has been "exiled" from the Garden of Eden, but also because her true self lies before her. This transcendental impulse shows and encapsulates how much where we are is not yet home. First theology, but now philosophy turns us homeless, in so far as we must reflect about where we are coming from and where we are going. Who are you? is a question whose answer is perpetually postponed.[11] Modernity is just another of philosophy's ways of exiling us from the world, of saying: "your time is not yet." Octavio Paz said of Modernity that it is a "tradition against itself" (Paz 1974).[12] What he meant is that Modernity is the asymptotic attempt of time to catch up with itself in order to devour itself. The temporal regime that characterizes the project of Modernity, which had its beginning in late antiquity with the ascendancy of Christianity to imperial religion, is defined by time's evisceration of itself. Just as the Messiah is the new beginning, the one who makes all things new, the most recent moment in history is the most forward point in the time-line of salvation history. Indeed, secular history is punctuated by the appearance of the new and the radical that point to a new society, just as *Heilsgeschichte* (salvation history) is punctuated by messianic ruptures that point in the direction of the eschaton.[13] Unless we are said to stand at the vanguard of time's deployment, we are not modern, but either ancient or primitive. When we fail to be with the movement of time we are either left behind (like Asia), or still to be embraced by time, (like America), as Hegel suggested in his lectures on world history.

To be the latest, the newest, the most modern means to enter into permanent crisis (the permanent revolution). The transformation of eschatology into permanent progress is the routinization and institutionalization of crisis. This transformation began with the transition from Jesus's proclamation of the kingdom of God, which was already at hand, to Paul's dispensation of the *parousia* through the *ekklesia*. The church became the site for the dispensation of the holy, the prolepsis of the coming city of God. While the church is the locus of the rupture of the transcendent into the city of man, Modernity appropriates this mission for itself in terms of the state and the law. The sovereign, after all, as Carl Schmitt had pointed out, is a poor copy of the divine sovereign.[14] Nonetheless, crisis and the eschaton are couplets of Modernity's temporal regime(s). To be modern is to approach the point of rupture when all things become

new again. Modernity therefore has always been in crisis. Crisis is
its essence. Crisis is the possibility of the imminent rupture of the
new into the established, the settled, the sedimented. This is the
ineluctable consequence of its temporal regime(s). As long as we
have to disavow the old in order to remain at the foremost boundary of time, crisis is but the necessary haste to shade the ancient or
primitive in order to remain moderns.[15] Indeed, we are defined by
our complete orientation towards the future. This is what Gehlen
had in mind when he defined our humanity in terms of our exocen-
tricity, i.e., by our lacks,[16] and what Gabriel Marcel had in mind
when he spoke of *homo viator,*[17] and what Heidegger had in mind
when he defined humanity's being, *Dasein,* in terms of our being-
onto-death.[18] Revolution is the *modus vivendi* of our societies. The
novum is our philosopher's stone.

Modernity has always had to justify itself. Just as crisis is its
essence, self-affirmation, self-justification, and self-legitimation
have been part and parcel of its having to maintain sovereignty over
the empire of the future.[19] Whether in Augustine's justification vis-
à-vis the fall of the Roman empire, or in Tertullian's question "what
does Athens have to do with Jerusalem?," or in Aquinas's use of
Aristotle, or in Schleiermacher's attempt to circumscribe an inner
dwelling for faith in the face of Hegel's and Kant's critiques, or in
the more recent polemics between Löwith, Blumemberg, Schmitt,
Lyotard, Habermas, et. al, Modernity's legitimacy has always had to
assert itself.[20] These self-affirmations and self-legitimations, however, have always been performed and exercised in the name of
Modernity itself. Modernity remains valid for it is the epitome of
time generating, regenerating, and consuming itself. Modernity, in
this fashion, begot modernism, avant-gardism, kitsch, retro, dada-
ism, surrealism, and the avant-gardes of Warhol, Duchamp, and
Dali,[21] just as it also parented Nietzsche, Freud, Marx (the philosophers of suspicion in Paul Ricoeur's phrasing[22]), Deleuze, Guatarri,
Derrida, Lyotard, and Levinas.[23] Postmodernity, in this vein, seems
to be the latest attempt of Modernity to catch up with itself. While
Adorno and Horkheimer proclaimed a dialectic of the Enlightenment, in which myth turned into reason just as reason reverted to
myth,[24] in the name of an enlightened Enlightenment (in Metz's
phrase[25]), the philosophers of suspicion unmasked Modernity in
the name of its own project: the unmasking of heteronomy, tyranny,
ignorance, arbitrary coercion in the name of autonomy, democracy,

edification (*Bildung*)[26], and the non-coercive coercion of Habermas's and Apel's ideal speech situation or ideal communication community, respectively.[27] Despite Habermas's warnings that the postmoderns are the Burkes of today, the young conservatives who in rejecting Modernity would want us to take two steps back to pre-Modernity,[28] postmodernity would seem to be the latest fashion in Modernity's market place of philosophical ideas.

Postmodernity is the legitimate child of Modernity, one that nevertheless would like to engage in parricide, for postmodernity disavows not only the tradition of the new as such, but the time that fueled Modernity, the *modernus*, the *novum*. As long as there was the possibility for transformation, regenerative ritual violence, our world-view, could embrace the time of novelty, of progress, of revolution, and of emancipatory metamorphosis. For Posmodernity, however, time seems to have finally caught up with itself.[29] Lyotard has starkly expressed this final self-cancellation of time when he characterized the post-modern condition as one in which meta-narratives have lost all legitimacy and power of convocation.[30] While it is hard to pin-point the moment when Modernity finally grew weary of its own time, we can mention Auschwitz, Hiroshima and Nagasaki, and the Soviet Gulags, as the three paradigmatic events that placed themselves at the most forward point in time. In the name of progress, freedom, revolution, transformation, regeneration, and elevation, time cancelled itself by turning into barbarity. Time—which thus far had been the story of liberation—turned into the time of perdition, *Verfallsgeschichte*, the history of humanity's fall. The future, which had been represented by the plentiful cornucopia, exquisitely and masterfully catalogued by Bloch in his three volume magnus opus *The Principle of Hope*,[31] has now turned into Walter Benjamin's angel, whose wings are caught open by the storm blowing from paradise that piles sky high the debris of history which we call progress.[32] Indeed, not even the "gods can save us now" (Heidegger), because the messiah has been sacrificed along with those sacrificed in his name. Few remembered that the messiah was a Jew, a poor fisherman's son in an occupied land, and that progress, redemption, and liberation were his namesakes.

The Postmodern, therefore, would appear finally to be the post-secular (John Milbank[33] and Mark C. Taylor[34]). Even if the time of Modernity was parasitic of Judeo-Christian notions of soteriology, praxeology, divine salvation history, etc. (Löwith[35]), Modernity's own project was the complete assimilation, consumption, and usurpation of divine transcendence. Secularization is the name for the process by which Modernity appropriated the transcendence of the divine into its own immanence. Progress, indeed, is but the secularization of divine eternity and perfection.[36] Modernity's continuous evisceration of time, however, was always contingent on the surplus of transcendence that remained beyond its own grasp. This is the meaning of Modernity's asymptotic attempt to cancel time. This surplus, at the same time, was always interpreted as a detritus, a residue of our immaturity (*Unmündigkeit*—to use Kant's word). Modernity saw the struggle between the darkness of belief and the light of reason. Enlightenment, *illuminismo*, *Aufklärung*, light is the motif; the light of reason makes the darkness of faith recede. Publicness, reason, and emancipation are all fundamental to the concept of enlightenment. The light shed by publicness (Habermas's *Öffenlichkeit*[37]) is the light of Enlightenment that emancipates the victims of superstition, fanatism, and despotism. Kant gave philosophical expression to the light of publicness and the illuminating function of reason in his essay, "What is the Enlightenment?" For Kant the point of the transcendental critique was to circumscribe the limits of reason from within so as to allow for faith, thus, making room for *Religion within the bounds of Reason alone*. Hegel in a different tactic, which encapsulates the parasitism of reason's transcendence on divine wholly otherness, subsumes theology into philosophy: God's death is philosophy's life. The idea of absolute freedom, or subjective self-affirmation is but the sublimation of the absolute passion and the good friday. History and knowledge are the secular images of recollection of suffering and the Golgotha of the Absolute Spirit. Modernity is the self-immolation of God, where secularization is her calvary. Habermas, the great defender of Modernity continues this motif. For him, religion is liquified in its linguistifications. The great motifs of otherness, suffering, universal injustice, are, in Habermas's view, redeemed and rendered liquid, the same way an asset is turned into currency in discourse ethics.[38] The *logos* of intersubjectivity and communicative action allows for a "transcendence from within" through its navigating between the extremes of a "transcendent-less" empiricism and a fetishistic glorification of pure transcendence. The question, nevertheless, that Modernity's often surreptitious, often blatant pillages of the transcendent, never faced is: will the secular, as well as the religious, withstand the onslaught of secularization?

Postmodernity does not declare the death of God, like Hegel, or Nietzsche, or Dostoyevsky, or Freud, or Altizer, may have done precisely because they were still (too) modern. Reversing John Milbank's argumentation, postmodernism is post-secular to the extent that it is post-theistic, where post-theistic refers to that "thinking" which is other than the onto-theological tradition that Heidegger had in mind when he denounced Hegel's ontological collapse of identity and difference. Postmodernity is the celebration of pagan polytheism. The world is no longer the inscription of some divine semiology, nor is the book of nature written in the language of mathematics, which is God's language, nor, much less, can we discern God's presence in the creative spewing forth of *natura naturans*, nor do we bother ourselves with the evil genius, nor with the presence of an absence, the *deus absconditus*. These, in the view of the "pagan" postmoderns, were all but forms of identity thinking, the onto-theological tradition, the metaphysics of presence,[39] the supremacy of the self-projecting imperial "I."[40]

Postmodernity's rejection of the temporal regime(s) of Modernity is also a rejection of its secular/spiritual, pious/pagan dichotomy. Postmodernity denounces Modernity's pillage of the divine, and wants no part in it. After all, postmoderns never tire of reminding us, how many people died in this war against faith, darkness, immaturity.

Postmodernity, as a condition and as a heuristic tool, is post-secular in that its reason's light has no darkness to dispel, to illuminate. For, as Adorno and Horkheimer already knew, reason is myth just as myth is reason. It is also post-secular because it no longer pretends to be the microphone of a voice from beyond, the transcendent that nevertheless was held in contempt. When God died in Modernity's sacrifice of the lamb at Auschwitz, the philosopher as Modernity's high priest, as Modernity's *kathechon*, also died. The office of the philosopher was vacated and rendered obsolete. Plato's philosopher-king, a figure still important to Hegel, has become postmodernity's D.J. rapper, and pop-psychology tv-show host.

This analysis of postmodernity, however, seems to be vitiated by the return of the sacred. Whereas the Enlightenment was partly understood as the further differentiation between state, church, public sphere, economy, etc. (Weber, Habermas), and postmodernity is understood as a questioning of these distinctions, the sacred returns to haunt our post-conventional, post-national, and post-industrial societies. How are we to understand the rise of the religious right in the United States, a revitalized "American Religion" (Bloom), the revival of Muslim fundamentalism, the theocratic revolution in Iran, the ethnic-religious war in Bosnia, and the spread of evangelical movements in Latin America? Above all, how are we to understand Latin American liberation theology, and its siblings, African, Asian, Black, and Feminist liberation theologies?[41] Either these movements are remnants from Modernity's dichotomy of the sacred and profane, the secular and the spiritual, or they are already proleptic forms of the postmodern. I would like to suggest that they are the latter. Liberation theologies are the manifestation not only of a postmodern condition but also the praxis of a new "theological paradigm" that would like to preserve and depart from Modernity's deceptive proclaiming of the secular and its pillaging of the sacred.

From Theology of Empire to Theology of Liberation

Johnann-Baptist Metz has suggested that the Enlightenment meant the end of the "cognitive innocence" of theology, although if we accept Küng's periodization we would have to extend this loss of innocence back to at least the 'hellenic patristic period' (3rd Century A.D.).[42] This loss of cognitive innocence translated into, on the one hand, the questioning of the *logos* of theology that resulted in its rationalistic reduction, and, on the other hand, the ghettoization (of religious experience) into the private life of individuals. In turn, theology has reacted by confronting society's mythologization of reason by a critique of ideology that unmasks this fetishization and by confronting the non-believer. This attitude can be summarized by the phrase "faith in search of reason" (Metz 1984).

This loss of innocence and its concomitant entrenched positioning of theology, however, cannot be understood without reference to the long history of oppositional attitudes that have characterized the construction and constitution of Europe.[43] The beginnings of this loss of innocence are in evidence in the attempt to homogenize and to level the sacred spaces of other religions within and outside of Europe. The *orbis christianus* is literally a site and time that excludes the heterogeneity of the non-christian.[44] Indeed, the story of the struggle against obscurantism and faith, as well as against apostasy, heresy, and heterodoxy, occupies a central place in the history of Europe, and the "Europanization of the world." The claims Spain made over the "new world," for instance, were sacralized by Pope Alexander the VI's bull *Inter caetera* of May 4 1493, which gave, granted, and assigned for eternity [*in perpetuum, tenore praesentium, donamus, et assignamus*] exclusive rights, authority, and legislation to the Catholic kings of Spain to evangelize the newly encountered Amerindians.[45] The sacralization of the violent evangelization of the new world was the background for one of the most important debates in the history of the mis-relationship between Europe and the new world. I am referring to the debate between Bartolomé de las Casas and Ginés Sepùlveda concerning the humanity of the "Indians," and the so-called right to wage just war against them on the grounds of their "savage" religious practices and infidelity.[46] Furthermore, this "evangelization" of "America" comes after the expulsion of the Jews from Spain and the culmination of about two centuries of crusades (1095–1291).[47] While infidels were to be rooted out from the holy land, unbelievers were to be excised from within. This was partly the function of the Inquisition, one of the great early forms of rationalized bureaucracy. The orthodox theologies that emerged from these struggles against infidels and barbarians have, therefore, looked at the problem of the Enlightenment's challenge to faith through the lens of the antagonism between theism and atheism. Their goal, since at least the councils of Nicaea (325) and Chalcedon (451), has been to construct a solid foundation that would support the edifice of systematic theologies designed with the expressed purpose of justifying a particular orthodoxy. This dogma established the univocality of belief and religious practice. The unity of the teachings of the Christian churches and the systematic affirmations of the theologies that underpin them, have been bought at the exacting prize of the excising of difference, heterogeneity, and heterodoxy.

This project of orthodoxy confronted its gravest crisis with the end of the European century, marked by the two World Wars. While Catholicism had turned its back on the modern world, Protestantism had made peace with it. The two world wars, nevertheless, represented as much a crisis of the modern outlook as a crisis of a spirituality that had either compromised too much with or removed itself too far from the world. The depth of this crisis, in fact, led Küng to date the birth of Postmodernity with the European experience of World War I.[48] The crisis theologies, such as Karl Barth's, which emerged between the two wars indicates an attempt to regain a new footing in the world, without being entirely subsumed by it. Be that as it may, there is a way in which the extermination of the Jews, and the dual war against soulless liberal democracy and atheistic Jewish Marxism, was partly a continuation of the idea of a Christian empire that needed to be defended from infidels, pagans and atheists. The Third Reich was to be the new Christendom, the rebirth, and out-shining of the holy Roman Empire.

The project of orthodoxy of European "Imperial" theologies, however, suffered its most acute crisis when a new theology, or theologies, emerged from an increasingly self-liberated and post-colonial non-Western world. Indeed, the end of the European century is not only marked by the devastation of Europe by two world wars, but also, and perhaps most significantly, by the "explosion of the third world."[49] Interestingly, while the end of the European century gives way to the American century, this latter is already haunted by the struggles for liberation of the subaltern, the oppressed, and the "Other" of Europe. As Dwight Hopkins illustrated in his essay "Black Theology and Globalization,"[50] the exposure of African-American soldiers during the war to the dignity and respect accorded to them by Europeans and other peoples of color, served as an impetus for their struggles for justice and political empowerment at home. At the same time, however, it is affirmation of sovereignty and autonomy of former colonies that begins a real as well as metaphorical resistance and liberation from Europe.

While the Middle East, Asia, and Africa were divided and configured according to post-war spheres of influence and power, thus creating the conditions for later projects of national liberation, Latin America underwent a rapid process of modernization and political liberation. These projects of political independence, popular sovereignty, and economic modernization, however, met their inner limits when confronted with the dependency and underdevelopment of Latin American economies. Kennedy's Alliance for Progress, a program designed by Washington to aid in modernization in Latin America, thus purportedly preempting "socialist" revolutions, met its failure with the growing impoverishment of the Latin American continent. The projects for a modernization of Latin America from the top culminated in a wave of revolutionary fervor throughout the continent. The many populisms of the sixties as well as the Cuban revolution, the democratic experiment in Chile, and eventually the Nicaraguan revolution, are some of the answers to the failure of technocratic visions of social modernization. It is against this historical background that we must understand the emergence of a new theological paradigm in Latin America.[51]

During the late sixties and early seventies, after decades of grass roots organizing and the emergence of a particular popular spirituality, a new theological paradigm began to be profiled in Latin America. This new theological paradigm begins with the affirmation of the personhood of the poor and the denunciation of those conditions in which their humanity is sacrificed and immolated to the gods of money, production, and progress. This new paradigm emerged as a reflection of the subjects of liberation on their own processes of liberation; Thus its name: liberation theology. This theology is as much about liberation as an object of speculation as it is about the process of liberation. This reflection on liberation, however, is not about liberation from heterodoxy and heresy, but from those conditions and systems of ideas that hide, occlude, and destroy the humanity of the "chosen ones of God," the poor. All reflection, including theological reflection, is situated, localized self-understanding. It is product of a given historical experience as it participates in the legitimation or critique of a given social status quo. Liberation theology, therefore, understands itself as both liberation *of* theology from its complicity with systems of exploitation and dehumanization, and liberation *of* the poor from these same systems.

Latin American liberation theology's point of departure is therefore entirely different from that of the European Imperial theologies of orthodoxy. In contrast to the latter, whose theological locus is the infidel or atheist, the *locus theologicus* of liberation theologies is the poor, the non-person. Liberation theology's *Ausgangspunkt*, its whence, is the immense and still growing poverty of the "wretched of the earth." Liberation theology begins not with the discovery of unbelief, skepticism, but with the discovery of the "absent ones of history", the despised Others. Its interlocutor is not the unbeliever but the hungry person, not the one who questions God, but the one whose carnality and survival is *the* question. While European theologies look at history through the prism of progress /modernization and atheism/theism, liberation theologies look at history from its "underside" (Gutiérrez, Dussel) through the prisms of oppression/liberation and idolatry/God of life.

The radical de-mythologizing of "Occidental Rationality" (Weber, Habermas), begun by Marx, Freud, and Nietzsche, later continued by Adorno and Horkheimer, is extended and actualized in the "concientization" (Friere, Mesters) practices of the ecclesiastical base communities. Liberation theologies, thus, do not reject the Enlightenment, but denounce its betrayal. While European theologies turn to philosophy as their dialogue partner, liberation theologies turn to the social sciences as theirs. Fetishization and idolatry occur not only, or not specially and most consequentially, in the realm of ideas, but in the realm of social reality. As Jon Sobrino suggested, whereas European theologies set out from the first Enlightenment (Kant, Rousseau, and Hegel), liberation theologies set out from the second Enlightenment (Marx).[52] Since liberation theologies take issue with Marx's eleventh thesis on Feuerbach ("Philosophers up to now have only interpreted the world, the point is to change it"), liberation theologies see their goal as orthopraxies—not orthodoxy. Their telos is the positive and humanizing transformation of the world, not its deciphering in terms of true and untrue belief.

These contrasts between European theologies and Third World liberation theologies illuminate their fundamental differences. I would like to focus on one pivotal difference: the shift in the conceptualizations of oikoumené (ecumene). This shift, I would like to argue, evidences an uncoupling between the *orbis christianus* and the ecumene, one that discloses the positive and negative dimension of a globalized planet. The shift in the conceptualizations of community of believers reflects not only a new site and locus for praxis and critical reflection but also the new global configurations of more entrenched dependencies and asymmetries. The site is the *reverso*, or underside, of history, as Gutiérrez has called it. The locus is the poor. In other words, liberation theology proclaims the localized and de-centered ecumene, as the dwelling of all humans with their histories of suffering, redemption, and liberation, while disavowing any claims to the *orbis christianus*, which was the nightmare of Imperial theology and Europe, its source.

The oikoumené of Western Christianity, as we noted above, divided the world into believers and infidels. After the first major paradigm of Jewish Christianity—which is also called the Apostolic period, when the ruling concept of oikoumené was Greco-Roman, which divided the world into citizens and barbarians—Christianity's ascendancy to imperial religion translated into the inauguration of Christendom. Christendom, as Pablo Richard defines it, is a particular configuration of the state, civil society, ideology, and the

Church in which power is articulated through the state in conjunction with its religious legitimation (Richard 1987: 1). Under Christendom the world was to be made after the image of Christ and Christian society. The church became the agent of the refashioning of the world after a divine semiology, or sacred symbolic order. We are all members of either the holy church or some sort of "invisible church." The church was the site for the dispensation of divine salvation, the locus for the construction of the city of God, as Augustine saw it in the fourth century. Its imperative was cultural monocentrism and substantive universalism (or what Krieger has also called "apologetic universalism"[53]): one true culture, one true church, one God actualizing itself in one true universal history. The oikoumené of Christendom had a telos, an alpha, and an omega; its history was the story of the excising of the primitive, the barbaric, the heterogeneous, the pagan, i.e., the domestication of God's otherness. The community of believers had as its antagonist the community of those beyond salvation, beyond history. Christendom was thus the reign of the homogeneous, the univocal, orthodoxy, sameness, the center of the world.

Inasmuch as liberation theologies begin not with the infidel but with the non-person, the *pauper*, their community or oikoumené is that of the dispossessed, the absent ones from history. The history of this community is not that of progress and modernization, but of oppression and liberation. By focusing on this dialectic, liberation theologies disclose that the history of modernization has been also the history of the impoverishment of the others of Europe's Christendom. Their oikoumené is not the universalizing of one God, the precensing of one substance, one principle, one history, but the earth as world-system. Liberation theologies's looking at history from its "underside" reveals the complementarity and internal entwinement between the wealth of one quarter of the First World and the poverty of three quarters of the World. Liberation theology discovers this through its appropriation of "dependency theory" and in its most recent reformulations in terms of "world-system" analysis (Wallerstein, Amin, Dussel).[54] In this way, liberation theologies disavowed the Enlightenment glorification of progress in order to affirm the historical memory of struggling people. The primitive, unmodern, or underdeveloped are not what comes before the civilized, modern, or developed. Both are sides of one and the same process of economic, political, social, and spiritual interdependence. The world is not the disjunction of space and time, which relegates the different to another country, in another time, as is suggested by Christendom, but the conjunction of both. Beyond and before, are always already, now, and still to come, here, there and yonder. In this sense, liberation theologies's concept of the human community is the true discovery of the world, the earth, the planet, as the home of all humanity. The world is not the site for the inscription of the universal, but the home of the suffering and living human being. Liberation theologies's critiques of dehumanizing social realities point at fetishization and idolatry as the presence of an absence, that is the presence of the negation of the God of life, the God of the poor, the God of Jesus, a poor, black Jew in a conquered land.

What Küng called the Postmodern ecumenical paradigm, and Metz the polycentric "universal" church, is practiced by liberation theologies in terms of their world-system analysis, which begins with the heterogeneity of histories, religions, cultures, and their economic, social, political, and cultural interdependencies. While progressive European theologies have been calling for a *Weltethos* (Küng 1991), a planetary ethics, and the inauguration of a truly ecumenical age, Latin American theologians at first, and other Third World theologians later, have been actualizing in practice this new world-perspective. Liberation theologies's turning to the social sciences and their appropriation of "dependency theory," as well as of "world-system" analysis, are paths to a post-modern understanding of a planetary and not universal oikoumené. Küng begins *Global Responsibility* with the sentence "No survival without a world ethic." How, however, is this "world" to be understood? Liberation theologies's world-system analysis and concept of the post-Christendom, polycentric oikoumené suggest that our world bears, diachronically and synchronically, the deep wounds of a long history of uneven development, unfair distribution of planetary wealth, pillage and waste of human life. Our world is this planet and its inhabitants are not the barbarians or infidels of Christendom but the "absent ones of history."

The new theological paradigm that emerged from the suffering humanity of Latin America, and the Third World in general, has articulated a new vision of our planet and the human community that inhabits it. It is a vision in which we are always already in a here and now that is both the continuity of the past and the futurity of what is to come. In this sense, and to conclude these *pautas*, liberation theologies were postmodern before Europeans thought of postmodernism. At the same time liberation theologies are beyond postmodernism, or rather, to use Dussel's term, they are trans-modern insofar as they think the exhaustion and end of these mythologies from their simultaneity as well as their *reverso*, their underside. And most importantly, they do not end up with a nihilistic skepticism, or abject stoicism; their localizing history and human suffering begin to profile an image of what we have not yet thought ourselves to be, or able to become: ". . . the situation calls imperatively for such knowledge, indeed because *consummate negativity*, once squarely faced, delineates the mirror image of its opposite" (Adorno 1978: 247, emphasis added).[55]

Notes

1. I would like to acknowledge the important criticism of David Batstone, Dwight Hopkins, and Lois Lorentzen on earlier versions of this essay. I am also very thankful to Cleo Kearns, Amós Nascimento, and Berit Bretthauer for their incisive and enlightening critical comments.

2. A non-eurocentric, methodologically reflexive view of Modernity would try to be more contentious concerning its periodization and chronology. Thus, it is incredible that most theorists dealing with the issue tend to view Modernity/Postmodernity as an exclusively central European phenomena. They either begin with the Reformation, or the French Revolution, or the *Aufklärung*, forgetting the Discovery/Invention of America, the debates between de las Casas and Sepúlveda, Vitorio and Suarez, as well as the declaration of Independence of the Twelve Colonies, and the struggle against Napoleon in the Hispanic Colonies (Haiti, etc.).

3. See Jane Flax, *Thinking Fragments: Psychoanalysis, Feminism and Postmodernism in the Contemporary West* (Berkeley: University of California Press, 1990), 32ff. See also Seyla Benhabib, "Epistemologies of Postmodernism: A Rejoinder to Jean-Francois Lyotard" in: *New German Critique*, No. 33 (Fall 1984), 103–126; and Seyla Benhabib, et. al., *Feminist Contentions: A Philosophical Exchange* (New York: Routledge, 1994).

4. Franz J. Hinkelammert, *Sacrificios humanos y sociedad occidental: Lucifer y la bestia* (San José, Costa Rica: Editorial DEI, 1991).

5. See Charles Taylor, *The Sources of the Self: The Making of the Modern Identity* (Cambridge: Harvard University Press, 1989); as well as his *The Ethics of Authenticity* (Cambridge: Harvard University Press, 1992). The letter this book appeared first in Canada under the title of *The Malaise of Modernity*. As important as Taylor's work is, a serious confrontation with its asssumptions and shortcomings, as well as its contributions has yet to be undertaken in the Northern part of the American continent. Enrique Dussel's essay is the one work I am aware of that has began this undertaking; see his *The Underside of Modernity: Apel, Ricoeur, Rorty, and the Philosophy of Liberation,*

edited and translated by Eduardo Mendieta (Atlantic Highlands: Humanities Press, 1995), chapter 7: "Modernity, Eurocentrism, and Transmodernity: In Dialogue with Charles Taylor's *Sources of The Self.*"

6. On the importance of the frontier and manifest destiny in the history of the making of the American "empire" see: Richard Slotkin, *Regeneration Through Violence: The Mythology of the American Frontier, 1600-1860* (Middletown, Connecticut: Wesleyan University Press, 1973), *The Fatal Environment: The Myth of the Frontier in the Age of Industrialization 1800-1890* (Middletown, Connecticut: Wesleyan University Press, 1986), *Gunfighter Nation: The Myth of the Frontier in Twentieth-Century America* (New York: Atheneum, 1992). William Appleman Williams' work on American history is also important for the the the analysis of the development of American Imperialism and the American Imperial way of life. See William Appleman Williams, *Empire as a Way of Life: An Essay on the Causes and Character of America's Present Predicament Along with a Few Thoughts About an Alternative* (Oxford and New York: Oxford University Press, 1980); see also Amy Kaplan and Donald E. Pease, eds., *Cultures of United States Imperialism* (Durham and London: Duke University Press, 1993); Jan Willem Schulte Nordholt, *The Myth of the West: America as the Last Empire*, trans. Herbert H. Rowen (Grand Rapids: Wm. B. Eerdmans Publishing Co., 1995).

7. See Eduardo Subirats, *El Continente Vacío: La Conquista del Nuevo Mundo y la conciencia moderna* (México: Siglo XXI, 1994) 114ff. This book, along with Enrique Dussel's *The Invention of the Americas: Eclipse of "the Other" and the Myth of Modernity*, trans. by Michael Barber (New York: Continuum, 1995), can help as rectifying spectacles for the naively eurocentric Charles Taylor.

8. I have dealt with the philosophical aspects of these claims in my essay "Modernity's When and Where: On the Spatial and Temporal regime(s) of Modernity" in Eduardo Mendieta and Pedro Lange-Churión, eds. *Latin America and Postmodernity: A Reader* (Atlantic Highlands: Humanities Press, Forthcoming). The main thinkers behind the inspiration for this thesis have been Anthony Giddens, Edward W. Soja, and Enrique Dussel. See Anthony Giddens, *A Contemporary Critique of Historical Materialism. Vol. 1: Power, Property and the State* (Berkeley: University of California Press, 1981), *The Constitution of Society: Outline of the Theory of Structuration*(Berkeley and Los Angeles: University of California Press, 1984), and in particular his recent *The Consequences of Modernity* (Stanford: Stanford University Press, 1990). See David Held and John B. Thompson, eds., *Social Theory of Modern Societies: Anthony Giddens and his Critics*, (Cambridge: Cambridge University Press, 1989) in particular the essays by Derek Gregory and Peter Saunders. Edward W. Soja, *Postmodern Geographies: The Reassertion of Space in Critical Social Theory* (London & New York: Verso, 1989). Enrique Dussel, *Philosophy of Liberation* (Maryknoll: Orbis Books, 1985), paragraphs 1.1–1.1.3.2: "Geopolitics and Philosophy"; as well as Dussel book I edited: *The Underside of Modernity*. See also Gilles Deleuze and Félix Guattari, *What is Philosophy?* (New York: Columbia University Press, 1994), chapter 4: "Geophilosophy," 85ff.

9. Jeffrey C. Alexander has captured, under a sociological perspective that is attentive to the religious, this same transformation. He writes: "Because the

contemporary re-coding of the antithesis of universalism can be *geographically* represented neither as non-Western nor *temporally* located in an earlier time, the social sacred of neo-modernism cannot, paradoxically, be represented as 'modernization'," in "Modern, Anti, Post and Neo" in *New Left Review*, No. 210 (March/April 1995), 93 (My emphasis). In other words, since the West can no longer code or map the anti-thesis of its universalistic claims (read: Imperialisms) in terms of its periphery (i.e. the frontier, the jungle, the desert, the sea, and outer space) or the non-contemporaneous (i.e. the primitive, the immature, the backward, the ancient, or its opposite, the ultramodern—in the sense of a future which is more modern than our own), its own center disentegrates. See also Homi K. Bhabha, *The Location of Culture* (New York: Routledge, 1994), chapter 11: "How newness enters the world: Postmodern space, postcolonial times and the trials of cultural translation," 212ff. Jeffrey C. Alexander's essay is a major contribution to the understanding of the terms Modernity, modernization, postmodern, etc. See the recently published book by Jeffrey Alexander, *Fin de Siècle Social Theory: Relativism, Reduction, and the Problem of Reason* (New York: Verso, 1995).

10. The German reads: "Die Philosophie ist eigentlich Heimweh-Trieb, überall zu Hause zu sein." Novalis, *Werke: in Einem Band* (Hamburg: Hoffmann und Campe Verlag, 1959), 379.

11. Along with Augustine's *Confessions*, we can also list Pico della Mirandola's *Oration on the Dignity of Man*, Juan Luis Vives's *A Fable About Man*, and Ernst Bloch's *The Spirit of Utopia*.

12. Octavio Paz, *Children of the Mire: Modern Poetry from Romanticism to the Avant-Garde* (Cambridge: Harvard University Press, 1974), first chapter. See also the more recent but equally magisterial collection of essays on the same thematic, *La Otra Voz: Poesia y fin de Siglo* (Barcelona: Seix Barral, 1990). This contains his Tanner lectures on "Poetry and Modernity."

13. See the magnificent work by Frank E. Manuel and Fritzie P. Manuel, *Utopian Thought in the Western World* (Cambridge: The Belknap Press of Harvard University Press, 1979), 33ff.

14. See Carl Schmitt, *Political Theology: Four Chapters on the Concept of Sovereignty* (Cambridge: The MIT Press, 1985), and *Politische Theologie II: Die Legende von der Erledigung jeder Politischen Theologie* (Berlin: Duncker & Humblot, 1984).

15. On the dialectic between the modern and the primitive, and the parasitism of the former on the latter, see Homi K. Bhabha, *The Location of Culture* (New York: Routledge, 1993), especially chapters seven, eight, and nine.

16. Arnold Gehlen, *Man: His Nature and Place in the World* (New York: Columbia University Press, 1988).

17. Gabriel Marcel, *Homo Viator: Introduction to a Metaphysic of Hope* (New York: Harper & Brothers, 1962)

18. Martin Heidegger, *Being and Time* (New York: Harper & Row, Publishers, 1962). Wolfhart Pannenberg's *Anthropology in Theological Perspective* (Philadelphia: The Westminster Press, 1985) still remains the best discussion of this fundamental future orientedness of humanity's *Dasein* with respect to theology and its sources therein.

19. I am using "self-legitimation" in the sense that Habermas suggests in

his *The Philosophical Discourses of Modernity: Twelve Lectures* (Cambridge: The MIT Press, 1987), 43ff.

20. See Hans Blumemberg, *The Legitimacy of the Modern Age* (Cambridge: The MIT Press, 1983), and Laurence Dickey, "Blumemberg and Secularization: 'Self-Assertion' and the Problem of Self-Realizing Teleology in History" in: *New German Critique*, No. 41 (Spring-Summer 1987), 151–165.

21. Matei Calinescu, *Five Faces of Modernity: Modernism, Avant-Garde, Decadence, Kitsch, Postmodernism* (Durham: Duke University Press, 1987).

22. Paul Ricoeur, *Freud and Philosophy: An Essay on Interpretation* (New Haven and London: Yale University Press, 1970), 32ff.

23. Luc Ferry and Alain Renaut, *French Philosophy of the Sixties: An Essay on Antihumanism* (Amherst: The University of Massachusetts Press, 1990).

24. Max Horkheimer and Theodor W. Adorno, *Dialectic of Enlightenment* (New York: Continuum, 1982).

25. Johann-Baptist Metz, "Theology in the Modern Age, and before its End" in: *Concilium*, No. 171 (1984), 13–17.

26. See Martin Jay's essay: "The Morals of Genealogy: Or Is There a Post-structuralist Ethics?" in Martin Jay, *Force Fields: Between Intellectual History and Cultural Critique* (New York: Routledge, 1992), 38–48.

27. See Seyla Benhabib and Fred Dallmayr, eds., *The Communicative Ethics Controversy* (Cambridge: The MIT Press, 1990).

28. Jürgen Habermas, "Modernity versus Postmodernity" in: *New German Critique*, No. 22 (Winter 1981), especially 11ff. This essay was delivered in 1980 on the ocassion of Habermas's receiving the T. W. Adorno prize. The original title was "Die Moderne -ein unvollendetes Projekt" [Modernity -an uncompleted project], now in the book by the same name [Leipzig: Reclam Verlag, 1992 (1990), 32–54].

29. Fredric Jameson, *Postmodernism: or, The Cultural Logic of Late Capitalism* (Durham: Duke University Press, 1991).

30. Jean-Francois Lyotard, *The Postmodern Condition: A Report on Knowledge* (Minneapolis: University of Minnesota Press, 1984).

31. Ernst Bloch, *The Principle of Hope* 3 Volumes (Cambridge: The MIT Press, 1986).

32. The reference is to Walter Benjamin's IX Thesis on the philosophy of history; see Walter Benjamin, *Illuminations: Essays and Reflections* (New York: Harcourt, Brace & World, Inc., 1968), 259–260.

33. See John Milbank, *Theology & Social Theory: Beyond Secular Reason* (Oxford & Cambridge: Blackwell, 1993), and his "The End of Enlightenment: Post-Modern or Post-Secular?" in *Concilium*, 1992/6, 39–48. This whole issue is dedicated to "The Debate on Modernity."

34. Mark C. Taylor, *Erring: A Postmodern A/theology* (Chicago and London: The University of Chicago Press, 1984).

35. Karl Löwith, *Meaning in History* (Chicago and London: The University of Chicago Press, 1949). See also Karl Löwith, *Martin Heidegger and European Nihilism*, edited by Richard Wolin and trans. by Gary Steiner (New York: Columbia University Press, 1995), "European Nihilism: Reflections on the Spiritual and Historical Background of the European War." pp. 173ff.

36. Octavio Paz, *Children of the Mire*, 23ff.

37. Jürgen Habermas, "Öffenlichkeit (ein Lexikonartikel) 1964" in J. Habermas, *Kultur und Kritik: Vestreute Aufsätze* (Frankfurt am Main: Suhrkamp Verlag, 1973), 61–69.

38. See Jürgen Habermas, "Israel and Athens, Or to Whom does Anamnestic Reason Belong? On Unity in the Multicultural Diversity" trans. Eduardo Mendieta, in this anthology. See also "Transcendence from Within, Transcendence in this World" in Don S. Browing and Francis Schüssler Fiorenza, eds. *Habermas, Modernity, and Public Theology* (New York: Crossroad, 1992), 226–250.

39 Jean-Luc Marion, *God Without Being: Hors-Texte* (Chicago and London: The University of Chicago Press, 1991).

40. Enrique Dussel, *1492: El Encubrimiento del Otro, Hacia El Origen del mito de la modernidad* (Madrid: Editorial Neuva Utopía, ca. 1992). See my review of this work in *The Journal of Hispanic/Latino Theology*, Vol. 2, No. 3, (February 1995), pp. 67–71.

41. See my co-authored introduction—with David Batstone, Lois Lorentzen and Dwight Hopkins—to the special issue of *Peace Review*, Vol 7, No. 1 (1995) on "Religion and Globalization."

42. Hans Küng, *Theology for the Third Millennium: An Ecumenical View* (New York: Doubleday, 1988).

43. See Denys Hay, *Europe: The Emergence of an Idea* (Edinburgh: The Edinburgh University Press, 1957), for a superb historical semantical reconstruction of an idea that has been neither solely geographical nor merely political, but an ideal that converges and overlaps with Christendom.

44 Samuel Purchas captured succinctly not only this imperialistic impulse but its foundational divinization, ideas shared by figures as important as Leonardo da Vinci, More, Erasmus, and later Leibniz, Kant, and Hegel. Purchas wrote: "Europe is taught the way to scale Heaven, not by Mathematicall principles [Bacon will reverse this argument], but by Divine veritie. Jesus Christ is their way, their truth, their life; who hath long since given a Bill of Divorce to ingratefull Asia where hee was borne, and Africa the prace of his flight and refuge, and is become almost wholly and onely Europaean. For little doe wee find of this name in Asia, lesse in Africa, and nothing at all in America, but later Europaean gleanings." quoted in Hay, *Europe: The Emergence of an Idea*, p. 110. Here the three-fold mythological division, stemming from the Bible (Genesis 9–10, where the textual beginnings of the myth of Japheth and the curse of Canaan, the people of Han, are established), and its patristic exegeses (Augustine, Jerome, etc), is modified to include the fourth part of the world—America. See Denys Hay, *Europe: The Emergence of an Idea*, 7-16, and Denis de Rougemont, *The Idea of Europe* (New York: The Macmillan Company, 1966), 19ff. Francisco Javier Hernáez, Volume 1, *Coleccion de Bulas, Breves y Otros Documentos relativos a la iglesia de America y Filipinas* (Vaduz: Kraus Reprint Ltd. 1964 [reprint of the 1879 edition by Imprenta de Alfredo Vromant, Bruselas), 13. An English translation may be found in John Tracy Ellis, ed., *Documents of American Catholic History* (Milwaukee: The Bruce Publishing Company, 1956), 1-3.

45. Francisco Javier Hernáez, Volume 1, *Coleccion de Bulas, Breves y Otros Documentos relativos a la iglesia de America y Filipinas* (Vaduz: Kraus Reprint

Ltd. 1964 [reprint of the 1879 edition by Imprenta de Alfredo Vromant, Bruselas), 13. An English translation can be found in John Tracy Ellis, ed., *Documents of American Catholic History* (Milwaukee: The Bruce Publishing Company, 1956), 1–3.

46. See Lewis Hanke, *All Mankind is One: A Study of the Disputation Between Bartolomé de Las Casas and Juan Ginés de Sepúlvada in 1550 on the Intellectual and Religious Capacity of the American Indians* (De Kalb: Northern Illinois University Press, 1974).

47. Luis N. Rivera, *A Violent Evangelism: The Political and Religious Conquest of the Americas* (Louisville: Westminster/John Knox Press, 1992), part I, 23 ff.

48. Hans Küng, *Theology for the Third Millennium: An Ecumenical View*, trans. Peter Heinegg (New York: Doubleday, 1988).

49. Cornel West, *Beyond Eurocentrism and Multiculturalism. Vol 1: Prophetic Thought in Postmodern Times* (Monroe: Common Courage Press, 1993), 7-30. See also Virginia Fabella, M. M. and Sergio Torres, eds., *Irruption of the Third World: Challenge to Theology* (Maryknoll: Orbis Books, 1983), and Eric Hobsbawm, *The Age of Extremes: A History of the World, 1914–1991* (New York: Pantheon Books, 1995), especially chap. 15.

50. Dwight Hopkins, "Black Theology and Globalization" in *Peace Review*, Vol. 7, No. 1 (1995), 41–45.

51. See my translator's preface to Enrique Dussel's book, *The Underside of Modernity* (op cit.).

52. Jon Sobrino, *The True Church and the Poor* (Maryknoll: Orbis Books, 1985), 10ff.

53. David J. Krieger, *The New Universalism: Foundations for a Global Theology* (Maryknoll: Orbis Books, 1991), see introduction.

54. See Enrique Dussel, "The 'world-system': Europe as 'Center' and Its 'Periphery.' Beyond Eurocentrism." Lecture presented at the Seminar on Globalization, Duke University, November 1994 (Forthcoming from Duke University Press).

55. Theodor W. Adorno, *Minima Moralia: Reflections from Damaged Life* (London: Verso, 1978), p 247 (my emphasis). This is the great challenge that liberation theology, as well as liberation philosophy, have taken up, namely how to think utopia without a teleology, ontological history, and without the deception of one subtance, one principle, one God that must actualize itself sacrificially in the horizon of human action. In other words, to think liberation without a teleological utopia. Adorno's negative dialectics and his "consumate negativity" are the nucleus of dangerous memory, memory of suffering, memory of fire, in Galeano's sense.

15

The Architectonic of the Ethics of Liberation
On Material Ethics and Formal Moralities[1]

Enrique Dussel

M y strategy of argumentation is as follows: In the *introduction* I will summarize the architectonic of discourse ethics [morality] and will demonstrate the difficulty in both its grounding and its application of its fundamental norm due to an originary dichotomy dating back to Kant. In §1, I will reformulate the meaning of material ethics, showing that it is possible to define the *universality* of material criteria, principles, and imperatives (which have been explained in diverse forms by the different material ethics and frequently quite reductively), but being clear that this is a *necessary but insufficient* moment within a comprehensive ethics.

In §2, I will reinterpret the meaning of formal moralities, since they are, in my opinion, the procedural dimension of the "application" of the material principle (completely inverting the traditional problem concerning this issue). This step must also be considered as a *necessary but insufficient* moment within any ethic worth its name. With these re-inscriptions I will have taken a fundamental step forward in the ongoing dialogue with discourse ethics.

In §3, I will integrate the procedural intention of Peirce's pragmatism, whose discourse ethics has been the first to articulate in its architectonic, but now diachronically as the institutionalization of the valid-good.

In §4, I will situate the transcendental place, the first place, of the historical consciousness of the main actors (the dominated and/or excluded) and of the recent "great critics" of the ruling ethical system. With this I will demonstrate the necessity of the thematic-scientific mediations used by these critics. Among those critics, which include Freud, Nietzsche, Foucault, Hinkelammert, and many others, I will give greater and fundamental relevance to Marx (for his clarity in pointing out the material-economic moment of every ethics of "content"), and to Levinas (in his critique of ethics and morality as such).

In § 5, having integrated the fallibilist thought of Karl-Otto Apel, I will show the meaning of the birth of a new intersubjective consensuality of the *dominated* majorities (domination that is justified by the majority of the material systems that now appear "hegemonic") and *excluded* (exclusion that is presupposed in the also "hegemonic" formal procedures). There thus emerges with clarity the sense of an *anti-hegemonic* intersubjectivity of the dominated and/or excluded before the hegemonic intersubjectivity. In this way we subsume and integrate critically the "democratic principle" in the critical processes, which can manifest itself either *normally* through the transformation of majority or popular movements, or *exceptionally* (a few time every century perhaps), through revolutionary movements. This is the theme of the future "institutionality," decided valid and consensually by the new intersubjectivity. I have not negated the intention of discourse ethics, but have subsumed it into a more complex architectonic that is also material, realistic, and critical. I believe that in this way I can show that the ethics of liberation is neither anarchist, nor reformist nor necessarily revolutionary.[2] This level will be denominated the "critical formal morality."

In §6, I will show how it is only now that the ethical-material and formal-moral consensual process of liberation can be understood. This process deconstructs the hegemonic system that excludes and dominates in order to re-construct or construct (in an exceptional case re-construction is not possible since the order is a new order), through "critical transformations" in the diverse "fronts"[3] of possible liberation (ecological, feminist, political, economic, pedagogical, racial, etc.), a "new order." All of these "transformations," or "constructions" of a "*new* order," will have to make use of the principle of consensuability, of the institutionalization of argumentation, i.e., formal principles that supersede in many aspects, but that do not invalidate the older principle of *phronesis* which continues to have validity in the individual order. Due to space constraints, this short contribution will be able only to advance some precise theses, situating the thematic without exhausting it. A more detailed analysis of this architectonic will be presented in the respective chapters of my *Ethics of Liberation (in the Epoch of Globalization and Exclusion)* that I am presently writing.

Introduction. The Formal Architectonic of Discourse Ethics

The architectonic of discourse ethics faces a critical knot (inasmuch as it is not undone) in the question of the application (*Anwendung*) of the basic norm of the procedural morality[4] (which has a different sense in Aristotle or Kant[5]). But this forced (or impossible) "landing" is the result of "taking off" from the ground in an ambiguous flight. The inadequacy of the "take off" determines the impossibility of the "landing." That is to say, the architectonic begins by not subsuming the ethical sense of the *materiality* of human life, and only considers the universal conditions of possibility of the moral validity of decisions, norms, or maxims that are adopted concretely. The empirical, historical, material is not negated; it is simply relegated since it has no relevance for the testing of the validity of rational universality of the formal intersubjective consensuability. The question of "validity" has absolute priority with respect to the question of "content" of every ethics of the "good."

Discourse ethics then, as with Kant, does not intend to ground a material ethics. This task is declared unnecessary and impossible, and for that reason both Apel and Habermas situate from the outset the entire problem of ethical philosophy at the level of formal morality, not seeing the importance of the indicated level of the "contents," of the material, of the *eu bíos* (good life) or the "bien (*good, das Gute*)." Is it because the death that faces life in the fields and streets of Mali, Haiti, or Bangladesh, the poverty and the state of no-right of the peripheral countries are not massive daily events in Europe or the United States? Kant clearly formulates the question: "All practical principles that presuppose an (material) object of the appetative faculty as determining foundation of the will, are empirical and can not *give practical laws*."[6]

In a prior text he expressed even more explicitly:

... to preserve one's life is a duty, and besides this every one has also an immediate inclination to do so. But on account of this the often anxious precautions taken by the greater part of mankind for this purpose have no inner worth, and the maxim of their action is without moral content. (Kant 1948, 65)

Discourse ethics shares this position with certain differences. This supposes three reductions: 1) The "inclinations" (the corporeality [*Leiblichkeit*]) are pathological, capricious, and, in the last instance, egotistical and particular—that is, not universal—and therefore do not enter into the determination of the basic norm. 2) The "good life" of each culture has its own characteristics without their being able to be grounded rationally, which furthermore makes it impossible to: a) ground the content of the particular *ethos*, and b) moreover, when a particular ethos is to be compared with the *ethos* of another culture (as it takes place in the "world-system" since 1492), it is impossible to carry out an inter-cultural dialogue (since there are no intrinsic trans-cultural criteria), or to reach an agreement on which of all the "good lives" is the best.[7] 3) The negation of survival as a material ethical principle.

In fact, after having defined the existence of a level A of the grounding of morality,[8] Apel asks himself how to "descend" to the concrete:

Indeed, already with the ultimate grounding [*Letztbegründung*] of the principle of ethics one must take into account *not only* the fundamental norm of the consensual grounding of norms which is acknowledged in the counterfactual anticipation of ideal relations of communication, *but also* simultaneously the fundamental norm of historically linked responsibility, indeed the care [*Sorge*] for the preservation of the natural conditions of living and the historical-cultural achievements of every now factically existing real community of communication. (Apel 1990, 22)

But when he turns to the application of this principle in order to preserve the concrete "natural conditions of living and the historical-cultural achievements," he confesses, "I must also admit that the elucidation of the reasons that lead me to make the distinction between a grounding part A and a grounding part B of discourse ethics, is not yet completely clear" (Apel 1990, 26).

Furthermore, "the conditions of application of an ethics of the

ideal communication community . . . *are not in any way given.*"[9]
That is, since the situational and contingent conditions are not
given[10] (one of them is the non participation of all the possibly
affected in their interests[11]), it is necessary to take recourse to an
"ethics of responsibility"—of a Weberian type—in order to create
the necessary conditions of equality and symmetry.[12]

Here we must note Franz Hinkelammert, who discovers in discourse ethics a lacking form for the articulation of material ethics,
writing:

> A norm is valid only to the extent that it is applicable, and it is
> applicable to the extent that *it allows us to live.* This does in no way
> challenge the validity of the norm as a point of departure, although
> it concerns the decision to apply it. In any event, a norm under
> which one could not live under any circumstance, would be *a priori*
> invalid. This is also true, for instance, in a universal decision for col-
> lective suicide. (Hinkelammert 1994, 137)

The reproduction and growth of human life is the first criterion
of truth (theoretical and practical). This is the absolute condition of
possibility of existence not only of the subjects of argumentation,
but also of the linguistic and conceptual processes themselves.
Seyla Benhabib makes approximately the same critique, given that
Habermas's *principle U* defines the rightful participants in argumentation as "the affected *in their interests*":

> The interests that participants in a discourse bring with them to the
> argumentation situation are ones that they already have as actors in
> the life-world. If, however, participants in discourses bring with
> them their own interpretation of their own interests, then the ques-
> tion immediately suggests itself: given that the satisfaction of the
> interests of *each* is to be viewed as a legitimate and reasonable
> *criterion* in establishing the *universality* of the norm, then is it not
> the case that universality can only result when a corresponding
> "compatibility" or even harmony of interests *really exists* in the life-
> world? (Benhabib 1986, 310–311, emphasis added)

Formal morality always presupposes a material ethics, which
determines it through its criteria of universal and concrete truth,
not only in the sense that it is *that "about" which one must argue,*
but still, and lastly, because of the fact that the validity of the

"agreement" is decided *from* (problematic horizon), *on* (ground), and *in* (the concretely agreed upon) the "content"—which has autonomy in its criteria, principles, or imperatives that one must know how to respect.

§1 The Material Aspect of Ethics: Is There a Universal Material Principle?

I have spoken with Apel of the need for a "transcendental economics" as a correlate to a "transcendental pragmatics."[13] I wanted to indicate that the formal (pragmatics) ought to be articulated with relationship to the material (a decisive example that I put forward was economics (*Oekonomik*), and that this *material* level was an ontological condition or condition of survival with respect to pragmatics (just like this is the *formal* condition of the former). In the same way, Karl Marx helped us to discover the lack of attention in pragmatics to the material conditions (of "content") of the subjects who argue. Now we can formulate the issue with greater precision.

In fact, our thesis could be formulated in the following manner: the "content" aspect of ethics,[14] abstractly, possesses its own universality and it always determines *materially* all the levels of formal morality. The "formal" aspect of morality (the *right, richtig*), the level of universal intersubjective validity (*Gültigkeit, validity*), abstractly, determine in turn *formally* all the levels of the material ethics. It is a matter of a mutual, constitutive and always present co-determination with *diverse senses* (one is "material," the other "formal," thus giving rise to a *real* unity: the valid-good [*el bien-válido*] and the good-validity [*válido-bueno*]). This is a fundamental thesis of the ethics of liberation, because in this way "poverty," the domination of women in their corporeality [*Leiblichkeit*], the discriminated non-white races, etc. could be interpreted ethically from the perspective of the material criteria always already presupposed in all critiques (a negative critique that departs from the "lack of" material realization of subjects; that is to say, from their unhappiness, suffering).

The material aspect of ethics (as Kant indicates) concerns in the last instance the reproduction and growth of human life.[15] For this reason we not only speak of "life" but also of "sur-vival" [*sobrevivencia*].[16] The material principle of ethics which fulfills the criteria of survival, could be enunciated in the following way:

Who acts (seriously or ethically) has already recognized *in actu* the requirements of the possible survival of humanity in a concrete *good human life* (happiness, values, cultural understandings of being [*Seinverständnis*], which is shared with all those who form part of a real, historical *community of life* which has a universality claim and co-solidarity with humanity as such.[17] (Apel 1986, 161)

Without taking recourse to the neo-aristotelians (from both sides of the Atlantic), I would like nevertheless to recall that Aristotle's *eudaimonia* was not the "end" of a Weberian instrumental reason, but instead the *telos*,[18] and as Heidegger put it, an "understanding-of-Being as potentiality-for-Being [*Seinsverständnis als Seinkön-nen*]."[19] In any event, that very same ontological "understanding of Being" presupposes an access to reality that we will call "originary ethical reason" (pre-ontological). This thematic requires that it be reviewed with care.[20]

Now I would like to refer to the utilitarians, who have been criticized since Moore up through Rawls. This position dates back to the empiricist tradition that takes pleasure as the exclusive moment (and in this reduction resides its error) for the material principle of ethics, as Locke indicated in his *An Essay Concerning Human Understanding*: "Good and evil are nothing but pleasure or pain, or that which occasions or procures pleasure or pain."[21] Jeremy Bentham's utilitarianism, so naive in many aspects, defines in the same fashion the ethical criteria: "[The] *fundamental axiom* . . . is the greatest happiness of the greatest number that is the measure of right and wrong (Bentham 1948, 3). John Stuart Mill, in turn, declares, "The creed which accepts as the foundation of moral *utility* or the *greatest happiness principle* holds that actions are right in proportion as they tend to promote happiness, wrong as they tend to produce the reverse of happiness" (Mill 1957, 10).

"Pleasure" (as mere sensation) or "happiness" (as "background feeling") certainly indicates a subjective aspect of the "content" of ethics—whose conflicts, contradictions, or exceptions ought to be treated by the "application" of the formal principle—but this is by no means the only aspect of every material ethics.

In fact, all material ethics[22] remind us of the pre-ontological condition of possibility as necessity of the reproduction or growth of human life, of "*sur*-vival" of every human act. A foundation of this material principle can also be argued against the skeptic[23] (who will present himself again[24]) in similar terms to the demonstration that is performed by discourse ethics of its principle through the medium of the performative self-contradiction: anyone who acts does so for the conservation and growth of human life, concretely for some "good,"[25] otherwise he ought to let himself die (and even he who would let himself die, would contradict himself performatively[26] if he tried to make explicit the motive of his suicide). But, above all, we must argue against the cynic who argues in favor of the death of those who are "superfluous," and who do not know or can not defend themselves (as F. Hayek expresses with reference to the market and competition). The problem is the position of the suicide. Who selects death, selects not to elect absolutely. In any event, all of these material aspects are *necessary but not sufficient*. For this reason we must not simply ignore the material aspect of the ethics of content, because then we would not be able to count on the criteria of survival that is the *foundation* with respect to every other formal criteria, principle, norm, decision, institution, argumentation, etc.

There are various objections. For instance, no one can indicate concretely and exhaustively the determinations that make up his own "good"[27]; it is difficult that here and now someone could say which type of historical cultural "good life" is the best; internal criteria to *Sittlichkeit* that would allow intercultural dialogue are not always available; etc.[28] Furthermore, there are persons who sacrifice their lives (for example, heroes), demonstrating that survival is not the first principle. To all of this we would answer that, in the first place, this principle is *fundamental* and *necessary*, but is far from being *sufficient*, and, for that reason, needs other criteria and principles for its concrete "application."

On the other hand, the question is not about determining the "content" of *this* "good life" or whether or not it has internal criteria[29] for the external intercultural dialogue (for which Habermas has given good reasons with respect to modernity[30]), but of simply affirming the fact that no one can act if he does not have in view a good or a good life. It does not matter which, but it has to be some. And, lastly, there is nothing further from egoism than this principle since it is also an intersubjective material principle that raises a *universal validity claim*[31] that can reach potentially co-solidarity with humanity (although this can restrict itself as egoism, ethnocentrism, totalitarian nationalism, etc. and in this case opposes itself to other criteria or co-determining principles. Here the *formal* rational "procedure" that reaches validity and judges as invalid the act that affirms the mere particularity over universality, is required). The moment of the content of ethics speaks of the question of *practical* truth; the formal moment refers to the moral theme of *validity*. Both moments are necessary and co-determine each other in order to reach a greater sufficiency (but not yet complete, as we will see).

Let us reiterate. The criteria of reproduction and growth of human life internal to every culture allows all, in the first place, to be self-critical with respect to the intrinsic moments that hinder this very life; and, in the second place, allows them from the universality of this criteria to establish a dialogue with other cultures (with respect to the valid or invalid of its manner of achieving the reproduction or growth of human life). This universality of material ethics has been negated by formal moralities and has been wrongly formulated by utilitarianism, communitarianism, axiologies, and other material ethics—and for this they have been justly criticized.

§2 The Function of the Formal Moment of Morality, Procedural Universality

Since the material principle is not sufficient for its own concrete "application,"[32] to explain its conflicts, contradictions, external confrontation with other conceptions of the ethical life, and exceptions, etc., it is *necessary* to exercise the formal consensual rational principle of intersubjectivity that can attain moral validity. But, in contrast to discourse ethics, which attempts to develop an ethics *exclusively* from out of the sole formal moral principle, liberation ethics attempts to subsume all that has been attained by discourse ethics (including its formal foundation) with respect especially to the pragmatic use of the intersubjective principle of universalization (transformed kantian principle of validity), but inverting its sense. It is not a question of applying the basic norm to the empirical-historical, but rather, conversely, the formal basic norm has as function to "apply" the material principle.[33] That is to say, procedurally adequate intersubjectivity attains the validity of a *material* "agreement" in as much as it departs from the criteria of survival and the ethical principle of content ("Who acts . . .").

The formal aspect of morality departs from the criteria of intersubjectivity, from the basic pragmatic norm or principle of universality that attains communitarian validity. But, reiterating, now it has inverted what has been affirmed with respect to it, given that it concerns a principle of "application" of the material norm. The material norm is the condition of possibility of a "content" of the "application" of the formal norm in as much as if one argues it is because one intends to know *how* one can (ought) to survive here and now: the material norm gives "content" to that which has been agreed upon through consensus (in the last instance, a mediation for survival of "needing" subjects and thus participants), within the horizon circumscribed by the "impossibility of selecting death."

The formulation of the basic norm or the moral-pragmatic principle of discourse ethics is the following:

> Who acts has already given evidence in *actu* that the *ideal rules of argumentation* in an, in principle unlimited, communication community of persons who recognize each other reciprocally as equals, represent *normative conditions of possibility of the decision on ethical validity claims*.[34] (Apel 1980, 161)

What has been gained in the analysis of discourse ethics we must subsume here, but with the caveat that it is not presented as the only principle; its function is also redefined.[35] And, lastly, the formal pragmatic morality is coordinated with material ethics (including its economic instances, as we will see below).

Here we must underscore that since Aristotle, the formal moment of validity (analyzed by the Latins in the theme of *conscientia*) was accomplished by the "practical argument." In fact, the understanding of the good (practical horizon that functions as major premise) was the point of departure. The act of practical reason guided by *phronesis* allowed for the application of the principle to a practical goal: the decision taken (*hypólepsis*[36]), whose validity was granted to it by the strength of the practical argument. As was the case for Hegel, practical reason (the *praktikós lógos* of the Greeks) worked from within the attainment of the "good." In other words, for the pre-modern ethicists[37] the formal-rational moment was always integrated within the internal constitution of the good or of its "material content." This "good," furthermore, is desired, but this desire was "selected"—it was never merely irrational as it was later for the empiricists. Practical reason had been analyzed and integrated in a far more complex fashion (but not so in Modernity, especially, since the dualist Kantian disjunction), and the ethical-material moment was coordinated with the formal-moral moment. Today, it is evident that we can accomplish radical transformations to these distinctions and attain a greater precision, but in the line of an organic subsumption, thus not perpetuating reductive rationalisms or irrational material ethics of incommunicability. Practical reason is that which unfolds the ultimate horizon (the intersubjective "understanding of Being," the material or the content, the "good" par excellance).[38] Theoretical reason functions within its horizon and only circumscribes abstract systems of greater precision and of lesser reality. Practical-ethical discursivity (formal-material) must be differentiated from the mere theoretical (or scientific) discursivity. On this point, discourse ethics ought to overcome a certain reductive rationalism.

§3 The Proceduralism of the Valid-Good: The Ethical-Moral Synthesis

In the prior sections we have considered synchronically and *abstractly* the material aspects of ethics and the formal aspects of morality. Now we will consider them concretely, subsumptively, procedurally, or *diachronically* in a more complex unity.

Determining the valid according to the consensual exigencies of intersubjectivity, which allows for the "application" of the criteria of survival under the communitarian principle of material ethics, we now ought to ascend toward the concrete. It is thus that we discover that the ethical is already procedural (Peirce's pragmatic principle). The following citation suggests for the theme:

> [The] Category the First is the Idea of that which is such as it is regardless of anything else . . . Category the second is the Idea of that which is such as it is as being Second to some First, regardless of anything else . . . it is *Reaction* . . . Category the Third is the Idea of that which is such as it is as being a Third,[39] or Medium, between a Second and its First. (Peirce 1960, 566)

Pragmatic proceduralism is mainly established at the level of what William James called *verification*. What is of interest to us here is the practical process of a material ethics of "contents" (of *liberation*), and moreover, consensual, formal, and critical, since the pragmatists, from Peirce, through James, up to Mead and Dewey will remain within the horizon of the North American *common sense*, though progressivist.[40]

The articulation of the valid-good (of the validity of the good) is not always given simultaneously in the diachronic process.

Possible Diachrony of Validity and the Good

Moments	§3	§4	§5	§6
The Formal	The hegemonic validity	The dominating validity	The anti-hegemonic validity	The new validity
The Material	The legitimate good	The illegitimate good	The future good	The legitimate good

Explanation of Schema: Moments §3-6 correspond to the same paragraphs in this work.

A good point of departure is Habermas's definition of legitimacy: "Legitimacy means that there are good arguments for a political order's claim to be recognized as right and just; a legitimate order deserves recognition" (Habermas 1979, 178).

Antonio Gramsci[41] differentiated between a hegemonic order (when it had ideological legitimacy, in Habermas's sense) and an order of domination (when legitimate coercion, in Weber's sense, becomes illegitimate coercion. This is the transition from level §3 of our Schema to level §4).

Procedurally, then, the concrete content of a project of reproduction and growth of human life, attains procedurally intersubjective validity thanks to the different modes of argumentation in the respective real communication community. The "good" is developed diachronically, historically, and concretely. At the political level of late capitalism [*Spätkapitalismus*] (it could also be the family-erotic sexism, or the pedagogical-cultural elitist culture, etc.), the "democracy principle" replaces the traditional treatment of *phronesis*. In any event, it is necessary to recall that the validity of consensual agreements (be they of norms, laws, institutions, actions, etc.) are about material contents. On this point, economics, and we do not speak of the sciences of economics[42] [*Oekonomik* and not *Wirtschaftswissenschaft*], obtains great significance in the debate. For this reason, I began this dialogue with the *material content* (technological economic of capitalism, from Marx's critical perspective[43]). Validity, politically speaking, ought to always have economic content, as reproduction and growth of human life, survival. The construction of a common good, intersubjective valid-good, is the diachronic effect of a historical process, in which the "rule of law" attains validity because a certain number of goods (vital, technical, economic, cultural, aesthetics, ethical, etc.) are effectively subsumed by the participants, thus creating a "common welfare" that makes the established order acceptable, which grounds *materially* the consensual legitimacy of the hegemonic system. In the case of capitalism, the project of the medieval past and of the first centuries of the bourgeois Modernity (liberty, equality, property for all) came to constitute the substratum on which the hegemonic validity is coordinated in a balanced fashion with the legitimate good in the majoritarian consensuality of the population of a nation or a state.

The process of constitution of a "rule of law" achieves a "classical" moment which all or the majority support with their consensus legitimacy.

The criteria of proceduralism is included in the definition of the respective principle: the valid-good, since it is diachronic, historical, dialectical, can never be assured to remain so for ever. Continuously, then, it can become invalid, illegitimate, unjust.

§4 The Architectonic Place of Critical Alterity

Only now can we begin to glimpse the specificity of liberation ethics. We could not understand its proposals before I explained them in the dialogue with discourse ethics. I believe that thus far I have failed because I have not presented clearly the phases of the theme. Only now can it be understood, for example, that the *"fact" of poverty*[44] in peripheral capitalism (in the epoch of central late capitalism) is not an immediate fact. Only now, in the light of the criteria and material principle (of the community of survival, of subjective happiness, and of the objective good, in the last instance, of the whole humanity), legitimated by the intersubjective validity of the ruling system, a massive fact can be discovered: the majority of this humanity finds itself sunk in "poverty," "unhappiness," "suffering," domination, and/or exclusion. The utopian project of the ruling system (economic, political, erotic, etc.) is discovered (in view of its own claims to freedom, equality, property for all, and other myths and symbols . . .) to be contradictory since the majority of its participants find themselves affected or deprived of the possibility of fullfilling the needs that the system itself has proclaimed as rights. It is from the *positivity* of the ethical criteria of survival (and its respective principle in concrete) that the *negativity* of death, of hunger, misery, the oppression of corporeality by work, the repression of the unconscious and the libido, particularly of women, the lack of power of the subjects over institutions, the ruling of inverted values, illiteracy, etc. can now attain an exact *ethical sense*. "The Other"—on whom I have so much insisted—appears as other of the "normality" presented in §1-3: the normal, ruling, "natural," legitimate system appears now as Marx's "fetishised capital," as Levinas's ethically perverse "totality," and as such it will lose its formal or intersubjective validity, its hegemony. It now appears before the eyes of the dominated and/or excluded only as imposed, as "dominating validity." Here can be situated Wellmer's[45] proposal with respect to the universal validity of the "negation of the non-generalizable maxim," Thou shall not make any one miserable!;[46] Thou shall not inmiserate any one! (Marx); Thou shall not take any one's life! (Hinkelammert).[47]

Here we can pause and underscore two essential moments: a) critical and ethical consciousness—which is to know to listen to the interpellation of the Other in her suffering corporeality—has as first subject the dominated and/or excluded. They, therefore, have a *concrete, historical, existential consciousness*, as is the case with Rigoberta Menchú.[48] This is the beginning of stage I of the process of *concientizacâo*.[49] b) In a second moment, and only for those who have some "experience"[50] of "us" *with* the dominated and/or excluded, can the misery of the other be thought reflexively: it is the thematic critique (scientific or philosophical, properly put, but where both are *critical*). It is the *explicit thematic critique* (the *krinêin*: to take distance in order to pronounce a "judgment" from the "tribunal") of the "great critics," even including the postmoderns.

In fact, for the rationalism of discourse ethics,[51] the postmodern critics appear only to launch themselves against reason *as such*. In part this is true, but one ought to distinguish between the critique of *dominating* reason as *dominating* (and that thus turns irrational) and the critique of reason *as such*. Extreme rationalism rejects all critiques of reason without taking note that the intention of some of these critics is directed against *dominating* reason (this is the case with Nietzsche, who does not distinguish clearly between mere reason and dominating reason), thus making itself complicit with the domination of modern reason (or at least it does not take sufficient note of eurocentric domination or that of capitalism since this system not only colonizes as "money" the life world, but above all materially, as the accumulation of surplus value of the workers and as transfer of value by peripheral capitalism[52]).

Liberation ethics can subsume the critique of the "great critics" (Nietzsche, Freud, Horkheimer, Adorno,[53] Foucault, Derrida, Lyotard, etc. and particularly Marx and Levinas) in as much as they criticized the "dominating" aspects of modern reason. But liberation ethics can just the same, against the irrationalism of some of these critics (especially against Nietzsche and the postmoderns), defend the *universality of reason* "as such." This double movement of subsumption and negation is possible (which is not possible for discourse ethics or the postmoderns) if we situate ourselves *outside*, *before* or transcendentally with respect to the system or life of the valid-good (capitalism, machismo, racism, etc.); that is from the perspective of the alterity of the dominated and/or exteriority of the excluded, with a critical and deconstructive position before the "hegemonic validity" of the system (now as *merely dominating*), and judging the "good" of the dominating/excluding system as illegitimate. Thus, although we had seen the importance of material ethics (of a MacIntyre or a Taylor), now this can be put in question from the perspective of *dominated*. The alterity of the dominated discovers as illegitimate the material sytem, the "content," the "good"[54] (what we have called in another work the *principium oppressionis*[55]). In the same way, the principle of intersubjective pragmatic validation can also be called into question from the standpoint of the necessary exclusion of the affected, not yet discovered as affected in their needs by the dominating system (what I have called the *principium exclusionis*). This concerns a critical intersubjective consensuability of *second degree*.

The "great critics" return to the scepticism that Levinas announces.[56] They are sceptics of the legitimacy of the ruling system. To know how to distinguish between the skepticism that emerges from the normality of the system (§2), from the scepticism of the system as dominating (§4), is to distinguish between a) the sceptic, who deserves to be refuted in order to retain the consistency of the discourse, b) the sceptic at the service of the cynic (who negates the rationality of the critique that struggles for the new future system, and c) the critical sceptic or liberator of a past agreement (today dominating), which has become invalid in view of the future validity of a new fairer agreement.

The strong point of departure, decisive in this entire critique, is, then, the contradiction that is produced in the suffering corporeality (*Leiblichkeit*) of the dominated (as worker, as Amerindian, as African slave, as dominated Asian of the colonial world, as feminine corporeality, as non-white race, as future generations that will suffer in their corporeality the ecological destruction that the present system inflicts on the planet). This suffering materiality becomes a criteria of material "content," of corporeality, of survival, of material ethics, at the level of the "good,"—which refuses validity to the system that produces the poverty or the unhappiness of the dominated or excluded (as negative universal imperative or prohibition of a maxim that is non-generalisable, or of the simple "impossibility to choose to die"), whether in the form of norms, acts, institutions, or arguments, as in the case of capital. Only Marx has demonstrated this *fact* in the last century[57]: the exploitation of the ethical subject, who is a member of the community of life, and who is affected in his corporeality thorugh daily work that is concretized in the non-fulfilled basic needs, that is, unhappiness (impossibility of living). The ethical subject of the poor finds itself materially oppressed and formally excluded. Therefore one would have to develop an analytic of the ethical-formal criteria and to define from it the critical principle. From the criteria of survival is now deduced a negative criteria or the *criteria of the prohibition of the non-survival*, of the ethical prohibition of the impoverishment of other, of the infliction of suffering, of the killing of the Other. The ethical-critical principle could be formulated in approximately the following way:

> Who acts *critically*-ethically has always already recognized *in actu* the dignity of the ethical subject that is negated in a hegemonic community of life that prevents the sur-vival of the dominated (impossibility of living), and in a real communication community that excludes them asymmetrically from argumentation.[58]

The above indicated critique is not possible without the recognition (*Anerkennung*) of the Other (of the dominated/excluded in the hegemonic sytem) as autonomous, free, equal, ethical subject, who is a possible origin of dissent or of consensus. The recognition of the Other, the "originary-ethical reason" (of Levinas), is prior to critique and prior to argument (to discursive or dialogic reason), and is at the origin of the process, prior to the interpellation or the call of the poor to solidarity in the system. This "ethical consciousness"[59] is attained, above all and before anyone else, in the intersubjective or communitarian subjectivity of the oppressed and/or excluded people itself (this is the origin of the *concientização* à la Paulo Freire, which is always political[60]).0

.§5 Anti-Hegemonic Formal Intersubjectivity

Now we enter stage II of the *cocientização*. The dominated and/or excluded (represented in popular movements, feminists, ecologists—the communitarian subjects) attain a *thematized critical consciousness*, thanks to the explicit critical contribution (scientific or philosophical of the organic intellectual). We recall that there are then three moments: a) An ethical critical consciousness of the dominated and/or excluded themselves, which is pre-thematic but substantively originary; b) a thematically explicit consciousness (critical scientific); c) an existential thematic critical consciousness, historical or practical of the people itself. From now forward spirals the communitarian intersubjective subject of the dominated and/or excluded in coordination with the "organic intellectuals" under different circumstances. This concerns the entire praxis-theory-praxis thematic that is now situated in an entirely different manner by the ethics of liberation.

Then, once the critique has been initiated in the dominated groups, an anti-hegemonic communication community starts to develop, which begins to work according to the "principle of democracy" (consensual intersubjectivity that replaces the older treatment of *phronesis*), a project of future good (not yet real but possible: the utopia of the realizable liberation[61]) from the perspective of a consensual proceduralism on the base of agreements not yet valid for the hegemonic, dominating society.

The existential-thematic *critical* proceduralism grows from the different "fronts of struggle" of domination and/or exclusion of alterity: from the erotic front (against male sexism), the ecological (against the destruction of the planet for future generation), the economic (against the capitalism destructive of humanity and the earth), etc. The pragmatic norm in a society in equilibrium, in "normal times" no longer applies. It ought to move on to an exceptional or "abnormal" application of the norm. When the majority of a people is dominated or excluded, the principle of universality changes subjects, and from the established hegemonic communication community it passes to be exercised by the anti-hegemonic communication community of the dominated and excluded. The reflexive and thematic, self-conscious (concienticized) intersubjectivity of the dominated and excluded begins now to behave as a new intersubjectivity of a future validity. This is the process of liberation proper at its formal-pragmatic level.

The materiality of the survival of the dominated and excluded once again repeats in an over-determined fashion in the moment analyzed in §1. To the extent that it is necessary to "apply" the criteria of survival against the established system, the intersubjectivity of the dominated and/or excluded utilizes formally the principle of universality (of the *new* universality against the older dominating intersubjectivity) and proceeds to criticize the ruling valid consensus. This entire formal process is now thematized; the deconstruction of domination counts with the *internal* articulation of the scientist and the critical philosopher (it is only in this fashion that the ethics of liberation can be practiced).

We have to distinguish clearly between the assuming of pre-thematic and implicit consciousness, but remembering that it is the radical ethical origin and the exercise of what we have called "the originary ethical reason," based on the recognition of the Other (analyzed in §4), and the moment at which we are not located. A pure and universal prohibition: "It is forbidden to empoverish any one!" is not the same as the complex and positive imperative, "Liberate the dominated, the poor, the excluded!" Now it is a call to action, to the operative responsibility, where the thematization, the scientific-philosophical articulation of the popular leaders, movements, or "organic intellectuals" ought to mediate. It is neither populist spontaneism nor elitist vanguardism. As critical material, the formal principle (the "liberation principle" [*das Befreiungsprinzip*]) could be formulated in the following manner, and this in turn subsumes all the prior principles: Who acts critically-ethically from the recognition of the dignity of every ethical subject, from the consciousness of the non-survival of the dominated (from the impossibility of choosing death) and from the non-participation of the excluded, has always already affirmed *in actu* the responsibility[62] that he shares in solidarity with all those who have reached the same degree of lucidity, and their obligation to realize transformations (normally) or systematic construction (exceptionally), through norms, actions, institutions, etc., of a new and more just future community of life and communication.

Before the "impossibility of choosing death,"[63] one must deploy critically, intersubjectively a concrete alternative for the "possibility of living." The "principle of hope" is the positive future horizon of something more complex: the "principle of liberation."

We have already demonstrated that the imperative: "liberate the excluded and/or oppressed!" (the "poor" of Levinas, as the common demonation for the dominated in general) presupposed always already different levels: (1) the comprehension of a material imperative good (happiness, wealth, etc.); (2) the validity of a consensual formal moral system; (3) the discovery of the non-fullfillment of this good with respect to the dominated themselves (misery, poverty, etc.) by the dominators themselves, first, and of the critical intellectuals, later: it is at this level that consciousness of "new rights" is born; (4) the negation of the hegemonic validity when the asymmetrical exclusion of the non-participating majorities is discovered; the thematizing critics incorporate themselves to the alterity of the dominated and to the exteriority of the excluded; (5) the organic creation of the new critical thematic intersubjectivity (this is the entire question of the relation between praxis-theory of the "organic intellectual" of Gramsci, analyzed ambigously in the problem of the party and "truth" in Lenin's vanguard[64]); (6) the acting communitarially for a project of liberation through a critique of utopias and through a praxis institutionally creative.

The concept of "fetishism" in Marx speaks to us of all of these levels of the naïve, false, or critical conciousness. The process of "concientization" (in its different phases and articulations, from the everyday existentiality of the poor to the thematic of the intellectual and their mutual and constant feedback) is the entire intersubjective formal and consensual movement of the oppressed that works *from within* the new project, the new, future, communitarian validity, in a participative, thematic and organizing fashion, at the political, consensual, thematic levels.

It is in relation and in the interior of this critical-communitarian intersubjectivity of the dominated and/or excluded that the ethics of liberation ought to function. It argues in favor of the ethical sense of the struggle for the sur-vival and for the moral validity of the praxis of liberation of the oppressed/excluded. The grounding of the material principle and the moral pragmatic norm is essential for the constitution of ethics as theory and as philosophy, but its ultimate historical and social function is directed to establishing the ethical validity of the survival, of the human life of the dominated and/or excluded.

§6 The Praxis of Liberation:
The New Democratic Institutionalization of the Future Valid-Good

We have finally arrived at the central theme.[65] If the material criteria is reproduction and growth of human life, then the praxis of liberation indicates the second moment: "growth of human life." The pure reproduction of "the Same"—as Levinas might say—can be fixation, stabilization, repetition, and domination. Only in the historical-cultural, ethical-political, erotic-pedagogical growth of human life, does human life express itself as *life in exercise*. Now praxis has become equivocal given that it can be domination and/or exclusion of the others (pure reproduction or decay), or it can be praxis of liberation (as critical transformation of growth or radical change of structure) that de-constructs actions, institutions, or systems of domination and/or exclusion. The praxis of liberation is the mediation of the critical transformation of institution or construction of the new system.

Here we can also deal with the most arduous ethical questions. Thus, for example, the legitimate coercion of the system becomes illegitimate when this is deployed against the dominated and/or excluded that take consciousness and struggle for the "new rights" (the levels analyzed in §4-5). Violence is force exercised against the legitimate right (valid) of the Other. Legitimate coercion thus turns violent domination (public repression) when this is exercised against those who have discovered "new rights." The ruling system does not perceive rapidly enough the changing situation. The older legitimate coercion becomes illegitimate in the face of a new social consciousness. In turn, the defense that the dominated and/or excluded make of their discovered "new rights" can not be violent (because it is not exercised against any rights of the Other), instead it is "just defense" with appropriate means (that mantain proportion with the illegitimate or violent coercion in order to be effectively a "realistic defense," strategically and tactically, of right [law] itself). The validation of this defensive action of the community of life and the anti-hegemonic communication community that promotes the sur-vival does not attain validity from the outset in the dominant community. This is not a question of a "just war,"[66] given that war is always unjust because it is violent, rather, it concerns the "just defense" (just coercion) of the oppressed, excluded or attacked in their rights.

Since ethical action is procedural, now we can see clearly that the critical-liberating point of departure is the "*unjust* normality" and the project is that of a more just society or institution, where the dominated and/or excluded will be constitutive and participant agents in a material justice (moments §5–6 of our schema).

The formal "application" of the principle of universality in the process of liberation, in the elaboration of a new type of society, etc. is played out at the formal level of the new inter-subjectivity, of the "principle of democracy." The new community (of yesterday's dominated and excluded) becomes with time in the new communication community, "normal." It is the social movements, pressure groups, critical political parties, etc., which triumph in social struggles.

The process continues uninterrupted in history. It is the history of individual, communitarian, institutional acts; it is the history of the struggle of ethnic subjects, of social movements of classes, of national, cultural, global movements. An act, an institutionalization or system, can be judged absolutely "good" or definitively "valid" only at the end of history; that is, the goodness and correctness of an act or an institution can never be validated *absolutely*: neither in its intention nor in its consequences, nor in the short term, midterm, or long term of global history. For this reason Hegel included in his ethics world history, but he pretended to be able to execute this judgment as the "court of world history"[67]: this is a dangerous illusion, one which Soviet stalinism also fell pray to, and which today neo-liberal capitalism also flirts with when it would like to eliminate all alternatives that could supersede it. In any event, material, formal, procedural, critical, and liberating criteria and principles guide behaviour that is oriented to the determination of the ethical validity of acts in that uninterrupted process of reflection, "application," and fullfillment of actions that is realized in view of the furtherance of a "valid-good," the "good-validity," from the standpoint of the criteria of sur-vival and under the light of the critical consensual intersubjectivity of the dominated and or excluded majorities.

Translated by Eduardo Mendieta

Notes

1. Paper presented at the Eichstätt seminar, April 4, 1995, in dialogue with K. O. Apel. I would like first of all to thank the participants in the seminar on the history of Latin American philosophy (UNAM, Mexico), especially Juan José Bautista, Enrique Gurría, Mario Rojas, Germán Gutiérrez, Rita Vergara, Marcio Luis Coasta, and many others. Furthermore, in this work, in order to facilitate dialogue, I will give to the word "ethics" its material sense of *ethos* or *Sittlichkeit*, and to "morality" its formal sense of intersubjective validity, leaving *"critical* ethics" for §4, on which the sense of an ethics of liberation is based. The ethics of liberation differs from other ethics because it formulates a critical transformation or revolution (both positions are possible for it) for society departing from the dominated and/or excluded as a formal criteria.

2. Again, and lastly, I would like to repeat that the specificity of the ethics of liberation is that it departs from the dominated and/or exluded in normal (here it is neither reformist nor meliorist, but formulates a partial, critical transformation) or exceptional times.

3. The "spheres" of justice of Walzer, are now transformed into the "fronts" of "struggle for recognition" (even more radical than that noted by Honneth, 1992).

4. We have already demonstrated how Apel includes at the level of the foundation material moments (e.g. the recognition of the dignity of the person) with which he falls into a certain contradiction (see Dussel 1993c and 1994).

5. See Apel, 1990, p. 24.

6. Kant, *Kritik der praktischen Vernunft*, A 38 (Kant, 1968, VI, 127.

7. Both arguments in b) can be refuted. The question is not whether there are criteria for an inter-cultural dialogue, nor which "good life" is better, but rather that every human act (here is universality) presupposes *a priori* (a historical but also ontological *apriori*) a "good life" as a horizon of ethical meaning out of which one can and ought to act. The universality of material ethics resides in the uncircumventability (*Nichthintergehbarkeit*) of this ontological presupposition.

8. In this essay we will not return to the theme of the foundation. In Dussel, 1993c and 1994, I have shown that Apel's formal foundation already includes material moments (such as the recognition of the other argumentation partners as "persons of equal dignity"), which would in turn imply a certain contradiction.

9. *Ibid.*, p. 32. "The reason for this is simply that the conditions for the application of discourse ethics have not yet been realized" (*Ibid.*, p. 32). "The application of the principle of discourse ethics—for example, the practice of a discursive-argumentative regulation of conflicts strictly separated from the

application of a rationality of strategic negotiation—can be attained only approximately where the relations of ethical life [*Sittlichkeit*] and law themselves make it possible" (*Ibid.*, 33). The formula is frequently repeated: application is impossible if the necessary conditions are not present.

10. See Apel 1985, p. 261.

11. In the Third World it is often the case that the conditions of *survival* (because of poverty) of the possible participants of the real community of communication are not given.

12. Concerning this problem, see my article, Dussel 1994, pp. 87–92.

13. See Dussel 1993.

14. It concerns the *good* (*das Gute*) (and the economic goods also) objectively, and of *happiness* subjectively, the *common good* (as synthesis) of the *community of life* (*Lebensgemeinschaft*) (as subject), and of evaluative *values* (this is the locus of the mediation for the preservation and enhancement of life), etc. When we speak of "life" in this work, it ought to be always understood as "human life," as cultural, institutional (familiar, political, etc.) life. With this we effectively abandon the "transcendental" level and we situate ourselves at a foundational *practical* level, which takes the material as point of departure.

15. Heidegger, commenting on Nietzsche, indicates that "value is the condition of the enhancement of life (*Steigerung des Lebens*)" (Heidegger, 1961, I, p. 488.); that is in Nietzsche's words, "The standpoint of "value" is the standpoint of conditions of preservation and enhancement for complex forms of relative life-duration within the flux of becoming." (F. Nietzsche, *Der Wille zur Macht*, 715, (Nov. 1887–March 1888); in Heidegger, 1961, II, pp. 101ff.). For Nietzsche, life is "will to power" and therefore domination. For the Latin American people, "life" in its strong sense is an instinct *(Trieb)* of extreme ethical positivity. In this sense, mediation has value insofar as it is real possibility for life. It is evident that there are no values without cultural intersubjectivity, and for the same reason they constitute an essential part of the "content" of a historical-concrete "ethical life."

16. The "sur [*sobre*]" of survival indicates, first, life from the perspective of the higher functions of the "mind" (such as conceptual categorization, conscience, linguistic competence, self-consciousness, autonomy, etc.), and second, enhancement, development, new processes of innovation or cultural invention, and the creation of new conditions for human *life*.

17. I have transformed the formulation of the procedural moral principle of discourse ethics into a possible formulation of the ethical material principle (see Apel 1986, p. 161).

18. ". . . Happiness [*eudaimonia*] is among the things that are prized and complete [*teleion*]. It seems to be so also from the fact that it is a first principle [*arkhé*]; for it is for the sake of this that we all do everything else, and the first principle and cause of goods [*agathôn*] is, we claim, something prized and divine." Aristotle, *Nichomechean Ethics*, I, 12, 1102a 1–4 [in *The Complete Works of Aristotle*, edited by Jonathan Barnes, Vol. 2 (Princenton: Princeton University Press, 1984), p. 1741]. See Dussel, 1973b.

19. See: "Un-derstanding as *potentiality for Being*" in my work Dussel, 1973, I, p. 47 ff, where we use Heidegger's theses on Volpi, 1992.

20. Discourse ethics does not have reflexive consciousness of its European presuppositions, of its historical "understanding of Being." As we will see later on, the maximum possible critique (due to the differentiation of the cultural world, the natural, and the subjective) allows for the possibility for a "distance" from the "life world" (*Lebenswelt*), but at the same time it requires that one have consciousness of eurocentrism (ethnocentrism of the world-system since 1492). This kind of awareness has not taken place explicitly.

21. Book 1, Chap. 28, # 5, in Locke 1975. In another text, Locke writes: "Things then are good or evil, only in reference to pleasure or pain" (*Ibid*, II, Chap. 20, # 2).

22. Today there exist some material ethics that give importance to history in order to rediscover the ethical sense, as is the case with MacIntyre (1981 and 1988) or Taylor (1975, 1989, and 1992). There are also those that describe some spheres of justice like Walzer (1983); and those of the Hegelian *Sittlichkeit*; etc. However, those already mentioned do not have what I will call the "critical" sense, perhaps with the exception of Walzer, although he still does not integrate sufficiently the formal procedural level of ethics. From a critical point of view (see §4 below), there are material ethics that develop ethics as a complete categorial system on the *intersubjective-communitarian materiality of corporality* of the alienating production and accumulation from out of the relation living-labour/value, as is the case with Marx's material ethics.

23. It is good to remember that discourse ethics is skeptical of material ethics, and these are required to refute this skepticism for the same reasons for which rationalist pragmatism refutes the skeptics of pragmatism.

24. See §4 below. Levinas notes this return, but now we know when this return takes place, and it is as a new "skepticism" that emerges before the ruling system *seen as* "hegemonic" or of "domination." This is the skepticism of the *dominating* reason. These, however, sometimes confuse it with reason *as such*. Yet, the anti-skeptics do not always differentiate between both types of skepticism and for that reason can fall into an a-critical rationalism that is complicit with cynical reason.

25. This argument, obviously, applies to Discourse Ethics, which would fall into a performative self-contradiction if it did not recognize that it *also* argues for ethical, material, biographical, and historical-cultural (European) motives (reasons, for a "good," although this is no more than the "ideal of a rational life," which is already a material content).

26. To act is to postpone death; it is to live; it is to affirm the "impossibility of choosing death." Death is the absolute preclusion of choosing. Suicide is not a mode of being (Heidegger's "being-towards-death"), but the mode through which one simply abandons existence.

27. Sartre, for instance, holds this view with respect to the impossibility of analyzing concretely, exhaustively, the horizon itself of the totality of being in the world, even with the psychoanalytical method. See Dussel 1973, I, pp. 50 and 57.

28. Some contemporary formal moralities list these objections without taking note that the post-conventional ethical consciousness itself (Kohlberg) is always a cultural product. Only in the case that eurocentrism is criticized explicitly, can one have a consciousness free of "conventionalism."

Furthermore, as we will see, the anti-hegemonic critical consciousness opposes the "universality" exercised by an autonoumously ethical individuality, but as ruling, dominating, and would thus be posterior to the stage 6 of Kohlberg, for instance. That is to say, the intent of a "post-conventional" ethics falls back into an "contemporary European conventionalism."

29. The universal principle of the reproduction and growth of human life is an "internal" principle to every culture that serves as a principle of self-correction when a culture "absolutizes" ethnocentrically its claims and negates other cultures. In other words, this principle is the horizon within which *each culture* (whether it be the aztec bantú or postconventional modern) circumscribes a concrete mode of realizing *human life*. This is dealt with in chapter 3 of the *Ethics of Liberation*, which I am presently writing.

30. See Habermas 1981, I, 2,3 (I, pp. 85ff) in the discussion with Peter Winch.

31. This "universal validity claim" would like to indicate that an Aztec or a Bantú or a Modern (with different consciousnesses of the natural, subjective, or social-critical-theoretical, or moral consciousnesses, but at the same time of the "systematic" or as "exteriority," in which case an Egyptian critic—practical critical consciousness of ethical alterity—of the Medium Empire can be more "critical" than a modern who supports "universally" the *status quo*) who grounds his existence from the perspective of a "good life," and which he tries to actualize *as valid for the whole of humanity*. It is clear that when another culture is confronted, or there is an irresolvable conflict, we must appeal to an argumentative or discursive intersubjectivity from out of our own "resources" (in the sense of Taylor 1989), given that no other resources are available. From this *honest and serious* "univerality claim" of every *ethos* as a concretization of the universal exigency for the reproduction and growth of human life present in each culture, it is possible to establish an intercultural dialogue (*from* whence the formal principle of the basic norm of discourse ethics ought to be applied). Ethnocentrism is the deformation of this honest and necessary "universality claim" of every "good life"—dogmatism or fundamentalism is the transition from the "honest universality claim" to the effective imposition through violence of this "world picture (*Weltbild*)" to others. In this last instance, the univerality claim is not demonstrated argumentatively (even if it is with mythical arguments, which are rational), it uses an irrational medium: force.

32. For now "application" will be written in quotes in order to indicate that it does not refer to the classical, kantian, or discourse ethics application (*application, Anwendung*). In these cases, application indicates a movement from above (the universal) downwards (the concrete maxim). Instead, dialectically, it *ascends from the partial abstract* (the maxim) *towards the universal concrete* (the principle): to situate the part in the whole. We ought to speak of a subsuming ascending the particular maxim in the universal whole: this which I have to do (partial, abstract, the maxim) as situated particularity in the whole of the survival of the community, of the nation, of humanity (the universal). From out of the horizon that opens up the "impossibility of chosing death," one argues intersubjectively about the *concrete* manner of accomplishing a norm, action, project, institution. To "apply" now is to situate in a

"whole" of *possibilities* for life. Furthermore, the Other as exteriority, as another "limit" rationality, prevents the traditional application. However, we shall retain the terminology in vogue in order not to confuse.

33. In this case the pragmatic norm (intersubjectively and symmetically procedural in order to attain acceptable validity) is a mediation that is neither autonomous nor indifferent to the content, whose function is to "apply" or to subsume the material concrete (the maxim) in the material universal (the "good").

34. Apel 1980, p. 161 [For full translation of text see Enrique Dussel, *The Underside of Modernity: Apel, Ricoeur, Rorty, Taylor, and the Philosophy of Liberation*, ed. and trans. by Eduardo Mendieta (Atlantic Highlands: Humanities Press, 1996), p. 45, endnote 69.]. For the formulation of the "U" principle in Habermas, see Habermas 1983 and 1991. See also the excellent critique by Wellmer 1986. See also Rehg, 1994, and the special issue of *The Philosophical Forum* edited by Kelly, 1989.

35. Given that if it attains intersubjective validity it is *about* that upon which the "agreement" of all falls: the ethical "content" that is object of argumentation. Without "content" there is neither agreement nor validity. An "empty" agreement can not have validity.

36. For Aristotle, furthermore, this act of "application" of the principle could be corrupted were there to be no "virtue" or "moderation" in the subject: ". . . (This is why we call temperance by this name; we imply that it preserves one's practical wisdom. Now what it preserves is a belief of the kind we have described.)" Aristotle, *Nichomechean Ethics*, 1140b 11–20 [*The Complete Works of Aristotle*, p. 1800].

37. For example, for Aquinas "the good does not fall within the election (*ultimus finis nullo modo sub electione cadit*)" (I–II, C. 13, a.3. c), since it is the first material principle and is always already presupposed. For this reason "the end is desired absolutely (*finis appetitur absolute*)" (*De Veritate*, c. 24, a.6, r.). On the contrary, "all of that which is labor by us is possibility (*possibilia*)" (*Ibid.*, a.5, c.). To apply the principle in a deliberation is "a syllogism of operatives (*operabilium*)" (*Ibid.*, c. 14, a.5, c.) on "the singular contingents (*singularia contingentia*)" (II–II, c. 49, a.5, c.).

38. See Dussel 1973, I, p. 64.

39. Already here we can anticipate that the "praxis of liberation" ought to situate itself in this "thirdness"; that is, from out of the life world (firstness), the other and its project of liberation irrupts (secondness) that from its exclusion and oppression brings about a *practical process* of liberation (thirdness). Liberation as process is mediation (thirdness), and moves from a situation of oppression in the world (firstness), which is negated from the counterfactual anticipation of utopia as a goal (secondness).

40. Cornel West 1989, executes an interesting effort to reconstitute pragmatism.

41. See Gramsci 1975, IV, pp. 3191ff.

42. See the work by Ulrich 1993, where one would have to distinguish instead between "economics" (*Oekonomik*) as philosophy (part of a material ethics), "economic pragmatics (*oekonomische Pragmatic*)," as economic-pragmatic science, and the properly economic (*oekonomisch*) level of the

effective materiality of production, distribution, and consumption as means for survival.

43. In all of my prior works presented with this ongoing dialogue, I have repeated this argument in order to demonstrate the importance of a material ethics, and especially the position of a non-*standard* Marx, but now reconstructed through a comprehensive and patient reading (see Dussel 1990 and 1993).

44. See my response to Apel in Dussel 1995, # 1, pp. 115ff.

45. See Wellmer 1986, I: "Kantian program."

46. Bentham proposed as an ought, the universalization of happiness. Wellmer's formulation is stronger. That is, the prohibition of the non-generalisable as negation allows for less exceptions (for example, it is non-generalisable: "Make others miserable!"). But what Wellmer does not indicate clearly is that this negation is determined from the standpoint of the material affirmation of what is negated: if to make miserable or to kill is judged ethically as non-generalizable is through comparison to the generalizable (happiness as universally attempted, but with a difficulty of concrete application). In other words, the material *positive* principle of ethics (described in §1) is on what is grounded its *negation* (only in this §4) as critique.

47. In a different way: The horizon of the material ethics remains circumscribed as *possible* by an empirical universal principle of impossibility, in this case as: It is impossible to choose death! Ethics presupposes this impossibility because in the case of suicide, the ethical subject is no longer alive and therefore can no longer chose. Ethics therefore disappears as a possibility. From this principle the following principle is derived: "Who acts affirms always the impossibility of choosing death." The *cynical principle* of the system of domination is formulated in the following manner: "In this system (i.e., capitalism) it is impossible for the majority to live (this is the impossibility of the impossibility of choosing death), therefore, let them die" (as is explicitly suggested by Friedrich Hayek, the father of neoliberal economics). From the contradiction between the "impossiblity of (choosing) death" and "the necessity to die" ("impossibility of living"), there emerges the critical consciousness and the recognition of the negated dignity of the victim. Dignity is discovered only through its negation, as the dignity of life before the possibility of losing it (before death through the robbery [a way of killing little by little] of the surplus value of the dominated, or also ethically as heroism or martyrdom of the liberating critic; and in all of these cases as effect of an unjust act that causes these deaths).

48. See Dussel 1994, # 2.

49. See Freire 1968; and in addition my essay, Dussel 1994, 2.

50. This "experience" is not that of Hegel's *Phenomenology of the Spirit*, but the "experience" of having taken over, submerged, and lived among the poor, the needy, the dominated, and excluded people. See Paulo Freire 1993. Many Euro-North American philosophers (and also from the peripheral world) have not "had" this experience or do not give it any ethical-philosophical value. But, none of the "great critics" to which we are refering have not had some "experience" (Marx as exiled and next to the workers in Paris, 1943, Levinas as uprooted Jew, Foucault as persecuted homosexual, etc.).

51. See Habermas 1988.

52. See Dussel 1988, Chap. 15.

53. These representatives of the "first Frankfurt School," critics of Modernity, lacked the possibility of linking up with historical groups (popular, social movements, or political parties) with whose communitarian subjectivity could have performed the function of "organic intellectuals." The Germany of their time did not grant them this possibility. In this they differ from liberation ethicists. Nevertheless, they were "critics."The "second" Frankfurt school, although it retains many merits, has lost its critical edge.

54. The "Good" becomes equivocal: the "good" of slavery of the Pharaons becomes a "dominating system" for its slaves. See Walzer 1985, when he writes: "So pharaonic oppression, deliverance, Sinai, and Canaan are still with us, powerful memories shaping our perceptions of the political world" (p. 149). Walzer recognizes his debt to Latin American thought of liberation when he cites my friend Severino Croatto (p. 4).

55. See Dussel, 1993c.

56. See Levinas 1974, pp. 210 ff, especially when he writes: "Le scepticisme qui traverse la rationalité ou la logigue du savoir, est un refus de *synchroniser* l'affirmation implicite contenue dans *le dire* et la *négation* que cette afirmation énonce dans *le Dit*" (p. 213). "The said" is expressed in the hegemonic system. "To say" is the interpellation of the Other, in §4, as exteriority that diachronically, from the future, for the system that turns from hegemonic into dominator and from legitimate into illegitimate because of the *negative* presence of the poor, of the women as sexual object, etc., demonstrates the non-coincidence of the "*dominating* reason as past" and "*liberating* reason as future." Who inhabits the new world, with object that are non-observable by the older paradigm (to speak like Thomas Kuhn), becomes sceptical of the prior moments of reason that begin to be superseded: scepticism makes itself present once again when there are radical historical changes. Now it is a scepticism that identifies with the ethical critique of the dominating order. For this reason it does not accept the "truth" or the "ratio" of domination. Is this not all found ambiguously in Nietzsche, for example?

57. A "Fact" is non-immediate and is mediated by the already indicated levels and formally by the *critical* material reconstructive sciences. Thus, Marx called "*Critique* of Political [capitalist] Economy" this ethical type of social science. Discourse ethics has provided us with sufficient criteria in order to perform a formal critique of validity (sociological, for example, but not economic). This is its Achilles' heel, which calls into question the entire project.

58. The hegemonic communication community leaves the dominated in the situation of the *impossibility of arguing* on the possibility of living.

59. For a long time we have already distinguished between "ethical consciousness" or critique, which "listen to the clamoring of the people," and the mere "moral consciousness" that applies the moral principles of the system (in §2). See Dussel 1973, II, pp. 52ff.

60. Paulo Freire begins his pedagogical experience in 1947 (See Freire 1993), which culminates with his seminal work (Freire, 1968). It could be said that Rousseau, with *Émile*, laid down the foundations for solipsistic

bourgeois education. Freire lays down the foundations for the critical inter-subjective and communitarian education of the oppressed. His entire work goes beyond the sixth stage of Kohlberg's developmental psychology (see Kohlberg 1981 and 1987; and Habermas 1983, pp. 127ff.), given that ethical consciousness reaches a stage that has not been described as of now; it con-cernes an "anti-hegemonic universal critical ethical consciousness of the oppressed." It is not only individual, autonomous, and universal (and in the case of Habermas, discursive in as much as it reaches for agreement), but in addition it transcends the *"dominating" universality*—of which Kohlberg does not take note—and that presupposes a "global *universality*" over and above post-conventional modern [eurocentric] consciousness. It demands from ethi-cal subjects an "ethical-critical consciousness" that also requires greater matu-rity since they must then oppose the *"ruling* universality*"*: the individuality and the communitarian intersubjectivity of this critic demands greater clarity, a social and historical judgment (scientific and political) of greater universality, and thus faces greater risks. This in the case of the heroes and martyrs, means their death, since they dared the "impudence" of going against the laws of the established order: they are the Washingtons (USA), or Hidalgos (Mexico), or the Lumumba (Zaire) or the "Resistence française" against Nazism, the resi-tance against Stalin; it is Oscar Romero (El Salvador) before the military dic-tatorships controlled by the United States; or the Amerindian rebellion in Chiapas (in 1994). We will articulate in our *Liberation Ethics* the question of a more critical and liberatory ethics in opposition to the mere post-conventional morality (which is, in any event, "conventionally" eurocentric without being aware of it, as we have noted repeatedly).

61. See Dussel 1973, II, # 25: "The Other, the common good and the infi-nite" (pp. 59ff).

62. This refers to Levinas's responsibility, see Levinas 1968.

63. Let us repeat. It is impossible to choose death because he who chooses death does not choose something, but chooses not to choose any more; he chooses not to choose. Thus, he falls practically in a performative contradic-tion if he were to pretend to provide an argument for his suicide. But what if he were not to pretend and were, without argument, to simply let himself die? He would not contradict himself, but he also would not be an opponent to the ultimate grouding of the material ethical principle.

64. Habermas studies this but without sufficient complexity (see Haber-mas 1963, 1968).

65. See Dussel 1973, II, pp. 65–127; 1994, # 2, b and c.

66. Walzer attempts to justify this ambigous alternative (Walzer 1977).

67. Hegel, *Elements of the Philosophy of Right*, # 347: "The nation [*Volk*] to which such a moment is allotted as a *natural* principle is given the task of implementing this principle in the course of the self-development of the world spirit's self-consciousness. This nation is the the *dominant* one in world history for this epoch, *and only once in history can it have this epoch-making role* (see # 346). In contrast with this absolute right that it possesses as bearer of the present state of the world spirit's development, the spirits of other nations are without rights, and they, like those whose epoch has passed, no longer count in world history." (p. 374; Hegel 1971, t. VII, pp. 505–506).

Works Cited

Apel, Karl-Otto. 1995 (1981). *Charles Peirce. From Pragmatism to Pragmaticism.* Atlantic Highlands, New Jersey: Humanities Press.

———. 1985. "¿Límites de la ética discursiva," in A. Cortina, 1985, pp. 233–262.

———. 1986. "Necesidad, dificultad y posibilidad de una fundamentación filosófica de la ética en la época de la ciencia," in *Estudios éticos,* trad. castellana, Editorial Alfa, Barcelona (German: "Notwendigkeit, Schwierigkeit und Möglichket einer philosophischen Begründung derEthik im Zeitalterder Wissenschaft", en *Festschrift Constantino Tzatzo,* Atenas, 1980).

———. 1990. "Diskursethik als Verantwortungsethik -eine postmetaphysiche Transformation der Ethik Kants," in Fornet-Betancourt, 1990, pp.10–40.

———, Enrique Dussel, and Raúl Fornet-Betancourt. 1992, *Fundamentación de la ética y la filosofía de la liberación,* Siglos XXI, México.

Arens, Edmund. 1995. *Anerkennung der Anderen.* Freiburg: Herder.

Benhabib, Seyla. 1986. *Critique, Norm, and Utopia. A Study of the Foundations of Critical Theory.* New York: Columbia University Press,.

Bentham, Jeremy. 1948. *A Fragment on Government and An Introduction to the Principles of Morals and Legislation.* Oxford: Basil Blackwell.

Boltvinik, Julio. 1995. "La Cumbre Social ¿Consolidación del neoliberalismo?" in *La Jornada* (México), marzo 3, p. 47.

Cortina, Adela. 1985. *Razón comunicativa y responsabilidad solidaria.* Madrid: Sígueme.

Dussel, Enrique. 1973. *Para una ética de la liberación latinoamericana,* Siglo XXI, Buenos Aires, t.-II.

———. 1973b. *Para una de-strucción de la historia de la ética,* Mendoza: Ser y Tiempo.

———. 1988. *Hacia un Marx desconocido. Un comentario de los Manuscritos del 61-63,* México: Siglo XXI.

———. 1990. "Die *Lebensgemeischaft* und die Interpellation des Armen," in Fornet-Betancourt, 1990, pp. 69–96.

———. 1993. *Apel, Ricoeur, Rorty y la filosofía de la liberación.* Guadalajara: Universidad de Guadalajara.

———. 1993b. *Von der Erfindung Amerikas zur Entdeckung des Anderen. Ein Projekt der Transmoderne.* Düsseldorf: Patmos (In English see: New York: Continuum, 1995).

———. 1993c. "Proyecto filosófico de Charles Taylor," in *Signos. Anuario de Humanidades* (UAM-I, México), VII–III, pp. 15–60.

———. 1994. "Ethik der Befreiung. Zum Ausgangspunkt als Vollzug der ursprünglichen ethischen Vernunft," in Fornet-Betancourt, 1994, pp. 83–110.

———. 1995. "Die Befreiungsethik gegenüber der Diskursethik," in Arens, 1995, pp.113–136.

Fornet-Betancourt, Raúl (Ed). 1990. *Ethik und Befreiung*. Aachen: Augustinus.

———. (Ed). 1994. *Konvergenz oder Divergenz?* Aachen: Augustinus.

Freire, Paulo. 1968. *Pedagogía del oprimido*. México: Siglo XXI.

———. 1993. *Pedagogía de la esperanza*. México: Siglo XXI.

Gramsci, Antonio. 1975. *Quaderni del Carcere*. Einaudi, Torino, t.I-IV.

Habermas, Jürgen. 1963. *Theorie und Praxis*, Suhrkamp, Frankfurt.

———. 1968. *Erkenntnis und Interesse*. Frankfurt: Suhrkamp.

———. 1976. *Zur Rekonstruktion des Historischen Materialismus*. Frankfurt: Suhrkamp.

———. 1981. *Theorie des kommunikativen Handelns*. Frankfurt: Suhrkamp, t.I-II.

———. 1983. *Moralbewußtsein und kommunikatives Handeln*. Frankfurt: Suhrkamp.

———. 1988. *Der philosophische Diskurs der Moderne*. Frankfurt: Suhrkamp.

———. 1991. *Erläuterungen zur Diskurethik*. Frankfurt: Suhrkamp.

Hegel, G. W. F. 1971. *G.W.F. Hegel Werke in zwanzig Bänden. Theorie Werkausgabe*. Frankfurt: Suhrkamp. t.I (1971)–XX (1979).

Hinkelammert, Franz. 1984. *Crítica a la razón utópica*. San José: DEI.

———. 1994. "Diskursethik und Verantwortungsethik," in Fornet-Betancourt, 1994, pp.111–150.

Honneth, Axel. 1992. *Kampf zum Anerkennung*. Frankfurt: Suhrkamp.

Jonas, Hans. 1982. *Prinzip Verantwortung*. Nördlingen: G.Wagner.

Kant, Immanuel. 1968. *Kant Werke*, Wissenschaftliche Buchgesellschaft, Darmstadt, t.I–X.

Kelly, Michael (Ed.). 1989. "Hermeneutics in Ethics and Social Theory," número completo de *The Philosophical Forum* (New York), XXI, 1–2 (1989–1990).

Kohlberg, Lawrence. 1981. *Essays on Moral Development*. Cambridge: Harper and Row, t.I–II(1984).

———. 1987. *The Measurement of Moral Judgement*. Cambridge: Cambridge University Press, t.I–II.

Levinas, Emmanuel. 1968. *Totalité et Infinit. Essai sur l'Extériorité*. 3era. ed., La Haye: Nijhoff.

———. 1974. *Autrement qu'être ou au-delà de l'essence*. La Haye: Nijhoff.

Locke, John. 1975. *An Essay concerning Human Understanding*, P. H. Nidditch, Ed., Oxford: Clarendon Press.

MacIntyre, A. 1981. *After Virtue. A Study in Moral Theory*. Notre Dame: University of Notre Dame Press.

———. 1988. *Whose Justice? Which Rationality?* Notre Dame: University of Notre Dame Press.

Marx, K. 1975. *Karl Marx-Friedrich Engels Gesamtausgabe (MEGA)*, Dietz, Berlin, t.I (1975)-ss (ed.cast. FCE, México, t.I (1982)-ss).

Mill, John Stuart. 1957. *Utilitarianism*. New York: The Liberal Arts Press.

Peirce, Charles S. 1931. *Collected Papers of Charles Peirce*, C. Hartshorne, P. Weiss, and A. Burks, Ed., Cambridge: Belknap Press, t.I (1960)–VIII (1966).

Rehg, William. 1994. *Insight and Solidarity. The Discourse Ethics of Jürgen Habermas*. Berkeley: University of California Press.

Sartre, Jean-Paul. 1960. *Critique de la raison dialectique. Théorie des ensembles pratiques*. Paris: Gallimard, t.I.

Scheler, Max. 1954. *Der Formalismus in der Ethik und die materiale Wertethik*. Berna: Francke.

Searle, J. 1984. *Minds, Brains and Science*, Cambridge: Harvard University Press.

———. 1994. *The Rediscovery of the Mind*. Cambridge: MIT Press.

Sidekum, Antonio (Ed). 1994. *Ética do Discurso e Filosofia da Libertacâo*. Sâo Leopoldo (Brasil): UNISINOS.

Taylor, Charles. 1975. *Hegel*. Cambridge: Cambridge University Press.

———. 1989. *Sources of the Self. The Making of the Modern Identity*. Cambridge: Cambridge University Press.

———. 1992. *The Ethics of Authenticity*. Cambridge: Harvard University Press.

Türcke, Christoph. 1994. "Diskursethik als Dauerbegründung ihrer selbst," in Fornet-B., 1994, pp. 235–246.

Ulrich, Peter. 1993. *Transformation der ökonomischen Vernunft*. Bern: Paul Haupt.

Volpi, Franco, 1992, "L'esistenza como *praxis*. Le radici aristoteliche della terminologia di *Esse e tempo*," in *Filosofia '91*, Roma: Laterza, pp. 215–254.

Walzer, Michael, 1977, *Just and Unjust Wars*. New York: Basic Books.

———. 1979, *Exodus and Revolution*. New York: Daniel Doron.

———. 1983, *Spheres of Justice. A Defense of Pluralism and Equality*. New York: Basic Books.

Wellmer, Albrecht, 1986, *Dialog und Diskurs*. Frankfurt: Suhrkamp.

West, Cornel, 1989, *The American Evasion of Philosophy. A Genealogy of Pragmatism*: Madison: The University of Wisconsin Press.

Zubiri, X. 1981, *Inteligencia sentiente*. Madrid: Alianza Editorial, Madrid.

———. 1986, *Sobre el hombre*. Madrid: Alianza Editorial, Madrid.

———. 1992, *Sobre el sentimiento y la volición*. Madrid: Alianza Editorial, Madrid.

Contributors

EDMUND ARENS, a Heisenberg Scholar of the German Research Foundation, has taught at Union Theological Seminary (NY), the Goethe University in Frankfurt, and the University of Münster. He is author of *The Logic of Pragmatic Thinking: From Pierce to Habermas* and *Christopraxis: A Theology of Praxis*, and has edited *Habermas und die Theologie*, a study of the theological reception of Habermas's work.

DAVID BATSTONE is Assistant Professor of Social Ethics at the University of San Francisco. He is author of *From Conquest to Struggle: Jesus of Nazareth in Latin America*, co-author of *Global Ethics: Theories and Practice* and editor of *New Visions for the Americas: Religious Engagement and Social Transformation*. In addition to his scholarly works, Batstone writes for several national media outlets, notably *SPIN*, *SOMA*, and the *Sunday Chicago Tribune*, and is the host of *BusStop RadioNet*.

MARÍA CLARA BINGEMAR is a Professor at the Pontifical Catholic University in Rio de Janeiro, Brazil. For several years she served as regional coordinator of Latin America for the Ecumenical Association of Third World Theologians (EATWOT). She is co-author, with Ivone Gebara, of *Mary: Mother of God, Mother of the Poor*.

ENRIQUE DUSSEL has authored over twenty books on religion, sociology, history, and law, including two recent works, *The Invention of the Americas* and *The Underside of Modernity*. A political refugee from his native Argentina, Dussel has lived in Mexico since 1975 and is currently Professor of Philosophy and Ethics at the Universidad Autonoma de México.

GUSTAVO GUTIÉRREZ is the author of *A Theology of Liberation*, the classic first exposition of liberation theology in Latin America. He lives and works in a poor *barrio* in Lima, Peru, dividing his time between pastoral work and teaching at the Catholic University. His other works include *The Power of the Poor in History*, *We Drink from Our Own Wells*, and *On Job: God-Talk and the Suffering of the Innocent*.

JÜRGEN HABERMAS taught for many years at the Goethe University in Frankfurt, Germany. His two-volume *The Theory of Communicative Action* is one of the most important works on social theory in the twentieth century. Among his other influential writings are *The Philosophical Discourse of Modernity*, *Moral Consciousness and Communicative Action*, and most recently, *Between Facts and Norms*.

FRANZ HINKELAMMERT, of German origin has lived in Central America for over 25 years and is an active member of Departamento Ecumenico de Investigaciones in Costa Rica. He is the author of *The Ideological Weapons of Death* and, most recently, *Critique of Utopian Reason*.

DWIGHT N. HOPKINS teaches systematic theology at the Divinity School of the University of Chicago. He is the co-editor of several texts including *Changing Conversations: Religious Reflection and Cultural Analysis*. Author of *Black Theology USA and South Africa*, and *Shoes That Fit Our Feet: Sources for a Constructive Black Theology*, he is the senior editor of the Henry McNeal Turner-Sojourner Truth Black religion book series for Orbis Books. His *American Culture and Black Theology* and *An Introduction to Black Theology* are both forthcoming.

LOIS ANN LORENTZEN is Associate Professor of Social Ethics at the University of San Francisco. Author of many articles on Central America and environmental ethics, she is co-editor of *The Gendered New World Order: Militarism, the Environment and Development*, associate editor of the journals *Terra Nova: nature and culture* (MIT Press) and *Peace Review: The International Quarterly of World Peace*, and co-author of *Global Ethics: Theories and Practice*.

EDUARDO MENDIETA is Assistant Professor of Philosophy and Ethics at the University of San Francisco. He edited and translated Enrique Dussel's *The Underside of Modernity*, which also contain essays by Karl-Otto Apel and Paul Ricoeur, and currently is writing a book entitled *The Geography of Utopia: Modernity's Spatio-Temporal Regimes.*

AMÓS NASCIMENTO, born in Brazil in 1965 has studied music, religion, social sciences, and philosophy in Buenos Aires, Sao Paulo, and Frankfurt. He has presented the results of his research on themes such as Discourse Theory, Postmodernism, and Latin American thinking at international conferences and has published in Brazil, the U.S., and Germany. His two most recent works are *Una Geneaolgia de la Postmodernidad* and *Grenzen der Moderne.*

ELSA TAMEZ is Professor of Biblical Studies at the Seminario Bíblico Latinamericano in San José, Costa Rica, and serves as a staff member of the Departamento Ecumenico de Investigaciones. Her books include *Through Her Eyes: Women's Theology in Latin America, Bible of the Oppressed, The Scandalous Message of James,* and *Against Machismo.*

JOSUÉ A. SATHLER, born in Brazil, has studied theology, religion, ethnology, and anthropology in Buenos Aires, Sao Paulo, Tuebingen, Marburg, and Freiburg. He has done research on 'Candombli' in Brazil and lectured on this subject in Europe and Latin America.

MARK McCLAIN TAYLOR is Associate Professor of Theology and Culture at Princeton Theological Seminary. He is author of *Remembering Esperanza: A Cultural Political Theology for North American Praxis; Beyond Explanation: Religious Dimensions in Cultural Anthropology; Paul Tillich: Theologian at the Boundaries,* and co-editor of *Reconstructing Christian Theology.* He is also founder and coordinator of AMAJ—Academics for Mumia Abu-Jamal.

ROBERT ALLEN WARRIOR, a citizen of the Osage Nation of Indians, teaches American Indian literature and intellectual history in the English Department of Stanford University. He is the author of *Tribal Secrets: Recovering American Indian Intellectual Traditions* and *Like a Hurricane; The Indian Movement from Alcatraz to Wounded Knee.*

SHARON WELCH is Associate Professor of Religious Studies and Women's Studies at the University of Missouri at Columbia, and regularly teaches workshops on racial diversity and multicultural education. Author of *A Feminist Ethic of Risk* and *Communities of Resistance and Solidarity,* she is currently writing a book on the confluence of jazz, ethics, and politics.

Index